Contents

PART III—WORKING WITH WOVENS

PART IV—FITTING AND GRADING

APPENDIXES

Preface

Complete Guide to Size Specification and Technical Design is an exciting new tool for fashion students and professionals to explore a segment of the industry that was once kept a secret to consumers. Private labels have come out of the closet and blossomed into "private brands." Offshore production, a necessity for many companies in today's economy, is utilized by both retailers and manufacturers. This text offers the basic knowledge needed to work as an industry liaison, in both retail and manufacturing, between design/product development staffs and production teams.

This text is a blueprint of size specification and technical design for the missy market. It has been laid out in a simple manner consistent with most industry spec manuals of its type. It includes an introduction to the industry, chapters on measuring (ordered for easy use), and instructions on creating specification sheets, fitting garments, and grading. Industry spec manuals are often as diverse in layout as garments are in design; therefore, this text is taken from what the author feels is the better of the biggest manuals combined into one easy-to-use guide. Appendixes and a glossary of terms and definitions (for important industry terminology) have been added for referencing.

This text is not a product development, patternmaking, production, or quality assurance tool. It does not cover material, trim, or color specifications (generally produced in product development); costing, piece lists, cut order sheets, assembly diagrams, order of operation sheets, or labor division instructions (generally produced in patternmaking and production); or garment inspection procedures (generally carried out in quality assurance departments). This text also does not propose computer applications. Companies vary in their computer software, ranging anywhere from purchased specification packages to spreadsheets and databases. The information enclosed can be inputted into many of those programs.

Using This Text

Companies vary in how they apprentice technical design and schools differ in how they present new material; therefore, the information in this text may not be presented in an order that follows everyone's criteria. For example, some prefer to present measuring woven garments first because the fabric is easier to handle. The industry often presents knit garments first because there are generally fewer style features to confuse the novice. Simply go to the section that makes you more comfortable. If needed, skip between knits and wovens, presenting the less complex garments first, then move on to the more complex garments.

Developing a first size specification sheet also varies in the industry. Spec sheets generated for offshore production generally start with a company sample. Private label spec sheets may begin with an evaluation of a designer sample (for copying), a factory sample, a sketch, a photograph, or a combination thereof. With the exception of a sketch or photograph, which requires the technician to use her experience and expertise to develop measurements without a garment, both the designer garment and the factory sample are usually measured first, fit onto a model or form, and then evaluated. This text works on the premise that a garment has been provided.

Part I: Getting Started

Chapter 1, Introduction to Size Specification and Technical Design: This chapter explores and offers the reader an overview of size specification and technical design as it relates to private label and offshore production. It also examines technical design skill requirements.

Chapter 2, Tools of the Trade: Chapter 2 offers the reader important information needed before beginning. It includes standardized body dimensions, shows the reader how to measure a live model/body form with a recording chart, plus how to read and use a generic spec sheet.

Chapter 3, Basic Measurement Points: Instructions are given to prepare a workstation for measuring and how to measure using step-by-step illustrated instructions for each basic measurement point.

Part II and Part III: Working with Knits and Working with Wovens

Chapters 4 through 15: Each chapter looks at specific garment types and the measurement points needed for each one. These chapters show the reader how to measure specific garments, with applicable measurement points. Basic garment spec sheets have been added for practical application and sample spec sheets for referencing.

Part IV: Fitting and Grading

Chapter 16, Achieving the Perfect Fit: This section should be explored only after one is comfortable with measuring. It offers common fit rules, common fit problems, and suggested solutions for correction.

Chapter 17, Grading: This chapter explores the last step in the technical design process. It offers grading spec sheet instructions for production, missy size grading guidelines, and tolerance allowances.

Appendix A, Basic Garment Croquis: This appendix includes a sampling of flat garment sketches used in technical design and directions for croquis use. A blank spec sheet is provided for the experienced user who wishes to design individual garment spec sheets using the croquis provided and the measurement point chapters.

Appendix B, Body Ease: This section is added as a reference for Chapter 16. Designing a good fit must include knowledge of body ease. A chart of ease is included.

Appendix C, Care Labeling: Formally a factory production step, many technical designers are getting involved with care labeling due to strict United States government regulations. ASTM care labeling instructions have been added for your reference.

Appendix D, Ordering a Body Form: This checklist has been added as a reference for those individuals who need to purchase a body form.

Glossary, Important Terms and Definitions: This glossary provides all the important vocabulary terms and definitions fashion students and professionals need to master.

Acknowledgments

I would first like to thank the wonderful staff at Fairchild Books, including, but not limited to, Olga Kontzias, Carolyn Purcell, and Amy Zarkos for their invaluable expertise and endless support. I am indebted to you for your patience.

To Matrix Art Services, a division of Matrix Publishing Services, and Clay Weldon of Clay Weldon Designs for the fantastic job of electronically rendering my original art, I say, "Thank you." This was not a small or easy task.

I am also indebted to the following educators and industry experts who reviewed my proposal and manuscript, offering many helpful suggestions and improvements: Catherine Black, Florida State University; Elizabeth Bye, University of Minnesota; Mary Ann Ferro, Fashion Institute of Technology; Cynthia

L. Istook, North Carolina State University; Jo Kallal, University of Delaware; Marycarol Miller, Parsons School of Design; Anita Racine, Cornell University; and Susan Suarez, Fashion Careers of California College. I would specifically like to thank Beth Black, NAP Inc., New York, NY, and Ronda Martinez, Senior Technical Designer, Philadelphia, PA, who always gave of their time to answer my questions, ensuring the accuracy of this text.

Lastly a big THANK YOU goes to my husband, Chris, and my son, Andrew, for their unwavering support, not only emotionally, but through their computer expertise, endless copy servicing, and more. This project would not have been possible without them.

Complete Guide to
Size Specification and Technical Design

PART 1

GETTING STARTED

This text is designed to offer students and professionals a comprehensive tool to size specification and technical design as it relates to the segment of the fashion industry known as private label and global garment production. By providing basic knowledge needed to measure a garment, create a spec sheet, fit a garment, and grade, it is my hope to help those fashion industry aspirants and professionals reach their goals in the exciting field of size specification and technical design and garment production.

Chapters 1 through 3 will explore the industry; "tools of the trade" used by size specification analysts and technical designers; basic specification sheets; tips needed before beginning; how to measure a model/form; how to prepare a workstation for measuring (giving systematically illustrated instructions for each basic measurement point); and basic measurement points for all garment types. Let's get started.

CHAPTER 1

Introduction to Size Specification and Technical Design

Brand Merchandise Versus Private Label

National and designer brand merchandise is owned by manufacturing companies called wholesalers. The brands are produced in factories owned or contracted by the wholesaler, then purchased by various retail establishments. Brands are widely recognized by consumers, in part due to national advertising. *MUDD*, *l.e.i.*, and *Tommy Hilfiger Collection* are brands popularized in the early 2000s by a youth market.

Private label refers to merchandise that is manufactured by or for a retailer under a label owned by that retailer. Merchandise that carries retailers' names or any other name owned by them was once kept secret from the consumer. However, as the idea of private label or store-owned branding became popular and increasingly lucrative, the industry exploded. Gap, Victoria's Secret, and Ann Taylor are well-known private label retailers. The retail store corporations own the labels. They have designers or product development staffs in the corporate offices develop merchandise for their stores; this merchandise is produced at independent manufacturing factories or production plants. Manufacturers that produce their own lines have also been known to develop private brands for retailers. After production,

the privately owned and labeled merchandise is shipped to distribution warehouses, and finally to their stores.

By the middle 1980s to the early 1990s, most fashion retail/buying offices were testing their own store labels. However, for retailers entering the manufacturing segment of the fashion industry, producing clothing under private labels posed certain problems. As a variety of manufacturers produced garments under retail contracts, the retailers were finding inconsistencies in sizing and quality. Each sewing plant or factory was constructing garments with its own set of specifications. As a result, specification buying and technical design began, meaning merchandise was manufactured to the store's standards, not the factories'. These private brand purchases allowed the stores to offer exclusive merchandise, giving them an edge over their competitors. It also offered the potential to increase profits, allowing a greater gross margin by cutting out the middleman, and enhance the store's image.

Today, private labels like Federated Department Stores' *I.N.C.*, Lord and Taylor's *Identity*, Nordstrom's *Frenchi*, and May Department Stores Co.'s *be* rival many of the designer labels. In some cases, these retailers are spending money on in-house design staffs, store presentations, and national ad cam-

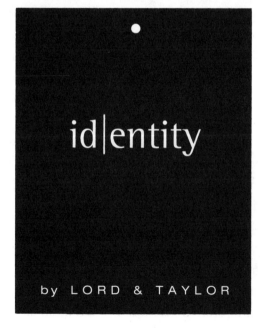

paigns. The result is exclusive private brands that differentiate stores from one another.

Basically, a retail technical designer's job is to create and maintain size standards for this private brand merchandise. Have you ever noticed that you might be able to wear a pair of jeans in one size from one designer, but need a different size from another? The reason for this is that designers pride themselves on a unique fit, or brand standard, which represents the body image and profile of their customer, called their target market. Retailers have adopted this same philosophy for private labels. One retailer's brand may cater to a junior's market, so the cut of its clothing may reflect a younger, slimmer figure. Another retailer's brand may cater to an entirely different market, petite's, for example. A petite figure, less than five foot four inches in height, is proportioned differently from a junior figure, so the retailer must adopt size and quality brand standards unique to its customer. These are called retail standards. Once the retailer establishes its desired measurements, dress forms are custom made and models hired so that garments can be checked against those standards.

Retail standards are important because a retailer wants a customer to be loyal to its store. One of the best ways to ensure loyalty is to offer quality merchandise. Quality merchandise must of course look good, be priced right, hold up in laundering, be comfortable, and fit well. If the garment is not comfortable, chances are it does not fit properly. When a consumer is constantly pulling on the sleeve because the armhole is too small or tugging at the hem because a skirt rises, that customer will not be happy with their purchase and may not want to buy that store brand again. In private label, where the store's name is associated with the merchandise, a good standard fit is imperative.

Many brands and the majority of private label merchandise are produced overseas because costs are lower; therefore, profits are higher. Retailers that produce private label merchandise have product development teams within their corporate offices that take care of production, while manufacturers have

production managers to do the same. Unless factories are owned by retailers or manufacturers, both use people called sourcers who must locate the factories/plants. Some larger companies have staff that do nothing but locate and visit plants (manufacturing sources) as potential manufacturers of their merchandise. Other companies may give the job of locating these plants to the product development staff or hire independent sourcing companies. The independent sourcer often acts as a broker or liaison between the retailer, the manufacturer, and the production plant. Lai Apparel of New York is an example of a sourcing company that has the prestigious TV retailer QVC as a client.

Once an agreement has been made between the retailer, the manufacturer, and the manufacturing plant, samples are produced. For private label companies, sample garments or prototypes can be created in several ways. The retailer might have staff designers create sketches of the desired garments, a product developer might find a great designer piece he or she would like to copy, or the factory might even offer design styles that it is currently producing. If samples are to be made from a sketch, specifications will be sent prior to the sample production. Sometimes samples are produced in advance of the retailer's finalized line in anticipation that they will be picked up (purchased under private label agreements), so style details may not be exact. Available buttons, zippers, fabrics, and trims that are close in style, type, and weight will be used for the first sample. However, sample styles that are copies or accepted from a manufacture line for private label usually go through the process of being line approved, then specification sheets are written.

Size Specification and Technical Design

Size specification is a term that has long been used in the fashion industry. It is simply a list of measurements for a particular size. Designers, patternmakers, and production personnel have all generated or used style sheets containing size specifications.

Size specifications, also called specs, are used by designers in several ways. One is to convey specific measurements to the draper or patternmaker. For example, if a designer wants the sweep of a specific garment to be 60 inches in circumference, she will note that on the spec sheet. A designer may also use a spec sheet if the garment is costing too much and needs to be scaled back. The designer may look at the measurements and trim details and make appropriate style changes to save money.

A patternmaker uses a spec sheet differently. When he is making a first pattern from a sketch, he might estimate measurements, make the pattern, then have a sample made from which a spec sheet is produced. On the other hand, a patternmaker may receive a set of specs that he must follow when drafting his first pattern.

Production personnel generally use specs for developing the cost of a garment; this is called costing.

Technical design is a new industry term. As retailers entered the private label industry, they hired personnel to create size specification sheets, thus a title for this developing position was needed. Early on, some retailers like May Department Stores Co., Merchandising Services used the title size specification analyst; Federated Department Stores and Macy's department stores use the title technical designer; Spiegel and J.C. Penney use the title quality assurance manager. Today, there is still variety in terminology. This text uses the term technical designer.

In retail, a technical designer is a person trained in design and patternmaking who can adjust garments to achieve a proper fit, compensate for variables such as movement, ease, and shrinkage, and act as a liaison between product development/design departments and manufacturers.

Some manufacturers hire technical designers to work with retailers estimating cost sheets or to oversee offshore production of their lines. Specs are also used by garment manufacturers for estimating garment price quotes. Obtaining accurate garment measurements allows the manufacturer to better estimate marker yardage, which can help designers make important design and style decisions.

Once the line has been developed, the individual garments are sent to the size specification/technical design department for analysis. In larger retail companies, this department may be part of quality assurance or quality control. Occasionally, some companies will misuse titles for appearance or perceived prestigious reasons, so let's look closely at those personnel.

❖ Style Clerk—A person working in a spec office who checks and records the style numbers of the garment for analysis. A secretary or assistant might also have this duty.

❖ Measurer—A person whose sole responsibility is to measure garments and record those measurements onto a spec sheet. This person reports to the size specification analyst/technical designer.

❖ Patternmaker—A person who can construct actual pattern pieces for a new style by adjusting a sloper (basic pattern) to meet the specifications required. The patternmaker who works in the specification/technical design/quality department often works with patternmakers at the manufacturing facilities.

❖ Size Specification Analyst—A person who analyzes garments, checking and adjusting the fit as required and writing specification sheets. This person knows how to measure garments.

❖ Assistant Size Specification Analyst—A person who performs clerical duties for the size specification analyst. This person knows how to measure and is apprenticing in fit analysis.

❖ Technical Designer—A person who analyzes garments, checking and adjusting fit as required and writing specification sheets. This person also has a design background and can offer style changes as needed to solve production problems. Larger companies may have different levels of technical designers, e.g., junior technical designer and senior technical designer. The pay scale and levels of responsibility often dictate the title.

❖ Assistant Technical Designer—A person who performs clerical duties for the technical designer. This person knows how to measure and is apprenticing in fit analysis and design.

❖ Technical Design Manager—A person who manages several technical designers, makes final fit decisions, writes specification sheets, and evaluates potential production risks. This person works closely with the general merchandise manager, may offer style or design changes as needed for production, and sets the fit schedule.

❖ Senior Technical Design Manager—A person who manages several technical design managers, makes executive department decisions, works with the divisional merchandise managers, and writes specification sheets as needed. This person reports to a vice president or quality assurance–oriented partner.

Now let's look at the people who are responsible for creating the garments that are sent to the size specification analysts/technical designers for analysis. Not all companies have every position listed below. Depending on the size of the company and the nature of its business, some of the following positions will differ from company to company. Some positions can be combined; therefore, job responsibilities may overlap.

❖ Designer—A person engaged in creating new and original clothing or accessories.

❖ Assistant Designer—A person who works for the designer and may do illustrating, patternmaking, or sewing. Depending on the company, this position may be more creative or more technical, whether the duties are more illustrative, designing or patternmaking, or sewing.

❖ First Patternmaker—A person who works with the designer or may be an assistant to the designer and who can construct actual pattern pieces for a new style by adjusting a sloper (basic pattern) for sample making. This person may also apply draping methods to create a first design or sample.

❖ Patternmaker—A person who is in charge of making a final pattern for grading and production. Depending on the size of the company, patternmakers may have computer-generated systems to aid in the patternmaking, but they must still know how to grade patterns and lay them onto a marker by hand. In smaller companies, the final patterns may be sent to an outside agency for grading and marker making.

❖ Illustrator/Sketcher—A person who illustrates/ sketches for the designer, product development team, or technical team. Many illustrators/ sketchers work freelance. In the past, illustrators were known for creating illustrations for ads, catalogs, or presentations, while sketchers did sketches for design, product development, and technical teams. The terms illustrator and sketcher have sometimes blurred in their definition, as some illustrators sketch and some sketchers illustrate.

❖ Product Developer—A person who develops exclusive private label merchandise.

❖ Product Development Manager—A person who oversees the development of exclusive private label merchandise and monitors its production to assure those garments meet the company's expectations.

❖ Product Manager—An executive who heads the product development team and is responsible for helping to plan, develop, and oversee the consistency of a style message for an exclusive product, product line, brand, or private label.

❖ Merchandiser—A person who makes decisions concerning the direction of the company's line. The merchandiser will study market trends, conduct market research, work with the sales staff, and oversee product development. This person is responsible for merchandise numbers in terms of the product and the stockkeeping units (SKUs).

❖ Fashion Director—A person who works closely with the merchandisers, supplying important forecast information on color, trends, new fabrications, and market insights. The fashion director must stay at least one year ahead of the current industry trends. In some companies, the fashion director may have some of the same responsibilities as the merchandiser, without the numbers consideration.

- Sourcer/Sourcing Agent—A person who locates manufacturing facilities/factories to produce apparel merchandise. This responsibility may be part of the product development team's duties or can be contracted to an outside agency.
- Stylist—A person who shops the market for style ideas that will fit the company's image. The stylist also translates those style ideas to fit the company's needs. A stylist often gives direction to the design department or product development staff and therefore must have a thorough knowledge of textiles and color.
- Assistant Merchandiser—A person who works for the merchandiser and is primarily responsible for clerical duties. This person is often an intermediary between the merchandiser and other company personnel.
- Department Merchandise Manager (DMM)—A person who manages a division or department of merchandise. This person manages several merchandisers and reports to a general merchandise manager.
- General Merchandise Manager (GMM)—A person who manages several divisions or departments of merchandise. This person reports to a vice president or a merchandise-oriented partner.

Whether you want to be a designer, buyer, merchandiser, patternmaker, or any number of other positions in the fashion business, chances are that you will encounter private label or offshore production in your career. Therefore, having knowledge of the workings of size specification/technical design can be useful in many ways. Here are a few examples.

Designers who work for manufacturers often work with buyers designing exclusive store merchandise. During a sales room showing, a buyer might see a beautiful Irish linen jacquard at a dress vendor's house, but she doesn't like the style of the dress designed. She would like to have something made in that linen, but it is exclusive to that vendor's house. The buyer has two options. Either have the jacquard copied at another fabric manufacturer or try to get an exclusively designed item by that vendor. If the vendor chooses to design and produce an exclusive item for the buyer, this merchandise will now compete with other merchandise that buyer can get through private labeling. As a result, it is important for the designer and vendor to know and understand the workings of private label in order to stay competitive.

Buyers at store and corporate levels must be in tune with the merchandise that they are buying and that is on their selling floor in order to offer their customer a good mix of merchandise. Many buyers will work directly with merchandisers that develop private label to ensure that key pieces and desired products are developed. Senior buyers often sit in on fittings with their merchandisers and occasionally measure garments in the store if there is a complaint. For example, a store's customers are complaining that a particular skirt style is too tight in the hips, even for the slimmest gal. None of these great skirts are selling, also hurting the sales of the coordinating tops. If the retail merchandising service that sold the skirt to its own store's buyer made the mistake, then the service is responsible, but if the manufacturer did not follow the specifications, then it is responsible. Either way, the buyer must get the situation resolved in order to move her merchandise. In this instance, the buyer may need to measure the hip area of the skirt and have the merchandiser check with the technical designer to verify that the skirt was made to specification. If it wasn't, the store and merchandising service may negotiate a markdown with the manufacturer or return the goods.

As you can see, the industry is complex. The more you know, the more successful you will be. So let's take a look at what you need to know to become a technical designer.

Becoming a Technical Designer

Basic knowledge of garment construction and patternmaking is essential to becoming a technical designer, even though few are ever asked to sew a garment or make a pattern. However, technical designers constantly work with creative designers and patternmakers; therefore, they need to be informed in these situations. In addition, fitting apparel requires knowledge of quality garment construction, patternmaking, and an eye for detail. Having these skills is imperative when troubleshooting potential fit problems. Common fit problems and adjustments will be discussed in detail later in this text.

Basic "flat" sketching skills are advised. Although a technical designer's sketches are often done by in-house or freelance artists, there are occasions, especially in smaller companies, when technicians must do their own sketches. This text offers basic style croquis (see Appendix A) to aid in drawing. Computer-generated sketches and digital photography are other tools used by technicians. Knowledge of computer photo and drawing programs (such as Illustrator, Corel, and PhotoShop) is advised. Companies vary in their computer software, ranging anywhere from purchased specification packages (Karat Software), proprietary programs (Gerber PDM) to spreadsheets (Excel) and databases (Access), so knowledge of those popular programs is advised as well. The majority of spec information is sent via e-mail worldwide. Therefore, e-mail communication skills are essential, including formatting and attachment capabilities.

Technical design requires an acute sense of detail. A person with an affinity to detail does well in this field. The pace is fast, and costly mistakes must be avoided. One incorrect or missed measurement can result in a neckline that doesn't fit or a bulging hipline.

It takes time and practice to become a technical designer. At first, measuring is difficult because there are so many points of measurement. Individual companies will have different measurement points and different ways of measuring. It is easy to miss measurements and make mistakes. Companies also differ in the way they record measurements. Some are recorded flat or singular, while others are recorded in the circumference, or doubled. It is believed that wovens were originally recorded in circumference measurements because woven blouses were sold by chest measurements (32, 34, 36, etc.) rather than sized (6, 8, 10, 12 . . .). It is also believed that knits were originally recorded flat because most knitting machines, circular and flat, use singular measurements. Today, there is great debate among technicians over the use of flat versus circumference. Some technicians prefer to record all measurements, knit or woven, flat, feeling there is less room for human error when recording. Other technicians prefer to record their measurements in the circumference because those numbers better relate to fit adjustments. Many of the large buying office's technicians use both methods, recording knit garments via flat and woven garments via circumference methods. Since you will need to learn both, this text follows the knit-flat, woven-circumference methodology.

A mastery of fractional math is imperative. Although many companies use computers for grading, manual manipulation of numbers is necessary. For example, a technician might need to add $\frac{5}{8}$ inch to a measurement of $12\frac{1}{2}$ inches to achieve a desired fit. Don't let that scare you—in time, fractional math will become as routine as simple addition.

Dedication is also an important aspect of technical design. Depending on the size of the company, a single technician may evaluate several thousand garments a year. Market weeks are especially busy and meeting deadlines is imperative. The technician must be a company person, putting the needs of the company first. Hours can be long and grueling, but beyond self-satisfaction the rewards may be vast. Most technicians are well paid and may have comprehensive benefits packages, including healthcare and retirement plans, especially in larger companies.

Some companies also offer bonuses, merchandise discounts, free or inexpensively priced samples, and dinner perks. There is often the opportunity for domestic and foreign travel. Technical designers are an integral part of the fashion business and are respected as such.

Any company that generates or utilizes specification sheets may hire a technical designer. The industry is widespread in the way it does business; manufacturers, consulting firms, sourcing offices, and warehouse quality control departments are just a few places where technical designers might work.

In the chapters that follow, you will learn how to measure models and body forms, measure garments, create spec sheets, fit garments for quality assurance, and grade sizes for production. It's a lot to learn. Patience and practice are essential to becoming a technical designer.

CHAPTER 1 TERMS

When working as a technical designer, you may come across the terms listed below. If you are unfamiliar with any of them, please look up the definitions in the glossary at the end of this text.

Brand/Branded merchandise
Private label merchandise
Retail standard
Size specification
Technical design
Technical designer

CHAPTER 2

Tools of the Trade

Before You Begin

It is important to know that not only the design of specification sheets (specs) vary within the industry but also the number of spec sheets that may be written per garment. Generally, there is a "first" or "working" spec sheet, a fully graded approval sheet, and as many in between as it takes to get the garment right. The method of developing a first size specification sheet also varies within the industry. Specs generated for offshore production generally start with a company sample. Private label specs may begin with an evaluation of a designer sample (for copying), a factory sample, a sketch, a photograph, or a combination thereof. With the exception of a sketch or photograph, requiring the technician to use her experience and expertise to develop measurements without a garment, both the designer garment and the factory sample are usually measured first, fit onto a model or form, and then evaluated. This text works on the premise that a garment has been provided.

Before any garments can be evaluated, the company will have set up their technical design department. This involves getting body dimensions from the designer, patternmaker, or product development team and having dress forms custom made. Spec sheets will be designed and measurement points will

be created. Apprenticing technicians will concentrate on measuring garments, while senior technicians will conduct fit sessions, evaluate garments using proper body ease, and grade approved sample specifications into a full size range.

In this chapter you will look at basic body dimensions, measuring a model or body form, and learn how to use a spec sheet. Chapters 3 through 15 concentrate on measuring and writing a first spec sheet. Fit is not covered until Chapter 16 to give the novice time to learn how to measure. Lastly, Chapter 17 covers grading and tolerance levels.

Basic Body Dimensions

Statistical tables compiled by the United States government have been adapted for most size categories used today in ready-to-wear apparel, whether designer, branded, or private label. Those tables reflect averages of body measurement of large, random groups of people. ASTM (American Society for Testing and Materials) has done further analysis and compiled the statistical table that follows (Table 2.1).

Neither ASTM nor the author proposes that these measurements are industry standards. They are simply an average of body measurements that may be used for individualized standardization. Further-

11

Table 2.1 STANDARD TABLE OF BODY MEASUREMENTS FOR ADULT FEMALE MISSES FIGURE TYPE, SIZES 2–20

Girth Measurements in inches.

Size	2	4	6	8	10	12	14	16	18	20
Bust	32	33	34	35	36	$37\frac{1}{2}$	39	$40\frac{1}{2}$	$42\frac{1}{2}$	$44\frac{1}{2}$
Waist	24	25	26	27	28	$29\frac{1}{2}$	31	$32\frac{1}{2}$	$34\frac{1}{2}$	$36\frac{1}{2}$
High hip	$31\frac{1}{2}$	$32\frac{1}{2}$	$33\frac{1}{2}$	$34\frac{1}{2}$	$35\frac{1}{2}$	37	$38\frac{1}{2}$	40	42	44
Hip	$34\frac{1}{2}$	$35\frac{1}{2}$	$36\frac{1}{2}$	$37\frac{1}{2}$	$38\frac{1}{2}$	40	$41\frac{1}{2}$	43	45	47
Mid-neck	13	$13\frac{1}{4}$	$13\frac{1}{2}$	$13\frac{3}{4}$	14	$14\frac{3}{8}$	$14\frac{3}{4}$	$15\frac{1}{8}$	$15\frac{5}{8}$	$16\frac{1}{8}$
Neck base	$13\frac{1}{2}$	$13\frac{3}{4}$	14	$14\frac{1}{4}$	$14\frac{1}{2}$	$14\frac{7}{8}$	$15\frac{1}{4}$	$15\frac{5}{8}$	$16\frac{1}{8}$	$16\frac{5}{8}$
Armscye	$14\frac{1}{4}$	$14\frac{5}{8}$	15	$15\frac{5}{8}$	$15\frac{3}{4}$	$16\frac{3}{8}$	17	$17\frac{5}{8}$	$18\frac{3}{8}$	$19\frac{1}{8}$
Upper arm	10	$10\frac{1}{4}$	$10\frac{1}{2}$	$10\frac{3}{4}$	11	$11\frac{3}{8}$	$11\frac{3}{4}$	$12\frac{1}{8}$	$12\frac{3}{4}$	$13\frac{3}{8}$
Elbow	$9\frac{3}{8}$	$9\frac{1}{2}$	$9\frac{5}{8}$	$9\frac{3}{4}$	$9\frac{7}{8}$	$10\frac{1}{8}$	$10\frac{3}{8}$	$10\frac{5}{8}$	11	$11\frac{3}{8}$
Wrist	$5\frac{5}{8}$	$5\frac{3}{4}$	$5\frac{7}{8}$	6	$6\frac{1}{8}$	$6\frac{1}{4}$	$6\frac{3}{8}$	$6\frac{1}{2}$	$6\frac{5}{8}$	$6\frac{3}{4}$
Thigh, max	$19\frac{1}{2}$	$20\frac{1}{4}$	21	$21\frac{3}{4}$	$22\frac{1}{2}$	$23\frac{1}{2}$	$24\frac{1}{2}$	$25\frac{1}{2}$	$26\frac{3}{4}$	28
Thigh, mid	$18\frac{1}{4}$	$18\frac{3}{4}$	$19\frac{1}{4}$	$19\frac{3}{4}$	20	21	$21\frac{3}{4}$	22	23	24
Knee	13	$13\frac{3}{8}$	$13\frac{3}{4}$	$14\frac{1}{8}$	$14\frac{1}{2}$	15	$15\frac{1}{2}$	16	$16\frac{1}{2}$	17
Calf	$12\frac{1}{2}$	$12\frac{7}{8}$	$13\frac{1}{4}$	$13\frac{5}{8}$	$14\frac{1}{8}$	$14\frac{1}{2}$	15	$15\frac{1}{2}$	16	$16\frac{1}{2}$
Ankle	$8\frac{3}{8}$	$8\frac{5}{8}$	$8\frac{7}{8}$	$9\frac{1}{8}$	$9\frac{3}{8}$	$9\frac{5}{8}$	$9\frac{7}{8}$	$10\frac{1}{8}$	$10\frac{3}{8}$	$10\frac{5}{8}$
Vertical trunk	56	$57\frac{1}{2}$	59	$60\frac{1}{2}$	62	$63\frac{1}{2}$	65	$66\frac{1}{2}$	68	$69\frac{1}{2}$
Total crotch	25	$25\frac{3}{4}$	$26\frac{1}{2}$	$27\frac{1}{4}$	28	$28\frac{3}{4}$	$29\frac{1}{2}$	$30\frac{1}{4}$	31	$31\frac{3}{4}$

Vertical Measurements in inches.

Size	2	4	6	8	10	12	14	16	18	20
Stature	$63\frac{1}{2}$	64	$64\frac{1}{2}$	65	$65\frac{1}{2}$	66	$66\frac{1}{2}$	67	$67\frac{1}{2}$	68
Cervical height	$54\frac{1}{2}$	55	$55\frac{1}{2}$	56	$56\frac{1}{2}$	57	$57\frac{1}{2}$	58	$58\frac{1}{2}$	59
Waist height	$39\frac{1}{4}$	$39\frac{1}{2}$	$39\frac{3}{4}$	40	$40\frac{1}{4}$	$40\frac{1}{2}$	$40\frac{3}{4}$	41	$41\frac{1}{4}$	$41\frac{1}{2}$
High hip height	$35\frac{1}{4}$	$35\frac{1}{2}$	$35\frac{3}{4}$	36	$36\frac{1}{4}$	$36\frac{1}{2}$	$36\frac{3}{4}$	37	$37\frac{1}{4}$	$37\frac{1}{2}$

Table 2.1 STANDARD TABLE OF BODY MEASUREMENTS FOR ADULT FEMALE MISSES FIGURE TYPE, SIZES 2–20

Girth Measurements in inches.

Size	2	4	6	8	10	12	14	16	18	20
Hip height	$31\frac{1}{4}$	$31\frac{1}{2}$	$31\frac{3}{4}$	32	$32\frac{1}{4}$	$32\frac{1}{2}$	$32\frac{3}{4}$	33	$33\frac{1}{4}$	$33\frac{1}{2}$
Crotch height	$29\frac{1}{2}$	$29\frac{1}{2}$	$29\frac{1}{2}$	$29\frac{1}{2}$	$29\frac{1}{2}$	$29\frac{1}{2}$	$29\frac{1}{2}$	$29\frac{1}{2}$	$29\frac{1}{2}$	$29\frac{1}{2}$
Knee height	$17\frac{5}{8}$	$17\frac{3}{4}$	$17\frac{7}{8}$	18	$18\frac{1}{8}$	$18\frac{1}{4}$	$18\frac{3}{8}$	$18\frac{1}{2}$	$18\frac{5}{8}$	$18\frac{3}{4}$
Ankle height	$2\frac{3}{4}$	$2\frac{3}{4}$	$2\frac{3}{4}$	$2\frac{3}{4}$	$2\frac{3}{4}$	$2\frac{3}{4}$	$2\frac{3}{4}$	$2\frac{3}{4}$	$2\frac{3}{4}$	$2\frac{3}{4}$
Waist length (front)	$13\frac{1}{2}$	$13\frac{3}{4}$	14	$14\frac{1}{4}$	$14\frac{1}{2}$	$14\frac{3}{4}$	15	$15\frac{1}{4}$	$15\frac{1}{2}$	$15\frac{3}{4}$
Waist length (back) (on Curve)	$15\frac{1}{2}$	$15\frac{3}{4}$	16	$16\frac{1}{4}$	$16\frac{1}{2}$	$16\frac{3}{4}$	17	$17\frac{1}{4}$	$17\frac{1}{2}$	$17\frac{3}{4}$
True rise	$9\frac{3}{4}$	10	$10\frac{1}{4}$	$10\frac{1}{2}$	$10\frac{3}{4}$	11	$11\frac{1}{4}$	$11\frac{1}{2}$	$11\frac{3}{4}$	12

Width and Length Measurements in inches.

Size	2	4	6	8	10	12	14	16	18	20
Across shoulder	$14\frac{3}{8}$	$14\frac{5}{8}$	$14\frac{7}{8}$	$15\frac{1}{8}$	$15\frac{3}{8}$	$15\frac{3}{4}$	$16\frac{1}{8}$	$16\frac{1}{2}$	17	$17\frac{1}{2}$
Cross-back width	$13\frac{7}{8}$	$14\frac{1}{8}$	$14\frac{3}{8}$	$14\frac{5}{8}$	$14\frac{7}{8}$	$15\frac{1}{8}$	$15\frac{5}{8}$	16	$16\frac{1}{2}$	17
Cross-chest width	$12\frac{7}{8}$	$13\frac{1}{8}$	$13\frac{3}{8}$	$13\frac{5}{8}$	$13\frac{7}{8}$	$14\frac{1}{4}$	$14\frac{5}{8}$	15	$15\frac{1}{2}$	16
Shoulder length	$4\frac{15}{16}$	5	$5\frac{1}{16}$	$5\frac{1}{8}$	$5\frac{3}{16}$	$5\frac{5}{16}$	$5\frac{7}{16}$	$5\frac{9}{16}$	$5\frac{3}{4}$	$5\frac{15}{16}$
Shoulder slope (degrees)	23	23	23	23	23	23	23	23	23	23
Arm length shoulder to wrist	$22\frac{15}{16}$	$23\frac{1}{8}$	$23\frac{5}{16}$	$23\frac{1}{2}$	$23\frac{11}{16}$	$23\frac{7}{8}$	$24\frac{1}{16}$	$24\frac{1}{4}$	$24\frac{7}{16}$	$24\frac{5}{8}$
Arm length shoulder to elbow	$13\frac{1}{4}$	$13\frac{3}{8}$	$13\frac{1}{2}$	$13\frac{5}{8}$	$13\frac{3}{4}$	$13\frac{7}{8}$	14	$14\frac{1}{8}$	$14\frac{1}{4}$	$14\frac{3}{8}$
Arm length center back neck to wrist	$30\frac{1}{8}$	$30\frac{7}{16}$	$30\frac{3}{4}$	$31\frac{1}{16}$	$31\frac{3}{8}$	$31\frac{3}{4}$	$32\frac{1}{8}$	$32\frac{1}{2}$	$32\frac{15}{16}$	$33\frac{3}{8}$
Bust point to bust point	7	$7\frac{1}{4}$	$7\frac{1}{2}$	$7\frac{3}{4}$	8	$8\frac{1}{4}$	$8\frac{1}{2}$	$8\frac{3}{4}$	9	$9\frac{1}{4}$
Neck to bust point	$9\frac{1}{4}$	$9\frac{1}{2}$	$9\frac{3}{4}$	10	$10\frac{3}{8}$	$10\frac{5}{8}$	11	$11\frac{3}{8}$	$11\frac{7}{8}$	$12\frac{3}{8}$
Scye depth	$7\frac{1}{8}$	$7\frac{1}{4}$	$7\frac{3}{8}$	$7\frac{1}{2}$	$7\frac{5}{8}$	$7\frac{3}{4}$	$7\frac{7}{8}$	8	$8\frac{1}{8}$	$8\frac{1}{4}$

Reprinted, with permission, from the Annual Book of ASTM Standards, copyright ASTM International, 100 Barr Harbor Drive, West Conshihocken, PA 19428.

more, very few individuals have body measurements that exactly reflect the measurements given in Table 2.1. Any number of women who customarily wear a given size will have certain measurements that differ in relation to the tables that follow. Posture and height will be additional differential factors.

Therefore, the body measurement points and dimensions listed have been added for your reference. Many companies have done private analysis or statistical gathering (possibly including this table) and have developed their own measurement tables. They use their own standards for sizing and an industry fit model that represents those standards. Nevertheless, these body dimensions are a good guide to use when analyzing size proportions. Classroom body forms are often donated by companies in the industry or are ordered according to individualized dress form company specifications. You may want to measure available forms against these measurements for size referencing.

Measuring a Model or Body Form

A body form will only need to be measured once since it will not change. However, if the form is subject to severe wear or abuse, it is advisable to spot-check it periodically or replace it. A model, on the other hand, needs to be measured thoroughly once a year and spot-checked monthly. It is important to use a fiberglass (plastic) measuring tape, as it will not stretch, and to have your model stand erect with a normal breathing pattern. The body points have been listed in order of measurement. A guide to body measurements and a chart for recording measurements (Figure 2.1) have been added for your reference. They are not suggested as industry standards for measuring a body, but are a combination of popular standards ussed in the industry. The following instructions can be used for a model or body form and may be changed or adapted to suit your needs.

Note: When measuring torso and leg circumference measurements, keep the tape measure parallel to the floor at all times; arms are down in a relaxed position.

a. Bust Circumference—Measure around fullest part of bust.

b. Waist Circumference—Measure around smallest part of waist.

c. High/Upper Hip Circumference—Measure around hip at a point 4" below waist.

d. Low Hip Circumference—Measure around hip at a point 7" below waist.

e. Mid Neck—Measure around middle of neck.

f. Armseye—Measure around armseye at a natural relaxed position.

g. Upper Arm—Measure around fullest part of upper arm without flexing the muscle.

h. Elbow—Measure around elbow, over elbow bone, and between arm crease.

i. Wrist—Measure around and over wrist bone.

j. Thigh—Measure around fullest part of thigh.

k. Mid Thigh—Measure around thigh at a point that is one-half length of thigh from crotch to knee.

l. Knee—Measure around knee, over knee bone, and between knee crease.

m. Calf—Measure around calf at fullest point.

n. Ankle—Measure around and over ankle bone.

o. Vertical Trunk—Measure from bottom of front neck at indentation down over front torso, through crotch, and back up back torso to top vertebra bone. Note: Some companies prefer to take this measurement from right shoulder neck point, down over front torso, through crotch, and back up to starting point at right shoulder.

p. Cross-back Width—Measure at a point 4" down from back neck bone straight across back from armseye to armseye.

q. Cross-chest Width—Measure at a point 4" down from shoulder at neck straight across chest from armseye to armseye.

r. Bust Point to Bust Point—Measure from one bust point apex straight across to other bust point apex.

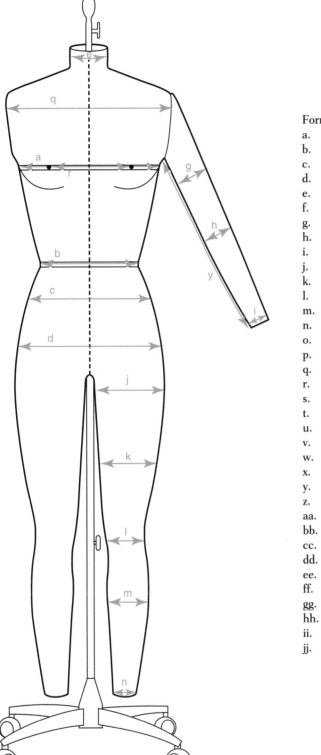

Figure 2.1

Form Measurement/Dimensions
a. Bust Circumference =
b. Waist Circumference =
c. High/Upper Hip Circumference =
d. Low Hip Circumference =
e. Mid Neck =
f. Armseye =
g. Upper Arm =
h. Elbow =
i. Wrist =
j. Thigh =
k. Mid Thigh =
l. Knee =
m. Calf =
n. Ankle =
o. Vertical Trunk =
p. Cross-back Width =
q. Cross-chest Width =
r. Bust Point to Bust Point =
s. Neck to Bust Point =
t. Armseye to Waist =
u. Waist to Hip =
v. Shoulder Length =
w. Arm Length, Shoulder to Wrist =
x. Arm Length, Shoulder to Elbow =
y. Underarm Length =
z. Waist Length Front =
aa. Waist Length Back =
bb. Stature =
cc. Shoulder Height =
dd. Bust Height =
ee. Waist Height =
ff. High Hip Height =
gg. Low Hip Height =
hh. Crotch Height =
ii. Knee Height =
jj. Ankle Height =

(continued)

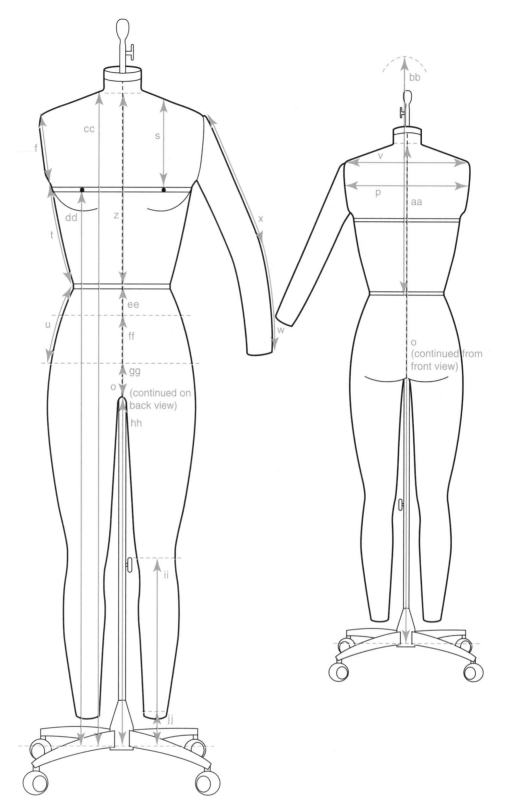

Figure 2.1 *Continued*

s. Neck to Bust Point—Measure from neck at shoulder straight down to bust point apex.

t. Armseye to Waist—Measure from the underarm, armseye, straight down side of body to smallest part of waist.

u. Waist to Hip—First mark hip at a point 7" below waist from bottom of waist at center front, then measure along side of body from waist at smallest part, down to hip at point that intersects with first point. Note: This measurement will be larger than 7" to accommodate hip curve.

v. Shoulder Length—Measure from right shoulder to left shoulder (feeling for shoulder bones) straight across the back.

w. Arm Length, Shoulder to Wrist—Hold your arm in a slightly bent position, then measure from top of shoulder at shoulder bone down outer arm, crossing top edge of the elbow bone slightly, continuing down to wrist bone.

x. Arm Length, Shoulder to Elbow—Hold your arm in a slightly bent position, then measure from top of shoulder at shoulder bone down outer arm, stopping at top edge of elbow bone.

y. Underarm Length—Hold your arm slightly away from body and measure from underarm straight down to palm side of wrist.

z. Waist Length Front—Measure from bottom of front neck at indentation straight down over front torso to waist at smallest part.

aa. Waist Length Back—Measure from bottom of back neck at neck bone straight down back to waist at smallest part.

bb. Stature—Measure from top of head straight down back to floor.

cc. Shoulder Height—Measure from right shoulder bone straight down front to floor.

dd. Bust Height—Measure from apex of bust straight down to floor.

ee. Waist Height—Measure from center front waist straight down to floor.

ff. High Hip Height—Measure from high hip from a point 4" below the center front of waist straight down to floor.

gg. Low Hip Height—Measure from low hip from a point 7" below center front of waist straight down to floor.

hh. Crotch Height—Measure from crotch from between legs straight down to floor.

ii. Knee Height—Measure from inside leg, inseam, at center of knee straight down to floor.

jj. Ankle Height—Measure from inside leg, inseam, at ankle bone straight down to floor.

Note: When taking measurements bb through jj on the form, be sure the form manufacturer has marked the floor point on your stand. If you do not have such a mark, be sure to ask the distance from the ankle to the floor (generally about $2\frac{3}{4}$"), then simply stop these measurements at the ankle and add the ankle floor measurement given.

Using a Spec Sheet

A specification sheet, or spec, is a technical rendering of a garment identifying the points of measurement and size ranges. Every garment on the line requires a new set of specs because each is unique. Larger companies are able to generate specs on computers, while in smaller companies the designers, technical designers, size specification analysts, merchandisers, or product managers are required to develop the specs by hand.

Developing a spec by hand or with the aid of a computer takes considerable training and experience. It is imperative that everyone in the production and manufacturing of clothing be able to read and use a spec sheet. Specs will vary in design throughout the industry. Let's look at the parts of a generic spec sheet (Figure 2.2).

❖ Style—A numerical code or name is used to identify each style. Style numbers or garment names are often designated according to department, grouping, or style type.

❖ Season—Most retailers and wholesalers track styles by season. Even if silhouettes are repeated

GENERIC SPEC SHEET		STYLE								
SEASON:		DESCRIPTION:								
LABEL: (SIZE CATEGORY)										
DATE:										
TECHNICAL SKETCH		SKETCH/PHOTO								

CODE	POINT OF MEASURE	TOL. +/–	4	S/6	8	M/10	12	L/14	16	XL/18
		°								

Figure 2.2

(continued)

GENERIC SPEC SHEET

STYLE

CODE	POINT OF MEASURE	TOL. +/–	4	S/6	8	M/10	12	L/14	16	XL/18

COMMENTS:

Figure 2.2 *Continued*

from season to season, a new style or color number/name is often assigned.

❖ Codes—Codes are used for the method of measurement. Notice on Figure 1.1 that the basic codes in the code column are the same as the codes on the technical sketch. There are more than 150 different codes used in the industry; only the most frequently used codes are printed on the spec sheets. Codes are important because they match the detailed measurement instructions found in the company's measurement manual. This text uses numbers 1 to 152. Some spec manuals use three-digit codes or code numbers and letters. However designated, codes on the spec sheet in the code column will always match codes on the technical sketch.

❖ Point of Measure (Measurement Method)—A brief description of the method of measurement is listed beside the code. A single industry standard for measuring has not been set; therefore, it cannot be assumed that everyone using the spec sheet will measure the same way. The description is very important for this reason. It is also important if a common method needs to be changed to accommodate a particular style. The change is then noted next to the description. You'll learn more about that later.

❖ Tolerance—Sewing garments is not an exact science. Although every step is taken to ensure accuracy, no two garments will ever be exactly alike. Therefore, tolerance measurements are given to indicate how much of a measurement deviation, on the plus or minus, will still be accepted. A tolerance chart has been added at the end of this text for your reference.

❖ Size Categories—There are a number of different size categories, each carrying a size range. The childrenswear category includes newborn 0 to 6 months, infant 6 to 24 months, toddler 2T to 4T, girls 4 to 6x, boys 4 to 7, girls 7 to 14, and boys 8 to 20. Preteen sizes 8 to 14 are sometimes categorized with childrenswear and other times considered prejuniors. Juniors are generally a separate category with sizes ranging from 2 to 10 or 3 to 11. Womenswear is broken into misses/missy sizes, generally ranging from size 6 to 16, and large/plus sizes ranging from 18 to 30. The menswear category breaks down its sizes by style, for example, neck and sleeve length for shirts, waist for pants, and chest for suit jackets. Spec sheets will generally indicate the size category by department name, e.g., missy.

❖ Size Range—Each size must be cut to its own measurements. The range of sizes (small, medium, large, extra large, for example) is listed across the top of the size columns. Generally, only the sizes that will actually be produced for that garment will be listed. A first or sample spec will only list the sample size measurements. Fully graded specs are developed after the sample has been approved for production. Chapter 15 covers grading instructions and includes grading charts for your reference.

❖ Sketch—A sketch or photo, often called a work sketch or work photo, is attached to the spec sheet. This gives everyone using the spec sheet a visual reference of the garment under production. It is important that exact style details are reflected on this sketch (the number of buttons, a pocket or a zipper, for example). Basic garment croquis can be found in Appendix B.

❖ Technical Sketch—The technical sketch is used as a key for visual code reference. The basic codes most frequently used are found on this sketch. If a style feature requires deviation from a basic or common code, then the new code must be added to the sketch for clarification. Details for clarification will be found in the Body Point of Measure and How to Measure portions of this text.

New to technical design is a working specification sheet also known as a fit session worksheet. It is just beginning to be incorporated into major buying offices' and offshore manufacturings' technical design departments. Essentially, the spec sheet looks the same, with the exception of the measuring boxes. In place of the boxes for the size range and fully graded measurements, the working specification/fit sheet has the following (see Figure 2.3):

- Prototype—The prototype column is for the first measurements that have been developed from a sketch or any garment under evaluation that is not from the contracted production plant.
- Revised Spec—The revised spec column is used after fitting a first garment. Changes or corrections are placed in this column. If first measurements are developed from a sketch, this column is not used.
- First Sample—The first sample column is used to list the measurements of the first sample as submitted by the contracted production plant. In some instances more than one sample will need to be submitted before production approval. If the garment is a second or third sample, the technician can simply make a note by changing this column or putting that designation in the comments column.
- Final Spec—The final spec column lists the approved specs decided upon after the sample evaluation. In most cases, these numbers will reflect the revised spec or the sample spec measurements. However, there will be instances when new measurements are given. These changes should be noted in the comments column.

- X—This is the "out-of-tolerance" column. This column is used by the technician to let the contractor know that a measurement is not within allowed limits for sewing discrepancies. It is used to flag potential fit and construction problems.
- Comments—Any comments that need to be indicated to the production plant by the technician can go in this column.

In the chapters that follow, you will learn how to measure garments. These measurements are recorded onto the spec sheets. Later, when you are ready to evaluate garments for fit, those measurements will be analyzed one by one and changed or corrected as needed. But for now, it's time to get familiar with measuring. Read through and practice the measurement points in Chapter 3, then move on to the individual garment chapters for more measuring practice and spec sheet recording.

CHAPTER 2 TERMS

When working as a technical designer, you will come across the terms listed below. If you are unfamiliar with any of them, please look up the definitions in the glossary at the end of this text.

Body dimension
Body form
Specification (spec) sheet

GENERIC SPEC SHEET   **STYLE**

SEASON:	DESCRIPTION:
LABEL: (SIZE CATEGORY)	
DATE:	
TECHNICAL SKETCH	SKETCH/PHOTO

CODE	POINT OF MEASURE	TOL. +/−	PROTO-TYPE	REVISED SPEC	FIRST SAMPLE	FINAL SPEC	X	COMMENTS
NOTE: X INDICATES THE SAMPLE IS OUT OF TOLERANCE								

(Tolerance $1/2$-$3/4$ S, M, L, XL = $3/4$" 4-18 = $1/2$")

The measured garment spec sheets are for *illustrative purposes only* and should not be used as industry standards

Figure 2.3

(continued)

GENERIC SPEC SHEET   **STYLE**

CODE	POINT OF MEASURE	TOL. +/−	PROTO-TYPE	REVISED SPEC	FIRST SAMPLE	FINAL SPEC	X	COMMENTS

COMMENTS:

Figure 2.3 *Continued*

CHAPTER 3

Basic Measurement Points

Measurement Preparation

Before starting to measure, it is important to read and follow the list of ten measurement preparations that follow. If these preparations are not followed each time the garment is measured, measurements may not be accurate. All garments should be measured to the nearest $\frac{1}{8}$ inch.

1. Always measure the garment lying flat, unless otherwise specified. The measuring surface must be clean and smooth without a rough texture or tabletop accoutrements. The area needs to be large enough to hold the entire garment lying flat without any folds or any part of the garment hanging over the edge of the table. A patternmaking table works well for measuring (see Figure 3.1).

2. Pick up the garment from the top, shake it gently to remove any folds, and lay it flat on the table in a natural relaxed position.

3. Gently pat and smooth out all the fabric wrinkles by hand. Do not pull or stretch the fabric beyond its natural condition to remove wrinkles. Also, do not compact the fabric beyond its natural condition by using inward hand strokes.

4. Take all the measurements with a plastic (fiberglass) tape measure. Do not use metal or fabric tape measures. Metal tape measures do not bend well when used on curves,

Figure 3.1 Always make sure your garmet is lying flat.

24

while fabric tape measures can stretch with use and, therefore, both may result in inaccurate measurements. Periodically check your plastic (fiberglass) tape against a metal ruler to ensure its accuracy and replace it when the numbers become worn.

5. All measurements are taken with the tape measure lying flat against the garment, unless measuring a curved seam/contour. To get an accurate measurement on a curved seam/contour, stand the tape measure on its side edge and proceed with the measurement (see Figures 3.2a and b).

6. Take all the measurements with the buttons, snaps, zippers, hooks, ties, pleats, and vents fully closed and in a natural relaxed position. This is especially important for flared or pleated edges. They must lie with the pleats closed (pinned if needed) or with the gathers softly folding. Do not pull or stretch the garment, unless otherwise specified by the design (see Figure 3.3).

7. Extended measurements will need to be taken on the waist, leg, and cuff openings when the elastic or drawstring draws areas or when a stretch fabric is used for contouring. Extended measurements are the only time a garment is to be stretched. However, do not stretch the fabric beyond the natural relaxed position of the garment. Gently pull the garment to get a measurement of the fabric width before it's drawn by the elastic, drawstring, or contouring fabric. Inert elastic should be measured with the garment extended until the fabric is smooth without breaking sewing stitches. Loosen the drawstrings and smooth out the gathers until the fabric is flat. Stretch materials are measured at a fully extended but not distorted position, without broken stitches.

8. For consistency, the front of the garment is always measured first, then the back. If the garment has a detachable item such as a collar or belt, it is measured last.

9. Always fold knitted garments for storage. Hanging knitted garments will cause them to stretch; therefore, measurements will not be accurate.

10. Before using a measurement method, be absolutely sure how that measurement is to be taken. Some garments may require a variation of that measurement due to highly detailed or unusual styling. Be sure to determine the measurement criteria and document the change on the specification sheet. Specific instructions for these changes will

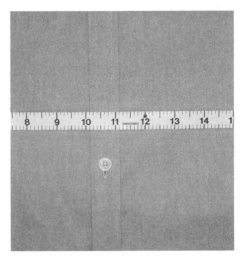

Figure 3.2a Your tape measure should lie flat against the garmet being measured.

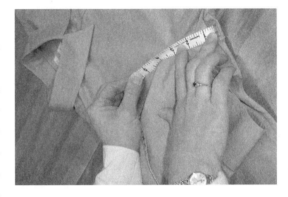

Figure 3.2b When measuring a curved seam, stand the tape measure on its side.

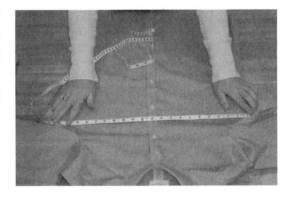

Figure 3.3 Make sure all buttons, snaps, zippers, etc. are closed when taking measurements.

be discussed in the How to Write a Spec Sheet section of this text.

A garment may contain a style or design feature that is not listed in the measurement terms and definitions section of this text. Those instances are very rare but are easily remedied by adding the required measurement method to your spec sheet. Specific instructions for these additions were discussed in the How to Write a Spec Sheet section of this text.

Basic Measurement Points

Basic measurement points refer to the point of each measurement for a particular style/garment. A standard measuring method will ensure that each person using the size specification, spec, will have the same understanding of the garment being created. This section consists of 152 basic measurement points. These points have been labeled, defined, and laid out in a manner consistent with top industry standards; however, this text does not propose to be a standard, but a reflection of other popular standards. These measurement points are offered in order of measurement, for example, length then width, rather then by garment style. Chapters 4 through 15 will regroup the basic body measurement points as required by a specific garment style.

It is an old industry practice for some measurement points to be taken flat, singular side to side, and some measurements to be taken in the circumference, also called total measurements. Circumference measurements are taken flat, then doubled. This may be confusing at first, but circumference measurements are clearly marked with doubling instructions. In many larger industry buying offices, knits are generally measured singularly and wovens are doubled.

A few garment or partial garment illustrations have been chosen for each measurement point that follows, best representing that particular point of measure. However, a wide variety of garments will be measured using these same measurement points. Again, this may be confusing at first, but further instructions for particular styles will be covered in Chapters 4 through 15.

Be sure you understand the ten measurement preparation instructions from the Measurement Preparation section before you begin to measure. At first, measuring may feel awkward. Practice each step until you feel comfortable with that mea-

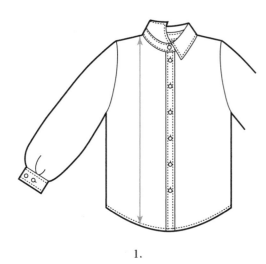

1.

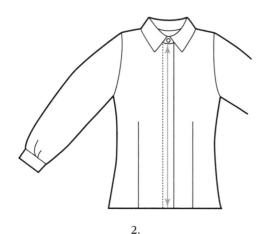

2.

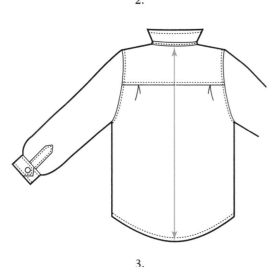

3.

surement point, then move on to the next step. You will need to have several garments available for measuring practice. Use garments from your own closet, if you are a student, or ask to borrow garments from a design, technical, or quality assurance department if you work in the industry.

1. *Front Length (garments with a front opening)*—Measure from high point shoulder at neck straight down, parallel to center front, to bottom of garment at front. If garment has a collar, gently lift it away from shoulder-neck measuring point.

2. *Center Front Length (garments with a plain front; no front opening)*—Measure from center front neck joining seams straight down to bottom of garment at center front. [Note: A garment without a front opening may still require use of Front Length if neckline is unusual.]

3. *Center Back Length*—Measure from center back neck joining seams straight down to bottom of garment at center back. If needed, gently lift collar away from back neck to expose joining seam.

4. *Side Length*—Measure from bottom of armhole/side seam straight down to bottom of garment along side of garment. Do not follow natural curve of garment's side seam, unless otherwise indicated. If needed, gently lift sleeve away from armhole/side seam joining seam.

5. *Front Bodice Length (garments with a front opening)*—Measure from high point shoulder at neck straight down, parallel to center front, to top edge of waistband, joining seam, or rib. If garment has a collar, gently lift it away from shoulder-neck measuring point.

6. *Center Front Bodice Length (garments with a plain front; no front opening)*—Measure from center front neck joining seam straight down to top edge of waistband, joining seam, or rib. [Note: A garment without a center opening may still require use of Front Bodice Length if neckline is unusual.]

7. *Center Back Bodice Length*—Measure from center back neck joining seams straight down to top edge of waistband, joining seam, or rib. If needed, gently lift collar away from back neck to expose joining seam.

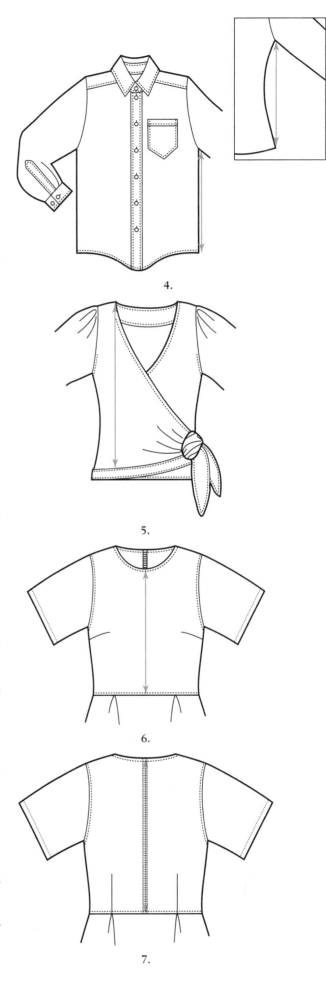

4.

5.

6.

7.

8.

9.

10.

11.

12.

13.

14.

15.

8. *Side Seam Bodice Length*—Measure from bottom of arm-hole/side seam straight down to top edge of waistband, joining seam, or rib, along side of garment, following natural curve of garment's side seam, unless otherwise indicated. If needed, gently lift sleeve away from armhole/side seam joining seam. [Note: You can take side seam bodice measurement straight rather than contoured if joining seam/rib can be extended, but indicate change on the spec sheet.]

9. *Chest Width (knit)*—Measure from edge of garment/side seam to edge of garment/side seam straight across garment at a point 1' below armhole.

10. *Chest Width Circumference (woven)*—Measure from edge of garment/side seam to edge of garment/side seam straight across garment at a point 1' below armhole. Double this measurement.

11. *Chest Width (raglan sleeve, knit)*—Measure from edge of garment/side seam to edge of garment/side seam straight across garment at a point _____" below high point shoulder. [Note: You will have to determine number of inches down from high point shoulder for each raglan sleeve style based on depth of sleeve. Then indicate this number on spec sheet.]

12. *Chest Width Circumference (raglan sleeve, woven)*—Measure from edge of garment/side seam to edge of garment/side seam straight across garment at a point _____" below high point shoulder. Double this measurement. [Note: You will have to determine number of inches down from high point shoulder for each raglan sleeve style based on depth of sleeve. Then indicate this number on spec sheet.]

13. *Across Shoulder*—Measure straight across front from arm-hole seam/edge to armhole seam/edge at shoulder seam or across natural shoulder fold line created if there is no seam.

14. *Shoulder Width*—Measure from neckband/collar/ribbing joining seam or neckline edge to top of armhole seam at shoulder, taken along shoulder seam or across natural shoulder fold line created if there is no seam.

15. *Across Chest*—Measure $2\frac{1}{2}$" down from collar/rib joining seam at center front straight across front of garment from arm-

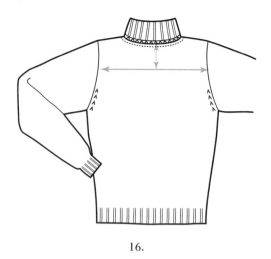

16.

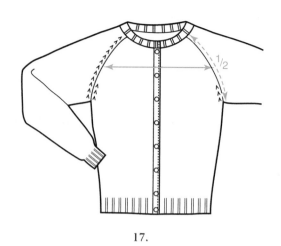

17.

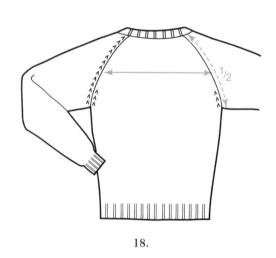

18.

19.

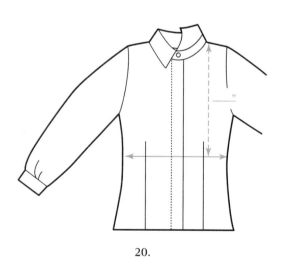

20.

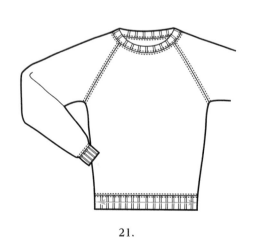

21.

hole seam/edge to armhole seam/edge. [Note: The $2\frac{1}{2}$" measurement point is for missywear only and may need to be adjusted up or down $\frac{1}{4}$" to $\frac{1}{2}$" accordingly for men's, children's, junior's, and large/plus womenswear. Indicate any changes on spec sheet.]

16. *Across Back*—Measure 4" down from collar/rib joining seam at center back straight across back of garment from armhole seam/edge to armhole seam/edge. [Note: The 4" measurement point is for missywear only and may need to be adjusted up or down $\frac{1}{4}$" to $\frac{1}{2}$" accordingly for men's, children's, junior's, and large/plus womenswear. Indicate any changes on spec sheet.]

17. *Across Chest/Center Armhole*—Measure at one-half depth of armhole straight across front of garment from armhole seam/edge to armhole seam/edge.

18. *Across Back/Center Armhole*—Measure at one-half depth of armhole straight across back of garment from armhole seam/edge to armhole seam/edge.

19. *Waist Width (knit)*—Measure from edge of garment/side seam to edge of garment/side seam straight across garment on seam or at narrowest point of waist taper at a point _____" below high point shoulder. [Note: You will have to determine number of inches down from high point shoulder for each raglan sleeve style based on depth of sleeve. Then indicate this number on spec sheet.]

20. *Waist Width Circumference (woven)*—Measure from edge of garment/side seam to edge of garment/side seam straight across garment on seam or at narrowest point of waist taper at a point _____" below high point shoulder. Double this measurement. [Note: You will have to determine number of inches down from high point shoulder for each raglan sleeve style based on depth of sleeve. Then indicate this number on spec sheet.]

21. *Bottom Band Width (knit top)*—Measure from side of bottom band to side of bottom band along center of band, following natural contour of waistband.

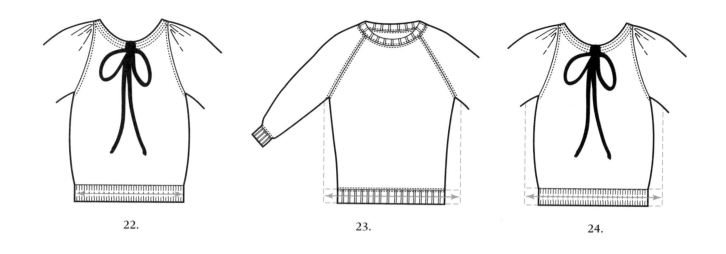

22.   23.   24.

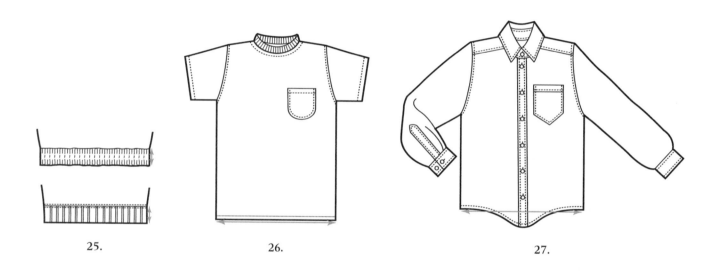

25.   26.   27.

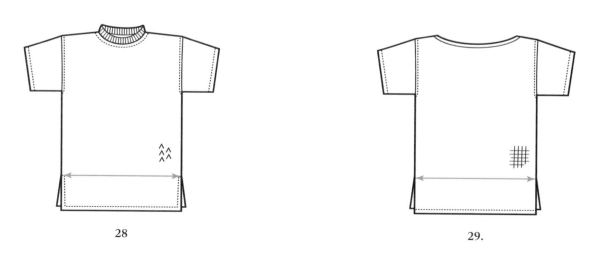

28   29.

22. *Bottom Band Circumference (woven top)*—Measure from side of bottom band to side of bottom band along center of band, following natural contour of waistband. Double this measurement.

23. *Bottom Band Width, Stretched (knit top)*—Measure from side of bottom band to side of bottom band straight across center of band in a fully extended position.

24. *Bottom Band Width Circumference Stretched (woven top)*—Measure from side of bottom band to side of bottom band straight across center of band in a fully extended position. Double this measurement.

25. *Bottom Band/Ribbing Height (knit or woven top)*—Measure from band/ribbing joining seam straight down to bottom edge of band/rib opening. [Note: If band is shaped or contoured, indicate special measurement instructions on spec sheet.]

26. *Bottom Opening/Sweep (knit top)*—Measure from edge of garment/side seam to edge of garment/side seam straight across garment at bottom opening. [Note: If sweep has pleats, measure with pleats closed or relaxed.]

27. *Bottom Opening/Sweep Width Circumference (woven top)*—Measure from edge of garment/side seam to edge of garment/side seam straight across garment at bottom opening. Double this measurement. [Note: If sweep has pleats, measure with pleats closed or relaxed.]

28. *Vented Bottom Opening/Sweep Width (knit top)*—Measure from edge of garment/side seam to edge of garment/side seam straight across garment at top of side vents. Do not follow natural curve of garment. [Note: If vents are too high to measure sweep, indicate opening at appropriate position, e.g., midriff opening.]

29. *Vented Bottom Opening/Sweep Width Circumference (woven top)*—Measure from edge of garment/side seam to edge of garment/side seam straight across garment at top of side vents. Do not follow natural curve of garment. Double this measurement. [Note: If vents are too high to measure sweep, indicate opening at appropriate position, e.g., midriff opening.]

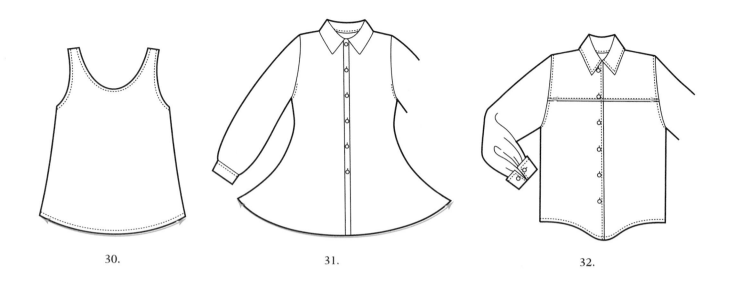

30.   31.   32.

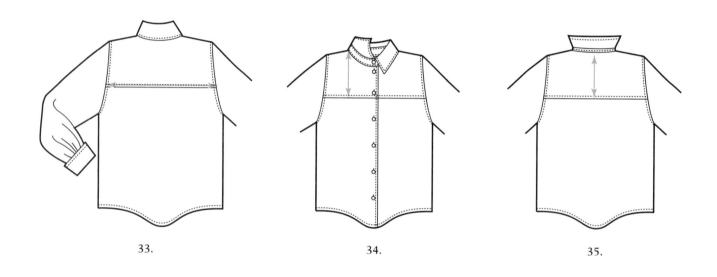

33.   34.   35.

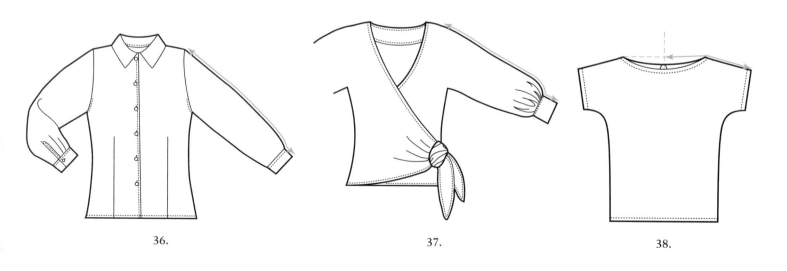

36.   37.   38.

30. *Circular Bottom Opening/Sweep Width (knit top)*—Measure from edge of garment/side seam to edge of garment/side seam, following natural contour of garment at bottom opening.

31. *Circular Bottom Opening/Sweep Width Circumference (woven top)*—Measure from edge of garment/side seam to edge of garment/side seam, following natural contour of garment at bottom opening. Double this measurement.

32. *Yoke Width Front*—Measure from armhole seam/edge to armhole seam/edge straight across front of garment, ignoring contours or points, at yoke-body joining seams. [Note: If yoke is asymmetrical, indicate changes in measuring as needed on spec sheet.]

33. *Yoke Width Back*—Measure from armhole seam/edge to armhole seam/edge straight across back of garment, ignoring contours or points, at yoke-body joining seams. [Note: If yoke is asymmetrical, indicate changes in measuring as needed on spec sheet.]

34. *Yoke Depth Front*—Measure from high point shoulder at neck straight down to bottom of front yoke-body joining seam. Be sure to gently lift collar away from shoulder-neck joining seam if needed.

35. *Yoke Back Depth*—Measure from center back neck joining seam straight down to bottom of back yoke-body joining seam. Gently lift collar away from back neck joining seam if needed.

36. *Sleeve Length Top Armhole*—Measure along top of sleeve/fold, following contour of sleeve from armhole seam at shoulder to bottom of sleeve opening, including cuff.

37. *Sleeve Length Top Neck*—Measure along top of sleeve/fold, following contour of sleeve from sleeve-neck joining seam/edge to edge of sleeve opening, including cuff. Gently lift away collar at sleeve-neck joining seam if needed.

38. *Sleeve Length Center Back*—Measure from center back neck joining seam or from a point above neck at an imaginary line, that of a joining seam, along top of sleeve/fold, following contour of sleeve to edge of sleeve opening, including cuff.

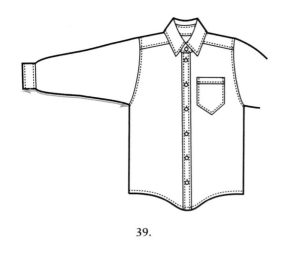

39.

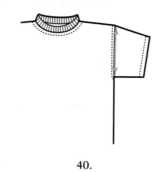

40.

41.

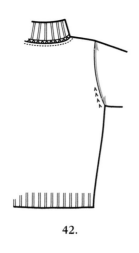

42.

43.

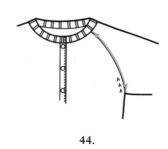

44.

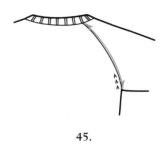

45.

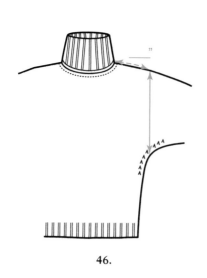

46.

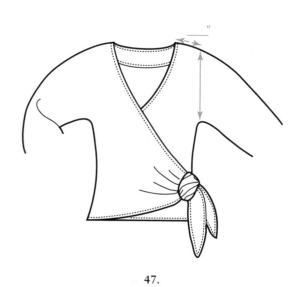

47.

39. *Sleeve Length Underarm*—Measure straight from bottom of armhole along sleeve seam to edge of sleeve opening, including cuff.

40. *Straight Armhole Width (knit)*—Measure from top of shoulder joining seam/edge straight down to bottom of armhole.

41. *Straight Armhole Width Circumference (woven)*—Measure from top of shoulder joining seam/edge straight down to bottom of armhole. Double this measurement.

42. *Curved Armhole Width (knit)*—Measure from top of shoulder joining seam/edge to bottom of armhole, following contour of armhole.

43. *Curved Armhole Width Circumference (woven)*—Measure from top of shoulder joining seam/edge to bottom of armhole, following contour of armhole. Double this measurement.

44. *Armhole Front*—Measure on front of garment from top of shoulder at neckline joining seam/edge to bottom of armhole, following contour of armhole. Gently lift collar away from neckline joining seam if needed.

45. *Armhole Back*—Measure on back of garment from top of shoulder at neck joining seam/edge to bottom of armhole, following contour of armhole. Gently lift collar away from neck joining seam if needed.

46. *Armhole Width Straight (knit)*—Measure from top of shoulder seam at a point _____" below neckline joining seam/edge straight down to bottom of armhole. [Note: Gently move collar away from neck joining seam if needed when measuring down _____" to armhole start point. Indicate number of inches measured down on spec sheet.]

47. *Armhole Width Circumference Straight (woven)*—Measure from top of shoulder seam at a point _____" below neckline joining seam/edge straight down to bottom of armhole. Double this measurement. [Note: Gently move collar away from neck joining seam if needed when measuring down _____" to armhole start point. Indicate number of inches measured down on spec sheet.]

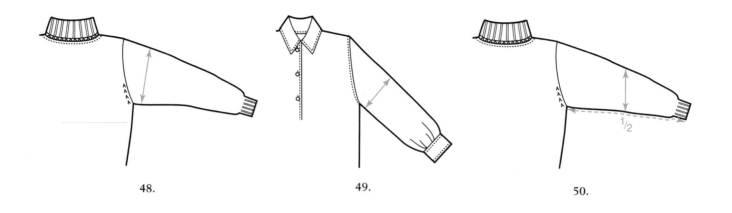

48.

49.

50.

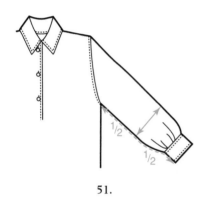

51.

52.

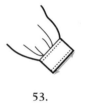

53.

54.

55.

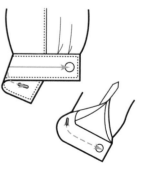

56.

48. *Muscle Width (knit)*—Measure from inner sleeve edge/seam to outer sleeve edge/fold at a point 1" below armhole and parallel to sleeve opening.

49. *Muscle Width Circumference (woven)*—Measure from inner sleeve edge/seam to outer sleeve edge/fold at a point 1" below armhole and parallel to sleeve opening. Double this measurement.

50. *Elbow Width (knit)*—Measure from inner sleeve edge/seam to outer sleeve edge/fold straight across sleeve at a point one-half of underarm sleeve length and parallel to sleeve opening at wrist or cuff. [Note: If sleeve is three-quarter length, indicate new point of measure on spec sheet.]

51. *Elbow Width Circumference (woven)*—Measure from inner sleeve edge/seam to outer sleeve edge/fold straight across sleeve at a point one-half of the underarm sleeve length and parallel to sleeve opening at wrist or cuff. Double this measurement. [Note: If sleeve is three-quarter length, indicate new point of measure on spec sheet.]

52. *Sleeve Opening Width (knit)*—Measure from inner sleeve edge/seam to outer sleeve edge/fold straight across bottom edge of sleeve opening.

53. *Sleeve Opening Width Circumference (woven)*—Measure from inner sleeve edge/seam to outer sleeve edge/fold straight across bottom edge of sleeve opening. Double this measurement.

54. *Sleeve Opening Width, Stretched (knit)*—Measure from inner sleeve edge/seam to outer sleeve edge/fold straight across bottom edge of sleeve opening in a fully extended position.

55. *Sleeve Opening Width Circumference, Stretched (woven)*—Measure from inner sleeve edge/seam to outer sleeve edge/fold straight across bottom edge of sleeve opening in a fully extended position. Double this measurement.

56. *Cuff Length Sleeve*—Measure from outside end of buttonhole to center of button straight along center of cuff. Open cuff out as flat as possible when measuring. [Note: If cuff length is contoured, measure along center-most point.]

57.

57. *Cuff/Ribbing Height Sleeve*—Measure from cuff joining seam or top of ribbing straight down to bottom edge of cuff or rib opening. [Note: If cuff is contoured, indicate changes made as needed to measurement on spec sheet.]

58.

58. *Neck Depth Front (garments with a plain front/asymmetrical front opening)*—Measure from center back neck joining seam/edge straight down to center front neck joining seam edge.

59.

59. *Neck Depth Center Front (garments with a center front opening)*—Measure from center back neck joining seam/edge straight down to center of first button at center front of garment.

60.

60. *Neck Drop Front*—Measure from an imaginary line connecting neckline edges straight down to center front neck opening edge. Use a ruler if needed to connect top neckline edges.

61.

61. *Neck Drop Back*—Measure from an imaginary line connecting neckline edges straight down to center back neck opening edge. This measurement is taken with front of garment facing up. Use a ruler to connect top neckline edges if needed.

62.

62. *Neck Width, No Collar*—Measure from inside neck edge/seam to inside neck edge/seam straight across back neck at widest point. This measurement is taken with front of garment facing up.

63.

63. *Neck Width, Collar*—Measure straight across back neck from neck-shoulder joining seam to neck-shoulder joining seam or natural shoulder line if no seam. This measurement is taken with back of garment faceup.

64.

64. *Neck Edge Width (knit)*—Measure from neck edge/seam/fold to neck edge/seam/fold along top opening edge, following natural contour of neck opening. Garment should be positioned with one shoulder on top of the other and with front and back neck edges meeting.

65.

65. *Neck Edge Width Circumference (woven)*—Measure from neck edge/seam/fold to neck edge/seam/fold along top opening edge, following natural contour of neck opening. Garment

should be positioned with one shoulder on top of the other and with front and back neck edges meeting. Double this measurement.

66. *Neck Edge Width, Stretched (knit)*—Measure from neck edge/seam/fold to neck edge/seam/fold along top opening edge in a fully extended position. Garment should be positioned with one shoulder on top of the other and with front and back neck edges meeting.

66.

67. *Neck Edge Width Circumference, Stretched (woven)*—Measure from neck edge/seam/fold to neck edge/seam/fold along top opening edge in a fully extended position. Garment should be positioned with one shoulder on top of the other and with front and back neck edges meeting. Double this measurement.

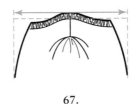

67.

68. *Neck Base (knit)*—Measure from neck edge/seam to neck edge/seam along collar/rib joining seam or neckline edge, following natural contour of neck opening. Garment should be buttoned or zippered, if applicable, with one shoulder seam positioned on top of the other and with front and back neck edges meeting.

68.

69. *Neck Base Circumference (woven)*—Measure from neck edge/seam to neck edge/seam along collar/rib joining seam or neckline edge, following natural contour of neck opening. Garment should be buttoned or zippered, if applicable, with one shoulder seam positioned on top of the other and with front and back neck edges meeting. Double this measurement.

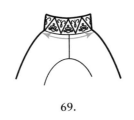

69.

70. *Neckband Length*—Measure from outside end of buttonhole to center of buttonhole across neckband, following contour of neckband.

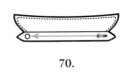

70.

71. *Collar Length*—Measure from one end of collar to other end of collar along neck joining seam.

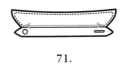

71.

72. *Collar Height*—Measure from collar/rib joining seam at center back neck straight up to outer edge of collar/rib.

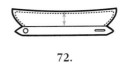

72.

73. *Collar Band Height*—Measure from collar joining seam at center back straight up to neckband joining seam at center back.

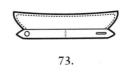

73.

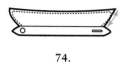

74.

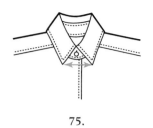

75.

Notched

Without
notches

76.

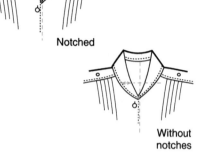

77.

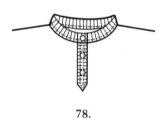

78.

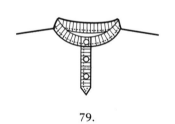

79.

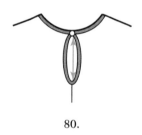

80.

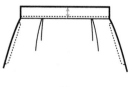

81.

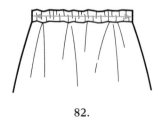

82.

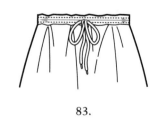

83.

74. *Collar Point Length*—Measure from collar joining seam to outer edge of collar along collar point edge. [Note: If collar is rounded, measure at a point parallel to center back and indicate change on spec sheet.]

75. *Collar Point Spread (pointed collars only)*—Measure, with collar band buttoned and collar in place, from collar point straight across collar edge to collar point.

76. *Lapel Width*
A. *Notched*—Measure from lower lapel notch straight across to lapel fold at a point perpendicular to garment center front.
B. *Without Notches*—Measure from lapel edge straight across widest point of lapel to lapel fold at a point _____" down from center back collar joining seam and perpendicular to front of garment.

77. *Center Front Extension*—Measure from an imaginary line at center front of garment horizontally to finished outer edge of front extended piece.

78. *Placket Length*—Measure from top edge of placket straight down to bottom of placket opening along center of placket.

79. *Placket Width*—Measure from placket joining seam straight across placket to placket edge at fold.

80. *Keyhole Length*—Measure from outer edge of neckline straight down to bottom of keyhole opening.

81. *Waistband Depth*—Measure from top of waistband edge straight down to bottom of waistband at waistband joining seam. [Note: If waistband is contoured, indicate measurement change on spec sheet.]

82. *Waistband Width (knit)*—Measure from side of bottom band to side of bottom band along center of band, following natural contour of waistband.

83. *Waistband Circumference (woven)*—Measure from side of bottom band to side of bottom band along center of band, following natural contour of waistband. Double this measurement.

84.

85.

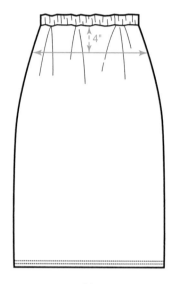

86.

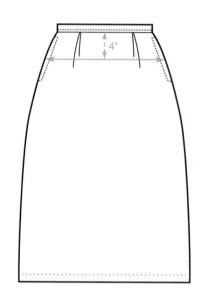

87.

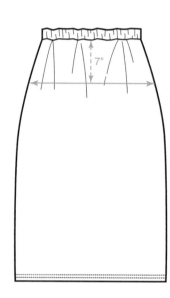

88.

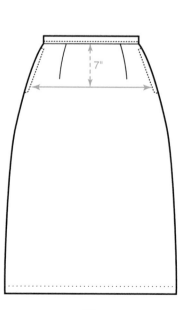

89.

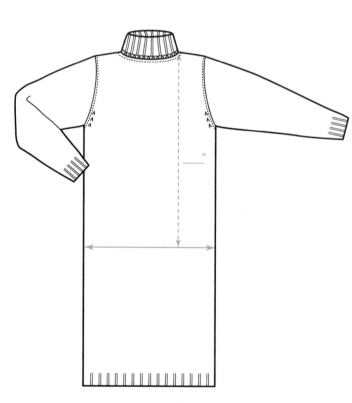

90.

84. *Waistband Width, Stretched (knit)*—Measure from side of bottom band to side of bottom band straight across center of band in a fully extended position.

85. *Waistband Width Circumference, Stretched (woven)*—Measure from side of bottom band to side of bottom band straight across center of band in a fully extended position. Double this measurement.

86. *High Hip Width (knit)*—Measure from edge of garment/side seam to edge of garment/side seam at a point 4" below bottom edge of waistband/seam, following contour of waist. [Note: The 4" point is for missywear only, adjust as needed $\frac{1}{2}$" to 1" up or down for children's, petite's, junior's or large/plus womenswear. Indicate change on spec sheet.]

87. *High Hip Width Circumference (woven)*—Measure from edge of garment/side seam to edge of garment/side seam at a point 4" below bottom edge of waistband/seam, following contour of waist. Double this measurement. [Note: The 4" point is for missywear only; adjust as needed $\frac{1}{2}$" to 1" up or down for children's, petite's, junior's, or large/plus womenswear. Indicate change on spec sheet.]

88. *Low Hip Width from Waist (knit)*—Measure from edge of garment/side seam to edge of garment/side seam at a point 7" below bottom edge of waistband/seam, following contour of waist. [Note: The 7" point is for missywear only; adjust as needed $\frac{1}{2}$" to 1" up or down for children's, petite's, junior's, or large/plus womenswear. Indicate change on spec sheet.]

89. *Low Hip Width Circumference from Waist (woven)*—Measure from edge of garment/side seam to edge of garment/side seam at a point 7" below bottom edge of waistband/seam, following contour of waist. Double this measurement. [Note: The 7" point is for missywear only; adjust as needed $\frac{1}{2}$" to 1" up or down for children's, petite's, junior's, or large/plus womenswear. Indicate change on spec sheet.]

90. *Hip Width from High Point Shoulder (knit)*—Measure from edge of garment/side seam to edge of garment/side seam straight across at a point _____" below high point shoulder. [Note: You will have to estimate low hip point on garment if there is no waistband and fill in _____" from high point shoul-

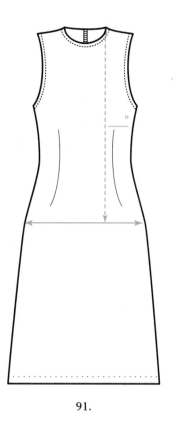

91.

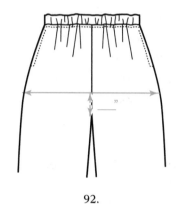

92.

93.

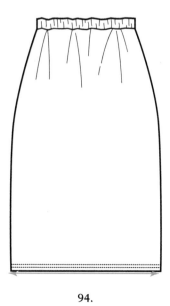

94.

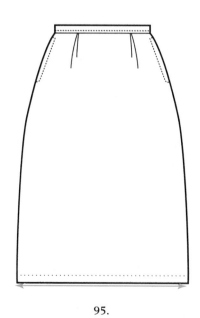

95.

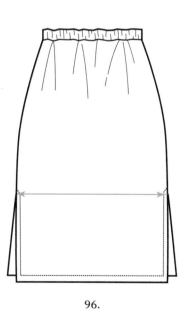

96.

der. This measurement will vary for children's, junior's, missy, and large/plus womenswear.]

91. *Hip Width from High Point Shoulder Circumference (woven)*—Measure from edge of garment/side seam to edge of garment/side seam straight across at a point _____" below high point shoulder. Double this measurement. [Note: You will have to estimate low hip point on garment if there is no waistband and fill in _____" from high point shoulder. This measurement will vary from children's, junior's, missy, and large/plus womenswear.]

92. *Hip Seat Width (knit pant)*—Measure from edge of garment/side seam to edge of garment/side seam at a point _____" up from crotch seam, following contour of waist. [Note 1: This measurement is useful when waistband sits below natural waistline. Note 2: Adjust _____" up from crotch as needed for junior's and large/plus womenswear. Note 3: A hip seat width of $2\frac{1}{2}$" up for children's and 3" up for menswear can take place of low hip width.]

93. *Hip Seat Width Circumference (woven pant)*—Measure from edge of garment/side seam to edge of garment/side seam at a point _____" up from crotch seam, following contour of waist. Double this measurement. [Note 1: This measurement is useful when waistband sits below natural waistline. Note 2: Adjust _____" up from crotch as needed for junior's and large/plus womenswear. Note 3: A hip seat width of $2\frac{1}{2}$" up for children's and 3" up for menswear can take place of low hip width.]

94. *Bottom Opening/Sweep Width (knit skirt)*—Measure from edge of garment/side seam to edge of garment/side seam straight across garment at bottom opening. [Note: If sweep has pleats, measure with pleats closed or relaxed.]

95. *Bottom Opening/Sweep Width Circumference (woven skirt)*—Measure from edge of garment/side seam to edge of garment/side seam straight across garment at bottom opening. Double this measurement. [Note: If sweep has pleats, measure with pleats closed or relaxed.]

96. *Vented Bottom Opening/Sweep Width (knit skirt)*—Measure from edge of garment/side seam to edge of garment/

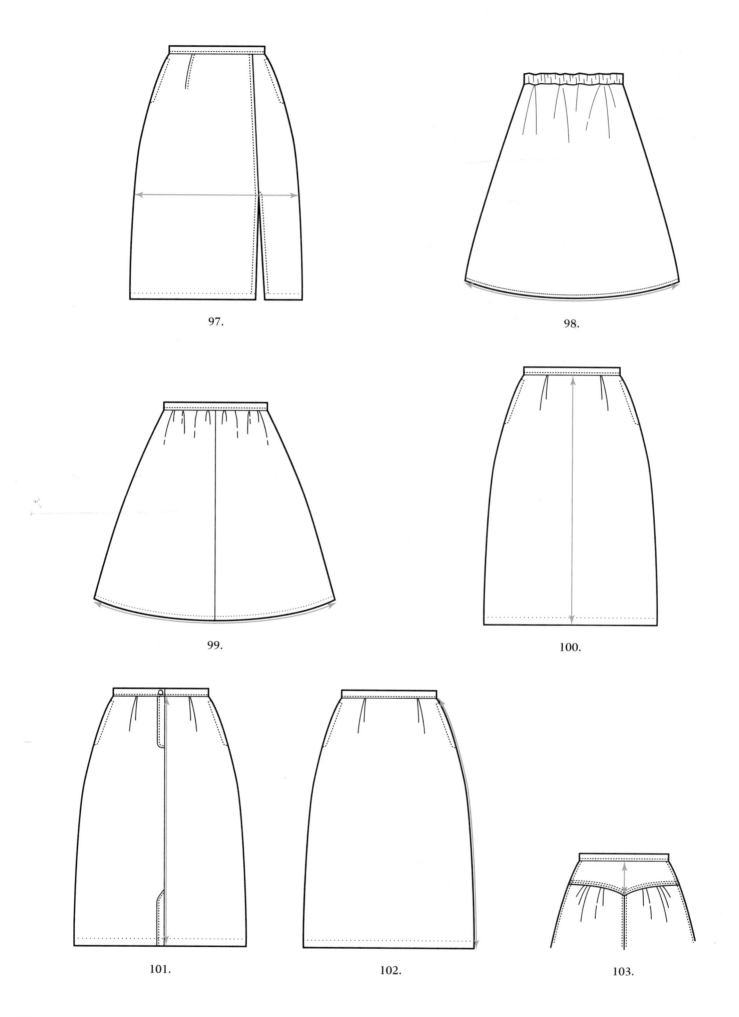

97.

98.

99.

100.

101.

102.

103.

side seam straight across garment at top of side vents. [Note: Indicate on spec sheet if there is only one vent or if vent hits at a point other than sweep, e.g., thigh opening.]

97. *Vented Bottom Opening/Sweep Width Circumference (woven skirt)*—Measure from edge of garment/side seam to edge of garment/side seam straight across garment at top of side vents. Double this measurement. [Note: Indicate on spec sheet if there is only one vent or if vent hits at a point other than sweep, e.g., thigh opening.]

98. *Circular Bottom Opening/Sweep Width (knit skirt)*—Measure from edge of garment/side seam to edge of garment/side seam, following natural contour of garment at bottom opening.

99. *Circular Bottom Opening/Sweep Width Circumference (woven skirt)*—Measure from edge of garment/side seam to edge of garment/side seam, following natural contour of garment at bottom opening. Double this measurement.

100. *Center Front Skirt Length*—Measure from bottom of waistband/seam (top edge if not banded or stitching if self-elastic/drawstring casing) straight down to bottom of garment at center front. [Note: A fashion-forward skirt may have an asymmetrical waist. Indicate top point of measure on spec sheet.]

101. *Center Back Skirt Length*—Measure from bottom of waistband/seam (top edge if not banded or stitching if self-elastic/drawstring casing) straight down to bottom of garment at center front. [Note: A fashion-forward skirt may have an asymmetrical waist. Indicate top point of measure on spec sheet.]

102. *Side Skirt Length*—Measure from bottom edge of waistband/seam (top edge if not banded or stitching if self-elastic/drawstring casing) to bottom of garment along side seam/fold of garment, following any contour.

103. *Skirt/Pant Yoke Depth Front*—Measure from bottom of waistband/seam (top edge if not banded or stitching if self-elastic/drawstring casing) straight down to bottom of yoke joining seam at center front. [Note: If yoke is contoured, indicate point of measure on spec sheet.]

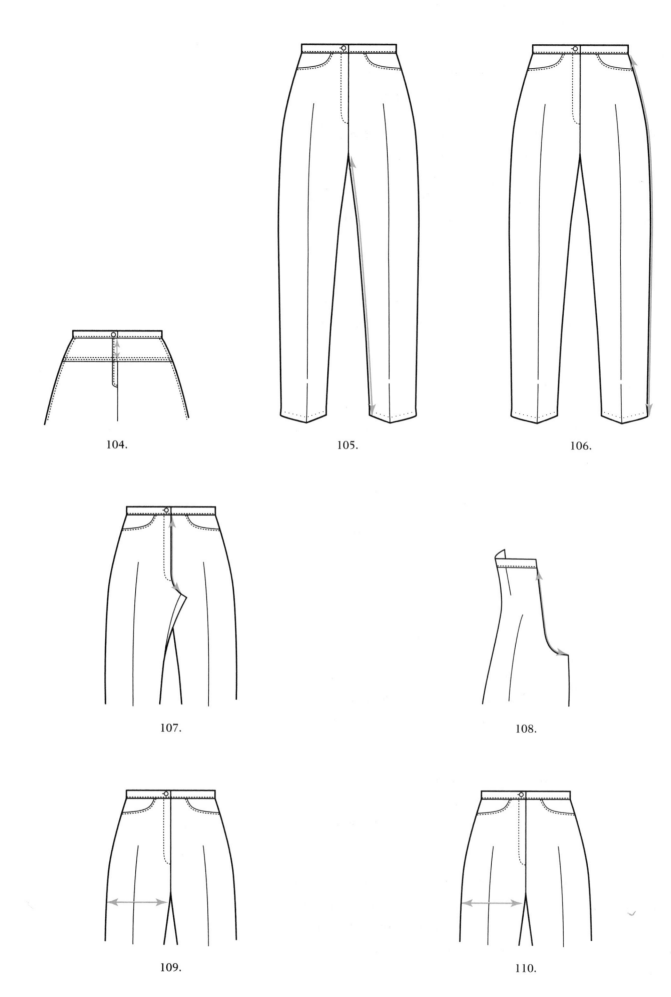

104.

105.

106.

107.

108.

109.

110.

104. *Skirt/Pant Yoke Depth Back*—Measure from bottom of waistband/seam (top edge if not banded or stitching if self-elastic/drawstring casing) straight down to bottom of yoke joining seam at center back. [Note: If yoke is contoured, indicate point of measure on spec sheet.]

105. *Inseam*—Measure from crotch joining seam to bottom of leg opening, following inseam/inner fold.

106. *Outseam*—Measure from bottom edge of waistband/seam (top edge if not banded or stitching if self-elastic/drawstring casing) to bottom of garment along side seam/fold of garment.

107. *Front Rise*—Measure from bottom edge of waistband/seam (top edge if not banded or stitching if self-elastic/drawstring casing) to crotch joining seam, following curve of front rise seam. [Note: Measure over zipper if in front rise seam.]

108. *Back Rise*—Measure from bottom edge of waistband/seam (top edge if not banded or stitching if self-elastic/drawstring casing) to crotch joining seam, following curve of back rise seam. [Note: Measure over zipper if in front back seam.]

109. *Thigh Width (knit)*—Measure from pant leg edge/seam to pant leg edge/seam straight across pant leg at a point 1" below crotch and parallel to leg opening. [Note: If leg opening is asymmetrical, measure to a point that would be parallel to the leg opening.]

110. *Thigh Width Circumference (woven)*—Measure from pant leg edge/seam to pant leg edge/seam straight across pant leg at a point 1" below crotch and parallel to leg opening. Double this measurement. [Note: If leg opening is asymmetrical, measure to a point that would be parallel to the leg opening.]

111. *Knee Width (knit)*—Measure from pant leg edge/seam to pant leg edge/seam at a point one-half of the inseam and parallel to leg opening. [Note 1: If leg opening is asymmetrical, measure to a point that would be parallel to leg opening. Note 2: If pant leg is three-quarter length, indicate point of measure on spec sheet. Note 3: A general knee measurement from crotch seam of missy 12", junior's 11", or large/plus women's 13" can be used. Indicate change on spec sheet. For childrenswear measure at one-half inseam minus $1\frac{1}{2}$", and for men's minus 2".]

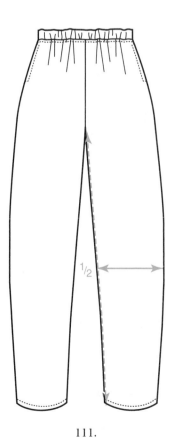

111.

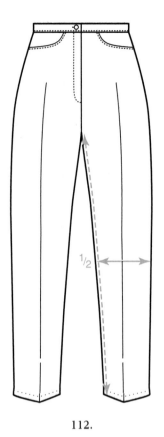

112.

113.

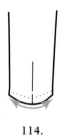

114.

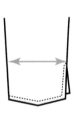

115.

116.

117.

118.

119.

120.

112. *Knee Width Circumference (woven)*—Measure from pant leg edge/seam to pant leg edge/seam at a point one-half of inseam and parallel to leg opening. Double this measurement. [Note 1: If leg opening is asymmetrical, measure to a point that would be parallel to leg opening. Note 2: If pant leg is three-quarter length, indicate point of measure on spec sheet. Note 3: A general knee measurement from crotch seam of missy 12", junior's 11", large/plus women's 13" can be used. Indicate change on spec sheet. Measure children's at one-half inseam minus $1\frac{1}{2}$", and for men's minus 2".]

113. *Leg Opening Width (knit)*—Measure from pant leg edge/seam to pant edge/seam straight across bottom edge of leg opening. [Note: If leg opening is contoured, follow contour and indicate measurement change on spec sheet.]

114. *Leg Opening Width Circumference (woven)*—Measure from pant leg edge/seam to pant leg edge/seam straight across bottom edge of leg opening. Double this measurement. [Note: If leg opening is contoured, follow contour and indicate measurement change on spec sheet.]

115. *Vented Leg Opening Width (knit)*—Measure from pant leg edge/seam to pant leg edge/seam straight across pant leg at top of side vents.

116. *Vented Leg Opening Circumference (woven)*—Measure from pant leg edge/seam to pant leg edge/seam straight across pant leg at top of side vents. Double this measurement.

117. *Leg Opening Width, Stretched (knit)*—Measure from pant leg edge/seam to pant leg edge/seam straight across bottom edge of leg opening in a fully extended position.

118. *Leg Opening Width Circumference, Stretched (woven)*—Measure from pant leg edge/seam to pant leg edge/seam straight across bottom edge of leg opening in a fully extended position. Double this measurement.

119. *Cuff Height Pants*—Measure from top of cuff edge straight down to bottom of cuff fold and leg opening.

120. *Bottom Band/Ribbing Height Pants*—Measure from cuff joining seam or top of ribbing straight down to bottom edge of

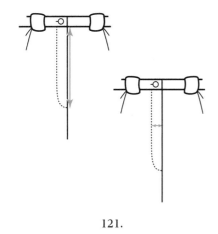

121.

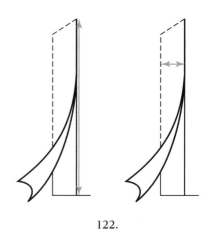

122.

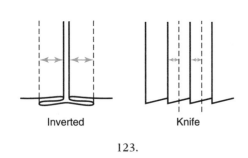

Inverted   Knife

123.

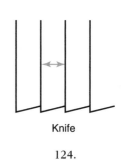

Knife

124.

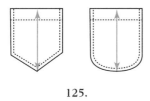

125.

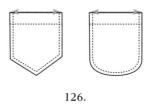

126.

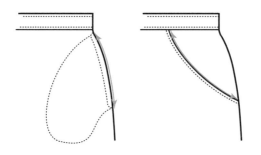

127.

cuff or rib opening. [Note: For fashion-forward pants, you may want to include a cuff length. See point of measure 56, Cuff Length Sleeve, for measuring instructions and indicate cuff length pant as needed on spec sheet.]

121. *Fly/Zipper*

A. *Length*—Measure from top of fly/zipper opening straight down to bottom of fly/zipper opening at zipper stop or bar tack.

B. *Fly/Zipper Width*—Measure top of fly/zipper at joining seam from edge/fold straight across to fly/zipper placket stitching.

122. *Vent/Slit*

A. *Height*—Measure from top of vent/slit straight down to bottom of vent/slit along edge of vent/slit.

B. *Width*—Measure top of vent/slit from edge/fold straight across to vent/slit placket stitching at a point parallel to garment hemline.

123. *Pleat Depth*—Measure from outer edge of pleat at fold/crease to inner fold of pleat. [Note 1: It is a good idea to indicate what type of pleat is being measured, e.g., box, inverted, knife, kick, kilt, or envelope. Note 2: If pleats are not parallel or symmetrical, indicate any special instructions on spec sheet.]

124. *Distance Between Pleats*—Measure from start of pleat to start of pleat, excluding pleat depth at a point directly below pleat joining seam. [Note: If pleats are not parallel or symmetrical, indicate any special instructions on spec sheet.]

125. *Applied Pocket Height*—Measure from top edge of pocket to bottom edge of pocket along center of pocket. [Note: For contoured or irregularly shaped pockets, take a second measurement and indicate point of measure on spec sheet.]

126. *Applied Pocket Width*—Measure from side of pocket to side of pocket along top edge of pocket. [Note: For contoured or irregularly shaped pockets, take a second measurement and indicate point of measure on spec sheet.]

127. *Pocket Opening Within a Seam*—Measure from top of pocket to bottom of pocket along edge of pocket opening.

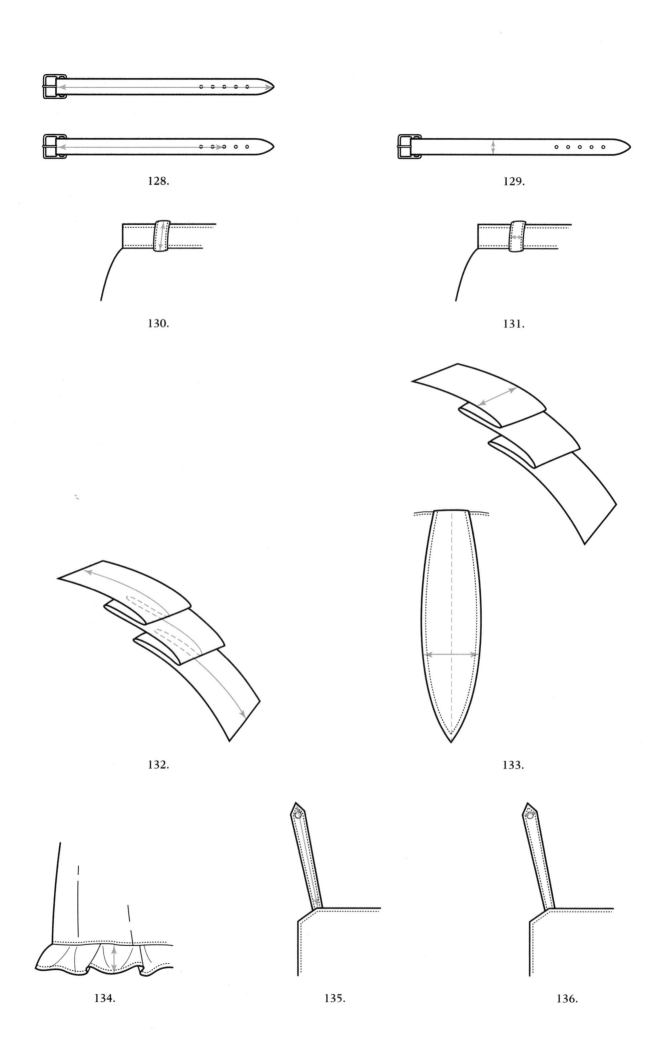

128.

129.

130.

131.

132.

133.

134.

135.

136.

128. *Belt Length*

A. *Total*—Measure from end of belt at buckle along center of belt to opposite end of belt, following contour.

B. *Circumference*—Measure from end of belt at buckle along center of belt to middle hole at opposite end.

129. *Belt Width (or Height)*—Measure from edge of belt straight across to edge of belt. [Note: If belt is contoured, indicate points of measure on spec sheet.]

130. *Belt Loop Length*—Measure from top of belt loop straight down/vertically to bottom of belt loop along center of belt loop. [Note: Fashion-forward or irregularly shaped belt loops may require further spec instructions. Indicate points of measure on spec sheet.]

131. *Belt Loop Width*—Measure belt loop from edge of belt loop straight across/horizontally to edge of belt loop. [Note: Fashion-forward or irregularly shaped belt loops may require further spec instructions. Indicate points of measure on spec sheet.]

132. *Tie Length*—Measure from end of tie/joining seam straight down to tie end along center of tie.

133. *Tie Width*

A. *Straight*—Measure from edge of tie straight across to edge of tie.

B. *Contoured*—Measure from edge of tie straight across to edge of tie at widest point of tie.

134. *Flounce/Ruffle Width*—Measure from flounce/ruffle joining seam straight across to outer edge of flounce/ruffle. [Note: If flounce/ruffle is contoured, measure along narrowest and widest points if possible and indicate changes on spec sheet.]

135. *Strap Length*—Measure from strap joining seam along center of strap to end of strap. [Note: If strap is contoured or has a contoured edge, measure along center, approximating center end point, or indicate instructions as needed on spec sheet.]

136. *Strap Width*—Measure from edge of strap straight across to edge of strap. [Note: If strap is contoured, measure along

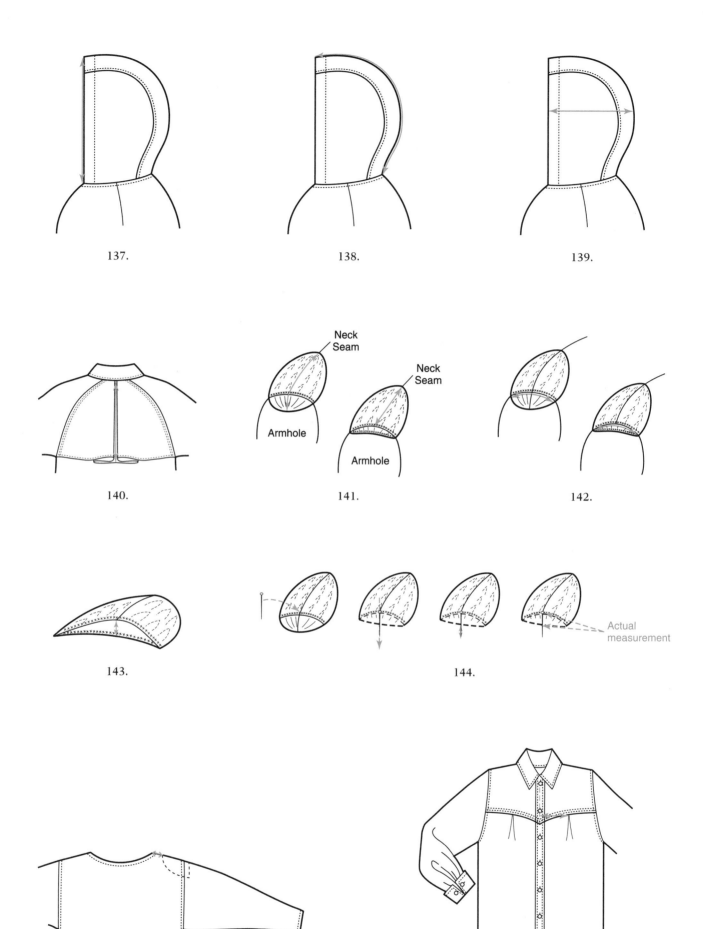

137.

138.

139.

140.

Neck
Seam

Armhole

141.

Neck
Seam

Armhole

142.

143.

Actual
measurement

144.

145.

146a.

narrowest and widest points if possible and indicate changes on spec sheet.]

137. *Front Hood Length*—Measure from top of hood to bottom of hood at center front joining seam along opening edge of hood.

138. *Back Hood Length*—Measure from top of hood at center front to bottom of hood at center back joining seam along outside curve of hood fold/seam.

139. *Hood Width*—Measure from front opening edge of hood straight across to back of hood along widest point of hood.

140. *Flange Depth*—Measure from center back neck joining seam straight down to bottom of flange at center back. [Note: If flange is contoured or asymmetrical, indicate point of measure on spec sheet.]

141. *Shoulder Pad Length*—Measure from edge of pad straight across to edge of pad along center of pad or natural shoulder line of pad.

142. *Shoulder Pad Width*—Measure from side of pad straight across to side of pad along edge of pad if straight or at widest point of pad if curved.

143. *Straight Edge Shoulder Pad Height*—Measure from top of pad straight down to bottom of pad along center of pad.

144. *Curved Edge Shoulder Pad Height*—Stick a one-inch straight pin into thickest part of shoulder pad. Push pin all way through pad until head of pin rests on top of pad. Be sure not to crush pad. Measure portion of pin sticking out of pad. Subtract this figure from one inch (length of pin) to get shoulder pad height.

145. *Shoulder Pad Placement*—Measure from neck edge or joining seam straight across shoulder seam or natural shoulder line to start of shoulder pad.

146. *Pleats Placement*
A. *Front Pleat Top*—Measure distance from center front of garment straight across to start of first pleat at a point par-

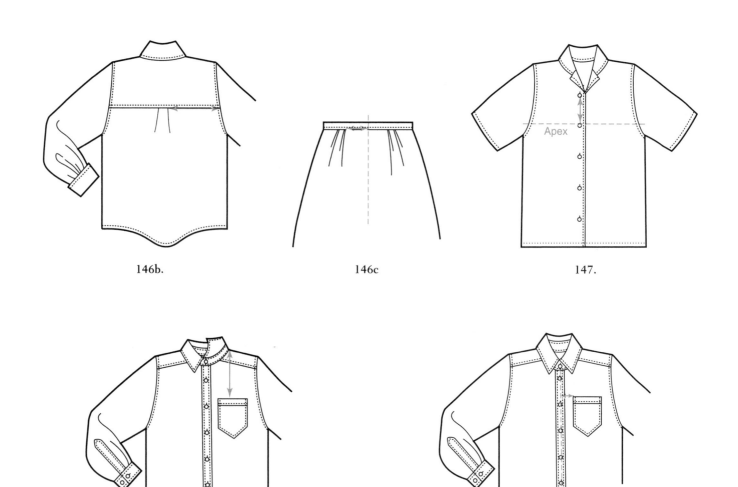

146b.

146c

147.

148a.

148b.

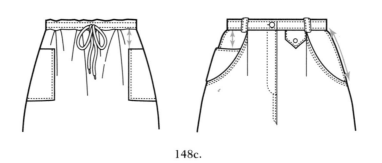

148c.

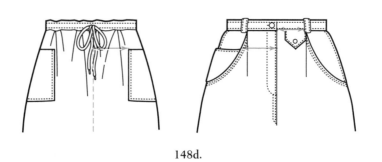

148d.

allel to garment hem. [Note: You may need to use armhole or side seam as a starting point if there is no center front seam or placket.]

B. *Back Pleat Top*—Measure distance from armholeseam/side seam (depending on pleat placement) to first pleat at a point parallel to garment hem.

C. *Front Pleat Skirt/Pant*—Measure distance from center front of garment waistband joining seam/edge straight across to start of first pleat.

148e.

147. *Button Placement*—Refer to measurement point 59, Neck Depth Center Front, for placement of first button. Then measure distance of first button to second button. Be sure when measuring that button at bust point is lined up to apex of bust. Adjust all buttons accordingly and respace as needed.

148f.

148. *Pocket Placement*

A. *Top Pocket Vertical*—Measure from shoulder-neck joining seam straight down to top edge of pocket.

B. *Top Pocket Horizontal*—Measure from center front straight across to side of pocket at top edge.

C. *Front Bottom Pocket Vertical*—Measure from waistband/ joining seam/edge straight down to top edge of pocket.

D. *Front Bottom Pocket Horizontal*—Measure from center front straight across to side of pocket at top edge.

E. *Back Bottom Pocket Vertical*—Measure from waistband/ joining seam/edge straight down to top edge of pocket.

F. *Back Bottom Pocket Horizontal*—Measure from center back straight across to side of pocket at top edge.

G. *Pocket from Side Seam*—Measure from side seam straight across to top of pocket. [Note: If pocket is contoured at sides, a top and bottom pocket size and placement must be measured and added to spec sheet.]

148g.

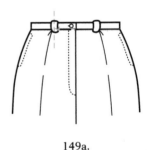

149a.

149. *Belt Loop Placement*

A. *Front*—Measure from center front of garment horizontally across to center of first front belt loop.

B. *Back*—Measure from center back of garment horizontally across to center of first back belt loop.

149b.

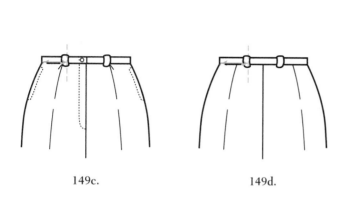

149c.

149d.

150a.

150b.

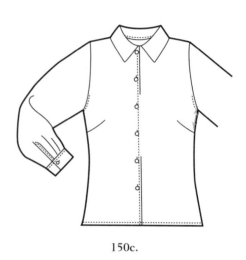

150c.

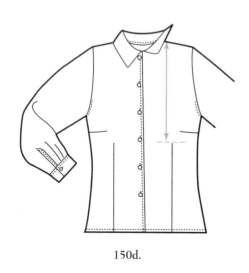

150d.

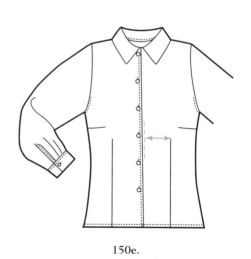

150e.

C. *Side Seam to Front*—Measure from center of side seam belt loop to center of front belt loop.

D. *Side Seam to Back*—Measure from center of side seam belt loop to center of back belt loop.

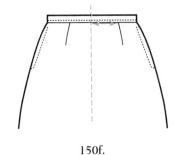

150f.

150. *Dart Placement*

A. *High Point Shoulder Bust Dart*—Measure from shoulder-neck joining seam or at a point _____" from shoulder-neck seam straight down, parallel to center front, to top of dart. [Note: The _____" from shoulder seam measurement is to be used for darts that are too short to be measured from high point shoulder. Be sure to indicate _____" measurement on spec sheet.]

B. *Center Front Bust Dart*—Measure from center front of garment straight across to top of dart.

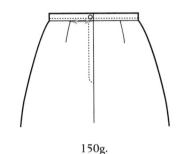

150g.

C. *Side Seam Bust Dart*—Measure from underarm/side seam joining seam down along contour of side seam to bottom of dart.

D. *High Point Shoulder Princess Dart*—Measure from shoulder-neck joining seam straight down to top of dart.

E. *Center Front Princess Dart*—Measure from center front of garment straight across to top of dart.

F. *Center Front Skirt/Pant*—Measure from center front of garment at waistband joining seam/edge straight across to top of dart.

G. *Center Back Skirt/Pant*—Measure from center back of garment at waistband joining seam/edge straight across to top of dart.

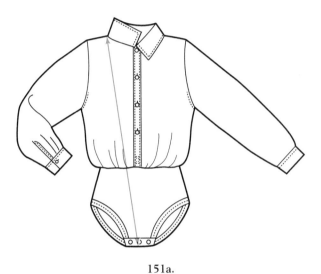

151a.

151. *Front Torso Length (Jumpsuits and One-Piece Garments)*

A. *Garments with a Front Opening, Relaxed*—Measure from high point shoulder at neck straight down to crotch joining seam with garment in a relaxed position.

B. *Garments with a Front Opening, Extended*—Measure from high point shoulder at neck straight down to crotch joining seam with garment in a fully extended position.

151b.

C. *Garments with a Plain Front, No Front Opening, Relaxed*—Measure from center front neck joining seam straight down to crotch joining seam with garment in a relaxed position.

D. *Garments with a Plain Front, No Front Opening, Extended*—Measure from center front neck joining seam straight down to crotch joining seam with garment in a fully extended position.

152. *Back Torso Length (Jumpsuits and One-Piece Garments)*

A. *Relaxed*—Measure from center back neck joining seam straight down to crotch joining seam with garment in a relaxed position.

B. *Extended*—Measure from center back neck joining seam straight down to crotch joining seam with garment in a fully extended position.

153. *High Point Shoulder Length (Jumpsuits and One-Piece Garments)*—Measure from high point shoulder straight down to bottom/hem of garment.

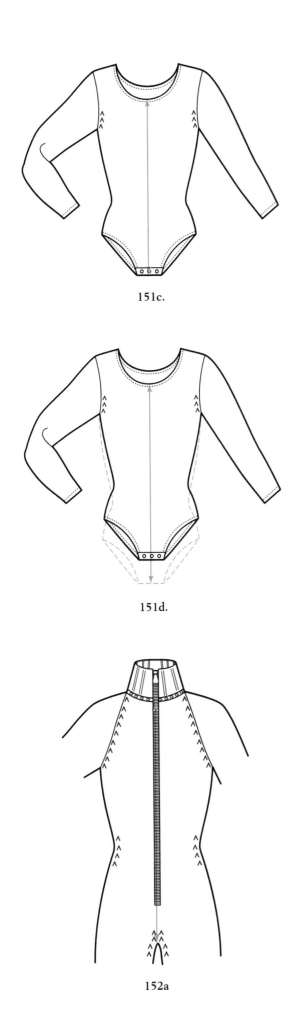

151c.

151d.

152a

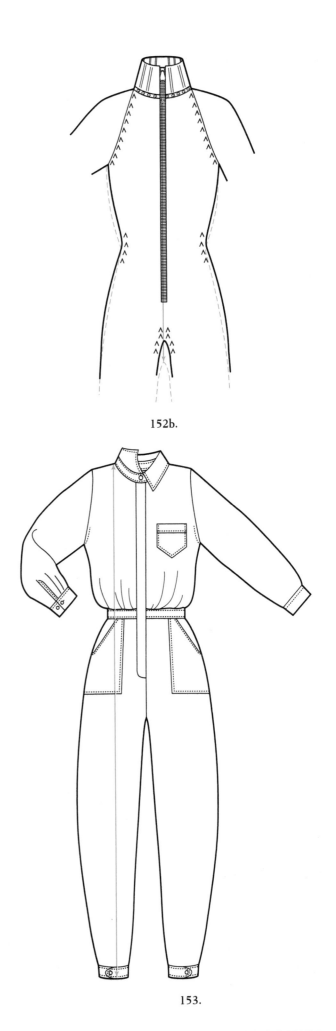

152b.

153.

154.

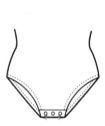

155.

154. *Center Back Garment Length (Jumpsuits and One-Piece Garments)*—Measure from center back neckline seam/edge straight down to bottom hem of garment. Note: For pant suits this point will intersect at an imaginary line formed by hemlines of pant legs and center of garment.

155. *Crotch Width*—Measure straight across crotch from side to side along seam/bottom edge/fold.

CHAPTER 3 TERMS

As you become more familiar with the measurement points, you will come across the following terms. If you are unfamiliar with any of them, please look up the definitions in the glossary at the end of this text.

Center back (CB)
Center front (CF)
Circumference
Extended measurement
High point shoulder (HPS)
Inert elastic
Measurement point (point of measure)
Natural relaxed position
Sweep
Total measurement

PART II

WORKING WITH KNITS

- Before starting Chapters 4 through 8, be sure to read the Measurement Preparation instructions listed in Chapter 3.
- Only those measurement points that are used when measuring basic garments are included in the respective chapters. Not every measurement point listed will be used on every garment; however, every measurement point for that type of garment has been listed in each chapter.
- Ignore any skipped numbers.
- You may want to try several different points of measure at first to see which one may yield the most accurate measurement. It takes time choosing the best point of measure for your garment, but it is imperative that you are consistent using the same method each time you measure that garment.
- Measuring knits will only include missy/contemporary sketches. Industry specification sheets are always specific to a single market and will only contain sketches for that market; however, this theory is easily adapted to other markets.
- A generic missy spec sheet has been added to each chapter for your use. Note that while some in the retail industry are starting to call their missy departments Contemporary, the sizing is still considered missy; therefore, this terminology will be used on all spec sheets.

- A completed example of a spec sheet, including a hand sketch and measurements, has been added to each chapter for your reference.
- Basic garment illustrations and a blank spec sheet can be found in the croquis section of Appendix A, Basic Garment Croquis, at the back of this text. These can be used to create your own spec sheets.

Chapters 4 through 8 have the user measure knits flat or singular to be consistent with many technicians in the industry. For those in the industry or in the classroom who prefer to measure all garment circumferences, you may simply double these measurements and change your spec sheets accordingly.

Knits in Review

Knit fabric is constructed by interlooping and continuously forming a series of new loops, consisting of one or more yarns. There are three classes of knit fabrics: circular knit, flat knit, and warp knit. This text does not entail fabric science but has listed several knit terms below that may be helpful as you work through Chapters 4 through 8.

Circular (tubular) knitting: the construction of a knitted fabric or garment on a knitting machine in a circular or tubular form.

Circular web: a fabric knitted in a tubular form, then cut and sewn to construct a garment.

Flat knit: the construction of a knitted fabric on a knitting machine in a flat form.

Full fashioned: a process of flat knitting in which the fabric is shaped by adding or reducing stitches.

Knitted courses (coarses): rows of interlooping loops.

Knitting in the round: a term for circular or tubular knitting.

Selvage: the finished edge on a cloth that prevents raveling or fraying.

Warp knit: knit produced with yarns running lengthwise, as warp on beams are prepared with one or more yarns per needle.

Weft knitting: knit produced on both flat and circular knitting machines using one continuous thread (yarn) making all the loops of a course.

CHAPTER 4

Knit Tops

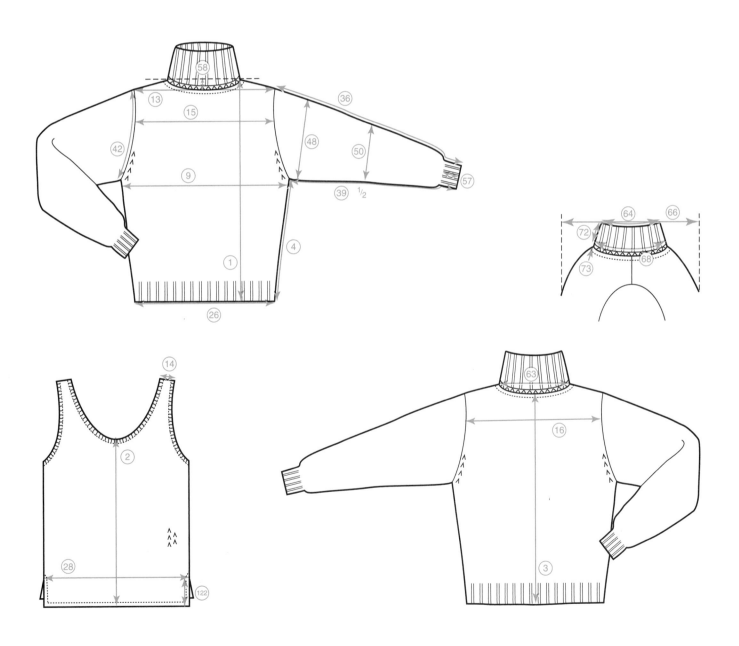

69

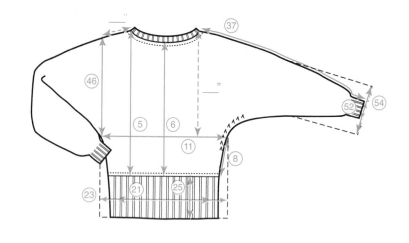

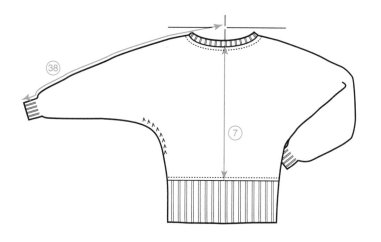

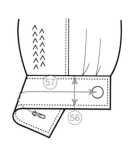

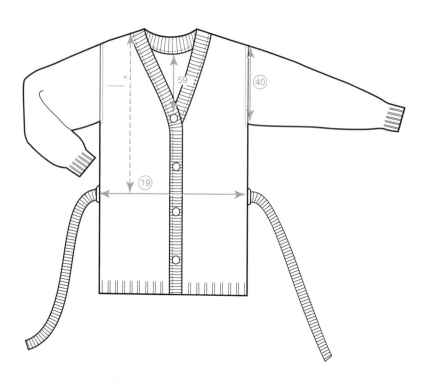

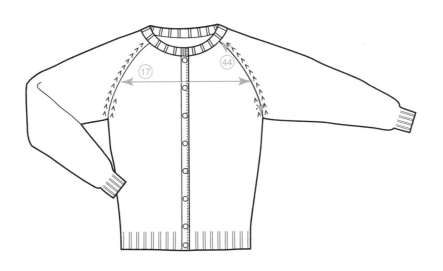

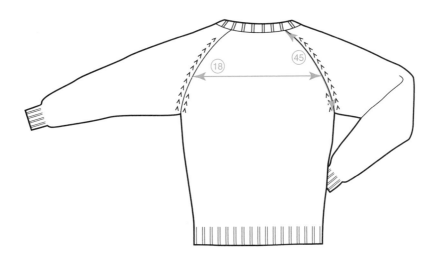

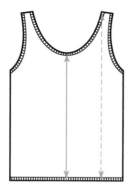

Figure 4.1

Measuring Knit Tops

Knit top spec sheets are used for knit garments including shirts, sweaters, and vests. As you measure, you will find some instances when more than one method can be used for taking a measurement. For example, a knit top's front length can be measured from the high point shoulder or the center front. Most knit tops are measured from the high point shoulder even though they do not have a front opening. However, there will be instances, for example, a tank top, when measuring from the center front is better than using the high point shoulder (Figure 4.1). As the technician, you must decide which measurement method would be better suited to your garment's style.

1. *Front Length (garments with a front opening)*—Measure from high point shoulder at neck straight down, parallel to center front, to bottom of garment at front. If garment has a collar, gently lift it away from shoulder-neck measuring point.

2. *Center Front Length (garments with a plain front; no front opening)*—Measure from center front neck joining seams straight down to bottom of garment at center front. [Note: A garment without a front opening may still require use of Front Length if neckline is unusual.]

3. *Center Back Length*—Measure from center back neck joining seams straight down to bottom of garment at center back. If needed, gently lift collar away from back neck to expose joining seam.

4. *Side Length*—Measure from bottom of armhole/side seam straight down to bottom of garment along side of garment. Do not follow natural curve of garment's side seam, unless otherwise indicated. If needed, gently lift sleeve away from armhole/side seam joining seam.

5. *Front Bodice Length (garments with a front opening)*—Measure from high point shoulder at neck

straight down, parallel to center front, to top edge of waistband, joining seam, or rib. If garment has a collar, gently lift it away from shoulder-neck measuring point.

6. *Center Front Bodice Length (garments with a plain front; no front opening)*—Measure from center front neck joining seam straight down to top edge of waistband, joining seam, or rib. [Note: A garment without a center opening may still require use of Front Bodice Length if neckline is unusual.]

7. *Center Back Bodice Length*—Measure from center back neck joining seams straight down to top edge of waistband, joining seam, or rib. If needed, gently lift collar away from back neck to expose joining seam.

8. *Side Seam Bodice Length*—Measure from bottom of armhole/side seam straight down to top edge of waistband, joining seam, or rib, along side of garment, following natural curve of garment's side seam, unless otherwise indicated. If needed, gently lift sleeve away from armhole/side seam joining seam. [Note: You can take side seam bodice measurement straight rather than contoured if joining seam/rib can be extended, but indicate change on spec sheet.]

9. *Chest Width (knit)*—Measure from edge of garment/side seam to edge of garment/side seam straight across garment at a point 1' below armhole.

11. *Chest Width (raglan sleeve, knit)*—Measure from edge of garment/side seam to edge of garment/side seam straight across garment at a point _____" below high point shoulder. [Note: You will have to determine number of inches down from high point shoulder for each raglan sleeve style based on depth of sleeve. Then indicate this number on spec sheet.]

13. *Across Shoulder*—Measure straight across front from armhole seam/edge to armhole seam/edge at shoulder seam or across natural shoulder fold line created if there is no seam.

14. *Shoulder Width*—Measure from neckband/collar/ribbing joining seam or neckline edge to top of armhole seam at shoulder, taken along shoulder seam or across natural shoulder fold line created if there is no seam.

15. *Across Chest*—Measure $2\frac{1}{2}$" down from collar/rib joining seam at center front straight across front of garment from armhole seam/edge to armhole seam/edge. [Note: The $2\frac{1}{2}$" measurement point is for missywear only and may need to be adjusted up or down $\frac{1}{4}$" to $\frac{1}{2}$" accordingly for men's, children's, junior's, and large/plus womenswear. Indicate any changes on spec sheet.]

16. *Across Back*—Measure 4" down from collar/rib joining seam at center back straight across back of garment from armhole seam/edge to armhole seam/edge. [Note: The 4" measurement point is for missywear only and may need to be adjusted up or down $\frac{1}{4}$" to $\frac{1}{2}$" accordingly for men's, children's, junior's, and large/plus womenswear. Indicate any changes on spec sheet.]

17. *Across Chest/Center Armhole*—Measure at one-half depth of armhole straight across front of garment from armhole seam/edge to armhole seam/edge.

18. *Across Back/Center Armhole*—Measure at one-half depth of armhole straight across back of garment from armhole seam/edge to armhole seam/edge.

19. *Waist Width (knit)*—Measure from edge of garment/side seam to edge of garment/side seam straight across garment on seam or at narrowest point of waist taper at a point _____" below high point shoulder. [Note: You will have to determine number of inches down from high point shoulder for each raglan sleeve style based on depth of sleeve. Then indicate this number on spec sheet.]

21. *Bottom Band Width (knit top)*—Measure from side of bottom band to side of bottom band along center of band, following natural contour of waistband.

23. *Bottom Band Width, Stretched (knit top)*—Measure from side of bottom band to side of bottom band straight across center of band in a fully extended position.

25. *Bottom Band/Ribbing Height (knit or woven top)*—Measure from band/ribbing joining seam straight down to bottom edge of band/rib opening. [Note: If band is shaped or contoured, indicate special measurement instructions on spec sheet.]

26. *Bottom Opening/Sweep (knit top)*—Measure from edge of garment/side seam to edge of garment/side seam straight across garment at bottom opening. [Note: If sweep has pleats, measure with pleats closed or relaxed.]

28. *Vented Bottom Opening/Sweep Width (knit top)*—Measure from edge of garment/side seam to edge of garment/side seam straight across garment at top of side vents. Do not follow natural curve of garment. [Note: If vents are too high to measure sweep, indicate opening at appropriate position, e.g., midriff opening.]

30. *Circular Bottom Opening/Sweep Width (knit top)*—Measure from edge of garment/side seam to edge of garment/side seam, following natural contour of garment at bottom opening.

32. *Yoke Width Front*—Measure from armhole seam/edge to armhole seam/edge straight across front of garment, ignoring contours or points, at yoke-body joining seams. [Note: If yoke is asymmetrical, indicate changes in measuring as needed on spec sheet.]

33. *Yoke Width Back*—Measure from armhole seam/edge to armhole seam/edge straight across back of garment, ignoring contours or points, at yoke-body joining seams. [Note: If yoke is asymmetrical, indicate changes in measuring as needed on spec sheet.]

34. *Yoke Depth Front*—Measure from high point shoulder at neck straight down to bottom of front yoke-body joining seam. Be sure to gently lift collar away from shoulder-neck joining seam if needed.

35. *Yoke Back Depth*—Measure from center back neck joining seam straight down to bottom of back yoke-body joining seam. Gently lift collar away from back neck joining seam if needed.

36. *Sleeve Length Top Armhole*—Measure along top of sleeve/fold, following contour of sleeve from armhole seam at shoulder to bottom of sleeve opening, including cuff.

37. *Sleeve Length Top Neck*—Measure along top of sleeve/fold, following contour of sleeve from sleeve-neck joining seam/edge to edge of sleeve opening, including cuff. Gently lift collar at sleeve-neck joining seam if needed.

38. *Sleeve Length Center Back*—Measure from center back neck joining seam or from a point above neck at an imaginary line, that of a joining seam, along top of sleeve/fold, following contour of sleeve to edge of sleeve opening, including cuff.

39. *Sleeve Length Underarm*—Measure straight from bottom of armhole along sleeve seam to edge of sleeve opening, including cuff.

40. *Straight Armhole Width (knit)*—Measure from top of shoulder joining seam/edge straight down to bottom of armhole.

42. *Curved Armhole Width (knit)*—Measure from top of shoulder joining seam/edge to bottom of armhole, following contour of armhole.

44. *Armhole Front*—Measure on front of garment from top of shoulder at neckline joining seam/edge to bottom of armhole, following contour of armhole. Gently lift collar away from neckline joining seam if needed.

45. *Armhole Back*—Measure on back of garment from top of shoulder at neck joining seam/edge to bottom of armhole, following contour of armhole. Gently lift collar away from neck joining seam if needed.

46. *Armhole Width Straight (knit)*—Measure from top of shoulder seam at a point _____" below neckline joining seam/edge straight down to bottom of armhole. [Note: Gently move collar away from neck joining seam if needed when measuring down _____" to armhole start point. Indicate number of inches measured down on spec sheet.]

48. *Muscle Width (knit)*—Measure from inner sleeve edge/seam to outer sleeve edge/fold at a point 1" below armhole and parallel to sleeve opening.

50. *Elbow Width (knit)*—Measure from inner sleeve edge/seam to outer sleeve edge/fold straight across sleeve at a point one-half of underarm sleeve length and parallel to sleeve opening at wrist or cuff. [Note: If sleeve is three-quarter length, indicate new point of measure on spec sheet.]

52. *Sleeve Opening Width (knit)*—Measure from inner sleeve edge/seam to outer sleeve edge/fold straight across bottom edge of sleeve opening.

54. *Sleeve Opening Width, Stretched (knit)*—Measure from inner sleeve edge/seam to outer sleeve edge/fold straight across bottom edge of sleeve opening in a fully extended position.

56. *Cuff Length Sleeve*—Measure from outside end of buttonhole to center of button straight along center of cuff. Open cuff out as flat as possible when measuring. [Note: If cuff length is contoured, measure along center-most point.]

57. *Cuff/Ribbing Height Sleeve*—Measure from cuff joining seam or top of ribbing straight down to bottom edge of cuff or rib opening. [Note: If cuff is con-

toured, indicate changes made as needed to measurement on spec sheet.]

58. *Neck Depth Front (garments with a plain front/asymmetrical front opening)*—Measure from center back neck joining seam/edge straight down to center front neck joining seam/edge.

59. *Neck Depth Center Front (garments with a center front opening)*—Measure from center back neck joining seam/edge straight down to center of first button at center front of garment.

60. *Neck Drop Front*—Measure from an imaginary line connecting neckline edges straight down to center front neck opening edge. Use a ruler if needed to connect top neckline edges.

61. *Neck Drop Back*—Measure from an imaginary line connecting neckline edges straight down to center back neck opening edge. This measurement is taken with front of garment facing up. Use a ruler to connect top neckline edges if needed.

62. *Neck Width, No Collar*—Measure from inside neck edge/seam to inside neck edge/seam straight across back neck at widest point. This measurement is taken with front of garment faceup.

63. *Neck Width, Collar*—Measure straight across back neck from neck-shoulder joining seam to neck-shoulder joining seam or natural shoulder line if no seam. This measurement is taken with back of garment faceup.

64. *Neck Edge Width (knit)*—Measure from neck edge/seam/fold to neck edge/seam/fold along top opening edge, following natural contour of neck opening. Garment should be positioned with one shoulder on top of the other and with front and back neck edges meeting.

66. *Neck Edge Width, Stretched (knit)*—Measure from neck edge/seam/fold to neck edge/seam/fold

along top opening edge in a fully extended position. Garment should be positioned with one shoulder on top of the other and with front and back neck edges meeting.

67. *Neck Edge Width Circumference, Stretched (woven)*—Measure from neck edge/seam/fold to neck edge/seam/fold along top opening edge in a fully extended position. Garment should be positioned with one shoulder on top of the other and with front and back neck edges meeting. Double this measurement.

68. *Neck Base (knit)*—Measure from neck edge/seam to neck edge/seam along collar/rib joining seam or neckline edge, following natural contour of neck opening. Garment should be buttoned or zippered, if applicable, with one shoulder seam positioned on top of the other and with front and back neck edges meeting.

70. *Neckband Length*—Measure from outside end of buttonhole to center of buttonhole across neckband, following contour of neckband.

71. *Collar Length*—Measure from one end of collar to other end of collar along neck joining seam.

72. *Collar Height*—Measure from collar/rib joining seam at center back neck straight up to outer edge of collar/rib.

73. *Collar Band Height*—Measure from collar joining seam at center back straight up to neckband joining seam at center back.

74. *Collar Point Length*—Measure from collar joining seam to outer edge of collar along collar point edge. [Note: If collar is rounded, measure at a point parallel to center back and indicate change on spec sheet.]

75. *Collar Point Spread (pointed collars only)*—Measure, with collar band buttoned and collar in place, from collar point straight across collar edge to collar point.

76. *Lapel Width*
A. *Notched*—Measure from lower lapel notch straight across to lapel fold at a point perpendicular to garment center front.
B. *Without Notches*—Measure from lapel edge straight across widest point of lapel to lapel fold at a point _____" down from center back collar joining seam and perpendicular to front of garment.

77. *Center Front Extension*—Measure from an imaginary line at center front of garment horizontally to finished outer edge of front extended piece.

78. *Placket Length*—Measure from top edge of placket straight down to bottom of placket opening along center of placket.

79. *Placket Width*—Measure from placket joining seam straight across placket to placket edge at fold.

80. *Keyhole Length*—Measure from outer edge of neckline straight down to bottom of keyhole opening.

81. *Waistband Depth*—Measure from top of waistband edge straight down to bottom of waistband at waistband joining seam. [Note: If waistband is contoured, indicate measurement change on spec sheet.]

122. *Vent/Slit*
A. *Height*—Measure from top of vent/slit straight down to bottom of vent/slit along edge of vent/slit.
B. *Width*—Measure top of vent slit from edge/fold straight across to vent/slit placket stitching at a point parallel to garment hemline.

123. *Pleat Depth*—Measure from outer edge of pleat at fold/crease to inner fold of pleat. [Note 1: It is a

good idea to indicate what type of pleat is being measured, e.g., box, inverted, knife, kick, kilt, or envelope. Note 2: If pleats are not parallel or symmetrical, indicate any special instructions on spec sheet.]

124. *Distance Between Pleats*—Measure from start of pleat to start of pleat, excluding pleat depth at a point directly below pleat joining seam. [Note: If pleats are not parallel or symmetrical, indicate any special instructions on spec sheet.]

125. *Applied Pocket Height*—Measure from top edge of pocket to bottom edge of pocket along center of pocket. [Note: For contoured or irregularly shaped pockets, take a second measurement and indicate point of measure on spec sheet.]

126. *Applied Pocket Width*—Measure from side of pocket to side of pocket along top edge of pocket. [Note: For contoured or irregularly shaped pockets, take a second measurement and indicate point of measure on spec sheet.]

127. *Pocket Opening Within a Seam*—Measure from top of pocket to bottom of pocket along edge of pocket opening.

128. *Belt Length*
A. *Total*—Measure from end of belt at buckle along center of belt to opposite end of belt, following contour.
B. *Circumference*—Measure from end of belt at buckle along center of belt to middle hole at opposite end.

129. *Belt Width (or Height)*—Measure from edge of belt straight across to edge of belt. [Note: If belt is contoured, indicate points of measure on spec sheet.]

130. *Belt Loop Length*—Measure from top of belt loop straight down/vertically to bottom of belt loop along center of belt loop. [Note: Fashion-forward or

irregularly shaped belt loops may require further spec instructions. Indicate points of measure on spec sheet.]

131. *Belt Loop Width*—Measure belt loop from edge of belt loop straight across/horizontally to edge of belt loop. [Note: Fashion-forward or irregularly shaped belt loops may require further spec instructions. Indicate points of measure on spec sheet.]

132. *Tie Length*—Measure from end of tie/joining seam straight down to tie end along center of tie.

133. *Tie Width*
A. *Straight*— Measure from edge of tie straight across to edge of tie.
B. *Contoured*—Measure from edge of tie straight across to edge of tie at widest point of tie.

134. *Flounce/Ruffle Width*—Measure from flounce/ruffle joining seam straight across to outer edge of flounce/ruffle. [Note: If flounce/ruffle is contoured, measure along narrowest and widest points if possible and indicate changes on spec sheet.]

135. *Strap Length*—Measure from strap joining seam along center of strap to end of strap. [Note: If strap is contoured or has a contoured edge, measure along center, approximating center end point, or indicate instructions as needed on spec sheet.]

136. *Strap Width*—Measure from edge of strap straight across to edge of strap. [Note: If strap is contoured, measure along narrowest and widest points if possible and indicate changes on spec sheet.]

137. *Front Hood Length*—Measure from top of hood to bottom of hood at center front joining seam along opening edge of hood.

138. *Back Hood Length*—Measure from top of hood at center front to bottom of hood at center back joining seam along outside curve of hood fold/seam.

139. *Hood Width*—Measure from front opening edge of hood straight across to back of hood along widest point of hood.

140. *Flange Depth*—Measure from center back neck joining seam straight down to bottom of flange at center back. [Note: If flange is contoured or asymmetrical, indicate point of measure on spec sheet.]

141. *Shoulder Pad Length*—Measure from edge of pad straight across to edge of pad along center of pad or natural shoulder line of pad.

142. *Shoulder Pad Width*—Measure from side of pad straight across to side of pad along edge of pad if straight or at widest point of pad if curved.

143. *Straight Edge Shoulder Pad Height*—Measure from top of pad straight down to bottom of pad along center of pad.

144. *Curved Edge Shoulder Pad Height*—Stick a one-inch straight pin into thickest part of shoulder pad. Push pin all way through pad until head of pin rests on top of pad. Be sure not to crush pad. Measure portion of pin sticking out of pad. Subtract this figure from one inch (length of pin) to get shoulder pad height.

145. *Shoulder Pad Placement*—Measure from neck edge or joining seam straight across shoulder seam or natural shoulder line to start of shoulder pad.

146. *Pleats Placement*
C. *Front Pleat Skirt/Pant*—Measure distance from center front of garment waistband joining seam/edge straight across to start of first pleat.
D. *Back Pleat Skirt*—Measure distance from center back of garment waistband joining seam/edge straight across to start of first pleat.

147. *Button Placement*—Refer to measurement point 59, Neck Depth Center Front, for placement of first button. Then measure distance of first button to second button. Be sure when measuring that button at bust point is lined up to apex of bust. Adjust all buttons accordingly and respace as needed.

148. *Pocket Placement*
A. *Top Pocket Vertical*—Measure from shoulder-neck joining seam straight down to top edge of pocket.
B. *Top Pocket Horizontal*—Measure from center front straight across to side of pocket at top edge.
C. *Front Bottom Pocket Vertical*—Measure from waistband/joining seam/edge straight down to top edge of pocket.
D. *Front Bottom Pocket Horizontal*—Measure from center front straight across to side of pocket at top edge.
E. *Back Bottom Pocket Vertical*—Measure from waistband/joining seam/edge straight down to top edge of pocket.
F. *Back Bottom Pocket Horizontal*—Measure from center back straight across to side of pocket at top edge.
G. *Pocket from Side Seam*—Measure from side seam straight across to top of pocket. [Note: If pocket is contoured at sides, a top and bottom pocket size and placement must be measured and added to spec sheet.]

149. *Belt Loop Placement*
A. *Front*—Measure from center front of garment horizontally across to center of first front belt loop.
B. *Back*—Measure from center back of garment horizontally across to center of first back belt loop.
C. *Side Seam to Front*—Measure from center of side seam belt loop to center of front belt loop.
D. *Side Seam to Back*—Measure from center of side seam belt loop to center of back belt loop.

150. *Dart Placement*
A. *High Point Shoulder Bust Dart*—Measure from shoulder-neck joining seam or at a point _____" from shoulder-neck seam straight down, parallel to center front, to top of dart. [Note: The _____" from shoulder seam measurement is to be used for darts that are too short to be measured from

high point shoulder. Be sure to indicate _____" measurement on spec sheet.]

B. *Center Front Bust Dart*—Measure from center front of garment straight across to top of dart.

C. *Side Seam Bust Dart*—Measure from under-arm/side seam joining seam down along contour of side seam to bottom of dart.

D. *High Point Shoulder Princess Dart*—Measure from shoulder-neck joining seam straight down to top of dart.

E. *Center Front Princess Dart*—Measure from center front of garment straight across to top of dart.

CHAPTER 4 TERMS

When working with knit tops, you may come across the garment terms listed here. If you are unfamiliar with any of them, please look up the definitions in the glossary at the end of this text.

Belted cardigan

Boat neck

Classic cardigan

Cowl neck

Crew neck

Cropped top

Dolman sleeve

Flashdance

Mock turtleneck

Shrink

T-shirt

Tube top

V neck

V-necked cardigan

Vest

SPEC SHEET: Knit top   **STYLE**

SEASON:	DESCRIPTION:
LABEL: (SIZE CATEGORY)	
DATE:	
TECHNICAL SKETCH Turtleneck	SKETCH/PHOTO

CODE	POINT OF MEASURE	TOL. +/−	4	S/6	8	M/10	12	L/14	16	XL/18
1.	Front length	$1/2$								
3.	Center back length	$1/2$								
4.	Side length	$1/4$								
9.	Chest width	$1/4$-$3/8$								
13.	Across shoulder	$1/4$								
15.	Across chest	$1/4$								
16.	Across back	$1/4$								
25.	Bottom band/ribbing height	$1/8$								
26.	Bottom opening/sweep	$1/4$-$3/8$								
36.	Sleeve length top armhole	$3/8$								
39.	Sleeve length underarm	$3/8$								
42.	Curved armhole width	$1/4$								
48.	Muscle width	$1/8$								
50.	Elbow width	$1/8$								
52.	Sleeve opening width	$1/8$								
54.	Sleeve opening width stretched	$1/8$								
57.	Cuff/ribbing height sleeve	$1/8$								
58.	Neck depth front	$1/8$								

(Tolerance $1/4$-$3/8$ S, M, L, XL = $3/8$" 4-18 = $1/4$")

The measured garment spec sheets are for *illustrative purposes only* and should not be used as industry standards

CODE	POINT OF MEASURE	TOL. +/−	4	S/6	8	M/10	12	L/14	16	XL/18
63.	Neck width collar	1/4								
64.	Neck edge width	1/4								
66.	Neck edge width stretched	1/4								
68.	Neck base	1/4								
72.	Collar height	1/8								
73.	Collar band height	1/8								

COMMENTS:

(Tolerance 1/4-3/8 S, M, L, XL = 3/8" 4-18 = 1/4")

SPEC SHEET:	Knit top	STYLE	

SEASON:	Early fall

DESCRIPTION: Sleeveless Turtleneck

LABEL: (SIZE CATEGORY) Missy

DATE:

TECHNICAL SKETCH   Turtleneck

SKETCH/PHOTO

CODE	POINT OF MEASURE	TOL. +/−	4	S/6	8	M/10	12	L/14	16	XL/18
1.	Front length	$1/2$				23				
3.	Center back length	$1/2$				$21 1/2$				
4.	Side length	$1/4$				14				
9.	Chest width	$1/4$-$3/8$				$18 1/2$				
13.	Across shoulder	$1/4$				$14 3/4$				
15.	Across chest	$1/4$				$13 3/4$				
16.	Across back	$1/4$				$13 3/4$				
25.	Bottom band/ribbing height	$1/8$				$3/8$				
26.	Bottom opening/sweep	$1/4$-$3/8$				$18 1/2$				
36.	Sleeve length top armhole	$3/8$								
39.	Sleeve length underarm	$3/8$								
42.	Curved armhole width (opening)	$1/4$				9				
48.	Muscle width	$1/8$								
50.	Elbow width	$1/8$								
52.	Sleeve opening width	$1/8$								
54.	Sleeve opening width stretched	$1/8$								
57.	Cuff/ribbing height sleeve (armhole)	$1/8$				$3/8$				
58.	Neck depth front	$1/8$				1				

(Tolerance $1/4$-$3/8$ S, M, L, XL = $3/8$"   4-18 = $1/4$")

The measured garment spec sheets are for *illustrative purposes only* and should not be used as industry standards

CODE	POINT OF MEASURE	TOL. +/−	4	S/6	8	M/10	12	L/14	16	XL/18
63.	Neck width collar	1/4				6½				
64.	Neck edge width	1/4				6½				
66.	Neck edge width stretched	1/4				13				
68.	Neck base	1/4				7½				
72.	Collar height	1/8				6				
73.	Collar band height	1/8				3/8				
122.	Side venT A. HeighT	1/4				2½				
	B. WidTh rib	1/8				3/8				

COMMENTS:

CHAPTER 5

Knit Skirts

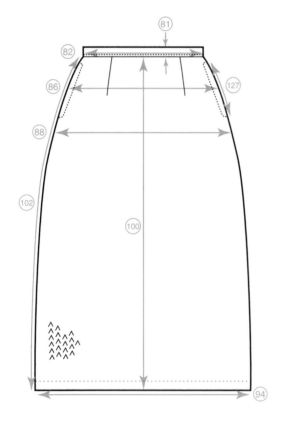

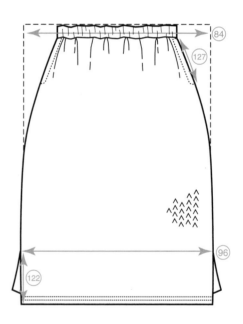

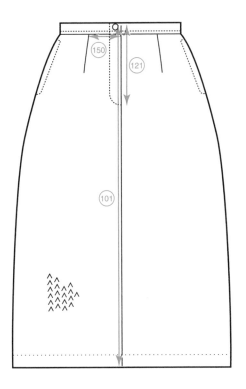

Optional

Figure 5.1

Measuring Knit Skirts

Knit skirts have become very popular over the last several years, in part due to increasing production costs and customer acceptance of elastic waistbands. Because styling is usually basic, knit skirts are one of the easiest garments to spec. However, there may be times when more than one method of measurement can be used for a measurement point (see Figure 5.1). As the technician, it is up to you to decide which measurement points are best suited to your garment style.

81. *Waistband Depth*—Measure from top of waistband edge straight down to bottom of waistband at waistband joining seam. [Note: If waistband is contoured, indicate measurement change on spec sheet.]

82. *Waistband Width (knit)*—Measure from side of bottom band to side of bottom band along center of band, following natural contour of waistband.

84. *Waistband Width, Stretched (knit)*—Measure from side of bottom band to side of bottom band straight across center of band in a fully extended position.

86. *High Hip Width (knit)*—Measure from edge of garment/side seam to edge of garment/side seam at a point 4" below bottom edge of waistband/seam, following contour of waist. [Note: The 4" point is for missywear only; adjust as needed $\frac{1}{2}$" to 1" up or down for children's, petite's, junior's, or large/plus womenswear. Indicate change on spec sheet.]

88. *Low Hip Width from Waist (knit)*—Measure from edge of garment/side seam to edge of garment/side seam at a point 7" below bottom edge of waistband/seam, following contour of waist. [Note: The 7" point is for missywear only; adjust as needed $\frac{1}{2}$" to 1" up or down for children's, petite's, junior's, or large/plus womenswear. Indicate change on spec sheet.]

90. *Hip Width from High Point Shoulder (knit)*—Measure from edge of garment/side seam to edge of garment/side seam straight across at a point _____" below high point shoulder. [Note: You will have to estimate low hip point on garment if there is no waistband and fill in _____" from high point shoulder. This measurement will vary from children's, junior's, missy, and large/plus womenswear.]

94. *Bottom Opening/Sweep Width (knit skirt)*—Measure from edge of garment/side seam to edge of garment/side seam straight across garment at bottom opening. [Note: If sweep has pleats, measure with pleats closed or relaxed.]

96. *Vented Bottom Opening/Sweep Width (knit skirt)*—Measure from edge of garment/side seam to edge of garment/side seam straight across garment at top of side vents. [Note: Indicate on spec sheet if there is only one vent or if vent hits at a point other than sweep, e.g., thigh opening.]

98. *Circular Bottom Opening/Sweep Width (knit skirt)*—Measure from edge of garment/side seam to edge of garment/side seam, following natural contour of garment at bottom opening.

100. *Center Front Skirt Length*—Measure from bottom of waistband/seam (top edge, if not banded or stitching if self-elastic/drawstring casing) straight down to bottom of garment at center front. [Note: A fashion-forward skirt may have an asymmetrical waist. Indicate top point of measure on spec sheet.]

101. *Center Back Skirt Length*—Measure from bottom of waistband/seam (top edge if not banded or stitching if self-elastic/drawstring casing) straight down to bottom of garment at center front. [Note: A fashion-forward skirt may have an asymmetrical waist. Indicate top point of measure on spec sheet.]

102. *Side Skirt Length*—Measure from bottom edge of waistband/seam (top edge if not banded or stitching if self-elastic/drawstring casing) to bottom of garment along side seam/fold of garment, following any contour.

103. *Skirt/Pant Yoke Depth Front*—Measure from bottom of waistband/seam (top edge if not banded or stitching if self-elastic/drawstring casing) straight down to bottom of yoke joining seam at center front. [Note: If yoke is contoured, indicate point of measure on spec sheet.]

104. *Skirt/Pant Yoke Depth Back*—Measure from bottom of waistband/seam (top edge if not banded or stitching if self-elastic/drawstring casing) straight

down to bottom of yoke joining seam at center back. [Note: If yoke is contoured, indicate point of measure on spec sheet.]

121. *Fly/Zipper*
A. *Length*—Measure from top of fly/zipper opening straight down to bottom of fly/zipper opening at zipper stop or bar tack.
B. *Fly/Zipper Width*—Measure top of fly/zipper at joining seam from edge/fold straight across to fly/zipper placket stitching.

122. *Vent/Slit*
A. *Height*—Measure from top of vent/slit straight down to bottom of vent/slit along edge of vent/slit.
B. *Width*—Measure top of vent/slit from edge/fold straight across to vent/slit placket stitching at a point parallel to garment hemline.

123. *Pleat Depth*—Measure from outer edge of pleat at fold/crease to inner fold of pleat. [Note 1: It is a good idea to indicate what type of pleat is being measured, e.g., box, inverted, knife, kick, kilt, or envelope. Note 2: If pleats are not parallel or symmetrical, indicate any special instructions on spec sheet.]

124. *Distance Between Pleats*—Measure from start of pleat to start of pleat, excluding pleat depth at a point directly below pleat joining seam. [Note: If pleats are not parallel or symmetrical, indicate any special instructions on spec sheet.]

125. *Applied Pocket Height*—Measure from top edge of pocket to bottom edge of pocket along center of pocket. [Note: For contoured or irregularly shaped pockets, take a second measurement and indicate point of measure on spec sheet.]

126. *Applied Pocket Width*—Measure from side of pocket to side of pocket along top edge of pocket. [Note: For contoured or irregularly shaped pockets, take a second measurement and indicate point of measure on spec sheet.]

127. *Pocket Opening Within a Seam*—Measure from top of pocket to bottom of pocket along edge of pocket opening.

128. *Belt Length*
A. *Total*—Measure from end of belt at buckle along center of belt to opposite end of belt, following contour.
B. *Circumference*—Measure from end of belt at buckle along center of belt to middle hole at opposite end.

129. *Belt Width (or Height)*—Measure from edge of belt straight across to edge of belt. [Note: If belt is contoured, indicate points of measure on spec sheet.]

130. *Belt Loop Length*—Measure from top of belt loop straight down/vertically to bottom of belt loop along center of belt loop. [Note: Fashion-forward or irregularly shaped belt loops may require further spec instructions. Indicate points of measure on spec sheet.]

131. *Belt Loop Width*—Measure belt loop from edge of belt loop straight across/horizontally to edge of belt loop. [Note: Fashion-forward or irregularly shaped belt loops may require further spec instructions. Indicate points of measure on spec sheet.]

132. *Tie Length*—Measure from end of tie/joining seam straight down to tie end along center of tie.

133. *Tie Width*
A. *Straight*—Measure from edge of tie straight across to edge of tie.
B. *Contoured*—Measure from edge of tie straight across to edge of tie at widest point of tie.

134. *Flounce/Ruffle Width*—Measure from flounce/ruffle joining seam straight across to outer edge of flounce/ruffle. [Note: If flounce/ruffle is contoured, measure along narrowest and widest points if possible and indicate changes on spec sheet.]

146. *Pleats Placement*

C. *Front Pleat Skirt/Pant*—Measure the distance from center front of garment waistband joining seam/edge straight across to start of first pleat.

D. *Back Pleat Skirt*—Measure the distance from center back of garment waistband joining seam/edge straight across to start of first pleat.

148. *Pocket Placement*

C. *Front Bottom Pocket Vertical*—Measure from waistband/joining seam/edge straight down to top edge of pocket.

D. *Front Bottom Pocket Horizontal*—Measure from center front straight across to side of pocket at top edge.

E. *Back Bottom Pocket Vertical*—Measure from waistband/joining seam/edge straight down to top edge of pocket.

F. *Back Bottom Pocket Horizontal*—Measure from center back straight across to side of pocket at top edge.

G. *Pocket from Side Seam*—Measure from side seam straight across to top of pocket. [Note: If pocket is contoured at sides, a top and bottom pocket size and placement must be measured and added to spec sheet.]

149. *Belt Loop Placement*

A. *Front*—Measure from center front of garment horizontally across to center of first front belt loop.

B. *Back*—Measure from center back of garment horizontally across to center of first back belt loop.

C. *Side Seam to Front*—Measure from center of side seam belt loop to center of front belt loop.

D. *Side Seam to Back*—Measure from center of side seam belt loop to center of back belt loop.

150. *Dart Placement*

F. *Center Front Skirt/Pant*—Measure from center front of garment at waistband joining seam/edge straight across to top of dart.

G. *Center Back Skirt/Pant*—Measure from center front of garment at waistband joining seam/edge straight across to top of dart.

CHAPTER 5 TERMS

When working with knit skirts, you may come across the garment terms listed below. If you are unfamiliar with any of them, please look up the definitions listed in the glossary at the end of this text.

Drawstring

Elastic waist

SPEC SHEET:	Knit skirt	STYLE	

SEASON:	DESCRIPTION:
LABEL: (SIZE CATEGORY)	
DATE:	

TECHNICAL SKETCH Pull on/elastic waist	SKETCH/PHOTO

CODE	POINT OF MEASURE	TOL. +/−	4	S/6	8	M/10	12	L/14	16	XL/18
81.	Waistband depth	$1/8$								
82.	Waistband width	$1/4$-$3/8$								
84.	Waistband width stretched	$1/4$-$3/8$								
88.	Low hip width	$1/4$-$3/8$								
94.	Bottom opening/sweep width	$1/4$-$3/8$								
96.	Vented bottom opening/sweep width	$1/4$-$3/8$								
98.	Circular bottom opening/sweep width	$1/4$-$3/8$								
100.	Center front skirt length	$3/8$								
101.	Center back skirt length	$3/8$								
102.	Side skirt length	$3/8$								
122.	Vent/slit A. Height	$1/4$								
	B. Width	$1/8$								
127.	Pocket opening	$1/4$								

(Tolerance $1/2$-$3/4$ S, M, L, XL = $3/8$" 4-18 = $1/4$")

The measured garment spec sheets are for *illustrative purposes only* and should not be used as industry standards

CODE	POINT OF MEASURE	TOL. +/−	4	S/6	8	M/10	12	L/14	16	XL/18
		TOL. +/−	4	S/6	8	M/10	12	L/14	16	XL/18

COMMENTS:

The measured garment spec sheets are for *illustrative purposes only* and should not be used as industry standards

SPEC SHEET: Knit skirt   **STYLE**

SEASON: Summer	DESCRIPTION: Short elastic waist skirt with two front pockets and decorative trim stitch.
LABEL: (SIZE CATEGORY) Missy	
DATE:	

TECHNICAL SKETCH   Pull on/elastic waist   SKETCH/PHOTO

CODE	POINT OF MEASURE	TOL. +/−	4	S/6	8	M/10	12	L/14	16	XL/18
81.	Waistband depth	$1/8$				1				
82.	Waistband width	$1/4$-$3/8$				14				
84.	Waistband width stretched	$1/4$-$3/8$				22				
88.	Low hip width	$1/4$-$3/8$				22				
94.	Bottom opening/sweep width	$1/4$-$3/8$				23				
96.	Vented bottom opening/sweep width	$1/4$-$3/8$								
98.	Circular bottom opening/sweep width	$1/4$-$3/8$								
100.	Center front skirt length	$3/8$				18				
101.	Center back skirt length	$3/8$				18				
102.	Side skirt length	$3/8$				19				
122.	Vent/slit A. Height	$1/4$								
	B. Width	$1/8$								
127.	Pocket opening	$1/4$				5				

(Tolerance $1/2$-$3/4$ S, M, L, XL = $3/8$" 4-18 = $1/4$")

The measured garment spec sheets are for *illustrative purposes only* and should not be used as industry standards

CODE	POINT OF MEASURE	TOL. +/−	4	S/6	8	M/10	12	L/14	16	XL/18

COMMENTS:

The measured garment spec sheets are for *illustrative purposes only* and should not be used as industry standards

CHAPTER 6

Knit Pants

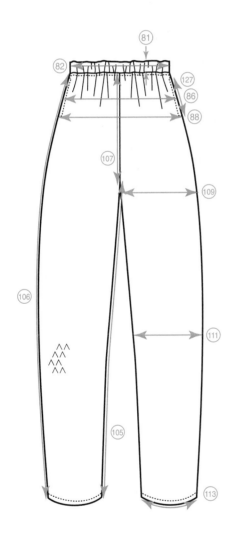

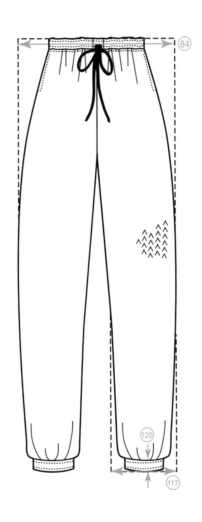

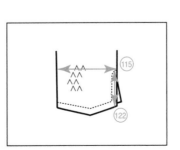

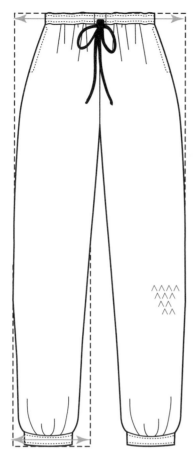

Figure 6.1

Measuring Knit Pants

Measuring knit pants is similar to measuring woven pants in theory, but generally with fewer style features. However, knit pants can be difficult to measure because of bulk in the rise. When measuring the waist and hip areas, line up the waistband at the center front and center back top edges, unless otherwise designed. The crotch/rise curve will not lie flat; simply let it lie in a natural position. When measuring a knit pant leg, lay one leg flat on the table, gently pushing the other aside. It is not necessary to measure both legs, but an occasional spot-check will ensure continuity. The front and back rises are measured separately and will have to be manipulated slightly in order to measure in a flat relaxed position. Although most knit pants do not have the construction details of woven pants, all style instructions have been included for the rare constructed knit pant. Pull-on styling is common with knit pants and is easy to spec. However, with all garments evaluated, you must be sure to choose and note the best measurement point for that garment to ensure consistency and accuracy.

81. *Waistband Depth*—Measure from top of waistband edge straight down to bottom of waistband at waistband joining seam. [Note: If waistband is contoured, indicate measurement change on spec sheet.]

82. *Waistband Width (knit)*—Measure from side of bottom band to side of bottom band along center of band, following natural contour of waistband.

84. *Waistband Width, Stretched (knit)*—Measure from side of bottom band to side of bottom band straight across center of band in a fully extended position.

86. *High Hip Width (knit)*—Measure from edge of garment/side seam to edge of garment/side seam at a point 4" below bottom edge of waistband/seam, following contour of waist. [Note: The 4" point is for

missywear only; adjust as needed $\frac{1}{2}$" to 1" up or down for children's, petite's, junior's, or large/plus womenswear. Indicate change on spec sheet.]

88. *Low Hip Width from Waist (knit)*—Measure from edge of garment/side seam to edge of garment/side seam at a point 7" below bottom edge of waistband/seam, following contour of waist. [Note: The 7" point is for missywear only; adjust as needed $\frac{1}{2}$" to 1" up or down for children's, petite's, junior's, or large/plus womenswear. Indicate change on spec sheet.]

90. *Hip Width from High Point Shoulder (knit)*—Measure from edge of garment/side seam to edge of garment/side seam straight across at a point _____" below high point shoulder. [Note: You will have to estimate low hip point on garment if there is no waistband and fill in _____" from high point shoulder. This measurement will vary for children's, junior's, missy, and large/plus womenswear.]

92. *Hip Seat Width (knit pant)*—Measure from edge of garment/side seam to edge of garment/side seam at a point _____" up from crotch seam, following contour of waist. [Note 1: This measurement is useful when waistband sits below natural waistline. Note 2: Adjust _____" up from crotch as needed for junior's and large/plus womenswear. Note 3: A hip seat width of $2\frac{1}{2}$" up for children's and 3" up for menswear can take place of low hip width.]

103. *Skirt/Pant Yoke Depth Front*—Measure from bottom of waistband/seam (top edge if not banded or stitching if self-elastic/drawstring casing) straight down to bottom of yoke joining seam at center front. [Note: If yoke is contoured, indicate point of measure on spec sheet.]

104. *Skirt/Pant Yoke Depth Back*—Measure from bottom of waistband/seam (top edge if not banded or stitching if self-elastic/drawstring casing) straight down to bottom of yoke joining seam at center back. [Note: If yoke is contoured, indicate point of measure on spec sheet.]

105. *Inseam*—Measure from crotch joining seam to bottom of leg opening, following inseam/inner fold.

106. *Outseam*—Measure from bottom edge of waistband/seam (top edge if not banded or stitching if self-elastic/drawstring casing) to bottom of garment along side seam/fold of garment.

107. *Front Rise*—Measure from bottom edge of waistband/seam (top edge if not banded or stitching if self-elastic/drawstring casing) to crotch joining seam, following curve of front rise seam. [Note: Measure over zipper if in front rise seam.]

108. *Back Rise*—Measure from bottom edge of waistband/seam (top edge if not banded or stitching if self-elastic/drawstring casing) to crotch joining seam, following curve of back rise seam. [Note: Measure over zipper if in front back seam.]

109. *Thigh Width (knit)*—Measure from pant leg edge/seam to pant leg edge/seam straight across pant leg at a point 1" below crotch and parallel to leg opening. [Note: If leg opening is asymmetrical, measure to a point that would be parallel to leg opening.]

111. *Knee Width (knit)*—Measure from pant leg edge/seam to pant leg edge/seam at a point one-half of inseam and parallel to leg opening. [Note 1: If leg opening is asymmetrical, measure to a point that would be parallel to leg opening. Note 2: If pant leg is three-quarter length, indicate point of measure on spec sheet. Note 3: A general knee measurement from crotch seam of missy 12", junior's 11", or large/plus women's 13" can be used. Indicate change on spec sheet. For childrenswear measure at one-half the inseam minus $1\frac{1}{2}$", and for men's minus 2".]

113. *Leg Opening Width (knit)*—Measure from pant leg edge/seam to pant edge/seam straight across bot-

tom edge of leg opening. [Note: If leg opening is contoured, follow contour and indicate measurement change on spec sheet.]

115. *Vented Leg Opening Width (knit)*—Measure from pant leg edge/seam to pant leg edge/seam straight across pant leg at top of side vents.

117. *Leg Opening Width, Stretched (knit)*—Measure from pant leg edge/seam to pant leg edge/seam straight across bottom edge of leg opening in a fully extended position.

119. *Cuff Height Pants*—Measure from top of cuff edge straight down to bottom of cuff fold and leg opening.

120. *Bottom Band/Ribbing Height Pants*—Measure from cuff joining seam or top of ribbing straight down to bottom edge of cuff or rib opening. [Note: For fashion-forward pants, you may want to include a cuff width. See point of measure 56, Cuff Length Sleeve, for measuring instructions and indicate cuff width pant as needed on spec sheet.]

121. *Fly/Zipper*
A. *Length*—Measure from top of fly/zipper opening straight down to bottom of fly/zipper opening at zipper stop or bar tack.
B. *Fly/Zipper Width*—Measure top of fly/zipper at joining seam from edge/fold straight across to fly/zipper placket stitching.

122. *Vent/Slit*
A. *Height*—Measure from top of vent/slit straight down to bottom of vent/slit along edge of vent/slit.
B. *Width*—Measure top of vent/slit from edge/fold straight across to vent/slit placket stitching at a point parallel to garment hemline.

123. *Pleat Depth*—Measure from outer edge of pleat at fold/crease to inner fold of pleat. [Note 1: It is a good idea to indicate what type of pleat is being mea-

sured, e.g., box, inverted, knife, kick, kilt, or envelope. Note 2: If pleats are not parallel or symmetrical, indicate any special instructions on spec sheet.]

124. *Distance Between Pleats*—Measure from start of pleat to start of pleat, excluding pleat depth at a point directly below pleat joining seam. [Note: If pleats are not parallel or symmetrical, indicate any special instructions on spec sheet.]

125. *Applied Pocket Height*—Measure from top edge of pocket to bottom edge of pocket along center of pocket. [Note: For contoured or irregularly shaped pockets, take a second measurement and indicate point of measure on spec sheet.]

126. *Applied Pocket Width*—Measure from side of pocket to side of pocket along top edge of pocket. [Note: For contoured or irregularly shaped pockets, take a second measurement and indicate point of measure on spec sheet.]

127. *Pocket Opening Within a Seam*—Measure from top of pocket to bottom of pocket along edge of pocket opening.

128. *Belt Length*
A. *Total*—Measure from end of belt at buckle along center of belt to opposite end of belt, following contour.
B. *Circumference*—Measure from end of belt at buckle along center of belt to middle hole at opposite end.

129. *Belt Width (or Height)*—Measure from edge of belt straight across to edge of belt. [Note: If belt is contoured, indicate points of measure on spec sheet.]

130. *Belt Loop Length*—Measure from top of belt loop straight down/vertically to bottom of belt loop along center of belt loop. [Note: Fashion-forward or irregularly shaped belt loops may require further spec instructions. Indicate points of measure on spec sheet.]

131. *Belt Loop Width*—Measure belt loop from edge of belt loop straight across/horizontally to edge of belt loop. [Note: Fashion-forward or irregularly shaped belt loops may require further spec instructions. Indicate points of measure on spec sheet.]

132. *Tie Length*—Measure from end of tie/joining seam straight down to tie end along center of tie.

133. *Tie Width*
A. *Straight*—Measure from edge of tie straight across to edge of tie.
B. *Contoured*—Measure from edge of tie straight across to edge of tie at widest point of tie.

134. *Flounce/Ruffle Width*—Measure from flounce/ruffle joining seam straight across to outer edge of flounce/ruffle. [Note: If flounce/ruffle is contoured, measure along narrowest and widest points if possible and indicate changes on spec sheet.]

146. *Pleats Placement*
C. *Front Pleat Skirt/Pant*—Measure distance from center front of garment waistband joining seam/edge straight across to start of first pleat.
D. *Back Pleat Skirt*—Measure distance from center back of garment waistband joining seam/edge straight across to start of first pleat.

148. *Pocket Placement*
C. *Front Bottom Pocket Vertical*—Measure from waistband/joining seam/edge straight down to top edge of pocket.
D. *Front Bottom Pocket Horizontal*—Measure from center front straight across to side of pocket at top edge.
E. *Back Bottom Pocket Vertical*—Measure from waistband/joining seam/edge straight down to top edge of pocket.

F. *Back Bottom Pocket Horizontal*—Measure from center back straight across to side of pocket at top edge.
G. *Pocket from Side Seam*—Measure from side seam straight across to top of pocket. [Note: If pocket is contoured at sides, a top and bottom pocket size and placement must be measured and added to spec sheet.]

149. *Belt Loop Placement*
A. *Front*—Measure from center front of garment horizontally across to center of first front belt loop.
B. *Back*—Measure from center back of garment horizontally across to center of first back belt loop.
C. *Side Seam to Front*—Measure from center of side seam belt loop to center of front belt loop.
D. *Side Seam to Back*—Measure from center of side seam belt loop to center of back belt loop.

150. *Dart Placement*
F. *Center Front Skirt/Pant*—Measure from center front of garment at waistband joining seam/edge straight across to top of dart.
G. *Center Back Skirt/Pant*—Measure from center front of garment at waistband joining seam/edge straight across to top of dart.

CHAPTER 6 TERMS

When working with knit pants, you may come across the garment terms listed below. If you are unfamiliar with any of them, please look up the definition in the glossary at the end of this text.

Pull-on pant
Warm-up pant

SPEC SHEET   Knit pant

STYLE	
SEASON:	DESCRIPTION:
LABEL: (SIZE CATEGORY)	
DATE:	

TECHNICAL SKETCH   Pull on pant

SKETCH/PHOTO

CODE	POINT OF MEASURE	TOL. +/−	4	S/6	8	M/10	12	L/14	16	XL/18
81.	Waistband depth	1/8								
82.	Waistband width	1/4-3/8								
84.	Waistband width stretched	1/4-3/8								
86.	High hip width	1/4-3/8								
88.	Low hip width	1/4-3/8								
105.	Inseam	3/8								
106.	Outseam	3/8								
107.	Front rise	3/8								
108.	Back rise	3/8								
109.	Thigh width	1/4								
111.	Knee width	1/4								
113.	Leg opening width	1/8								

(Tolerance 1/4-3/8 S, M, L, XL = 3/8" 4-18 = 1/4")

The measured garment spec sheets are for *illustrative purposes only* and should not be used as industry standards

CODE	POINT OF MEASURE	TOL. +/–	4	S/6	8	M/10	12	L/14	16	XL/18
120.	Bottom band/ribbing height	1/8								
127.	Pocket opening	1/4								
			TOL. +/–	4	S/6	8	M/10	12	L/14	16	XL/18

COMMENTS:

SPEC SHEET Knit pant

STYLE

SEASON: Fall/Winter	DESCRIPTION: Pull on wool pant with rib covered
LABEL: (SIZE CATEGORY) Missy	elastic waistband
DATE:	

TECHNICAL SKETCH Pull on pant

SKETCH/PHOTO

CODE	POINT OF MEASURE	TOL. +/−	4	S/6	8	M/10	12	L/14	16	XL/18
81.	Waistband depth	1/8				1				
82.	Waistband width	1/4-3/8				14				
84.	Waistband width stretched	1/4-3/8				19 1/2				
86.	High hip width	1/4-3/8				18 1/2				
88.	Low hip width	1/4-3/8				20 1/2				
105.	Inseam	3/8				28				
106.	Outseam	3/8				38 1/2				
107.	Front rise	3/8				11 1/2				
108.	Back rise	3/8				13 1/2				
109.	Thigh width	1/4				24				
111.	Knee width	1/4				10 1/4				
113.	Leg opening width	1/8				8				

(Tolerance 1/4-3/8 S, M, L, XL = 3/8" 4-18 = 1/4")

The measured garment spec sheets are for *illustrative purposes only* and should not be used as industry standards

CODE	POINT OF MEASURE	TOL. +/−	4	S/6	8	M/10	12	L/14	16	XL/18
120.	Bottom band/ribbing height	1/8				1/8				
127.	Pocket opening	1/4				—				

COMMENTS:

The measured garment spec sheets are for *illustrative purposes only* and should not be used as industry standards

CHAPTER 7

Knit Dresses

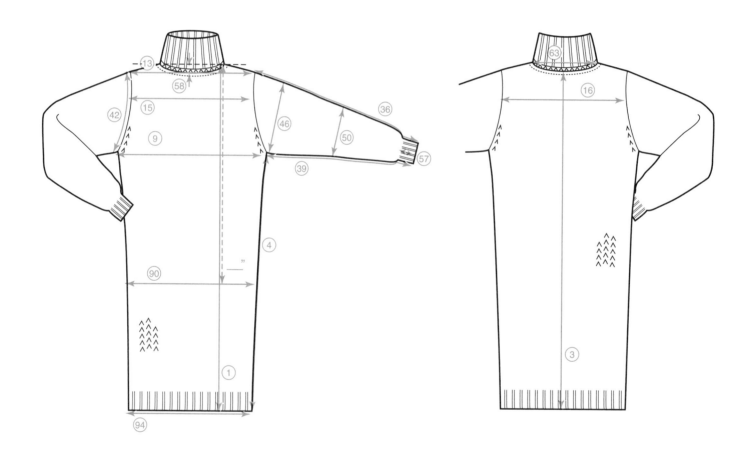

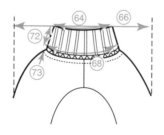

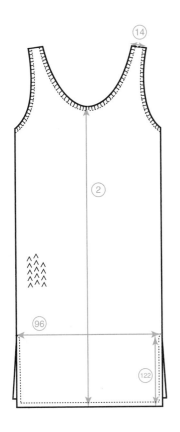

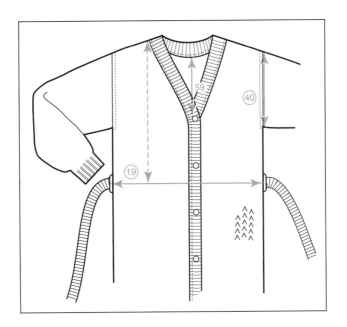

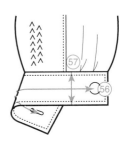

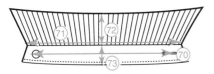

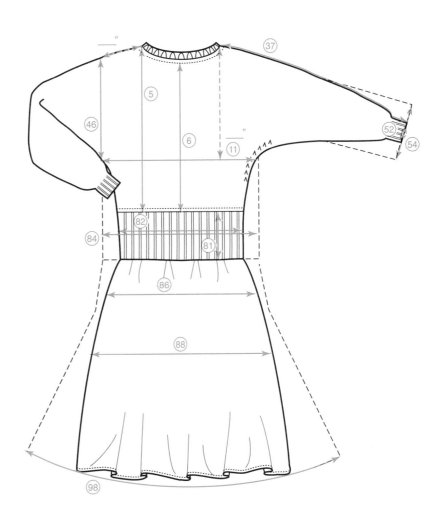

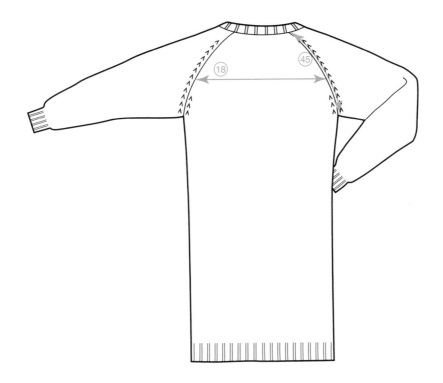

Measuring Knit Dresses

Many knit dresses are simply designed as long versions of T-shirts or sweaters, combining the measurements of a knit top and a knit skirt. Therefore, the rules you learned for each of those styles will be used here as well. If needed, look back over those chapters.

1. *Front Length (garments with a front opening)*—Measure from high point shoulder at neck straight down, parallel to center front, to bottom of garment at front. If garment has a collar, gently lift it away from shoulder-neck measuring point.

2. *Center Front Length (garments with a plain front; no front opening)*—Measure from center front neck joining seams straight down to bottom of garment at center front. [Note: A garment without a front open-

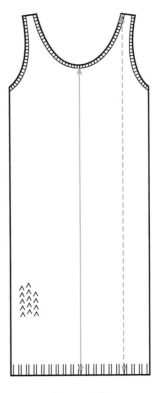

Figure 7.1

ing may still require use of Front Length if neckline is unusual.]

3. *Center Back Length*—Measure from center back neck joining seams straight down to bottom of garment at center back. If needed, gently lift collar away from back neck to expose joining seam.

4. *Side Length*—Measure from bottom of armhole/side seam straight down to bottom of garment along side of garment. Do not follow natural curve of garment's side seam, unless otherwise indicated. If needed, gently lift sleeve away from armhole/side seam joining seam.

5. *Front Bodice Length (garments with a front opening)*—Measure from high point shoulder at neck straight down, parallel to center front, to top edge of waistband, joining seam, or rib. If garment has a collar, gently lift it away from shoulder-neck measuring point.

6. *Center Front Bodice Length (garments with a plain front; no front opening)*—Measure from center front neck joining seam straight down to top edge of waistband, joining seam, or rib. [Note: A garment without a center opening may still require use of Front Bodice Length if neckline is unusual.]

7. *Center Back Bodice Length*—Measure from center back neck joining seams straight down to top edge of waistband, joining seam, or rib. If needed, gently lift collar away from back neck to expose joining seam.

8. *Side Seam Bodice Length*—Measure from bottom of armhole/side seam straight down to top edge of waistband, joining seam, or rib, along side of garment, following natural curve of garment's side seam, unless otherwise indicated. If needed, gently lift sleeve away from armhole/side seam joining seam. [Note: You can take side seam bodice measurement straight rather than contoured if joining seam/rib can be extended, but indicate change on spec sheet.]

9. *Chest Width (knit)*—Measure from edge of garment/side seam to edge of garment/side seam straight across garment at a point 1' below armhole.

11. *Chest Width (raglan sleeve, knit)*—Measure from edge of garment/side seam to edge of garment/side seam straight across garment at a point _____" below high point shoulder. [Note: You will have to determine number of inches down from high point shoulder for each raglan sleeve style based on depth of sleeve. Then indicate this number on spec sheet.]

13. *Across Shoulder*—Measure straight across front from armhole seam/edge to armhole seam/edge at shoulder seam or across natural shoulder fold line created if there is no seam.

14. *Shoulder Width*—Measure from neckband/collar/ribbing joining seam or neckline edge to top of armhole seam at shoulder, taken along shoulder seam or across natural shoulder fold line created if there is no seam.

15. *Across Chest*—Measure $2\frac{1}{2}$" down from collar/rib joining seam at center front straight across front of garment from armhole seam/edge to armhole seam/edge. [Note: The $2\frac{1}{2}$" measurement point is for missywear only and may need to be adjusted up or down $\frac{1}{4}$" to $\frac{1}{2}$" accordingly for men's, children's, junior's, and large/plus womenswear. Indicate any changes on spec sheet.]

16. *Across Back*—Measure 4" down from collar/rib joining seam at center back straight across back of garment from armhole seam/edge to armhole seam/edge. [Note: The 4" measurement point is for missywear only and may need to be adjusted up or down $\frac{1}{4}$" to $\frac{1}{2}$" accordingly for men's, children's, junior's, and large/plus womenswear. Indicate any changes on spec sheet.]

17. *Across Chest/Center Armhole*—Measure at one-half depth of armhole straight across front of garment from armhole seam/edge to armhole seam/edge.

18. *Across Back/Center Armhole*—Measure at one-half depth of armhole straight across back of garment from armhole seam/edge to armhole seam/edge.

19. *Waist Width (knit)*—Measure from edge of garment/side seam to edge of garment/side seam straight across garment on seam or at narrowest point of waist taper at a point _____" below high point shoulder. [Note: You will have to determine number of inches down from high point shoulder for each raglan sleeve style based on depth of sleeve. Then indicate this number on spec sheet.]

32. *Yoke Width Front*—Measure from armhole seam/edge to armhole seam/edge straight across front of garment, ignoring contours or points, at yoke-body joining seams. [Note: If yoke is asymmetrical, indicate changes in measuring as needed on spec sheet.]

33. *Yoke Width Back*—Measure from armhole seam/edge to armhole seam/edge straight across back of garment, ignoring contours or points, at yoke-body joining seams. [Note: If yoke is asymmetrical, indicate changes in measuring as needed on spec sheet.]

34. *Yoke Depth Front*—Measure from high point shoulder at neck straight down to bottom of front yoke-body joining seam. Be sure to gently lift collar away from shoulder-neck joining seam if needed.

35. *Yoke Back Depth*—Measure from center back neck joining seam straight down to bottom of back yoke-body joining seam. Gently lift collar away from back neck joining seam if needed.

36. *Sleeve Length Top Armhole*—Measure along top of sleeve/fold following contour of sleeve from armhole seam at shoulder to bottom of sleeve opening, including cuff.

37. *Sleeve Length Top Neck*—Measure along top of sleeve/fold following contour of sleeve from sleeve-neck joining seam/edge to edge of sleeve opening, including cuff. Gently lift away collar at sleeve-neck joining seam if needed.

38. *Sleeve Length Center Back*—Measure from center back neck joining seam or from a point above neck at an imaginary line, that of a joining seam, along top of sleeve/fold, following contour of sleeve to edge of sleeve opening, including cuff.

39. *Sleeve Length Underarm*—Measure straight from bottom of armhole along sleeve seam to edge of sleeve opening, including cuff.

40. *Straight Armhole Width (knit)*—Measure from top of shoulder joining seam/edge straight down to bottom of armhole.

42. *Curved Armhole Width (knit)*—Measure from top of shoulder joining seam/edge to bottom of armhole, following contour of armhole.

44. *Armhole Front*—Measure on front of garment from top of shoulder at neckline joining seam/edge to bottom of armhole, following contour of armhole. Gently lift collar away from neckline joining seam if needed.

45. *Armhole Back*—Measure on back of garment from top of shoulder at neck joining seam/edge to bottom of armhole, following contour of armhole. Gently lift collar away from neck joining seam if needed.

46. *Armhole Width Straight (knit)*—Measure from top of shoulder seam at a point _____" below neckline joining seam/edge straight down to bottom of armhole. [Note: Gently move collar from neck joining seam if needed when measuring down _____" to armhole start point. Indicate number of inches measured down on spec sheet.]

48. *Muscle Width (knit)*—Measure from inner sleeve edge/seam to outer sleeve edge/fold at a point 1" below armhole and parallel to sleeve opening.

50. *Elbow Width (knit)*—Measure from inner sleeve edge/seam to outer sleeve edge/fold straight across sleeve at a point one-half of underarm sleeve length and parallel to sleeve opening at wrist or cuff. [Note: If sleeve is three-quarter length, indicate new point of measure on spec sheet.]

52. *Sleeve Opening Width (knit)*—Measure from inner sleeve edge/seam to outer sleeve edge/fold straight across bottom edge of sleeve opening.

54. *Sleeve Opening Width, Stretched (knit)*—Measure from inner sleeve edge/seam to outer sleeve edge/fold straight across bottom edge of sleeve opening in a fully extended position.

56. *Cuff Length Sleeve*—Measure from outside end of buttonhole to center of button straight along center of cuff. Open cuff out as flat as possible when measuring. [Note: If cuff length is contoured, measure along center-most point.]

57. *Cuff/Ribbing Height Sleeve*—Measure from cuff joining seam or top of ribbing straight down to bottom edge of cuff or rib opening. [Note: If cuff is contoured, indicate changes made as needed to measurement on spec sheet.]

58. *Neck Depth Front (garments with a plain front/asymmetrical front opening)*—Measure from center back neck joining seam/edge straight down to center front neck joining seam/edge.

59. *Neck Depth Center Front (garments with a center front opening)*—Measure from center back neck joining seam/edge straight down to center of first button at center front of garment.

60. *Neck Drop Front*—Measure from an imaginary line connecting neckline edges straight down to center front neck opening edge. Use a ruler if needed to connect top neckline edges.

61. *Neck Drop Back*—Measure from an imaginary line connecting neckline edges straight down to center back neck opening edge. This measurement is taken with front of garment facing up. Use a ruler to connect top neckline edges if needed.

62. *Neck Width, No Collar*—Measure from inside neck edge/seam to inside neck edge/seam straight across back neck at widest point. This measurement is taken with front of garment faceup.

63. *Neck Width, Collar*—Measure straight across back neck from neck-shoulder joining seam to neck-shoulder joining seam or natural shoulder line if no seam. This measurement is taken with back of garment face up.

64. *Neck Edge Width (knit)*—Measure from neck edge/seam/fold to neck edge/seam/fold along top opening edge, following natural contour of neck opening. Garment should be positioned with one shoulder on top of the other and with front and back neck edges meeting.

66. *Neck Edge Width, Stretched (knit)*—Measure from neck edge/seam/fold to neck edge/seam/fold along top opening edge in a fully extended position. Garment should be positioned with one shoulder on top of the other and with front and back neck edges meeting.

68. *Neck Base (knit)*—Measure from neck edge/seam to neck edge/seam along collar/rib joining seam or neckline edge, following natural contour of neck opening. Garment should be buttoned or zippered, if applicable, with one shoulder seam positioned on top of the other, and with front and back neck edges meeting.

70. *Neckband Length*—Measure from outside end of buttonhole to center of buttonhole across neckband, following contour of neckband.

71. *Collar Length*—Measure from one end of collar to other end of collar along neck joining seam.

72. *Collar Height*—Measure from collar/rib joining seam at center back neck straight up to outer edge of collar/rib.

73. *Collar Band Height*—Measure from collar joining seam at center back straight up to neckband joining seam at center back.

74. *Collar Point Length*—Measure from collar joining seam to outer edge of collar along collar point edge. [Note: If collar is rounded, measure at a point parallel to center back and indicate change on spec sheet.]

75. *Collar Point Spread (pointed collars only)*—Measure, with collar band buttoned and collar in place, from collar point straight across collar edge to collar point.

76. *Lapel Width*
A. *Notched*—Measure from lower lapel notch straight across to lapel fold at a point perpendicular to garment center front.
B. *Without Notches*—Measure from lapel edge straight across widest point of lapel to lapel fold at a point _____" down from center back collar joining seam and perpendicular to front of garment.

77. *Center Front Extension*—Measure from an imaginary line at center front of garment horizontally to finished outer edge of front extended piece.

78. *Placket Length*—Measure from top edge of placket straight down to bottom of placket opening along center of placket.

79. *Placket Width*—Measure from placket joining seam straight across placket to placket edge at fold.

80. *Keyhole Length*—Measure from outer edge of neckline straight down to bottom of keyhole opening.

81. *Waistband Depth*—Measure from top of waistband edge straight down to bottom of waistband at waistband joining seam. [Note: If waistband is contoured, indicate measurement change on spec sheet.]

82. *Waistband Width (knit)*—Measure from side of bottom band to side of bottom band along center of band, following natural contour of waistband.

84. *Waistband Width, Stretched (knit)*—Measure from side of bottom band to side of bottom band straight across center of band in a fully extended position.

86. *High Hip Width (knit)*—Measure from edge of garment/side seam to edge of garment/side seam at a point 4" below bottom edge of waistband/seam, following contour of waist. [Note: The 4" point is for missywear only; adjust as needed $\frac{1}{2}$" to 1" up or down for children's, petite's, junior's, or large/plus womenswear. Indicate change on spec sheet.]

88. *Low Hip Width from Waist (knit)*—Measure from edge of garment/side seam to edge of garment/side seam at a point 7" below bottom edge of waistband/seam, following contour of waist. [Note: The 7" point is for missywear only; adjust as needed $\frac{1}{2}$" to 1" up or down for children's, petite's, junior's, or large/plus womenswear. Indicate change on spec sheet.]

90. *Hip Width from High Point Shoulder (knit)*—Measure from edge of garment/side seam to edge of garment/side seam straight across at a point _____" below high point shoulder. [Note: You will have to estimate low hip point on garment if there is no waistband and fill in _____" from high point shoulder. This measurement will vary for children's, junior's, missy, and large/plus womenswear.]

94. *Bottom Opening/Sweep Width (knit skirt)*—Measure from edge of garment/side seam to edge of garment/side seam straight across garment at bottom

opening. [Note: If sweep has pleats, measure with pleats closed or relaxed.]

96. *Vented Bottom Opening/Sweep Width (knit skirt)*—Measure from edge of garment/side seam to edge of garment/side seam straight across garment at top of side vents. [Note: Indicate on spec sheet if there is only one vent or if vent hits at a point other than sweep, e.g., thigh opening.]

98. *Circular Bottom Opening/Sweep Width (knit skirt)*—Measure from edge of garment/side seam to edge of garment/side seam, following natural contour of garment at bottom opening.

100. *Center Front Skirt Length*—Measure from bottom of waistband/seam (top edge if not banded or stitching if self-elastic/drawstring casing) straight down to bottom of garment at center front. [Note: A fashion-forward skirt may have an asymmetrical waist. Indicate top point of measure on spec sheet.]

101. *Center Back Skirt Length*—Measure from bottom of waistband/seam (top edge if not banded or stitching if self-elastic/drawstring casing) straight down to bottom of garment at center front. [Note: A fashion-forward skirt may have an asymmetrical waist. Indicate top point of measure on spec sheet.]

102. *Side Skirt Length*—Measure from bottom edge of waistband/seam (top edge if not banded or stitching if self-elastic/drawstring casing) to bottom of garment along side seam/fold of garment, following any contour.

103. *Skirt/Pant Yoke Depth Front*—Measure from bottom of waistband/seam (top edge if not banded or stitching if self-elastic/drawstring casing) straight down to bottom of yoke joining seam at center front. [Note: If yoke is contoured, indicate point of measure on spec sheet.]

104. *Skirt/Pant Yoke Depth Back*—Measure from bottom of waistband/seam (top edge if not banded

or stitching if self-elastic/drawstring casing) straight down to bottom of yoke joining seam at center back. [Note: If yoke is contoured, indicate point of measure on spec sheet.]

121. *Fly/Zipper*
A. *Length*—Measure from top of fly/zipper opening straight down to bottom of fly/zipper opening at zipper stop or bar tack.
B. *Fly/Zipper Width*—Measure top of fly/zipper at joining seam from edge/fold straight across to fly/zipper placket stitching.

122. *Vent/Slit*
A. *Height*—Measure from top of vent/slit straight down to bottom of vent/slit along edge of vent/slit.
B. *Width*—Measure top of vent/slit from edge/fold straight across to vent/slit placket stitching at a point parallel to garment hemline.

123. *Pleat Depth*—Measure from outer edge of pleat at fold/crease to inner fold of pleat. [Note 1: It is a good idea to indicate what type of pleat is being measured, e.g., box, inverted, knife, kick, kilt, or envelope. Note 2: If pleats are not parallel or symmetrical, indicate any special instructions on spec sheet.]

124. *Distance Between Pleats*—Measure from start of pleat to start of pleat, excluding pleat depth at a point directly below pleat joining seam. [Note: If pleats are not parallel or symmetrical, indicate any special instructions on spec sheet.]

125. *Applied Pocket Height*—Measure from top edge of pocket to bottom edge of pocket along center of pocket. [Note: For contoured or irregularly shaped pockets, take a second measurement and indicate point of measure on spec sheet.]

126. *Applied Pocket Width*—Measure from side of pocket to side of pocket along top edge of pocket. [Note: For contoured or irregularly shaped pockets, take a second measurement and indicate point of measure on spec sheet.]

127. *Pocket Opening Within a Seam*—Measure from top of pocket to bottom of pocket along edge of pocket opening.

128. *Belt Length*
A. *Total*—Measure from end of belt at buckle along center of belt to opposite end of belt, following contour.
B. *Circumference*—Measure from end of belt at buckle along center of belt to middle hole at opposite end.

129. *Belt Width (or Height)*—Measure from edge of belt straight across to edge of belt. [Note: If belt is contoured, indicate points of measure on spec sheet.]

130. *Belt Loop Length*—Measure from top of belt loop straight down/vertically to bottom of belt loop along center of belt loop. [Note: Fashion-forward or irregularly shaped belt loops may require further spec instructions. Indicate points of measure on spec sheet.]

131. *Belt Loop Width*—Measure belt loop from edge of belt loop straight across/horizontally to edge of belt loop. [Note: Fashion-forward or irregularly shaped belt loops may require further spec instructions. Indicate points of measure on spec sheet.]

132. *Tie Length*—Measure from end of tie/joining seam straight down to tie end along center of tie.

133. *Tie Width*
A. *Straight*—Measure from edge of tie straight across to edge of tie.
B. *Contoured*—Measure from edge of tie straight across to edge of tie at widest point of tie.

134. *Flounce/Ruffle Width*—Measure from flounce/ruffle joining seam straight across to outer edge of flounce/ruffle. [Note: If flounce/ruffle is contoured, measure along narrowest and widest points if possible and indicate changes on spec sheet.]

135. *Strap Length*—Measure from strap joining seam along center of strap to end of strap. [Note: If a strap is contoured or has a contoured edge, measure along center, approximating center end point, or indicate instructions as needed on spec sheet.]

136. *Strap Width*—Measure from edge of strap straight across to edge of strap. [Note: If strap is contoured, measure along narrowest and widest points if possible and indicate changes on spec sheet.]

137. *Front Hood Length*—Measure from top of hood to bottom of hood at center front joining seam along opening edge of hood.

138. *Back Hood Length*—Measure from top of hood at center front to bottom of hood at center back joining seam along outside curve of hood fold/seam.

139. *Hood Width*—Measure from front opening edge of hood straight across to back of hood along widest point of hood.

140. *Flange Depth*—Measure from center back neck joining seam straight down to bottom of flange at center back. [Note: If flange is contoured or asymmetrical, indicate point of measure on spec sheet.]

141. *Shoulder Pad Length*—Measure from edge of pad straight across to edge of pad along center of pad or natural shoulder line of pad.

142. *Shoulder Pad Width*—Measure from side of pad straight across to side of pad along edge of pad if straight or at widest point of pad if curved.

143. *Straight Edge Shoulder Pad Height*—Measure from top of pad straight down to bottom of pad along center of pad.

144. *Curved Edge Shoulder Pad Height*—Stick a one-inch straight pin into thickest part of shoulder pad. Push pin all way through pad until head of pin rests on top of pad. Be sure not to crush pad. Measure

portion of pin sticking out of pad. Subtract this figure from one inch (length of pin) to get shoulder pad height.

145. *Shoulder Pad Placement*—Measure from neck edge or joining seam straight across shoulder seam or natural shoulder line to start of shoulder pad.

146. *Pleats Placement*
A. *Front Pleat Top*—Measure the distance from center front of garment straight across to start of first pleat at a point parallel to garment hem. [Note: You may need to use armhole or side seam as a starting point if there is no center front seam or placket.]
B. *Back Pleat Top*—Measure distance from armhole seam/side seam (depending on pleat placement) to first pleat at a point parallel to garment hem.
C. *Front Pleat Skirt/Pant*—Measure distance from center front of garment waistband joining seam/edge straight across to start of first pleat.
D. *Back Pleat Skirt*—Measure distance from center back of garment waistband joining seam/edge straight across to start of first pleat.

147. *Button Placement*—Refer to measurement point 59, Neck Depth Center Front, for placement of first button. Then measure distance of first button to second button. Be sure when measuring that button at bust point is lined up to apex of the bust. Adjust all buttons accordingly and respace as needed.

148. *Pocket Placement*
A. *Top Pocket Vertical*—Measure from shoulder-neck joining seam straight down to top edge of pocket.
B. *Top Pocket Horizontal*—Measure from center front straight across to side of pocket at top edge.
C. *Front Bottom Pocket Vertical*—Measure from waistband/joining seam/edge straight down to top edge of pocket.
D. *Front Bottom Pocket Horizontal*—Measure from center front straight across to side of pocket at top edge.

E. *Back Bottom Pocket Vertical*—Measure from waistband/joining seam/edge straight down to top edge of pocket.
F. *Back Bottom Pocket Horizontal*—Measure from center back straight across to side of pocket at top edge.
G. *Pocket from Side Seam*—Measure from side seam straight across to top of pocket. [Note: If pocket is contoured at sides, a top and bottom pocket size and placement must be measured and added to spec sheet.]

149. *Belt Loop Placement*
A. *Front*—Measure from center front of garment horizontally across to center of first front belt loop.
B. *Back*—Measure from center back of garment horizontally across to center of first back belt loop.
C. *Side Seam to Front*—Measure from center of side seam belt loop to center of front belt loop.
D. *Side Seam to Back*—Measure from center of side seam belt loop to center of back belt loop.

150. *Dart Placement*
A. *High Point Shoulder Bust Dart*—Measure from shoulder-neck joining seam or at a point _____" from shoulder-neck seam straight down, parallel to center front, to top of dart. [Note: The _____" from shoulder seam measurement is to be used for darts that are too short to be measured from high point shoulder. Be sure to indicate _____" measurement on spec sheet.]
B. *Center Front Bust Dart*—Measure from center front of garment straight across to top of dart.
C. *Side Seam Bust Dart*—Measure from underarm/side seam joining seam down along contour of side seam to bottom of dart.
D. *High Point Shoulder Princess Dart*—Measure from shoulder-neck joining seam straight down to top of dart.
E. *Center Front Princess Dart*—Measure from center front of garment straight across to top of dart.
F. *Center Front Skirt/Pant*—Measure from center

front of garment at waistband joining seam/edge straight across to top of dart.

G. *Center Back Skirt/Pant*—Measure from center back of garment at waistband joining seam/edge straight across to top of dart.

CHAPTER 7 TERMS

When working with knit dresses, you may come across the garment terms listed below. If you are unfamiliar with any of them, please look up the definitions in the glossary at the end of this text.

Dress:
   Cardigan
   Polo shirt
   Poor-boy shift
   Sweater
   T-shirt

SPEC SHEET Knit dress	STYLE
SEASON:	DESCRIPTION:
LABEL: (SIZE CATEGORY)	
DATE:	

TECHNICAL SKETCH Turtleneck dress	SKETCH/PHOTO

CODE	POINT OF MEASURE	TOL. +/−	4	S/6	8	M/10	12	L/14	16	XL/18
1.	Front length	$1/2$								
3.	Center back length	$1/2$								
4.	Side length	$1/4$								
9.	Chest width	$1/4$-$3/8$								
13.	Across shoulder	$1/4$								
15.	Across chest	$1/4$								
16.	Across back	$1/4$								
25.	Bottom band/ribbing height	$1/8$								
36.	Sleeve length top armhole	$3/8$								
39.	Sleeve length underarm	$3/8$								
42.	Curved armhole width	$1/4$								
48.	Muscle width	$1/8$								

(Tolerance $1/4$-$3/8$ S, M, L, XL = $3/8$" 4-18 = $1/4$")

The measured garment spec sheets are for *illustrative purposes only* and should not be used as industry standards

CODE	POINT OF MEASURE	TOL. +/−	4	S/6	8	M/10	12	L/14	16	XL/18
50.	Elbow width	$1/8$								
52.	Sleeve opening width	$1/8$								
54.	Sleeve opening width stretched	$1/8$								
57.	Cuff/ribbing height sleeve	$1/8$								
58.	Neck depth front	$1/8$								
63.	Neck width collar	$1/4$								
64.	Neck edge width	$1/4$								
66.	Neck edge width stretched	$1/4$								
68.	Neck base	$1/4$								
72.	Collar height	$1/8$								
73.	Collar band height	$1/8$								
90.	Hip width from H.P.S. _____ "	$1/4$-$3/8$								
94.	Bottom opening sweep width	$1/4$-$3/8$								

COMMENTS:

The measured garment spec sheets are for *illustrative purposes only*
and should not be used as industry standards

STYLE

SEASON: Fall

DESCRIPTION: Sleeveless Turtleneck dress

LABEL: (SIZE CATEGORY) Missy

DATE:

TECHNICAL SKETCH Turtleneck dress

SKETCH/PHOTO

CODE	POINT OF MEASURE	TOL. +/−	4	S/6	8	M/10	12	L/14	16	XL/18
1.	Front length	$1/2$				34				
3.	Center back length	$1/2$				$32^{3/4}$				
4.	Side length	$1/4$				25				
9.	Chest width	$1/4$-$3/8$				19				
13.	Across shoulder	$1/4$				$14^{3/4}$				
15.	Across chest	$1/4$				$13^{3/4}$				
16.	Across back	$1/4$				$13^{3/4}$				
25.	Bottom band/ribbing height	$1/8$				$3/8$				
36.	Sleeve length top armhole	$3/8$								
39.	Sleeve length underarm	$3/8$								
42.	Curved armhole width	$1/4$				9				
48.	Muscle width	$1/8$								

(Tolerance $1/4$-$3/8$ S, M, L, XL = $3/8$" 4-18 = $1/4$")

The measured garment spec sheets are for *illustrative purposes only* and should not be used as industry standards

CODE	POINT OF MEASURE	TOL. +/–	4	S/6	8	M/10	12	L/14	16	XL/18
50.	Elbow width	$1/8$								
52.	Sleeve opening width	$1/8$								
54.	Sleeve opening width stretched	$1/8$								
57.	Cuff/ribbing height sleeve	$1/8$				$3/8$				
58.	Neck depth front	$1/8$				1				
63.	Neck width collar	$1/4$				$6 1/2$				
64.	Neck edge width	$1/4$				$6 1/2$				
66.	Neck edge width stretched	$1/4$				13				
68.	Neck base	$1/4$				$7 1/2$				
72.	Collar height	$1/8$				6				
73.	Collar band height	$1/8$				$3/8$				
90.	Hip width from H.P.S. ___21 "	$1/4$-$3/8$				19				
94.	Bottom opening sweep width	$1/4$-$3/8$				$18 1/2$				

COMMENTS:

CHAPTER 8

Knit Jumpsuits and One-Piece Garments

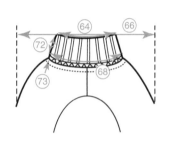

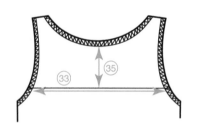

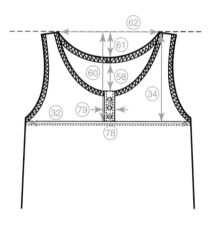

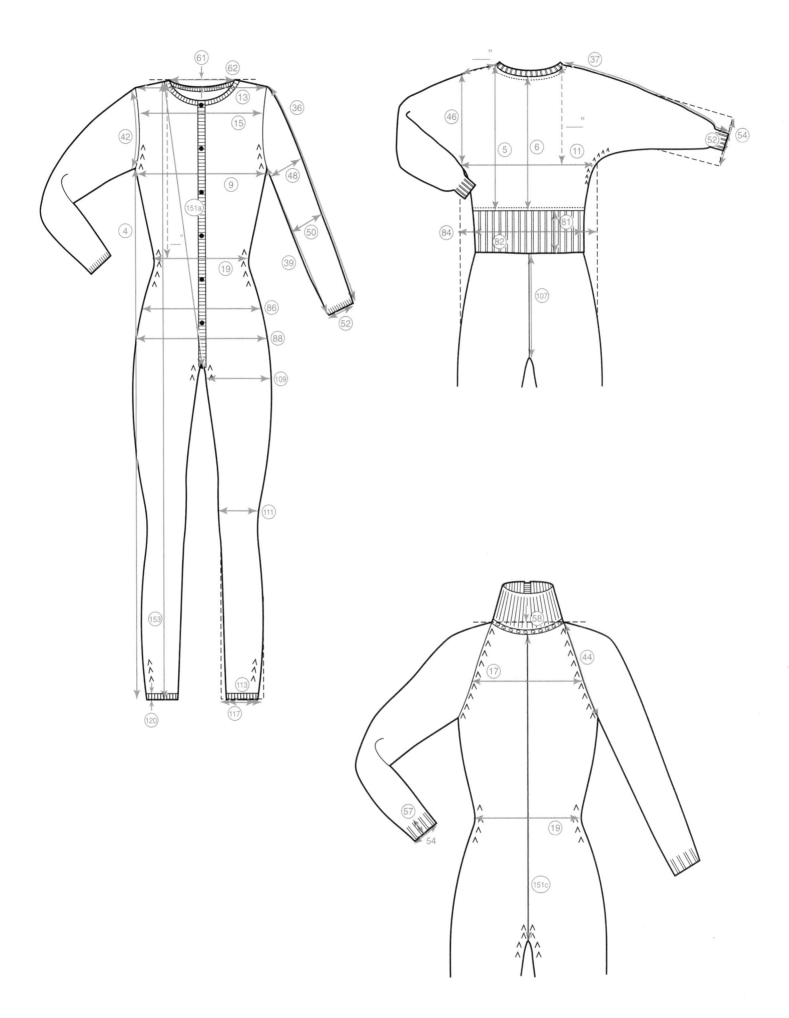

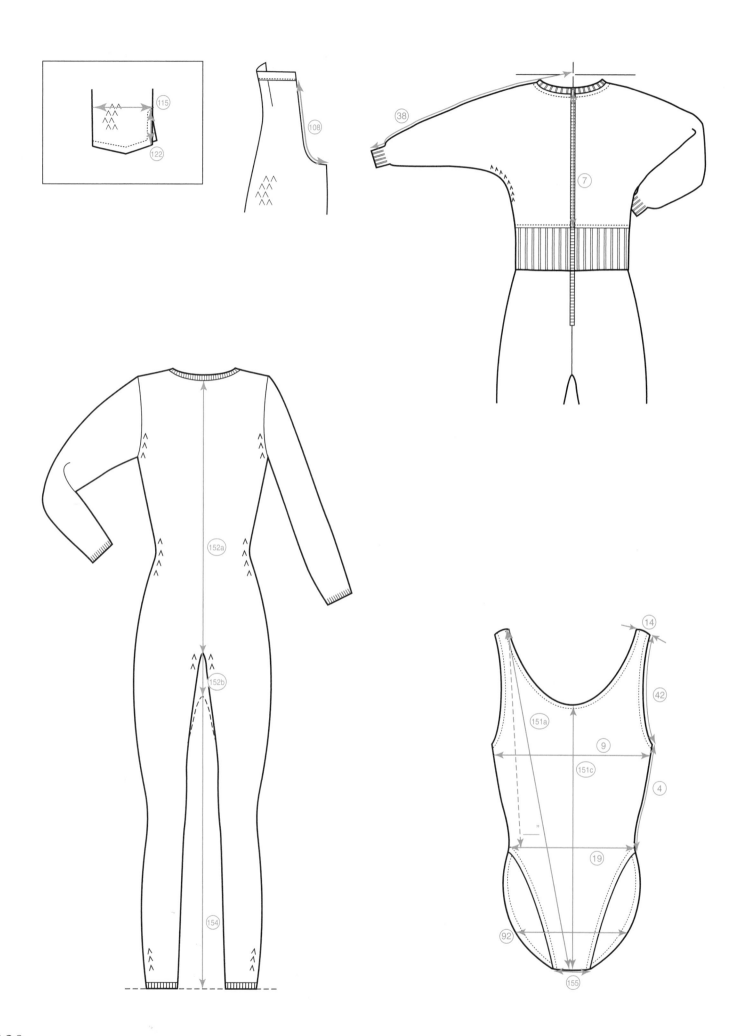

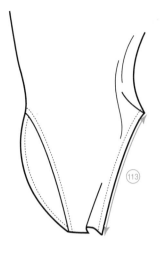

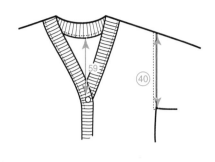

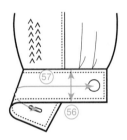

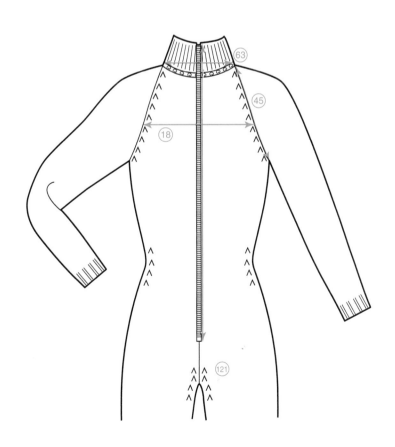

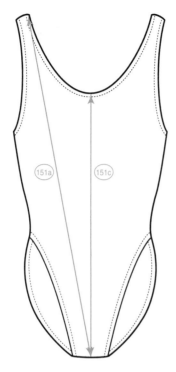

Figure 8.1

Measuring Knit Jumpsuits and One-Piece Garments

Knit jumpsuit and one-piece garment specification sheets are common in the swimwear and children's industries. This chapter is written for the missy market. However, the spec sheet provided can be easily adapted to any market. Common one-piece garments include bodysuits, one-piece swimsuits, and bunny suits and union suits. Measuring a bodysuit or one-piece garment basically combines the measurement points of a knit top and a knit pant. However, a one-piece swimsuit can be measured from point 1, Front Length, the high point shoulder to the bottom of the garment, or using point 151, Front Torso Length, the high point shoulder to the crotch joining seam. Depending on styling, it may be a good idea to use both.

1. *Front Length (garments with a front opening)*—Measure from high point shoulder at neck straight down, parallel to center front, to bottom of garment at front. If garment has a collar, gently lift it away from shoulder-neck measuring point.

2. *Center Front Length (garments with a plain front; no front opening)*—Measure from center front neck joining seams straight down to bottom of garment at center front. [Note: A garment without a front opening may still require use of Front Length if neckline is unusual.]

3. *Center Back Length*—Measure from center back neck joining seams straight down to bottom of garment at center back. If needed, gently lift collar away from back neck to expose joining seam.

4. *Side Length*—Measure from bottom of armhole/side seam straight down to bottom of garment along side of garment; do not follow natural curve of garment's side seam, unless otherwise indicated. If needed, gently lift sleeve away from armhole/side seam joining seam.

5. *Front Bodice Length (garments with a front opening)*—Measure from high point shoulder at neck

straight down, parallel to center front, to top edge of waistband, joining seam, or rib. If garment has a collar, gently lift it away from shoulder-neck measuring point.

6. *Center Front Bodice Length (garments with a plain front; no front opening)*—Measure from center front neck joining seam straight down to top edge of waistband, joining seam, or rib. [Note: A garment without a center opening may still require use of Front Bodice Length if neckline is unusual.]

7. *Center Back Bodice Length*—Measure from center back neck joining seams straight down to top edge of waistband, joining seam, or rib. If needed, gently lift collar away from back neck to expose joining seam.

8. *Side Seam Bodice Length*—Measure from bottom of armhole/side seam straight down to top edge of waistband, joining seam, or rib, along side of garment, following natural curve of garment's side seam, unless otherwise indicated. If needed, gently lift sleeve away from armhole/side seam joining seam. [Note: You can take side seam bodice measurement straight rather than contoured if joining seam/rib can be extended, but indicate change on spec sheet.]

9. *Chest Width (knit)*—Measure from edge of garment/side seam to edge of garment/side seam straight across garment at a point 1' below armhole.

11. *Chest Width (raglan sleeve, knit)*—Measure from edge of garment/side seam to edge of garment/side seam straight across garment at a point _____" below high point shoulder. [Note: You will have to determine number of inches down from high point shoulder for each raglan sleeve style based on depth of sleeve. Then indicate this number on spec sheet.]

13. *Across Shoulder*—Measure straight across front from armhole seam/edge to armhole seam/edge at shoulder seam or across natural shoulder fold line created if there is no seam.

14. *Shoulder Width*—Measure from neckband/collar/ribbing joining seam or neckline edge to top of armhole seam at shoulder, taken along shoulder seam or across natural shoulder fold line created if there is no seam.

15. *Across Chest*—Measure $2\frac{1}{2}$" down from collar/rib joining seam at center front straight across front of garment from armhole seam/edge to armhole seam/edge. [Note: The $2\frac{1}{2}$" measurement point is for missywear only and may need to be adjusted up or down $\frac{1}{4}$" to $\frac{1}{2}$" accordingly for men's, children's, junior's, and large/plus womenswear. Indicate any changes on spec sheet.]

16. *Across Back*—Measure 4" down from collar/rib joining seam at center back straight across back of garment from armhole seam/edge to armhole seam/edge. [Note: The 4" measurement point is for missywear only and may need to be adjusted up or down $\frac{1}{4}$" to $\frac{1}{2}$" accordingly for men's, children's, junior's, and large/plus womenswear. Indicate any changes on spec sheet.]

17. *Across Chest/Center Armhole*—Measure at one-half depth of armhole straight across front of garment from armhole seam/edge to armhole seam/edge.

18. *Across Back/Center Armhole*—Measure at one-half depth of armhole straight across back of garment from armhole seam/edge to armhole seam/edge.

19. *Waist Width (knit)*—Measure from edge of garment/side seam to edge of garment/side seam straight across garment on seam or at narrowest point of waist taper at a point _____" below high point shoulder. [Note: You will have to determine number of inches down from high point shoulder for each raglan sleeve style based on depth of sleeve. Then indicate this number on spec sheet.]

32. *Yoke Width Front*—Measure from armhole seam/edge to armhole seam/edge straight across front of garment, ignoring contours or points, at yoke-

body joining seams. [Note: If yoke is asymmetrical, indicate changes in measuring as needed on spec sheet.]

33. *Yoke Width Back*—Measure from armhole seam/edge to armhole seam/edge straight across back of garment, ignoring contours or points, at yoke-body joining seams. [Note: If yoke is asymmetrical, indicate changes in measuring as needed on spec sheet.]

34. *Yoke Depth Front*—Measure from high point shoulder at neck straight down to bottom of front yoke-body joining seam. Be sure to gently lift collar away from shoulder-neck joining seam if needed.

35. *Yoke Back Depth*—Measure from center back neck joining seam straight down to bottom of back yoke-body joining seam. Gently lift collar away from back neck joining seam if needed.

36. *Sleeve Length Top Armhole*—Measure along top of sleeve/fold following contour of sleeve from armhole seam at shoulder to bottom of sleeve opening, including cuff.

37. *Sleeve Length Top Neck*—Measure along top of sleeve/fold, following contour of sleeve from sleeve-neck joining seam/edge to edge of sleeve opening, including cuff. Gently lift collar away at sleeve-neck joining seam if needed.

38. *Sleeve Length Center Back*—Measure from center back neck joining seam or from a point above neck at an imaginary line, that of a joining seam, along top of sleeve/fold, following contour of sleeve to edge of sleeve opening, including cuff.

39. *Sleeve Length Underarm*—Measure straight from bottom of armhole along sleeve seam to edge of sleeve opening, including cuff.

40. *Straight Armhole Width (knit)*—Measure from top of shoulder joining seam/edge straight down to bottom of armhole.

42. *Curved Armhole Width (knit)*—Measure from top of shoulder joining seam/edge to bottom of armhole, following contour of armhole.

44. *Armhole Front*—Measure on front of garment from top of shoulder at neckline joining seam/edge to bottom of armhole, following contour of armhole. Gently lift collar away from neckline joining seam if needed.

45. *Armhole Back*—Measure on back of garment from top of shoulder at neck joining seam/edge to bottom of armhole, following contour of armhole. Gently lift collar away from neck joining seam if needed.

46. *Armhole Width Straight (knit)*—Measure from top of shoulder seam at a point _____" below neckline joining seam/edge straight down to bottom of armhole. [Note: Gently move collar from neck joining seam if needed when measuring down _____" to armhole start point. Indicate number of inches measured down on spec sheet.]

48. *Muscle Width (knit)*—Measure from inner sleeve edge/seam to outer sleeve edge/fold at a point 1" below armhole and parallel to sleeve opening.

50. *Elbow Width (knit)*—Measure from inner sleeve edge/seam to outer sleeve edge/fold straight across sleeve at a point one-half of the underarm sleeve length and parallel to sleeve opening at wrist or cuff. [Note: If sleeve is three-quarter length, indicate new point of measure on spec sheet.]

52. *Sleeve Opening Width (knit)*—Measure from inner sleeve edge/seam to outer sleeve edge/fold straight across bottom edge of sleeve opening.

54. *Sleeve Opening Width, Stretched (knit)*—Measure from inner sleeve edge/seam to outer sleeve edge/fold straight across bottom edge of sleeve opening in a fully extended position.

56. *Cuff Length Sleeve*—Measure from outside end of buttonhole to center of button straight along center of cuff. Open cuff out as flat as possible when measuring. [Note: If cuff length is contoured, measure along center-most point.]

57. *Cuff/Ribbing Height Sleeve*—Measure from cuff joining seam or top of ribbing straight down to bottom edge of cuff or rib opening. [Note: If cuff is contoured, indicate changes made as needed to measurement on spec sheet.]

58. *Neck Depth Front (garments with a plain front/asymmetrical front opening)*—Measure from center back neck joining seam/edge straight down to center front neck joining seam/edge.

59. *Neck Depth Center Front (garments with a center front opening)*—Measure from center back neck joining seam/edge straight down to center of first button at center front of garment.

60. *Neck Drop Front*—Measure from an imaginary line connecting neckline edges straight down to center front neck opening edge. Use a ruler if needed to connect top neckline edges.

61. *Neck Drop Back*—Measure from an imaginary line connecting neckline edges straight down to center back neck opening edge. This measurement is taken with front of garment facing up. Use a ruler to connect top neckline edges if needed.

62. *Neck Width, No Collar*—Measure from inside neck edge/seam to inside neck edge/seam straight across back neck at widest point. This measurement is taken with front of garment faceup.

63. *Neck Width, Collar*—Measure straight across back neck from neck-shoulder joining seam to neck-shoulder joining seam or natural shoulder line if no seam. This measurement is taken with back of garment faceup.

64. *Neck Edge Width (knit)*—Measure from neck edge/seam/fold to neck edge/seam/fold along top opening edge, following natural contour of neck opening. Garment should be positioned with one shoulder on top of the other and with front and back neck edges meeting.

66. *Neck Edge Width, Stretched (knit)*—Measure from neck edge/seam/fold to neck edge/seam/fold along top opening edge in a fully extended position. Garment should be positioned with one shoulder on top of the other and with front and back neck edges meeting.

68. *Neck Base (knit)*—Measure from neck edge/seam to neck edge/seam along collar/rib joining seam or neckline edge, following natural contour of neck opening. Garment should be buttoned or zippered, if applicable, with one shoulder seam positioned on top of the other and with front and back neck edges meeting.

70. *Neckband Length*—Measure from outside end of buttonhole to center of buttonhole across neckband, following contour of neckband.

71. *Collar Length*—Measure from one end of collar to other end of collar along neck joining seam.

72. *Collar Height*—Measure from collar/rib joining seam at center back neck straight up to outer edge of collar/rib.

73. *Collar Band Height*—Measure from collar joining seam at center back straight up to neckband joining seam at center back.

74. *Collar Point Length*—Measure from collar joining seam to outer edge of collar along collar point edge. [Note: If collar is rounded, measure at a point parallel to center back and indicate change on spec sheet.]

75. *Collar Point Spread (pointed collars only)*—Measure, with collar band buttoned and collar in place,

from collar point straight across collar edge to collar point.

76. *Lapel Width*

A. *Notched*—Measure from lower lapel notch straight across to lapel fold at a point perpendicular to garment center front.

B. *Without Notches*—Measure from lapel edge straight across widest point of lapel to lapel fold at a point ____" down from center back collar joining seam and perpendicular to front of garment.

77. *Center Front Extension*—Measure from an imaginary line at center front of garment horizontally to finished outer edge of front extended piece.

78. *Placket Length*—Measure from top edge of placket straight down to bottom of placket opening along center of placket.

79. *Placket Width*—Measure from placket joining seam straight across placket to placket edge at fold.

80. *Keyhole Length*—Measure from outer edge of neckline straight down to bottom of keyhole opening.

81. *Waistband Depth*—Measure from top of waistband edge straight down to bottom of waistband at waistband joining seam. [Note: If waistband is contoured, indicate measurement change on spec sheet.]

82. *Waistband Width (knit)*—Measure from side of bottom band to side of bottom band along center of band, following natural contour of waistband.

84. *Waistband Width, Stretched (knit)*—Measure from side of bottom band to side of bottom band straight across center of band in a fully extended position.

86. *High Hip Width (knit)*—Measure from edge of garment/side seam to edge of garment/side seam at

a point 4" below bottom edge of waistband/seam, following contour of waist. [Note: The 4" point is for missywear only; adjust as needed $\frac{1}{2}$" to 1" up or down for children's, petite's, junior's, or large/plus womenswear. Indicate change on spec sheet.]

88. *Low Hip Width from Waist (knit)*—Measure from edge of garment/side seam to edge of garment/side seam at a point 7" below bottom edge of waistband/seam, following contour of waist. [Note: The 7" point is for missywear only; adjust as needed $\frac{1}{2}$" to 1" up or down for children's, petite's, junior's, or large/plus womenswear. Indicate change on spec sheet.]

90. *Hip Width from High Point Shoulder (knit)*—Measure from edge of garment/side seam to edge of garment/side seam straight across at a point ____" below high point of shoulder. [Note: You will have to estimate low hip point on garment if there is no waistband and fill in ____" from high point shoulder. This measurement will vary for children's, junior's, missy, and large/plus womenswear.]

92. *Hip Seat Width (knit pant)*—Measure from edge of garment/side seam to edge of garment/side seam at a point ____" up from crotch seam, following contour of waist. [Note 1: This measurement is useful when waistband sits below natural waistline. Note 2: Adjust the ____" up from crotch as needed for junior's and large/plus womenswear. Note 3: A hip seat width of $2\frac{1}{2}$" up for children's and 3" up for menswear can take place of low hip width.]

103. *Skirt/Pant Yoke Depth Front*—Measure from bottom of waistband/seam (top edge if not banded or stitching if self-elastic/drawstring casing) straight down to bottom of yoke joining seam at center front. [Note: If yoke is contoured, indicate point of measure on spec sheet.]

104. *Skirt/Pant Yoke Depth Back*—Measure from bottom of waistband/seam (top edge if not banded or stitching if self-elastic/drawstring casing) straight

down to bottom of yoke joining seam at center back. [Note: If yoke is contoured, indicate point of measure on spec sheet.]

105. *Inseam*—Measure from crotch joining seam to bottom of leg opening, following inseam/inner fold.

106. *Outseam*—Measure from bottom edge of waistband/seam (top edge if not banded or stitching if self-elastic/drawstring casing) to bottom of garment along side seam/fold of garment.

107. *Front Rise*—Measure from bottom edge of waistband/seam (top edge if not banded or stitching if self-elastic/drawstring casing) to crotch joining seam, following curve of front rise seam. [Note: Measure over zipper if in front rise seam.]

108. *Back Rise*—Measure from bottom edge of waistband/seam (top edge if not banded or stitching if self-elastic/drawstring casing) to crotch joining seam, following curve of back rise seam. [Note: Measure over zipper if in front back seam.]

109. *Thigh Width (knit)*—Measure from pant leg edge/seam to pant leg edge/seam straight across pant leg at a point 1" below crotch and parallel to leg opening. [Note: If leg opening is asymmetrical, measure to a point that would be parallel to leg opening.]

111. *Knee Width (knit)*—Measure from pant leg edge/seam to pant leg edge/seam at a point one-half of inseam and parallel to leg opening. [Note 1: If leg opening is asymmetrical, measure to a point that would be parallel to leg opening. Note 2: If pant leg is three-quarter length, indicate point of measure on spec sheet. Note 3: A general knee measurement from crotch seam of missy 12", junior's 11", or large/plus women's 13" can be used. Indicate change on spec sheet. For childrenswear measure at one-half inseam minus $1\frac{1}{2}$" and for men's minus 2".]

113. *Leg Opening Width (knit)*—Measure from pant leg edge/seam to pant edge/seam straight across bot-tom edge of leg opening. [Note: If leg opening is contoured, follow contour and indicate measurement change on spec sheet.]

115. *Vented Leg Opening Width (knit)*—Measure from pant leg edge/seam to pant leg edge/seam straight across pant leg at top of side vents.

117. *Leg Opening Width, Stretched (knit)*—Measure from pant leg edge/seam to pant leg edge/seam straight across bottom edge of leg opening in a fully extended position.

119. *Cuff Height Pants*—Measure from top of cuff edge straight down to bottom of cuff fold and leg opening.

120. *Bottom Band/Ribbing Height Pants*—Measure from cuff joining seam or top of ribbing straight down to bottom edge of cuff or rib opening. [Note: For fashion-forward pants, you may want to include a cuff width. See point of measure 56, Cuff Length Sleeve, for measuring instructions and indicate cuff width pant as needed on spec sheet.]

121. *Fly/Zipper*
A. *Length*—Measure from top of fly/zipper opening straight down to bottom of fly/zipper opening at zipper stop or bar tack.
B. *Fly/Zipper Width*—Measure top of fly/zipper at joining seam from edge/fold straight across to fly/zipper placket stitching.

122. *Vent/Slit*
A. *Height*—Measure from top of vent/slit straight down to bottom of vent/slit along edge of vent/slit.
B. *Width*—Measure top of vent/slit from edge/fold straight across to vent/slit placket stitching at a point parallel to garment hemline.

123. *Pleat Depth*—Measure from outer edge of pleat at fold/crease to inner fold of pleat. [Note 1: It is a good idea to indicate what type of pleat is being mea-

sured, e.g., box, inverted, knife, kick, kilt, or envelope. Note 2: If pleats are not parallel or symmetrical, indicate any special instructions on spec sheet.]

124. *Distance Between Pleats*—Measure from start of pleat to start of pleat, excluding pleat depth at a point directly below pleat joining seam. [Note: If pleats are not parallel or symmetrical, indicate any special instructions on spec sheet.]

125. *Applied Pocket Height*—Measure from top edge of pocket to bottom edge of pocket along center of pocket. [Note: For contoured or irregularly shaped pockets, take a second measurement and indicate point of measure on spec sheet.]

126. *Applied Pocket Width*—Measure from side of pocket to side of pocket along top edge of pocket. [Note: For contoured or irregularly shaped pockets, take a second measurement and indicate point of measure on spec sheet.]

127. *Pocket Opening Within a Seam*—Measure from top of pocket to bottom of pocket along edge of pocket opening.

128. *Belt Length*
A. *Total*—Measure from end of belt at buckle along center of belt to opposite end of belt, following contour.
B. *Circumference*—Measure from end of belt at buckle along center of belt to middle hole at opposite end.

129. *Belt Width (or Height)*—Measure from edge of belt straight across to edge of belt. [Note: If belt is contoured, indicate points of measure on spec sheet.]

130. *Belt Loop Length*—Measure from top of belt loop straight down/vertically to bottom of belt loop along center of belt loop. [Note: Fashion-forward or irregularly shaped belt loops may require further spec instructions. Indicate points of measure on spec sheet.]

131. *Belt Loop Width*—Measure belt loop from edge of belt loop straight across/horizontally to edge of belt loop. [Note: Fashion-forward or irregularly shaped belt loops may require further spec instructions. Indicate points of measure on spec sheet.]

132. *Tie Length*—Measure from end of tie/joining seam straight down to tie end along center of tie.

133. *Tie Width*
A. *Straight*—Measure from edge of tie straight across to edge of tie.
B. *Contoured*—Measure from edge of tie straight across to edge of tie at widest point of tie.

134. *Flounce/Ruffle Width*—Measure from flounce/ruffle joining seam straight across to outer edge of flounce/ruffle. [Note: If flounce/ruffle is contoured, measure along narrowest and widest points if possible and indicate changes on spec sheet.]

135. *Strap Length*—Measure from strap joining seam along center of strap to end of strap. [Note: If a strap is contoured or has a contoured edge, measure along center, approximating center end point, or indicate instructions as needed on spec sheet.]

136. *Strap Width*—Measure from edge of strap straight across to edge of strap. [Note: If strap is contoured, measure along narrowest and widest points if possible and indicate changes on spec sheet.]

137. *Front Hood Length*—Measure from top of hood to bottom of hood at center front joining seam along opening edge of hood.

138. *Back Hood Length*—Measure from top of hood at center front to bottom of hood at center back joining seam along outside curve of hood fold/seam.

139. *Hood Width*—Measure from front opening edge of hood straight across to back of hood along widest point of hood.

140. *Flange Depth*—Measure from center back neck joining seam straight down to bottom of flange at center back. [Note: If flange is contoured or asymmetrical, indicate point of measure on spec sheet.]

141. *Shoulder Pad Length*—Measure from edge of pad straight across to edge of pad along center of pad or natural shoulder line of pad.

142. *Shoulder Pad Width*—Measure from side of pad straight across to side of pad along edge of pad if straight or at widest point of pad if curved.

143. *Straight Edge Shoulder Pad Height*—Measure from top of pad straight down to bottom of pad along center of pad.

144. *Curved Edge Shoulder Pad Height*—Stick a one-inch straight pin into thickest part of shoulder pad. Push pin all way through pad until head of pin rests on top of pad. Be sure not to crush pad. Measure portion of pin sticking out of pad. Subtract this figure from one inch (length of pin) to get shoulder pad height.

145. *Shoulder Pad Placement*—Measure from neck edge or joining seam straight across shoulder seam or natural shoulder line to start of shoulder pad.

146. *Pleats Placement*
A. *Front Pleat Top*—Measure distance from the center front of garment straight across to start of first pleat at a point parallel to garment hem. [Note: You may need to use armhole or side seam as a starting point if there is no center front seam or placket.]
B. *Back Pleat Top*—Measure distance from armhole seam/side seam (depending on pleat placement) to first pleat at a point parallel to garment hem.
C. *Front Pleat Skirt/Pant*—Measure distance from center front of garment waistband joining seam/edge straight across to start of first pleat.
D. *Back Pleat Skirt*—Measure distance from center back of garment waistband joining seam/edge straight across to start of first pleat.

147. *Button Placement*—Refer to measurement point 59, Neck Depth Center Front, for placement of first button. Then measure distance of first button to second button. Be sure when measuring that button at bust point is lined up to apex of bust. Adjust all buttons accordingly and respace as needed.

148. *Pocket Placement*
A. *Top Pocket Vertical*—Measure from shoulder-neck joining seam straight down to top edge of pocket.
B. *Top Pocket Horizontal*—Measure from center front straight across to side of pocket at top edge.
C. *Front Bottom Pocket Vertical*—Measure from waistband/joining seam/edge straight down to top edge of pocket.
D. *Front Bottom Pocket Horizontal*—Measure from center front straight across to side of pocket at top edge.
E. *Back Bottom Pocket Vertical*—Measure from waistband/joining seam/edge straight down to top edge of pocket.
F. *Back Bottom Pocket Horizontal*—Measure from center back straight across to side of pocket at top edge.
G. *Pocket from Side Seam*—Measure from side seam straight across to top of pocket. [Note: If pocket is contoured at sides, a top and bottom pocket size and placement must be measured and added to spec sheet.]

149. *Belt Loop Placement*
A. *Front*—Measure from center front of garment horizontally across to center of first front belt loop.
B. *Back*—Measure from center back of garment horizontally across to center of first back belt loop.
C. *Side Seam to Front*—Measure from center of side seam belt loop to center of front belt loop.
D. *Side Seam to Back*—Measure from center of side seam belt loop to center of back belt loop.

150. *Dart Placement*
A. *High Point Shoulder Bust Dart*—Measure from shoulder-neck joining seam or at a point _____"

from shoulder-neck seam straight down, parallel to center front, to top of dart. [Note: The _____" from shoulder seam measurement is to be used for darts that are too short to be measured from high point shoulder. Be sure to indicate _____" measurement on spec sheet.]

B. *Center Front Bust Dart*—Measure from center front of garment straight across to top of dart.

C. *Side Seam Bust Dart*—Measure from underarm/side seam joining seam down along contour of side seam to bottom of dart.

D. *High Point Shoulder Princess Dart*—Measure from shoulder-neck joining seam straight down to top of dart.

E. *Center Front Princess Dart*—Measure from center front of garment straight across to top of dart.

F. *Center Front Skirt/Pant*—Measure from center front of garment at waistband joining seam/edge straight across to top of dart.

G. *Center Back Skirt/Pant*—Measure from center back of garment at waistband joining seam/edge straight across to top of dart.

151. *Front Torso Length (Jumpsuits and One-Piece Garments)*

A. *Garments with a Front Opening, Relaxed*—Measure from high point shoulder at neck straight down to crotch joining seam with garment in a relaxed position.

B. *Garments with a Front Opening, Extended*—Measure from high point shoulder at neck straight down to crotch joining seam with garment in a fully extended position.

C. *Garments with a Plain Front, No Front Opening, Relaxed*—Measure from center front neck joining seam straight down to crotch joining seam with the garment in a relaxed position.

D. *Garments with a Plain Front, No Front Opening, Extended*—Measure from center front neck join-ing seam straight down to crotch joining seam with garment in a fully extended position.

152. *Back Torso Length (Jumpsuits and One-Piece Garments)*

A. *Relaxed*—Measure from center back neck join-ing seam straight down to crotch joining seam with garment in a relaxed position.

B. *Extended*—Measure from center back neck join-ing seam straight down to crotch joining seam with garment in a fully extended position.

153. *High Point Shoulder Length (Jumpsuits and One-Piece Garments)*—Measure from high point shoulder straight down to bottom/hem of garment.

154. *Center Back Garment Length (Jumpsuits and One-Piece Garments)*—Measure from center back neckline seam/edge, straight down to bottom hem of garment. [Note: For pant suits this point will inter-sect at an imaginary line formed by hemlines of pant legs and center of garment.]

155. *Crotch Width*—Measure straight across crotch from side to side along seam/bottom edge/fold.

CHAPTER 8 TERMS

When working with knit jumpsuits and one-piece garments, you may come across the garment terms listed below. If you are unfamiliar with any of them, please look up the definitions in the glossary at the end of this text.

Body stocking
Bodysuit
Bunny suit
One-piece swimsuit (bathing suit)

SPEC SHEET: One-peice knit garment   **STYLE**

SEASON:	DESCRIPTION:
LABEL: (SIZE CATEGORY)	
DATE:	

TECHNICAL SKETCH   One-peice swimsuit   SKETCH/PHOTO

CODE	POINT OF MEASURE	TOL. +/−	4	S/6	8	M/10	12	L/14	16	XL/18
4.	Side length	1/4								
9.	Chest width	1/4-3/8								
14.	Shoulder width	1/4								
19.	Waist width	1/4-3/8								
42.	Curved armhole width	1/4								
60.	Neck drop front	1/8								
61.	Neck drop back	1/8								
62.	Neck width, no collar	1/4								
92.	Hip seat width _____ " up from crotch	1/4-3/8								
113.	Leg opening width	1/8								
117.	Leg opening width stretched	1/8								
151.	Front torso length A. H.P.S. to crotch	1/2								
	B. H.P.S. to crotch stretched	1/2								
	C. C.F. neck to crotch	1/2								
	D. C.F. neck stretched	1/2								
155.	Crotch width	1/8								

(Tolerance 1/4-3/8 S, M, L, XL = 3/8"   4-18 = 1/4")

The measured garment spec sheets are for *__illustrative purposes only__* and should not be used as industry standards

CODE	POINT OF MEASURE	TOL. +/−	4	S/6	8	M/10	12	L/14	16	XL/18

COMMENTS:

The measured garment spec sheets are for *illustrative purposes only*
and should not be used as industry standards

SPEC SHEET: One-peice knit garment

STYLE	
DESCRIPTION: Updated Tank style swimsuit with self binding	

SEASON: Summer

LABEL: (SIZE CATEGORY) Missy

DATE:

TECHNICAL SKETCH One-peice swimsuit

SKETCH/PHOTO

CODE	POINT OF MEASURE	TOL. +/-	4	S/6	8	M/10	12	L/14	16	XL/18
4.	Side length	$1/4$				12				
9.	Chest width	$1/4$-$3/8$				$15^{1/2}$				
14.	Shoulder width	$1/4$								
19.	Waist width from C.F. neck $9^{1/4}$ "	$1/4$-$3/8$				12				
42.	Curved armhole width Excluding strap	$1/4$				$3^{1/2}$				
60.	Neck drop front	$1/8$				$5^{1/2}$				
61.	Neck drop back	$1/8$				$12^{1/4}$				
62.	Neck width, no collar Strap To Strap	$1/4$				$9^{1/4}$				
92.	Hip seat width __4__ " up from crotch	$1/4$-$3/8$				$11^{1/2}$				
113.	Leg opening width	$1/8$				$10^{1/2}$				
117.	Leg opening width stretched	$1/8$				$14^{1/2}$				
151.	Front torso length A. H.P.S. to crotch	$1/2$								
	B. H.P.S. to crotch stretched	$1/2$								
	C. C.F. neck to crotch	$1/2$				21				
	D. C.F. neck stretched	$1/2$				25				
155.	Crotch width	$1/8$				3				
135.	Strap length Total front to back	$1/4$				$12^{3/4}$				
136.	Strap width	$1/8$				$3/8$				

(Tolerance $1/4$-$3/8$ S, M, L, XL = $3/8$" 4-18 = $1/4$")

The measured garment spec sheets are for *illustrative purposes only* and should not be used as industry standards

KNIT JUMPSUITS AND ONE-PIECE GARMENTS 133

CODE	POINT OF MEASURE	TOL. +/−	4	S/6	8	M/10	12	L/14	16	XL/18

COMMENTS:

The measured garment spec sheets are for *illustrative purposes only* and should not be used as industry standards

134 WORKING WITH KNITS

PART III

WORKING WITH WOVENS

Wovens in Review

Weaving is one of the oldest arts known to humankind, dating back to ancient Egypt. Woven fabric is constructed by interlocking or interlacing two basic series of yarn, a warp and a weft, or filling. There are three basic weaves: plain, twill, and satin. This text does not entail fabric science but has listed several woven terms below that may be helpful as you work through Chapters 9 to 15.

Basket weave: a variation of the plain weave construction by passing weft yarns over and under warp yarns, two or more warps up and two or more warps down, in alternating rows.

Plain weave: the construction of a woven fabric by passing weft yarns over and under warp yarns, one warp up and one warp down, in alternating rows.

Satin weave: the construction of a woven fabric by passing weft yarns over and under warp yarns; this weave is generally constructed with five warps up and one warp down, repeating, creating a smooth surface.

Selvage: the finished edge on a cloth that prevents raveling or fraying.

Thread count (count of cloth): the number, or count, of warp and weft yarns per inch.

Twill weave: the construction of a woven fabric by passing filling yarns over and under warp yarns, two warps up and one warp down, creating a diagonal effect.

Weft yarns (filling yarns): the set of yarns in a woven fabric that run from selvage edge to selvage edge.

Warp yarns: the set of yarns in a woven fabric that run lengthwise or parallel to the selvage.

❖ Before starting Chapters 9 through 15, be sure to read the measurement preparation instructions listed in Chapter 3.
❖ Only those measurement points that are used when measuring basic garments are included in the respective chapters. Not every measurement point listed will be used on every garment; however, every measurement point for that type of garment has been listed in each chapter.
❖ Ignore any skipped numbers.
❖ You may want to try several different points of measure at first to see which one may yield the most accurate measurement. It takes time choosing the best point of measure for your garment,

135

but it is imperative that you are consistent in using the same method each time you measure that garment.

❖ Measuring wovens will only include missy/contemporary sketches. Industry specification sheets are always specific to a single market and will only contain sketches for that market; however, this theory is easily adapted to other markets.

❖ A generic missy spec sheet has been added to each chapter for your use. Note that while some in the retail industry are starting to call their missy departments Contemporary, the sizing is still considered missy; therefore, this terminology will be used on all spec sheets.

❖ A completed example of a spec sheet, including a hand sketch and measurements, has been added to each chapter for your reference.

❖ Basic garment illustrations and a blank spec sheet can be found in the croquis section of Appendix A: Basic Garment Croquis at the back of this text. These can be used to create your own spec sheets.

Chapters 9 through 15 have the user measure wovens in the circumference to be consistent with many technicians in the industry. Measurements are to be taken flat, across the front, and then only doubled as indicated in the instructions that follow. There is no need to remeasure a circumference measurement from the back; it would be redundant. For those in the industry or in the classroom who prefer to measure all garments flat or singularly, you may simply ignore the instructions to double measurements and change your spec sheets accordingly.

CHAPTER 9

Woven Tops

137

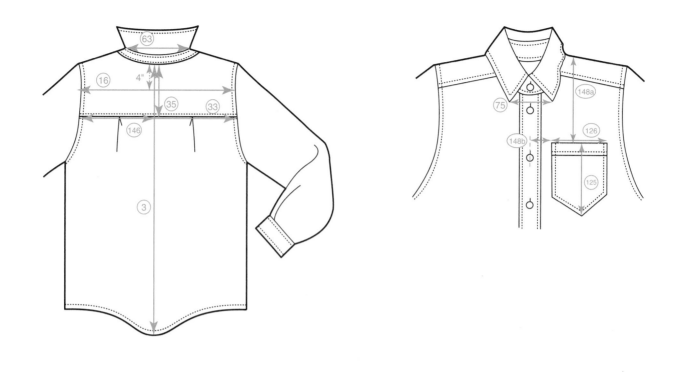

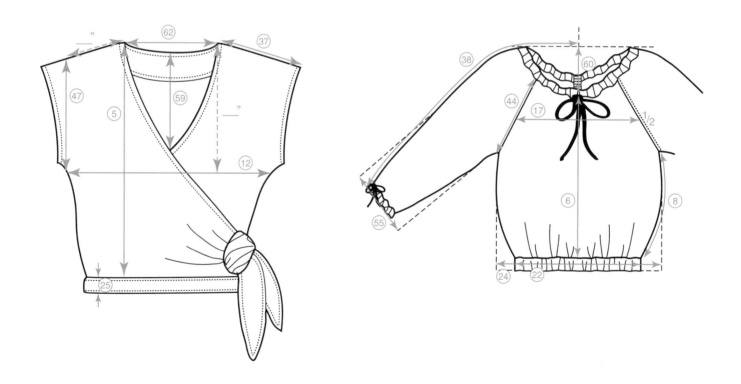

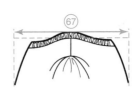

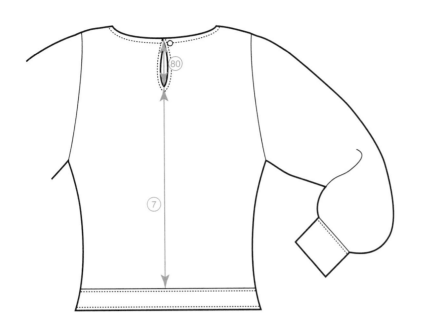

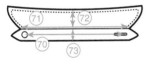

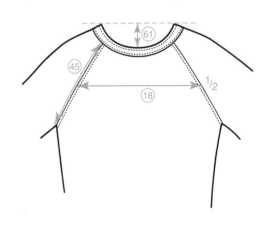

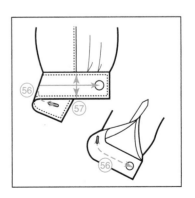

Measuring Woven Tops

Woven top spec sheets are used for woven garments, including blouses, shirts, and vests (though companies may have separate spec sheets for vests). As you measure, there will be instances when more than one method can be used for taking a measurement. You learned in Chapter 3 that the high point shoulder measurement is good for blouses with a front opening and the center front measurement is for a blouse without one. However, a top with a loop closure on the center front opening falls between the two definitions (Figure 9.1). In this instance, it is difficult to accurately measure the front length at the center front; therefore, the high point shoulder would be a better measurement. Conversely, if there is ruffling down the sides of the blouse (as shown in Figure 9.2), it would be better to measure using the center front point rather than measuring over the bulk of the ruffle at the high point shoulder. It is up to you, the technician, to make the decision as to which measurement method would be better suited to your garment style.

Figure 9.1

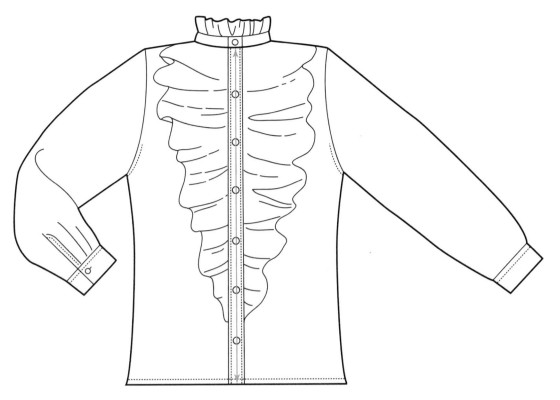

Figure 9.2

1. *Front Length (garments with a front opening)*—Measure from high point shoulder at neck straight down, parallel to center front, to bottom of garment at front. If garment has a collar, gently lift it away from shoulder-neck measuring point.

2. *Center Front Length (garments with a plain front; no front opening)*—Measure from center front neck joining seams straight down to bottom of garment at center front. [Note: A garment without a front opening may still require use of Front Length if neckline is unusual.]

3. *Center Back Length*—Measure from center back neck joining seams straight down to bottom of garment at center back. If needed, gently lift collar away from back neck to expose joining seam.

4. *Side Length*—Measure from bottom of armhole/side seam straight down to bottom of garment along side of garment. Do not follow natural curve of garment's side seam, unless otherwise indicated. If needed, gently lift sleeve away from armhole/side seam joining seam.

5. *Front Bodice Length (garments with a front opening)*—Measure from high point shoulder at neck straight down, parallel to center front, to top edge of waistband, joining seam, or rib. If garment has a collar, gently lift it away from shoulder-neck measuring point.

6. *Center Front Bodice Length (garments with a plain front; no front opening)*—Measure from center front neck joining seam straight down to top edge of waistband, joining seam, or rib. [Note: A garment without a center opening may still require use of Front Bodice Length if neckline is unusual.]

7. *Center Back Bodice Length*—Measure from center back neck joining seams straight down to top edge of waistband, joining seam, or rib. If needed, gently lift collar away from back neck to expose joining seam.

8. *Side Seam Bodice Length*—Measure from bottom of armhole/side seam straight down to top edge of waistband, joining seam, or rib, along side of garment, following natural curve of garment's side seam, unless otherwise indicated. If needed, gently lift sleeve away from armhole/side seam joining seam. [Note: You can take side seam bodice measurement straight rather than contoured if joining seam/rib can be extended, but indicate change on spec sheet.]

10. *Chest Width Circumference (woven)*—Measure from edge of garment/side seam to edge of garment/side seam straight across garment at a point 1' below armhole. Double this measurement.

12. *Chest Width Circumference (raglan sleeve, woven)*—Measure from edge of garment/side seam to edge of garment/side seam straight across garment at a point _____" below high point shoulder. Double this measurement. [Note: You will have to determine number of inches down from high point shoulder for each raglan sleeve style based on depth of sleeve. Then indicate this number on spec sheet.]

13. *Across Shoulder*—Measure straight across front from armhole seam/edge to armhole seam/edge at shoulder seam or across natural shoulder fold line created if there is no seam.

14. *Shoulder Width*—Measure from neckband/collar/ribbing joining seam or neckline edge to top of armhole seam at shoulder, taken along shoulder seam or across natural shoulder fold line created if there is no seam.

15. *Across Chest*—Measure $2\frac{1}{2}$" down from collar/rib joining seam at center front straight across front of garment from armhole seam/edge to armhole seam/edge. [Note: The $2\frac{1}{2}$" measurement point is for missywear only and may need to be adjusted up or down $\frac{1}{4}$" to $\frac{1}{2}$" accordingly for men's, children's, junior's, and large/plus womenswear. Indicate any changes on spec sheet.]

16. *Across Back*—Measure 4" down from collar/rib joining seam at center back straight across back of garment from armhole seam/edge to armhole seam/edge. [Note: The 4" measurement point is for missy-wear only and may need to be adjusted up or down $\frac{1}{4}$" to $\frac{1}{2}$" accordingly for men's, children's, junior's, and large/plus womenswear. Indicate any changes on spec sheet.]

17. *Across Chest/Center Armhole*—Measure at one-half depth of armhole straight across front of garment from armhole seam/edge to armhole seam/edge.

18. *Across Back/Center Armhole*—Measure at one-half depth of armhole straight across back of garment from armhole seam/edge to armhole seam/edge.

20. *Waist Width Circumference (woven)*—Measure from edge of garment/side seam to edge of garment/side seam straight across garment on seam or at narrowest point of waist taper at a point _____" below high point shoulder. Double this measurement. [Note: You will have to determine number of inches down from high point shoulder for each raglan sleeve style based on depth of sleeve. Then indicate this number on spec sheet.]

22. *Bottom Band Circumference (woven top)*—Measure from side of bottom band to side of bottom band along center of band, following natural contour of waistband. Double this measurement.

24. *Bottom Band Width Circumference, Stretched (woven top)*—Measure from side of bottom band to side of bottom band straight across center of band in a fully extended position. Double this measurement.

25. *Bottom Band/Ribbing Height (knit or woven top)*—Measure from band/ribbing joining seam straight down to bottom edge of band/rib opening. [Note: If band is shaped or contoured, indicate special measurement instructions on spec sheet.]

27. *Bottom Opening/Sweep Width Circumference (woven top)*—Measure from edge of garment/side seam to edge of garment/side seam straight across garment at bottom opening. Double this measurement. [Note: If sweep has pleats, measure with pleats closed or relaxed.]

29. *Vented Bottom Opening/Sweep Width Circumference (woven top)*—Measure from edge of garment/side seam to edge of garment/side seam straight across garment at top of side vents. Do not follow natural curve of garment. Double this measurement. [Note: If vents are too high to measure sweep, indicate opening at appropriate position, e.g., midriff opening.]

31. *Circular Bottom Opening/Sweep Width Circumference (woven top)*—Measure from edge of garment/side seam to edge of garment/side seam, following natural contour of garment at bottom opening. Double this measurement.

32. *Yoke Width Front*—Measure from armhole seam/edge to armhole seam/edge straight across front of garment, ignoring contours or points, at yoke-body joining seams. [Note: If yoke is asymmetrical, indicate changes in measuring as needed on spec sheet.]

33. *Yoke Width Back*—Measure from armhole seam/edge to armhole seam/edge straight across back of garment, ignoring contours or points, at yoke-body joining seam. [Note: If yoke is asymmetrical, indicate changes in measuring as needed on spec sheet.]

34. *Yoke Depth Front*—Measure from high point shoulder at neck straight down to bottom of front yoke-body joining seam. Gently lift collar away from shoulder-neck joining seam if needed.

35. *Yoke Back Depth*—Measure from center back neck joining seam straight down to bottom of back yoke-body joining seam. Be sure to gently lift collar away from back neck joining seam if needed.

36. *Sleeve Length Top Armhole*—Measure along top of sleeve/fold, following contour of sleeve from armhole seam at shoulder to bottom of sleeve opening, including cuff.

37. *Sleeve Length Top Neck*—Measure along top of sleeve/fold, following contour of sleeve from sleeve-neck joining seam/edge to edge of sleeve opening, including cuff. Gently lift collar at sleeve-neck joining seam if needed.

38. *Sleeve Length Center Back*—Measure from center back neck joining seam or from a point above neck at an imaginary line, that of a joining seam, along top of sleeve/fold, following contour of sleeve to edge of sleeve opening, including cuff.

39. *Sleeve Length Underarm*—Measure straight from the bottom of armhole along sleeve seam to edge of sleeve opening, including cuff.

41. *Straight Armhole Width Circumference (woven)*—Measure from top of shoulder joining seam/edge straight down to bottom of armhole. Double this measurement.

43. *Curved Armhole Width Circumference (woven)*—Measure from top of shoulder joining seam/edge to bottom of armhole, following contour of armhole. Double this measurement.

44. *Armhole Front*—Measure on front of garment from top of shoulder at neckline joining seam/edge to bottom of armhole, following contour of armhole. Gently lift collar away from neckline joining seam if needed.

45. *Armhole Back*—Measure on back of garment from top of shoulder at neck joining seam/edge to bottom of armhole, following contour of armhole. Gently lift collar away from neck joining seam if needed.

47. *Armhole Width Circumference Straight (woven)*—Measure from top of shoulder seam at a point _____" below neckline joining seam/edge straight down to bottom of armhole. Double this measurement. [Note: Gently move collar away from neck joining seam if needed when measuring down _____" to armhole start point. Indicate number of inches measured down on spec sheet.]

49. *Muscle Width Circumference (woven)*—Measure from inner sleeve edge/seam to outer sleeve edge/fold at a point 1" below armhole and parallel to sleeve opening. Double this measurement.

51. *Elbow Width Circumference (woven)*—Measure from inner sleeve edge/seam to outer sleeve edge/fold straight across sleeve at a point one-half of the underarm sleeve length and parallel to sleeve opening at wrist or cuff. Double this measurement. [Note: If sleeve is three-quarter length, indicate new point of measure on spec sheet.]

53. *Sleeve Opening Width Circumference (woven)*—Measure from inner sleeve edge/seam to outer sleeve edge/fold straight across bottom edge of sleeve opening. Double this measurement.

55. *Sleeve Opening Width Circumference, Stretched (woven)*—Measure from inner sleeve edge/seam to outer sleeve edge/fold straight across bottom edge of sleeve opening in a fully extended position. Double this measurement.

56. *Cuff Length Sleeve*—Measure from outside end of buttonhole to center of button straight along center of cuff. Open cuff out as flat as possible when measuring. [Note: If cuff length is contoured, measure along center most point.]

57. *Cuff/Ribbing Height Sleeve*—Measure from cuff joining seam or top of ribbing straight down to bottom edge of cuff or rib opening. [Note: If cuff is contoured, indicate changes made as needed to measurement on spec sheet.]

58. *Neck Depth Front (garments with a plain front/asymmetrical front opening)*—Measure from center back neck joining seam/edge straight down to center front neck joining seam/edge.

59. *Neck Depth Center Front (garments with a center front opening)*—Measure from center back neck joining seam/edge straight down to center of first button at center front of garment.

60. *Neck Drop Front*—Measure from an imaginary line connecting neckline edges straight down to center front neck opening edge. Use a ruler if needed to connect top neckline edges.

61. *Neck Drop Back*—Measure from an imaginary line connecting neckline edges straight down to center back neck opening edge. This measurement is taken with front of garment facing up. Use a ruler to connect top neckline edges if needed.

62. *Neck Width, No Collar*—Measure from inside neck edge/seam to inside neck edge/seam straight across back neck at widest point. This measurement is taken with front of garment faceup.

63. *Neck Width, Collar*—Measure straight across back neck from neck-shoulder joining seam to neck-shoulder joining seam or natural shoulder line if no seam. This measurement is taken with back of garment faceup.

65. *Neck Edge Width Circumference (woven)*—Measure from neck edge/seam/fold to neck edge/seam/fold along top opening edge, following natural contour of neck opening. Garment should be positioned with one shoulder on top of the other and with front and back neck edges meeting. Double this measurement.

66. *Neck Edge Width, Stretched (knit)*—Measure from neck edge/seam/fold to neck edge/seam/fold along top opening edge in a fully extended position. Garment should be positioned with one shoulder on top of the other and with front and back neck edges meeting.

67. *Neck Edge Width Circumference, Stretched (woven)*—Measure from neck edge/seam/fold to neck edge/seam/fold along top opening edge in a fully extended position. Garment should be positioned with one shoulder on top of the other and with front and back neck edges meeting. Double this measurement.

69. *Neck Base Circumference (woven)*—Measure from neck edge/seam to neck edge/seam along collar/rib joining seam or neckline edge, following natural contour of neck opening. Garment should be buttoned or zippered, if applicable, with one shoulder seam positioned on top of the other and with front and back neck edges meeting. Double this measurement.

70. *Neckband Length*—Measure from outside end of buttonhole to center of buttonhole across neckband, following contour of neckband.

71. *Collar Length*—Measure from one end of collar to other end of collar along neck joining seam.

72. *Collar Height*—Measure from collar/rib joining seam at center back neck straight up to outer edge of collar/rib.

73. *Collar Band Height*—Measure from collar joining seam at center back straight up to neck band joining seam at center back.

74. *Collar Point Length*—Measure from collar joining seam to outer edge of collar along collar point edge. [Note: If collar is rounded, measure at a point parallel to center back and indicate change on spec sheet.]

75. *Collar Point Spread (pointed collars only)*—Measure, with collar band buttoned and collar in place, from collar point straight across collar edge to collar point.

76. *Lapel Width*

A. *Notched*—Measure from lower lapel notch straight across to lapel fold at a point perpendicular to garment center front.

B. *Without Notches*—Measure from lapel edge straight across widest point of lapel to lapel fold at a point _____" down from center back collar joining seam and perpendicular to front of garment.

77. *Center Front Extension*—Measure from an imaginary line at center front of garment horizontally to finished outer edge of front extended piece.

78. *Placket Length*—Measure from top edge of placket straight down to bottom of placket opening along center of placket.

79. *Placket Width*—Measure from placket joining seam straight across placket to placket edge at fold.

80. *Keyhole Length*—Measure from outer edge of neckline straight down to bottom of keyhole opening.

122. *Vent/Slit*

A. *Height*—Measure from top of vent/slit straight down to bottom of vent/slit along edge of vent/slit.

B. *Width*—Measure top of vent/slit from edge/fold straight across to vent/slit placket stitching at a point parallel to garment hemline.

123. *Pleat Depth*—Measure from outer edge of pleat at fold/crease to inner fold of pleat. [Note 1: It is a good idea to indicate what type of pleat is being measured, e.g., box, inverted, knife, kick, kilt, or envelope. Note 2: If pleats are not parallel or symmetrical, indicate any special instructions on spec sheet.]

124. *Distance Between Pleats*—Measure from start of pleat to start of pleat, excluding pleat depth at a point directly below pleat joining seam. [Note: If pleats are not parallel or symmetrical, indicate any special instructions on spec sheet.]

125. *Applied Pocket Height*—Measure from top edge of pocket to bottom edge of pocket along center of pocket. [Note: For contoured or irregularly shaped pockets, take a second measurement and indicate point of measure on spec sheet.]

126. *Applied Pocket Width*—Measure from side of pocket to side of pocket along top edge of pocket. [Note: For contoured or irregularly shaped pockets, take a second measurement and indicate point of measure on spec sheet.]

127. *Pocket Opening Within a Seam*—Measure from top of pocket to bottom of pocket along edge of pocket opening.

128. *Belt Length*

A. *Total*—Measure from end of belt at buckle along center of belt to opposite end of belt, following contour.

B. *Circumference*—Measure from end of belt at buckle along center of belt to middle hole at opposite end.

129. *Belt Width (or Height)*—Measure from edge of belt straight across to edge of belt. [Note: If belt is contoured, indicate points of measure on spec sheet.]

130. *Belt Loop Length*—Measure from top of belt loop straight down/vertically to bottom of belt loop along center of belt loop. [Note: Fashion-forward or irregularly shaped belt loops may require further spec instructions. Indicate points of measure on spec sheet.]

131. *Belt Loop Width*—Measure belt loop from edge of belt loop straight across/horizontally to edge of belt loop. [Note: Fashion-forward or irregularly shaped belt loops may require further spec instructions. Indicate points of measure on spec sheet.]

132. *Tie Length*—Measure from end of tie/joining seam straight down to tie end along center of tie.

133. *Tie Width*
A. *Straight*—Measure from edge of tie straight across to edge of tie.
B. *Contoured*—Measure from edge of tie straight across to edge of tie at widest point of tie.

134. *Flounce/Ruffle Width*—Measure from flounce/ruffle joining seam straight across to outer edge of flounce/ruffle. [Note: If flounce/ruffle is contoured, measure along narrowest and widest points if possible and indicate changes on spec sheet.]

135. *Strap Length*—Measure from strap joining seam along center of strap to end of strap. [Note: If a strap is contoured or has a contoured edge, measure along center, approximating center end point, or indicate instructions as needed on spec sheet.]

136. *Strap Width*—Measure from edge of strap straight across to edge of strap. [Note: If strap is contoured, measure along narrowest and widest points if possible and indicate changes on spec sheet.]

137. *Front Hood Length*—Measure from top of hood to bottom of hood at center front joining seam along opening edge of hood.

138. *Back Hood Length*—Measure from top of hood at center front to bottom of hood at center back joining seam along outside curve of hood fold/seam.

139. *Hood Width*—Measure from front opening edge of hood straight across to back of hood along widest point of hood.

140. *Flange Depth*—Measure from center back neck joining seam straight down to bottom of flange at center back. [Note: If flange is contoured or asymmetrical, indicate point of measure on spec sheet.]

141. *Shoulder Pad Length*—Measure from edge of pad straight across to edge of pad along center of pad or natural shoulder line of pad.

142. *Shoulder Pad Width*—Measure from side of pad straight across to side of pad along edge of pad if straight or at widest point of pad if curved.

143. *Straight Edge Shoulder Pad Height*—Measure from top of pad straight down to bottom of pad along center of pad.

144. *Curved Edge Shoulder Pad Height*—Stick a one-inch straight pin into thickest part of shoulder pad. Push pin all way through pad until head of pin rests on top of pad. Be sure not to crush pad. Measure portion of pin sticking out of pad. Subtract this figure from one inch (length of pin) to get shoulder pad height.

145. *Shoulder Pad Placement*—Measure from neck edge or joining seam straight across shoulder seam or natural shoulder line to start of shoulder pad.

146. *Pleats Placement*
A. *Front Pleat Top*—Measure distance from center front of garment straight across to start of first pleat at a point parallel to garment hem. [Note: You may need to use armhole or side seam as a starting point if there is no center front seam or placket.]
B. *Back Pleat Top*—Measure distance from armhole seam/side seam (depending on pleat placement) to first pleat at a point parallel to garment hem.

147. *Button Placement*—Refer to measurement point 59, Neck Depth Center Front, for placement of first button. Then measure distance of first button to second button. Be sure when measuring that button at bust point is lined up to apex of bust. Adjust all buttons accordingly and respace as needed.

148. *Pocket Placement*
A. *Top Pocket Vertical*—Measure from shoulder-neck joining seam straight down to top edge of pocket.
B. *Top Pocket Horizontal*—Measure from center front straight across to side of pocket at top edge.

C. *Front Bottom Pocket Vertical*—Measure from waistband/joining seam/edge straight down to top edge of pocket.

D. *Front Bottom Pocket Horizontal*—Measure from center front straight across to side of pocket at top edge.

E. *Back Bottom Pocket Vertical*—Measure from waistband/joining seam/edge straight down to top edge of pocket.

F. *Back Bottom Pocket Horizontal*—Measure from center back straight across to side of pocket at top edge.

G. *Pocket from Side Seam*—Measure from side seam straight across to top of pocket. [Note: If pocket is contoured at sides, a top and bottom pocket size and placement must be measured and added to spec sheet.]

149. *Belt Loop Placement*
A. *Front*—Measure from center front of garment horizontally across to center of first front belt loop.

B. *Back*—Measure from center back of garment horizontally across to center of first back belt loop.

C. *Side Seam to Front*—Measure from center of side seam belt loop to center of front belt loop.

D. *Side Seam to Back*—Measure from center of side seam belt loop to center of back belt loop.

150. *Dart Placement*
A. *High Point Shoulder Bust Dart*—Measure from shoulder-neck joining seam or at a point _____" from shoulder-neck seam straight down, parallel to center front, to top of dart. [Note: The _____" from shoulder seam measurement is to be used for darts that are too short to be measured from high point shoulder. Be sure to indicate _____" measurement on spec sheet.]

B. *Center Front Bust Dart*—Measure from center front of garment straight across to top of dart.

C. *Side Seam Bust Dart*—Measure from under-arm/side seam joining seam down along contour of side seam to bottom of dart.

D. *High Point Shoulder Princess Dart*—Measure from shoulder-neck joining seam straight down to top of dart.

E. *Center Front Princess Dart*—Measure from center front of garment straight across to top of dart.

CHAPTER 9 TERMS

When working with woven tops, you may come across the garment terms listed below. If you are unfamiliar with any of them, please look up the definitions listed in the glossary at the end of this text.

Blouse:
  Basic or front buttoning
  Body shirt or fitted
  Bow
  Cossack
  Cowboy (Western)
  Drawstring
  Dress Shirt
  Epaulet
  Guayabera
  Hawaiian
  Jabot
  Nautical/Middy
  Oversized
  Peasant
  Stock-tie
  Tunic
  Wrap

SPEC SHEET: Woven top	**STYLE**
SEASON:	DESCRIPTION:
LABEL: (SIZE CATEGORY)	
DATE:	
TECHNICAL SKETCH Basic blouse	SKETCH/PHOTO

CODE	POINT OF MEASURE	TOL. +/-	4	S/6	8	M/10	12	L/14	16	XL/18
1.	Front length	$1/2$								
2.	Center front length	$1/2$								
3.	Center back length	$1/2$								
4.	Side length	$1/4$								
10.	Chest width circumference	$1/2$								
13.	Across shoulder	$1/4$								
15.	Across chest	$1/4$								
16.	Across back	$1/4$								
27.	Bottom opening/sweep width circumference	$1/2$-$3/4$								
32.	Yoke width front	$1/4$								
33.	Yoke width back	$1/4$								
34.	Yoke depth front	$1/8$								
35.	Yoke depth back	$1/8$								
36.	Sleeve length top armhole	$3/8$								
39.	Sleeve length underarm	$3/8$								
43.	Curved armhole width circumference	$3/8$								
49.	Muscle width circumference	$1/4$								
51.	Elbow width circumference	$1/4$								

(Tolerance $1/4$-$3/8$ S, M, L, XL = $3/8$"   4-18 = $1/4$")

The measured garment spec sheets are for *illustrative purposes only* and should not be used as industry standards

CODE	POINT OF MEASURE	TOL. +/−	4	S/6	8	M/10	12	L/14	16	XL/18
53.	Sleeve opening width circumference	1/4								
56.	Cuff length sleeve	1/4								
57.	Cuff/ribbing height sleeve	1/8								
58.	Neck depth front	1/8								
63.	Neck width collar	1/8								
69.	Neck base circumference	1/4								
70.	Neckband length	1/4								
71.	Collar length	1/4								
72.	Collar height	1/8								
73.	Collar band height	1/16								
74.	Collar point length	1/8								
75.	Collar point spread	1/4								
77.	Center front extension	1/8								
78.	Placket length	1/4								
79.	Placket width	1/8								
123.	Pleat depth	1/8								
124.	Distance between pleats	1/16								
125.	Applied pocket height	1/4								
126.	Applied pocket width	1/4								
146.	Pleats placement A. Front pleat top	1/4								
	B. Back pleat top	1/4								
147.	Button placement	1/8								
148.	Pocket placement A. Top pocket vertical	1/8								
	B. Top pocket horizontal	1/8								
	C. Pocket from side seam	1/8								

COMMENTS:

The measured garment spec sheets are for *illustrative purposes only* and should not be used as industry standards

STYLE

SEASON: Spring	DESCRIPTION: Oversized Blouse
LABEL: (SIZE CATEGORY) Missy	
DATE:	

TECHNICAL SKETCH Basic Blouse	SKETCH/PHOTO

CODE	POINT OF MEASURE	TOL. +/−	4	S/6	8	M/10	12	L/14	16	XL/18
1.	Front length	$1/2$				$30\tfrac{1}{2}$				
2.	Center front length	$1/2$								
3.	Center back length	$1/2$				$30\tfrac{1}{2}$				
4.	Side length	$1/4$				20				
10.	Chest width circumference	$1/2$-$3/4$				$48\tfrac{1}{2}$				
13.	Across shoulder	$1/4$				$18\tfrac{1}{4}$				
15.	Across chest 6" from H.P.S.	$1/4$				$17\tfrac{1}{4}$				
16.	Across back	$1/4$								
27.	Bottom opening/sweep width circumference	$1/2$-$3/4$				$48\tfrac{1}{2}$				
32.	Yoke width front	$1/4$				$6\tfrac{1}{4}$				
33.	Yoke width back	$1/4$				19				
34.	Yoke depth front	$1/8$				$3\tfrac{1}{2}$				
35.	Yoke depth back	$1/8$				$\tfrac{1}{2}$				
36.	Sleeve length top armhole	$3/8$				$23\tfrac{1}{2}$				
39.	Sleeve length underarm	$3/8$				19				
43.	Curved armhole width circumference	$3/8$				$20\tfrac{1}{4}$				
49.	Muscle width circumference	$1/4$				$17\tfrac{3}{4}$				
51.	Elbow width circumference	$1/4$				$15\tfrac{1}{2}$				

(Tolerance $1/2$-$3/4$ S, M, L, XL = $3/4$" 4-18 = $1/2$")

The measured garment spec sheets are for *illustrative purposes only* and should not be used as industry standards

SPEC SHEET: Woven top   **STYLE**

CODE	POINT OF MEASURE	TOL. +/−	4	S/6	8	M/10	12	L/14	16	XL/18
53.	Sleeve opening width circumference	1/4				8				
56.	Cuff length sleeve	1/4				8 1/2				
57.	Cuff/ribbing height sleeve	1/8				2 3/4				
58.	Neck depth front	1/8				1 1/8				
63.	Neck width collar	1/8				7				
69.	Neck base circumference	1/4				18				
70.	Neckband length	1/4				17				
71.	Collar length	1/4				15 3/4				
72.	Collar height	1/8				2 1/8				
73.	Collar band height	1/8				1 1/8				
74.	Collar point length	1/8				3				
75.	Collar point spread	1/4				3				
77.	Center front extension	1/8				5/8				
78.	Placket length	1/4				4 1/4				
79.	Placket width	1/8				1				
123.	Pleat depth (2 pleats, sleeve)	1/8				3/4				
124.	Distance between pleats	1/8				1				
125.	Applied pocket width	1/8								
126.	Applied pocket height	1/8								
146.	Pleats placement A. Front pleat top	1/4								
	B. Back pleat top	1/4								
147.	Button placement	1/8				3 3/4				
148.	Pocket placement A. Top pocket vertical	1/8								
	B. Top pocket horizontal	1/8								
	G. Pocket from side seam	1/8								
122	Vent/slit A. Height	1/4				10				
123.	Pleat depth (back yoke box pleat)	1/8				3/4				
124.	Distance between pleats (back yoke box pleat)	1/8				2				

COMMENTS: All Topstiching is 1/16" from edge/seams
          hem depth rolled and stitched is 1/2" wide

The measured garment spec sheets are for ***illustrative purposes only***
and should not be used as industry standards

CHAPTER 10

Woven Skirts

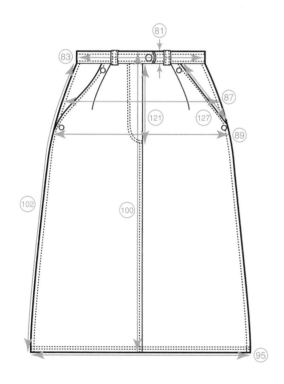

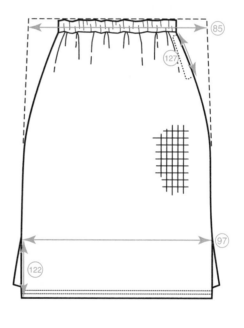

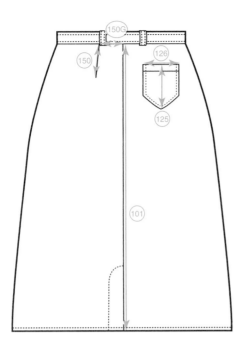

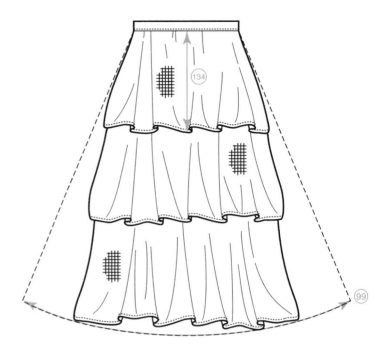

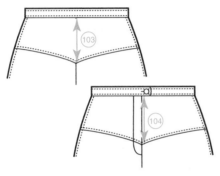

Measuring Woven Skirts

A-line, kick-pleat, straight, and wrap are just a few of the woven skirts that can be evaluated using the woven skirt spec sheet. Just like measuring a top, there are times that more than one method of measurement can be used for a measurement point. For example, most skirts are measured at both the high and low hip points. If you are measuring a granny skirt with a large amount of shirring at the waist (Figure 10.1), the high point measurement will be difficult to obtain accurately. In that situation, as the technician, you may choose to eliminate the high hip measurement and add an additional low hip or across thigh measurement.

Figure 10.1

81. *Waistband Depth*—Measure from top of waist-band edge straight down to bottom of waistband at waistband joining seam. [Note: If waistband is contoured, indicate measurement change on spec sheet.]

83. *Waistband Circumference (woven)*—Measure from side of bottom band to side of bottom band along center of band, following natural contour of waistband. Double this measurement.

85. *Waistband Width Circumference, Stretched (woven)*—Measure from side of bottom band to side of bottom band straight across center of band in a fully extended position. Double this measurement.

87. *High Hip Width Circumference (woven)*—Measure from edge of garment/side seam to edge of garment/side seam at a point 4" below bottom edge of waistband/seam, following contour of waist. Double this measurement. [Note: The 4" point is for missy-wear only; adjust as needed $\frac{1}{2}$" to 1" up or down for children's, petite's, junior's, or large/plus womens-wear. Indicate change on spec sheet.]

89. *Low Hip Width Circumference from Waist (woven)*—Measure from edge of garment/side seam to edge of garment/side seam at a point 7" below bottom edge of waistband/seam, following contour of waist. Double this measurement. [Note: The 7" point is for missywear only; adjust as needed $\frac{1}{2}$" to 1" up or down for children's, petite's, junior's, or large/plus womenswear. Indicate change on spec sheet.]

91. *Hip Width from High Point Shoulder Circumference (woven)*—Measure from edge of garment/side seam to edge of garment/side seam straight across at a point _____" below high point shoulder. Double this measurement. [Note: You will have to estimate low hip point on garment if there is no waistband and fill in _____" from high point shoulder. This measurement will vary from children's, junior's, missy, and large/plus womenswear.]

95. *Bottom Opening/Sweep Width Circumference (woven skirt)*—Measure from edge of garment/side seam to edge of garment/side seam straight across garment at bottom opening. Double this measurement. [Note: If sweep has pleats, measure with pleats closed or relaxed.]

97. *Vented Bottom Opening/Sweep Width Circumference (woven skirt)*—Measure from edge of garment/side seam to edge of garment/side seam straight across garment at top of side vents. Double this measurement. [Note: Indicate on spec sheet if there is only one vent or if vent hits at a point other than sweep, e.g., thigh opening.]

99. *Circular Bottom Opening/Sweep Width Circumference (woven skirt)*—Measure from edge of garment/side seam to edge of garment/side seam, following natural contour of garment at bottom opening. Double this measurement.

100. *Center Front Skirt Length*—Measure from bottom of waistband/seam (top edge if not banded or stitching if self-elastic/drawstring casing) straight down to bottom of garment at center front. [Note: A fashion-forward skirt may have an asymmetrical waist. Indicate top point of measure on spec sheet.]

101. *Center Back Skirt Length*—Measure from the bottom of the waistband/seam (top edge if not banded or stitching if self-elastic/drawstring casing) straight down to the bottom of garment at center front. [Note: A fashion-forward skirt may have an asymmetrical waist. Indicate top point of measure on spec sheet.]

102. *Side Skirt Length*—Measure from bottom edge of waistband/seam (top edge if not banded or stitching if self-elastic/drawstring casing) to bottom of garment along side seam/fold of garment, following any contour.

103. *Skirt/Pant Yoke Depth Front*—Measure from bottom of waistband/seam (top edge if not banded

or stitching if self-elastic/drawstring casing) straight down to bottom of yoke joining seam at center front. [Note: If yoke is contoured, indicate point of measure on spec sheet.]

104. *Skirt/Pant Yoke Depth Back*—Measure from bottom of waistband/seam (top edge if not banded or stitching if self-elastic/drawstring casing) straight down to bottom of yoke joining seam at center back. [Note: If yoke is contoured, indicate point of measure on spec sheet.]

121. *Fly/Zipper*
A. *Length*—Measure from top of fly/zipper opening straight down to bottom of fly/zipper opening at zipper stop or bar tack.
B. *Fly/Zipper Width*—Measure top of fly/zipper at joining seam from edge/fold straight across to fly/zipper placket stitching.

122. *Vent/Slit*
A. *Height*—Measure from top of vent/slit straight down to bottom of vent/slit along edge of vent/slit.
B. *Width*—Measure top of vent/slit from edge/fold straight across to vent/slit placket stitching at a point parallel to garment hemline.

123. *Pleat Depth*—Measure from outer edge of pleat at fold/crease to inner fold of pleat. [Note 1: It is a good idea to indicate what type of pleat is being measured, e.g., box, inverted, knife, kick, kilt, or envelope. Note 2: If pleats are not parallel or symmetrical, indicate any special instructions on spec sheet.]

124. *Distance Between Pleats*—Measure from start of pleat to start of pleat, excluding pleat depth at a point directly below pleat joining seam. [Note: If pleats are not parallel or symmetrical, indicate any special instructions on spec sheet.]

125. *Applied Pocket Height*—Measure from top edge of pocket to bottom edge of pocket along center of pocket. [Note: For contoured or irregularly shaped

pockets, take a second measurement and indicate point of measure on spec sheet.]

126. *Applied Pocket Width*—Measure from side of pocket to side of pocket along top edge of pocket. [Note: For contoured or irregularly shaped pockets, take a second measurement and indicate point of measure on spec sheet.]

127. *Pocket Opening Within a Seam*—Measure from top of pocket to bottom of pocket along edge of pocket opening.

128. *Belt Length*
A. *Total*—Measure from end of belt at buckle along center of belt to opposite end of belt, following contour.
B. *Circumference*—Measure from end of belt at buckle along center of belt to middle hole at opposite end.

129. *Belt Width (or Height)*—Measure from edge of belt straight across to edge of belt. [Note: If belt is contoured, indicate points of measure on spec sheet.]

130. *Belt Loop Length*—Measure from top of belt loop straight down/vertically to bottom of belt loop along center of belt loop. [Note: Fashion-forward or irregularly shaped belt loops may require further spec instructions. Indicate points of measure on spec sheet.]

131. *Belt Loop Width*—Measure belt loop from edge of belt loop straight across/horizontally to edge of belt loop. [Note: Fashion-forward or irregularly shaped belt loops may require further spec instructions. Indicate points of measure on spec sheet.]

132. *Tie Length*—Measure from end of tie/joining seam straight down to tie end along center of tie.

133. *Tie Width*
A. *Straight*—Measure from edge of tie straight across to edge of tie.

B. *Contoured*—Measure from edge of tie straight across to edge of tie at widest point of tie.

134. *Flounce/Ruffle Width*—Measure from flounce/ruffle joining seam straight across to outer edge of flounce/ruffle. [Note: If flounce/ruffle is contoured, measure along narrowest and widest points if possible and indicate changes on spec sheet.]

146. *Pleats Placement*
C. *Front Pleat Skirt/Pant*—Measure distance from center front of garment waistband joining seam/edge straight across to start of first pleat.
D. *Back Pleat Skirt*—Measure distance from center back of garment waistband joining seam/edge straight across to start of first pleat.

148. *Pocket Placement*
C. *Front Bottom Pocket Vertical*—Measure from waistband/joining seam/edge straight down to top edge of pocket.
D. *Front Bottom Pocket Horizontal*—Measure from center front straight across to side of pocket at top edge.
E. *Back Bottom Pocket Vertical*—Measure from waistband/joining seam/edge straight down to top edge of pocket.
F. *Back Bottom Pocket Horizontal*—Measure from center back straight across to side of pocket at top edge.
G. *Pocket from Side Seam*—Measure from side seam straight across to top of pocket. [Note: If pocket is contoured at sides, a top and bottom pocket size and placement must be measured and added to spec sheet.]

149. *Belt Loop Placement*
A. *Front*—Measure from center front of garment horizontally across to center of first front belt loop.
B. *Back*—Measure from center back of garment horizontally across to center of first back belt loop.
C. *Side Seam to Front*—Measure from center of side seam belt loop to center of front belt loop.
D. *Side Seam to Back*—Measure from center of side seam belt loop to center of back belt loop.

150. *Dart Placement*
F. *Center Front Skirt/Pant*—Measure from center front of garment at waistband joining seam/edge straight across to top of dart.
G. *Center Back Skirt/Pant*—Measure from center back of garment at waistband joining seam/edge straight across to top of dart.

CHAPTER 10 TERMS

When working woven skirts, you may come across the garment terms listed below. If you are unfamiliar with any of them, please look up the definitions in the glossary at the end of this text.

Skirt:
   A-line
   Asymmetric
   Fitted (straight)
   Gored
   Granny
   Jean/Denim
   Kick pleated
   Layered/Tiered
   Pleated
   Slit
   Wrap
   Yoke

SPEC SHEET:	Woven skirt	STYLE	
SEASON:		DESCRIPTION:	
LABEL: (SIZE CATEGORY)			
DATE:			

TECHNICAL SKETCH   Basic skirt

SKETCH/PHOTO

CODE	POINT OF MEASURE	TOL. +/−	4	S/6	8	M/10	12	L/14	16	XL/18
81.	Waistband depth	1/8								
83.	Waistband width circumference	1/2-3/4								
87.	High hip width circumference	1/2-3/4								
89.	Low hip width circumference	1/2-3/4								
95.	Bottom opening/sweep width circumference	1/2-3/4								
100.	Center front skirt length	3/8								
101.	Center back skirt length	3/8								
102.	Side length skirt	3/8								
121.	Fly/zipper A. Length	1/4								
	B. Width	1/8								
122.	Vent/slit A. Height	1/4								
	B. Width	1/8								
123.	Pleat depth	1/8								
125.	Applied pocket height	1/8								
126.	Applied pocket width	1/8								
127.	Pocket opening	1/4								
146.	Pleats placement C. Front pleat skirt	1/4								
148.	Pocket placement C. Front vertical	1/8								

(Tolerance 1/2-3/4 S, M, L, XL = 3/4"   4-18 = 1/2")

The measured garment spec sheets are for *illustrative purposes only* and should not be used as industry standards

CODE	POINT OF MEASURE	TOL. +/–	4	S/6	8	M/10	12	L/14	16	XL/18
	D. Front horizontal	1/8								
	E. Back vertical	1/8								
	F. Back horizontal	1/8								
	G. From side seam	1/8								
149.	Belt loop A. Length	1/8								
	B. Width	1/8								
	C. Placement C.F.	1/8								
	D. Placement C.B.	1/8								
150.	Dart length front	1/8								
	Back	1/8								
	F. Placement C.F.	1/8								
	G. Placement C.B.	1/8								

COMMENTS:

SPEC SHEET: Woven skirt	STYLE
SEASON: Early fall	DESCRIPTION: Knee length skirt with a Tailored buttonhole
LABEL: (SIZE CATEGORY) Missy	pocket side zipper opening and back kick vent.
DATE:	

TECHNICAL SKETCH   Basic skirt

SKETCH/PHOTO

CODE	POINT OF MEASURE	TOL. +/–	4	S/6	8	M/10	12	L/14	16	XL/18
81.	Waistband depth	$1/8$				1				
83.	Waistband width circumference	$1/2$-$3/4$				29				
87.	High hip width circumference	$1/2$-$3/4$				36				
89.	Low hip width circumference	$1/2$-$3/4$				40				
95.	Bottom opening/sweep width circumference	$1/2$-$3/4$				39				
100.	Center front skirt length	$3/8$				20				
101.	Center back skirt length	$3/8$				20				
102.	Side length skirt	$3/8$				20				
121.	Fly/zipper A. Length	$1/4$				7				
	B. Width (invisible)	$1/8$				–				
122.	Vent/slit A. Height	$1/4$				7				
	B. Width	$1/8$				$11/2$				
123.	Pleat depth	$1/8$								
125.	Applied pocket height (buttonhole)	$1/8$				$1/2$				
126.	Applied pocket width	$1/8$								
127.	Pocket opening	$1/4$				$41/2$				
146.	Pleats placement C. Front pleat skirt	$1/4$								
148.	Pocket placement C. Front vertical	$1/8$				$11/4$				

(Tolerance $1/2$-$3/4$ S, M, L, XL = $1/2$" 4-18 = $3/4$")

The measured garment spec sheets are for *illustrative purposes only* and should not be used as industry standards

CODE	POINT OF MEASURE	TOL. +/−	4	S/6	8	M/10	12	L/14	16	XL/18
	D. Front horizontal	1/8								
	E. Back vertical	1/8								
	F. Back horizontal	1/8								
	G. From side seam	1/8				1/2				
149.	Belt loop A. Length	1/8								
	B. Width	1/8								
	C. Placement C.F.	1/8								
	D. Placement C.B.	1/8								
150.	Dart length front	1/8				4 1/2				
	Back (2 back darts)	1/8				4				
	F. Placement C.F.	1/8				6 1/2				
	G. Placement C.B.	1/8				4 5/8				
	Distance between back darts	1/8				1 3/8				

COMMENTS:

The measured garment spec sheets are for *illustrative purposes only* and should not be used as industry standards

CHAPTER 11

Woven Pants

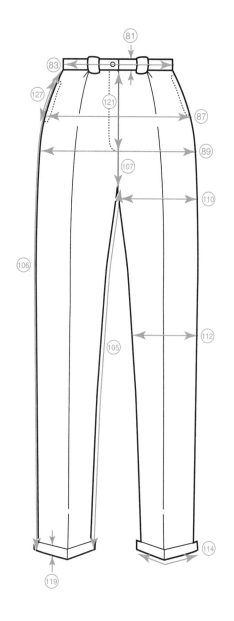

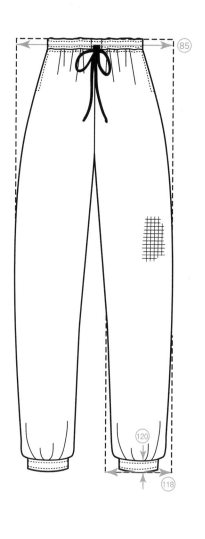

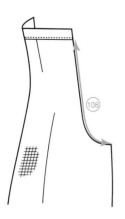
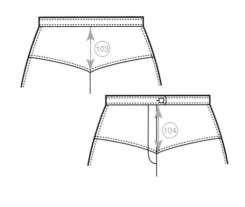
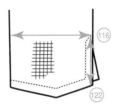

Measuring Woven Pants

The three most common types of woven pant construction are pleated, darted, and flat front. The waistlines may be high, low, or anywhere in between. Leg widths may be anywhere from slim/stovepipe to full palazzo. Because of such variety there will be instances when more than one point of measurement can be used when evaluating a woven pant. For example, the woven pant shown below should be measured at the low hip and seat rather than at the high hip and low hip, because of the low-rise design (Figure 11.1). As always, you will need to pick the measurement point that best represents a specific garment's features.

Unless otherwise stated, woven pants are measured flat, and then the measurement is doubled. When measuring the waist and hip areas, the waistband should line up at the center front and center back top edges, unless the design prohibits that. Pants can be difficult to measure because of the rise. The crotch/rise curve will not lay flat; let it lay in a natural position. When measuring the pant leg, lay one flat, gently pushing the other aside. It is not necessary to measure both legs; however, an occasional spot-check will ensure continuity. Front and back rises are measured separately and will have to be manipulated slightly in order to measure in a flat relaxed position.

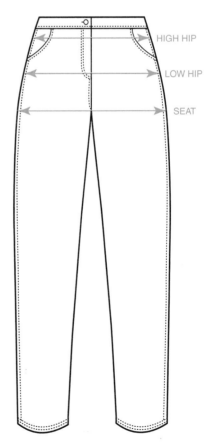

Figure 11.1

81. *Waistband Depth*—Measure from top of waistband edge straight down to bottom of waistband at waistband joining seam. [Note: If waistband is contoured, indicate measurement change on spec sheet.]

83. *Waistband Circumference (woven)*—Measure from side of bottom band to side of bottom band along center of band, following natural contour of waistband. Double this measurement.

85. *Waistband Width Circumference, Stretched (woven)*—Measure from side of bottom band to side of bottom band straight across center of band in a fully extended position. Double this measurement.

87. *High Hip Width Circumference (woven)*—Measure from edge of garment/side seam to edge of garment/side seam at a point 4" below bottom edge of waistband/seam, following contour of waist. Double this measurement. [Note: The 4" point is for missywear only; adjust as needed $\frac{1}{2}$" to 1" up or down for children's, petite's, junior's, or large/plus womenswear. Indicate change on spec sheet.]

89. *Low Hip Width Circumference from Waist (woven)*—Measure from edge of garment/side seam to edge of garment/side seam at a point 7" below bottom edge of waistband/seam, following contour of waist. Double this measurement. [Note: The 7" point is for missywear only; adjust as needed $\frac{1}{2}$" to 1" up or down for children's, petite's, junior's, or large/plus womenswear. Indicate change on spec sheet.]

91. *Hip Width from High Point Shoulder Circumference (woven)*—Measure from edge of garment/side seam to edge of garment/side seam straight across at a point _____" below high point shoulder. Double this measurement. [Note: You will have to estimate low hip point on garment if there is no waistband and fill in _____" from high point shoulder. This measurement will vary from children's, junior's, missy, and large/plus womenswear.]

93. *Hip Seat Width Circumference (woven pant)*—Measure from edge of garment/side seam to edge of garment/side seam at a point _____" up from crotch seam, following contour of waist. Double this measurement. [Note 1: This measurement is useful when waistband sits below natural waistline. Note 2: Adjust the _____" up from crotch as needed for junior's and large/plus womenswear. Note 3: A hip seat width of $2\frac{1}{2}$" up for children's and 3" up for menswear can take the place of low hip width.

103. *Skirt/Pant Yoke Depth Front*—Measure from bottom of waistband/seam (top edge if not banded or stitching if self-elastic/drawstring casing) straight down to bottom of yoke joining seam at center front. [Note: If yoke is contoured, indicate point of measure on spec sheet.]

104. *Skirt/Pant Yoke Depth Back*—Measure from bottom of waistband/seam (top edge if not banded or stitching if self-elastic/drawstring casing) straight down to bottom of yoke joining seam at center back. [Note: If yoke is contoured, indicate point of measure on spec sheet.]

105. *Inseam*—Measure from crotch joining seam to bottom of leg opening, following inseam/inner fold.

106. *Outseam*—Measure from bottom edge of waistband/seam (top edge if not banded or stitching if self-elastic/drawstring casing) to bottom of garment along side seam/fold of garment.

107. *Front Rise*—Measure from bottom edge of waistband/seam (top edge if not banded or stitching if self-elastic/drawstring casing) to crotch joining seam, following curve of front rise seam. [Note: Measure over zipper if in front rise seam.]

108. *Back Rise*—Measure from bottom edge of waistband/seam (top edge if not banded or stitching if self-elastic/drawstring casing) to crotch joining seam, following curve of back rise seam. [Note: Measure over zipper if in front back seam.]

109. *Thigh Width (knit)*—Measure from pant leg edge/seam to pant leg edge/seam straight across pant leg at a point 1" below crotch and parallel to leg opening. [Note: If leg opening is asymmetrical, measure to a point that would be parallel to leg opening.]

110. *Thigh Width Circumference (woven)*—Measure from pant leg edge/seam to pant leg edge/seam straight across pant leg at a point 1" below crotch and parallel to leg opening. Double this measurement. [Note: If leg opening is asymmetrical, measure to a point that would be parallel to leg opening.]

112. *Knee Width Circumference (woven)*—Measure from pant leg edge/seam to pant leg edge/seam at a point one-half of the inseam and parallel to leg opening. Double this measurement. [Note 1: If leg opening is asymmetrical, measure to a point that would be parallel to leg opening. Note 2: If pant leg is three-quarter length, indicate point of measure on spec sheet. Note 3: A general knee measurement from crotch seam of missy 12", junior's 11", large/plus women's 13" can be used. Indicate change on spec sheet. Measure children's at one-half inseam minus $1\frac{1}{2}$", and for men's minus 2".]

114. *Leg Opening Width Circumference (woven)*—Measure from pant leg edge/seam to pant leg edge/seam straight across bottom edge of leg opening. Double this measurement. [Note: If leg opening is contoured, follow contour and indicate measurement change on spec sheet.]

116. *Vented Leg Opening Circumference (woven)*—Measure from pant leg edge/seam to pant leg edge/seam straight across pant leg at top of side vents. Double this measurement.

118. *Leg Opening Width Circumference, Stretched (woven)*—Measure from pant leg edge/seam to pant leg edge/seam straight across bottom edge of leg opening in a fully extended position. Double this measurement.

119. *Cuff Height Pants*—Measure from top of cuff edge straight down to bottom of cuff fold and leg opening.

120. *Bottom Band/Ribbing Height Pants*—Measure from cuff joining seam or top of ribbing straight down to bottom edge of cuff or rib opening. [Note: For fashion-forward pants, you may want to include a cuff width. See point of measure 56, Cuff Length Sleeve, for measuring instructions and indicate cuff width pant as needed on spec sheet.]

121. *Fly/Zipper*
A. *Length*—Measure from top of fly/zipper opening straight down to bottom of fly/zipper opening at zipper stop or bar tack.
B. *Fly/Zipper Width*—Measure top of fly/zipper at joining seam from edge/fold straight across to fly/zipper placket stitching.

122. *Vent/Slit*
A. *Height*—Measure from top of vent/slit straight down to bottom of vent/slit along edge of vent/slit.
B. *Width*—Measure top of vent/slit from edge/fold straight across to vent/slit placket stitching at a point parallel to garment hemline.

123. *Pleat Depth*—Measure from outer edge of pleat at fold/crease to inner fold of pleat. [Note 1: It is a good idea to indicate what type of pleat is being measured, e.g., box, inverted, knife, kick, kilt, or envelope. Note 2: If pleats are not parallel or symmetrical, indicate any special instructions on spec sheet.]

124. *Distance Between Pleats*—Measure from start of pleat to start of pleat, excluding pleat depth at a point directly below pleat joining seam. [Note: If pleats are not parallel or symmetrical, indicate any special instructions on spec sheet.]

125. *Applied Pocket Height*—Measure from top edge of pocket to bottom edge of pocket along center of pocket. [Note: For contoured or irregularly shaped

pockets, take a second measurement and indicate point of measure on spec sheet.]

126. *Applied Pocket Width*—Measure from side of pocket to side of pocket along top edge of pocket. [Note: For contoured or irregularly shaped pockets, take a second measurement and indicate point of measure on spec sheet.]

127. *Pocket Opening Within a Seam*—Measure from top of pocket to bottom of pocket along edge of pocket opening.

128. *Belt Length*
A. *Total*—Measure from end of belt at buckle along center of belt to opposite end of belt, following contour.
B. *Circumference*—Measure from end of belt at buckle along center of belt to middle hole at opposite end.

129. *Belt Width (or Height)*—Measure from edge of belt straight across to edge of belt. [Note: If belt is contoured, indicate points of measure on spec sheet.]

130. *Belt Loop Length*—Measure from top of belt loop straight down/vertically to bottom of belt loop along center of belt loop. [Note: Fashion-forward or irregularly shaped belt loops may require further spec instructions. Indicate points of measure on spec sheet.]

131. *Belt Loop Width*—Measure belt loop from edge of belt loop straight across/horizontally to edge of belt loop. [Note: Fashion-forward or irregularly shaped belt loops may require further spec instructions. Indicate points of measure on spec sheet.]

132. *Tie Length*—Measure from end of tie/joining seam straight down to tie end along center of tie.

133. *Tie Width*
A. *Straight*—Measure from edge of tie straight across to edge of tie.

B. *Contoured*—Measure from edge of tie straight across to edge of tie at widest point of tie.

134. *Flounce/Ruffle Width*—Measure from flounce/ruffle joining seam straight across to outer edge of flounce/ruffle. [Note: If flounce/ruffle is contoured, measure along narrowest and widest points if possible and indicate changes on spec sheet.]

146. *Pleats Placement*
A. *Front Pleat Top*—Measure distance from center front of garment straight across to start of first pleat at a point parallel to garment hem. [Note: You may need to use armhole or side seam as a starting point if there is no center front seam or placket.]
B. *Back Pleat Top*—Measure distance from armhole seam/side seam (depending on pleat placement) to first pleat at a point parallel to garment hem.
C. *Front Pleat Skirt/Pant*—Measure distance from center front of garment waistband joining seam/edge straight across to start of first pleat.
D. *Back Pleat Skirt*—Measure distance from center back of garment waistband joining seam/edge straight across to start of first pleat.

148. *Pocket Placement*
C. *Front Bottom Pocket Vertical*—Measure from waistband/joining seam/edge straight down to top edge of pocket.
D. *Front Bottom Pocket Horizontal*—Measure from center front straight across to side of pocket at top edge.
E. *Back Bottom Pocket Vertical*—Measure from waistband/joining seam/edge straight down to top edge of pocket.
F. *Back Bottom Pocket Horizontal*—Measure from center back straight across to side of pocket at top edge.
G. *Pocket from Side Seam*—Measure from side seam straight across to top of pocket. [Note: If pocket is contoured at sides, a top and bottom pocket size and placement must be measured and added to spec sheet.]

149. *Belt Loop Placement*

A. *Front*—Measure from center front of garment horizontally across to center of first front belt loop.

B. *Back*—Measure from center back of garment horizontally across to center of first back belt loop.

C. *Side Seam to Front*—Measure from center of side seam belt loop to center of front belt loop.

D. *Side Seam to Back*—Measure from center of side seam belt loop to center of back belt loop.

150. *Dart Placement*

F. *Center Front Skirt/Pant*—Measure from center front of garment at waistband joining seam/edge straight across to top of dart.

G. *Center Back Skirt/Pant*—Measure from center back of garment at waistband joining seam/edge straight across to top of dart.

CHAPTER 11 TERMS

When working with woven pants, you may come across the garment terms listed below. If you are unfamiliar with any of them, please look up the definitions in the glossary at the end of this text.

Pants:

    Baggy (baggies)

    Bell-bottom (bell-bottoms)

    Continental

    Cropped

    Hip-hugger (low rise)

    Oxford

    Palazzo

    Sailor

    Stovepipe

    Western

Seat

SPEC SHEET	Woven pant	STYLE	

SEASON:

DESCRIPTION:

LABEL: (SIZE CATEGORY)

DATE:

TECHNICAL SKETCH Classic cuffed pant

SKETCH/PHOTO

CODE	POINT OF MEASURE	TOL. +/–	4	S/6	8	M/10	12	L/14	16	XL/18
81.	Waistband depth	1/8								
83.	Waistband circumference	1/2-3/4								
85.	Waistband circumference stretched	1/2-3/4								
87.	High hip width	1/2-3/4								
89.	Low hip width	1/2-3/4								
105.	Inseam	3/8								
106.	Outseam	3/8								
107.	Front rise	3/8								
108.	Back rise	3/8								
110.	Thigh width circumference	3/8								
112.	Knee width circumference	3/8								
114.	Leg opening width circumference	1/4								

(Tolerance 1/2-3/4 S, M, L, XL = 3/4" 4-18 = 1/2")

The measured garment spec sheets are for *illustrative purposes only* and should not be used as industry standards

CODE	POINT OF MEASURE	TOL. +/−	4	S/6	8	M/10	12	L/14	16	XL/18
119.	Cuff height pants	1/8								
121.	Fly/zipper A. Length	1/4								
	B. Width	1/8								
123.	Pleat depth	1/8								
124.	Distance between pleats	1/8								
127.	Pocket opening	1/4								
130.	Belt loop length	1/8								
131.	Belt loop width	1/8								
150.	Dart length	1/8								

COMMENTS:

The measured garment spec sheets are for *illustrative purposes only* and should not be used as industry standards

SPEC SHEET Woven pant

STYLE	
SEASON: Early fall	**DESCRIPTION:** Updated classic pant with cuff, front dart,
LABEL: (SIZE CATEGORY) Missy	and pleat back buttoned vent pocket
DATE:	

TECHNICAL SKETCH Classic cuffed pant

SKETCH/PHOTO

CODE	POINT OF MEASURE		TOL. +/−	4	S/6	8	M/10	12	L/14	16	XL/18
81.	Waistband depth	To stitching	1/8			1 1/2					
83.	Waistband circumference		1/2-3/4			30					
85.	Waistband circumference stretched		1/2-3/4								
87.	High hip width	Below stitching	1/2-3/4			38 1/4					
89.	Low hip width	Below stitching	1/2-3/4			43					
105.	Inseam		3/8			31					
106.	Outseam	Below stitching	3/8			41					
107.	Front rise	Below stitching	3/8			12 1/2					
108.	Back rise	Below stitching	3/8			14 3/4					
110.	Thigh width circumference		3/8			28					
112.	Knee width circumference		3/8			22					
114.	Leg opening width circumference		1/4			18 1/2					

(Tolerance 1/2-3/4 S, M, L, XL = 3/4" 4-18 = 1/2")

The measured garment spec sheets are for illustrative purposes only
and should not be used as industry standards

CODE	POINT OF MEASURE		TOL. +/−	4	S/6	8	M/10	12	L/14	16	XL/18
119.	Cuff height pants		$1/8$			$1\frac{1}{2}$					
121.	Fly/zipper A. Length	Below stitching	$1/2$-$3/4$			7					
	B. Width		$1/2$-$3/4$			$1\frac{1}{8}$					
123.	Pleat depth		$1/2$-$3/4$			$1\frac{1}{8}$					
124.	Distance between pleats		$1/2$-$3/4$								
127.	Pocket opening	Side seam	$1/4$			6					
130.	Belt loop length		$1/8$			2					
131.	Belt loop width		$1/8$			$3/8$					
150.	Dart length	Front below stitching	$1/8$			4					
		Back below stitching	$1/8$			$4\frac{1}{8}$					
127.	Pocket opening back vent height		$1/4$			$3/8$					
		Length/width	$1/8$			$4\frac{1}{2}$					
146.	Pleats placement from C.F.		$1/4$			$4\frac{1}{8}$					
148.	Pocket placement E. Back vertical		$1/8$			$2\frac{3}{8}$					
	F. Back horizontal		$1/8$			$1\frac{3}{8}$					
149.	Belt loop placement A. C.F. to loop		$1/8$			$4\frac{1}{8}$					
	B. C.B. to loop		$1/8$			$3/4$					
	Distance between back darts		$1/8$			$1\frac{3}{4}$					
150.	Dart placement F. C.F. to dart		$1/8$			$5\frac{3}{4}$					
	G. C.B. to 1st dart		$1/8$			$2\frac{1}{2}$					

COMMENTS:

CHAPTER 12

Woven Dresses

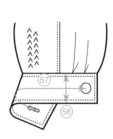

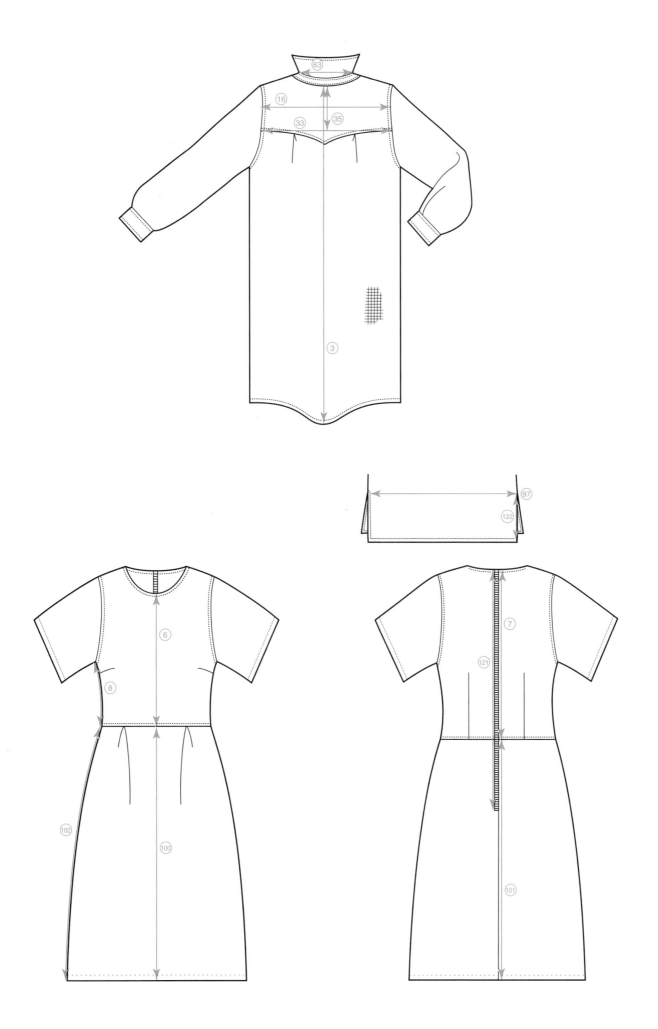

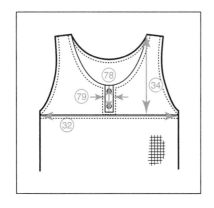

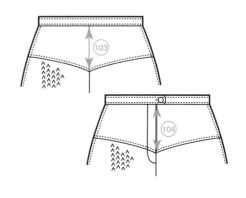

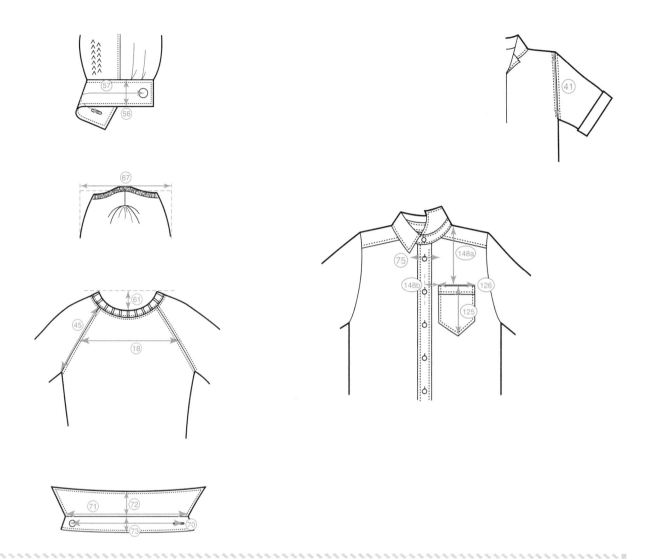

Measuring Woven Dresses

Measuring a woven dress basically combines the measurements of a woven blouse and a woven skirt; therefore, the rules you learned for each of those styles will be used here as well. If needed, look back over those chapters. However, there will be measurement points unique to dresses not covered in those chapters; measurement point 91, Hip Width from High Point Shoulder Circumference (Figure 12.1), is an example. As the technician, be sure to decide which measurements are best suited to the garment under evaluation.

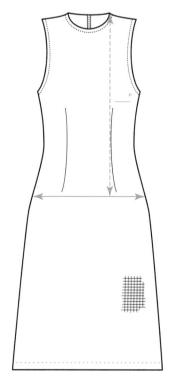

Figure 12.1

1. *Front Length (garments with a front opening)*—Measure from high point shoulder at neck straight down, parallel to center front, to bottom of garment at front. If garment has a collar, gently lift it away from shoulder-neck measuring point.

2. *Center Front Length (garments with a plain front; no front opening)*—Measure from center front neck joining seams straight down to bottom of garment at center front. [Note: A garment without a front opening may still require use of Front Length if neckline is unusual.]

3. *Center Back Length*—Measure from center back neck joining seams straight down to bottom of garment at center back. If needed, gently lift the collar away from back neck to expose joining seam.

4. *Side Length*—Measure from bottom of armhole/side seam straight down to bottom of garment along side of garment. Do not follow natural curve of garment's side seam, unless otherwise indicated. If needed, gently lift sleeve away from armhole/side seam joining seam.

5. *Front Bodice Length (garments with a front opening)*—Measure from high point shoulder at neck straight down, parallel to center front, to top edge of waistband, joining seam, or rib. If garment has a collar, gently lift it away from shoulder-neck measuring point.

6. *Center Front Bodice Length (garments with a plain front; no front opening)*—Measure from center front neck joining seam straight down to top edge of waistband, joining seam, or rib. [Note: A garment without a center opening may still require use of Front Bodice Length if neckline is unusual.]

7. *Center Back Bodice Length*—Measure from center back neck joining seams straight down to top edge of waistband, joining seam, or rib. If needed, gently lift collar away from back neck to expose joining seam.

8. *Side Seam Bodice Length*—Measure from bottom of armhole/side seam straight down to top edge of waistband, joining seam, or rib, along side of garment, following natural curve of garment's side seam, unless otherwise indicated. If needed, gently lift sleeve away from armhole/side seam joining seam. [Note: You can take side seam bodice measurement straight rather than contoured if joining seam/rib can be extended, but indicate change on spec sheet.]

10. *Chest Width Circumference (woven)*—Measure from edge of garment/side seam to edge of garment/side seam straight across garment at a point 1' below armhole. Double this measurement.

12. *Chest Width Circumference (raglan sleeve, woven)*—Measure from edge of garment/side seam to edge of garment/side seam straight across garment at a point _____" below high point shoulder. Double this measurement. [Note: You will have to determine number of inches down from high point shoulder for each raglan sleeve style based on depth of sleeve. Then indicate this number on spec sheet.]

13. *Across Shoulder*—Measure straight across front from armhole seam/edge to armhole seam/edge at shoulder seam or across natural shoulder fold line created if there is no seam.

14. *Shoulder Width*—Measure from neckband/collar/ribbing joining seam or neckline edge to top of armhole seam at shoulder, taken along shoulder seam or across natural shoulder fold line created if there is no seam.

15. *Across Chest*—Measure $2\frac{1}{2}$" down from collar/rib joining seam at center front straight across front of garment from armhole seam/edge to armhole seam/edge. [Note: The $2\frac{1}{2}$" measurement point is for missy-wear only and may need to be adjusted up or down $\frac{1}{4}$" to $\frac{1}{2}$" accordingly for men's, children's, junior's, and large/plus womenswear. Indicate any changes on spec sheet.]

16. *Across Back*—Measure 4" down from collar/rib joining seam at center back straight across back of garment from armhole seam/edge to armhole seam/edge. [Note: The 4" measurement point is for missywear only and may need to be adjusted up or down $\frac{1}{4}$" to $\frac{1}{2}$" accordingly for men's, children's, junior's, and large/plus womenswear. Indicate any changes on spec sheet.]

17. *Across Chest/Center Armhole*—Measure at one-half depth of armhole straight across front of garment from armhole seam/edge to armhole seam/edge.

18. *Across Back/Center Armhole*—Measure at one-half depth of armhole straight across back of garment from armhole seam/edge to armhole seam/edge.

20. *Waist Width Circumference (woven)*—Measure from edge of garment/side seam to edge of garment/side seam straight across garment on seam or at narrowest point of waist taper at a point _____" below high point shoulder. Double this measurement. [Note: You will have to determine number of inches down from high point shoulder for each raglan sleeve style based on depth of sleeve. Then indicate this number on spec sheet.]

32. *Yoke Width Front*—Measure from armhole seam/edge to armhole seam/edge straight across front of garment, ignoring contours or points, at yoke-body joining seams. [Note: If yoke is asymmetrical, indicate changes in measuring as needed on spec sheet.]

33. *Yoke Width Back*—Measure from armhole seam/edge to armhole seam/edge straight across back of garment, ignoring contours or points, at yoke-body joining seams. [Note: If yoke is asymmetrical, indicate changes in measuring as needed on spec sheet.]

34. *Yoke Depth Front*—Measure from high point shoulder at neck straight down to bottom of front yoke-body joining seam. Be sure to gently lift collar away from shoulder-neck joining seam if needed.

35. *Yoke Back Depth*—Measure from center back neck joining seam straight down to bottom of back yoke-body joining seam. Gently lift collar away from back neck joining seam if needed.

36. *Sleeve Length Top Armhole*—Measure along top of sleeve/fold, following contour of sleeve from armhole seam at shoulder to bottom of sleeve opening, including cuff.

37. *Sleeve Length Top Neck*—Measure along top of sleeve/fold, following contour of sleeve from sleeve-neck joining seam/edge to edge of sleeve opening, including cuff. Gently lift collar at sleeve-neck joining seam if needed.

38. *Sleeve Length Center Back*—Measure from center back neck joining seam or from a point above neck at an imaginary line, that of a joining seam, along top of sleeve/fold, following contour of sleeve to edge of sleeve opening, including cuff.

39. *Sleeve Length Underarm*—Measure straight from bottom of armhole along sleeve seam to edge of sleeve opening, including cuff.

41. *Straight Armhole Width Circumference (woven)*—Measure from top of shoulder joining seam/edge straight down to bottom of armhole. Double this measurement.

43. *Curved Armhole Width Circumference (woven)*—Measure from top of shoulder joining seam/edge to bottom of armhole, following contour of armhole. Double this measurement.

44. *Armhole Front*—Measure on front of garment from top of shoulder at neckline joining seam/edge to bottom of armhole, following contour of armhole. Gently lift collar away from neckline joining seam if needed.

45. *Armhole Back*—Measure on back of garment from top of shoulder at neck joining seam/edge to

bottom of armhole, following contour of armhole. Gently lift collar away from neck joining seam if needed.

47. *Armhole Width Circumference Straight (woven)*—Measure from top of shoulder seam at a point _____" below neckline joining seam/edge straight down to bottom of armhole. Double this measurement. [Note: Gently move collar away from neck joining seam if needed when measuring down _____" to armhole start point. Indicate number of inches measured down on spec sheet.]

49. *Muscle Width Circumference (woven)*—Measure from inner sleeve edge/seam to outer sleeve edge/fold at a point 1" below armhole and parallel to sleeve opening. Double this measurement.

51. *Elbow Width Circumference (woven)*—Measure from inner sleeve edge/seam to outer sleeve edge/fold straight across sleeve at a point one-half of underarm sleeve length and parallel to sleeve opening at wrist or cuff. Double this measurement. [Note: If sleeve is three-quarter length, indicate new point of measure on spec sheet.]

53. *Sleeve Opening Width Circumference (woven)*—Measure from inner sleeve edge/seam to outer sleeve edge/fold straight across bottom edge of sleeve opening. Double this measurement.

55. *Sleeve Opening Width Circumference, Stretched (woven)*—Measure from inner sleeve edge/seam to outer sleeve edge/fold straight across bottom edge of sleeve opening in a fully extended position. Double this measurement.

56. *Cuff Length Sleeve*—Measure from outside end of buttonhole to center of button straight along center of cuff. Open cuff out as flat as possible when measuring. [Note: If cuff length is contoured, measure along center-most point.]

57. *Cuff/Ribbing Height Sleeve*—Measure from cuff joining seam or top of ribbing straight down to bottom edge of cuff or rib opening. [Note: If cuff is contoured, indicate changes made as needed to measurement on spec sheet.]

58. *Neck Depth Front (garments with a plain front/asymmetrical front opening)*—Measure from center back neck joining seam/edge straight down to center front neck joining seam/edge.

59. *Neck Depth Center Front (garments with a center front opening)*—Measure from center back neck joining seam/edge straight down to center of first button at center front of garment.

60. *Neck Drop Front*—Measure from an imaginary line connecting neckline edges straight down to center front neck opening edge. Use a ruler if needed to connect top neckline edges.

61. *Neck Drop Back*—Measure from an imaginary line connecting neckline edges straight down to center back neck opening edge. This measurement is taken with front of garment facing up. Use a ruler to connect top neckline edges if needed.

62. *Neck Width, No Collar*—Measure from inside neck edge/seam to inside neck edge/seam straight across back neck at widest point. This measurement is taken with front of garment faceup.

63. *Neck Width, Collar*—Measure straight across back neck from neck-shoulder joining seam to neck-shoulder joining seam or natural shoulder line if no seam. This measurement is taken with back of garment faceup.

65. *Neck Edge Width Circumference (woven)*—Measure from neck edge/seam/fold to neck edge/seam/fold along top opening edge, following natural contour of neck opening. Garment should be positioned with one shoulder on top of the other and

with front and back neck edges meeting. Double this measurement.

67. *Neck Edge Width Circumference, Stretched (woven)*—Measure from neck edge/seam/fold to neck edge/seam/fold along top opening edge in a fully extended position. Garment should be positioned with one shoulder on top of the other and with front and back neck edges meeting. Double this measurement.

69. *Neck Base Circumference (woven)*—Measure from neck edge/seam to neck edge/seam along collar/rib joining seam or neckline edge, following natural contour of neck opening. Garment should be buttoned or zippered, if applicable, with one shoulder seam positioned on top of the other and with front and back neck edges meeting. Double this measurement.

70. *Neckband Length*—Measure from outside end of buttonhole to center of buttonhole across neckband, following contour of neckband.

71. *Collar Length*—Measure from one end of collar to other end of collar along neck joining seam.

72. *Collar Height*—Measure from collar/rib joining seam at center back neck straight up to outer edge of collar/rib.

73. *Collar Band Height*—Measure from collar joining seam at center back straight up to neckband joining seam at center back.

74. *Collar Point Length*—Measure from collar joining seam to outer edge of collar along collar point edge. [Note: If collar is rounded, measure at a point parallel to center back and indicate change on spec sheet.]

75. *Collar Point Spread (pointed collars only)*—Measure, with collar band buttoned and collar in place, from collar point straight across collar edge to collar point.

76. *Lapel Width*
A. *Notched*—Measure from lower lapel notch straight across to lapel fold at a point perpendicular to garment center front.
B. *Without Notches*—Measure from lapel edge straight across widest point of lapel to lapel fold at a point _____" down from center back collar joining seam and perpendicular to front of garment.

77. *Center Front Extension*—Measure from an imaginary line at center front of garment horizontally to finished outer edge of front extended piece.

78. *Placket Length*—Measure from top edge of placket straight down to bottom of placket opening along center of placket.

79. *Placket Width*—Measure from placket joining seam straight across placket to placket edge at fold.

80. *Keyhole Length*—Measure from outer edge of neckline straight down to bottom of keyhole opening.

81. *Waistband Depth*—Measure from top of waistband edge straight down to bottom of waistband at waistband joining seam. [Note: If waistband is contoured, indicate measurement change on spec sheet.]

83. *Waistband Circumference (woven)*—Measure from side of bottom band to side of bottom band along center of band, following natural contour of waistband. Double this measurement.

85. *Waistband Width Circumference, Stretched (woven)*—Measure from side of bottom band to side of bottom band straight across center of band in a fully extended position. Double this measurement.

87. *High Hip Width Circumference (woven)*—Measure from edge of garment/side seam to edge of garment/side seam at a point 4" below bottom edge of

waistband/seam, following contour of waist. Double this measurement. [Note: The 4" point is for missy-wear only; adjust as needed $\frac{1}{2}$" to 1" up or down for children's, petite's, junior's, or large/plus womens-wear. Indicate change on spec sheet.]

89. *Low Hip Width Circumference from Waist (woven)*—Measure from edge of garment/side seam to edge of garment/side seam at a point 7" below bottom edge of waistband/seam, following contour of waist. Double this measurement. [Note: The 7" point is for missywear only; adjust as needed $\frac{1}{2}$" to 1" up or down for children's, petite's, junior's, or large/plus womenswear. Indicate change on spec sheet.]

91. *Hip Width from High Point Shoulder Circumference (woven)*—Measure from edge of garment/side seam to edge of garment/side seam straight across at a point _____" below high point shoulder. Double this measurement. [Note: You will have to estimate low hip point on garment if there is no waistband and fill in _____" from high point shoulder. This measurement will vary from children's, junior's, missy, and large/plus womenswear.]

95. *Bottom Opening/Sweep Width Circumference (woven skirt)*—Measure from edge of garment/side seam to edge of garment/side seam straight across garment at bottom opening. Double this measurement. [Note: If sweep has pleats, measure with pleats closed or relaxed.]

97. *Vented Bottom Opening/Sweep Width Circumference (woven skirt)*—Measure from edge of garment/side seam to edge of garment/side seam straight across garment at top of side vents. Double this measurement. [Note: Indicate on spec sheet if there is only one vent or if vent hits at a point other than sweep, e.g., thigh opening.]

99. *Circular Bottom Opening/Sweep Width Circumference (woven skirt)*—Measure from edge of garment/side seam to edge of garment/side seam, fol-lowing natural contour of garment at bottom opening. Double this measurement.

100. *Center Front Skirt Length*—Measure from bottom of waistband/seam (top edge if not banded or stitching if self-elastic/drawstring casing) straight down to bottom of garment at center front. [Note: A fashion-forward skirt may have an asymmetrical waist. Indicate top point of measure on spec sheet.]

101. *Center Back Skirt Length*—Measure from bottom of waistband/seam (top edge if not banded or stitching if self-elastic/drawstring casing) straight down to bottom of garment at center front. [Note: A fashion-forward skirt may have an asymmetrical waist. Indicate top point of measure on spec sheet.]

102. *Side Skirt Length*—Measure from bottom edge of waistband/seam (top edge if not banded or stitching if self-elastic/drawstring casing) to bottom of garment along side seam/fold of garment, following any contour.

103. *Skirt/Pant Yoke Depth Front*—Measure from bottom of waistband/seam (top edge if not banded or stitching if self-elastic/drawstring casing) straight down to bottom of yoke joining seam at center front. [Note: If yoke is contoured, indicate point of measure on spec sheet.]

104. *Skirt/Pant Yoke Depth Back*—Measure from bottom of waistband/seam (top edge if not banded or stitching if self-elastic/drawstring casing) straight down to bottom of yoke joining seam at center back. [Note: If yoke is contoured, indicate point of measure on spec sheet.]

121. *Fly/Zipper*
A. *Length*—Measure from top of fly/zipper opening straight down to bottom of fly/zipper opening at zipper stop or bar tack.
B. *Fly/Zipper Width*—Measure top of fly/zipper at joining seam from edge/fold straight across to fly/zipper placket stitching.

122. *Vent/Slit*

A. *Height*—Measure from top of vent/slit straight down to bottom of vent/slit along edge of vent/slit.

B. *Width*—Measure top of vent/slit from edge/fold straight across to vent/slit placket stitching at a point parallel to garment hemline.

123. *Pleat Depth*—Measure from outer edge of pleat at fold/crease to inner fold of pleat. [Note 1: It is a good idea to indicate what type of pleat is being measured, e.g., box, inverted, knife, kick, kilt, or envelope. Note 2: If pleats are not parallel or symmetrical, indicate any special instructions on spec sheet.]

124. *Distance Between Pleats*—Measure from start of pleat to start of pleat, excluding pleat depth at a point directly below pleat joining seam. [Note: If pleats are not parallel or symmetrical, indicate any special instructions on spec sheet.]

125. *Applied Pocket Height*—Measure from top edge of pocket to bottom edge of pocket along center of pocket. [Note: For contoured or irregularly shaped pockets, take a second measurement and indicate point of measure on spec sheet.]

126. *Applied Pocket Width*—Measure from side of pocket to side of pocket along top edge of pocket. [Note: For contoured or irregularly shaped pockets, take a second measurement and indicate point of measure on spec sheet.]

127. *Pocket Opening within a Seam*—Measure from top of pocket to bottom of pocket along edge of pocket opening.

128. *Belt Length*

A. *Total*—Measure from end of belt at buckle along center of belt to opposite end of belt, following contour.

B. *Circumference*—Measure from end of belt at buckle along center of belt to middle hole at opposite end.

129. *Belt Width (or Height)*—Measure from edge of belt straight across to edge of belt. [Note: If belt is contoured, indicate points of measure on spec sheet.]

130. *Belt Loop Length*—Measure from top of belt loop straight down/vertically to bottom of belt loop along center of belt loop. [Note: Fashion-forward or irregularly shaped belt loops may require further spec instructions. Indicate points of measure on spec sheet.]

131. *Belt Loop Width*—Measure belt loop from edge of belt loop straight across/horizontally to edge of belt loop. [Note: Fashion-forward or irregularly shaped belt loops may require further spec instructions. Indicate points of measure on spec sheet.]

132. *Tie Length*—Measure from end of tie/joining seam straight down to tie end along center of tie.

133. *Tie Width*

A. *Straight*—Measure from edge of tie straight across to edge of tie.

B. *Contoured*—Measure from edge of tie straight across to edge of tie at widest point of tie.

134. *Flounce/Ruffle Width*—Measure from flounce/ruffle joining seam straight across to outer edge of flounce/ruffle. [Note: If flounce/ruffle is contoured, measure along narrowest and widest points if possible and indicate changes on spec sheet.]

135. *Strap Length*—Measure from strap joining seam along center of strap to end of strap. [Note: If a strap is contoured or has a contoured edge, measure along center, approximating center end point, or indicate instructions as needed on spec sheet.]

136. *Strap Width*—Measure from edge of strap straight across to edge of strap. [Note: If strap is contoured, measure along narrowest and widest points if possible and indicate changes on spec sheet.]

137. *Front Hood Length*—Measure from top of hood to bottom of hood at center front joining seam along opening edge of hood.

138. *Back Hood Length*—Measure from top of hood at center front to bottom of hood at center back joining seam along outside curve of hood fold/seam.

139. *Hood Width*—Measure from front opening edge of hood straight across to back of hood along widest point of hood.

140. *Flange Depth*—Measure from center back neck joining seam straight down to bottom of flange at center back. [Note: If flange is contoured or asymmetrical, indicate point of measure on spec sheet.]

141. *Shoulder Pad Length*—Measure from edge of pad straight across to edge of pad along center of pad or natural shoulder line of pad.

142. *Shoulder Pad Width*—Measure from side of pad straight across to side of pad along edge of pad if straight or at widest point of pad if curved.

143. *Straight Edge Shoulder Pad Height*—Measure from top of pad straight down to bottom of pad along center of pad.

144. *Curved Edge Shoulder Pad Height*—Stick a one-inch straight pin into thickest part of shoulder pad. Push pin all way through pad until head of pin rests on top of pad. Be sure not to crush pad. Measure portion of pin sticking out of pad. Subtract figure from 1" (length of pin) to get shoulder pad height.

145. *Shoulder Pad Placement*—Measure from neck edge or joining seam straight across shoulder seam or natural shoulder line to start of shoulder pad.

146. *Pleats Placement*
A. *Front Pleat Top*—Measure distance from center front of garment straight across to start of first pleat at a point parallel to garment hem. [Note: You may need to use armhole or side seam as a starting point if there is no center front seam or placket.]
B. *Back Pleat Top*—Measure distance from armhole seam/side seam (depending on pleat placement) to first pleat at a point parallel to garment hem.
C. *Front Pleat Skirt/Pant*—Measure distance from center front of garment waistband joining seam/edge straight across to start of first pleat.
D. *Back Pleat Skirt*—Measure distance from center back of garment waistband joining seam/edge straight across to start of first pleat.

147. *Button Placement*—Refer to measurement point 59, Neck Depth Center Front, for placement of first button. Then measure distance of first button to second button. Be sure when measuring that button at bust point is lined up to apex of bust. Adjust all buttons accordingly and respace as needed.

148. *Pocket Placement*
A. *Top Pocket Vertical*—Measure from shoulder-neck joining seam straight down to top edge of pocket.
B. *Top Pocket Horizontal*—Measure from center front straight across to side of pocket at top edge.
C. *Front Bottom Pocket Vertical*—Measure from waistband/joining seam/edge straight down to top edge of pocket.
D. *Front Bottom Pocket Horizontal*—Measure from center front straight across to side of pocket at top edge.
E. *Back Bottom Pocket Vertical*—Measure from waistband/joining seam/edge straight down to top edge of pocket.
F. *Back Bottom Pocket Horizontal*—Measure from center back straight across to side of pocket at top edge.
G. *Pocket from Side Seam*—Measure from side seam straight across to top of pocket. [Note: If pocket is contoured at sides, a top and bottom pocket size and placement must be measured and added to spec sheet.]

149. *Belt Loop Placement*

A. *Front*—Measure from center front of garment horizontally across to center of first front belt loop.

B. *Back*—Measure from center back of garment horizontally across to center of first back belt loop.

C. *Side Seam to Front*—Measure from center of side seam belt loop to center of front belt loop.

D. *Side Seam to Back*—Measure from center of side seam belt loop to center of back belt loop.

150. *Dart Placement*

A. *High Point Shoulder Bust Dart*—Measure from shoulder-neck joining seam or at a point _____" from shoulder-neck seam straight down, parallel to center front, to top of dart. [Note: The _____" from shoulder seam measurement is to be used for darts that are too short to be measured from high point shoulder. Be sure to indicate _____" measurement on spec sheet.]

B. *Center Front Bust Dart*—Measure from center front of garment straight across to top of dart.

C. *Side Seam Bust Dart*—Measure from underarm/side seam joining seam down along contour of side seam to bottom of dart.

D. *High Point Shoulder Princess Dart*—Measure from shoulder-neck joining seam straight down to top of dart.

E. *Center Front Princess Dart*—Measure from center front of garment straight across to top of dart.

F. *Center Front Skirt/Pant*—Measure from center front of garment at waistband joining seam/edge straight across to top of dart.

G. *Center Back Skirt/Pant*—Measure from center back of garment at waistband joining seam/edge straight across to top of dart.

CHAPTER 12 TERMS

When working with woven dresses, you may come across the garment terms listed below. If you are unfamiliar with any of them, please look up the definitions in the glossary at the end of this text.

Dress:
Basic A-line (shift)
Caftan
Coat
Safari
Sheath
Shirt (shirtdress)
Slip
Wedge
Wrap

SPEC SHEET	Woven dress	STYLE

SEASON:	DESCRIPTION:
LABEL: (SIZE CATEGORY)	
DATE:	

TECHNICAL SKETCH Basic/shift dress

SKETCH/PHOTO

CODE	POINT OF MEASURE	TOL. +/−	4	S/6	8	M/10	12	L/14	16	XL/18
1.	Front length	$1/2$								
2.	Center front length	$1/2$								
3.	Center back length	$1/2$								
4.	Side length	$1/4$								
10.	Chest width circumference	$1/2$-$3/4$								
13.	Across shoulder	$1/4$								
14.	Shoulder width	$1/8$								
15.	Across chest	$1/4$								
16.	Across back	$1/4$								
20.	Waist width circumference	$1/2$-$3/4$								
43.	Curved arm hole width circumference	$3/8$								
60.	Neck drop front	$1/8$								

(Tolerance $1/2$-$3/4$ S, M, L, XL = $3/4$" 4-18 = $1/2$")

The measured garment spec sheets are for *illustrative purposes only*
and should not be used as industry standards

CODE	POINT OF MEASURE	TOL. +/−	4	S/6	8	M/10	12	L/14	16	XL/18
61.	Neck drop back	$1/8$								
62.	Neck width, no collar	$1/4$								
91.	Hip width from H.P.S. circumference _____	$1/2\text{-}3/4$								
95.	Bottom opening sweep width circumference	$1/2\text{-}3/4$								
121.	Fly/zipper A. Length	$1/8$								
122.	Vent/slit A. Height	$1/4$								
	B. Width	$1/8$								
150.	Dart length	$1/8$								

COMMENTS:

The measured garment spec sheets are for *illustrative purposes only*
and should not be used as industry standards

SPEC SHEET	Woven dress	STYLE	
SEASON:	Summer	DESCRIPTION: Floral print shift with lace inset hem.	
LABEL: (SIZE CATEGORY) Missy			
DATE:			

TECHNICAL SKETCH   **Basic/shift dress**

SKETCH/PHOTO

CODE	POINT OF MEASURE	TOL. +/−	4	S/6	8	M/10	12	L/14	16	XL/18
1.	Front length	$1/2$			37					
2.	Center front length	$1/2$			30 3/4					
3.	Center back length	$1/2$			36 1/2					
4.	Side length	$1/4$			29 1/2					
10.	Chest width circumference	$1/2$-$3/4$			38					
13.	Across shoulder	$1/4$								
14.	Shoulder width	$1/8$			1 1/8					
15.	Across chest * 5" from HPS	$1/4$			13 1/2					
16.	Across back	$1/4$			35					
20.	Waist width circumference * 14" from HPS	$1/2$-$3/4$			20					
43.	Curved arm hole width circumference	$3/8$			7 1/2					
60.	Neck drop front	$1/8$			1 1/2					

(Tolerance $1/2$-$3/4$ S, M, L, XL = $3/4$" 4-18 = $1/2$")

The measured garment spec sheets are for *illustrative purposes only* and should not be used as industry standards

CODE	POINT OF MEASURE		TOL. +/−	4	S/6	8	M/10	12	L/14	16	XL/18
61.	Neck drop back		1/8			1¹/₂					
62.	Neck width, no collar		1/4			12					
91.	Hip width from H.P.S. circumference __21__ "		1/2-3/4			41					
95.	Bottom opening sweep width circumference		1/2-3/4			45					
121.	Fly/zipper A. Length		1/8			20					
122.	Vent/slit A. Height		1/4								
	B. Width		1/8								
150.	Dart length	Front bust	1/8			5					
		Front princess	1/8			10					
		Back princess	1/8			11¹/₂					
150.	Dart placement	A. H.P.S. To bust dart	1/8			9³/₄					
		D. H.P.S. To front princess	1/8			11					
		H.P.S. To back princess	1/8			9⁵/₈					
		E. C.F. To front princess	1/8			4					
		C.B. To back princess	1/8			4					
	Distance from hem To lace insert		1/8			1⁵/₈					

COMMENTS:

CHAPTER 13

Woven Jumpsuits and One-Piece Garments

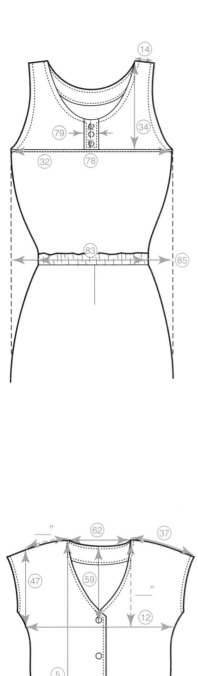

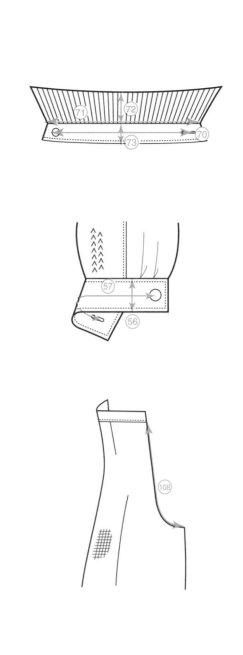

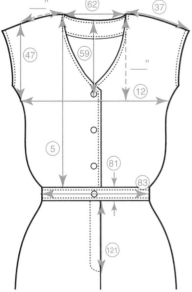

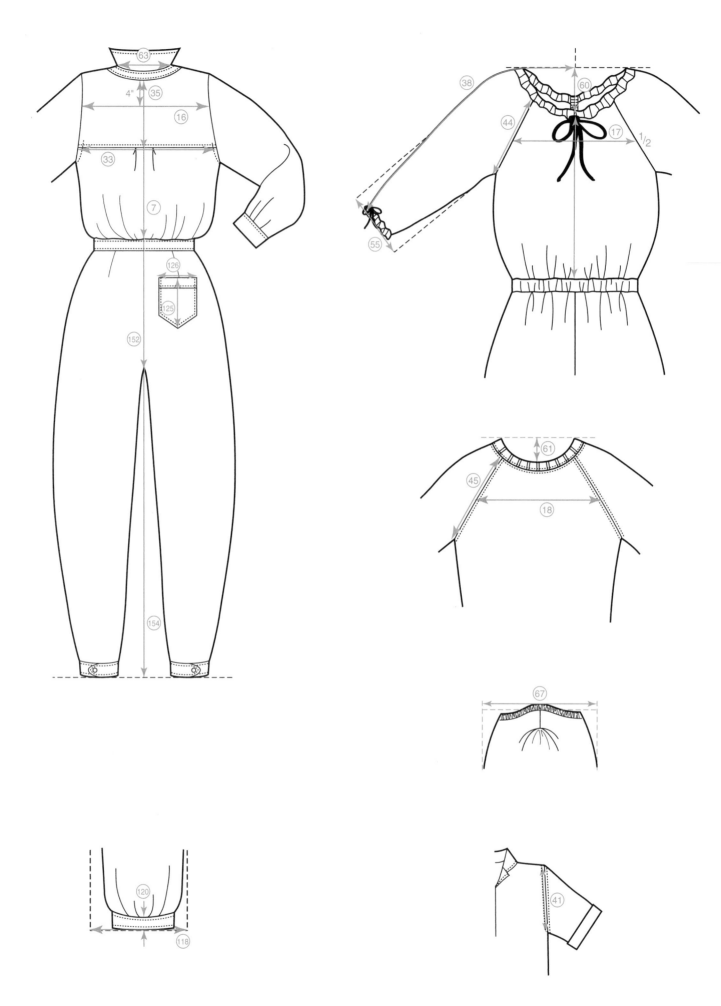

Measuring Woven Jumpsuits and One-Piece Garments

Overalls and safari-style jumpsuits are two of the most frequently specced missy garments in this category. This chapter is written for the missy market; however, the spec sheet provided can be easily adapted to any market. Measuring woven one-piece garments or jumpsuits basically combines the measurements of a woven blouse and a woven pant. Therefore, the rules you learned for each of those styles will be used here as well. You may want to look back over those chapters. The sketch below (Figure 13.1) shows that a jumpsuit can be measured from point 1, Front Length, from the high point shoulder to the bottom of the garment, or from point 151, Front Torso Length, from the high point shoulder to the crotch joining seam. Some technicians choose to use both measurements. As always, you will decide which measurement points work best for the style under evaluation.

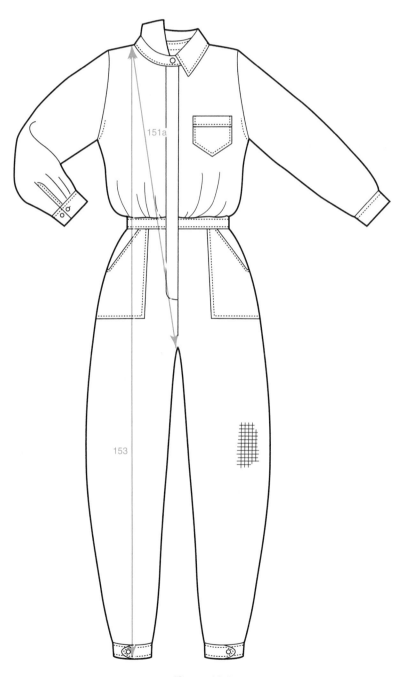

Figure 13.1

1. *Front Length (garments with a front opening)*—Measure from high point shoulder at neck straight down, parallel to center front, to bottom of garment at front. If garment has a collar, gently lift it away from shoulder-neck measuring point.

2. *Center Front Length (garments with a plain front; no front opening)*—Measure from center front neck joining seams straight down to bottom of garment at center front. [Note: A garment without a front opening may still require use of Front Length if neckline is unusual.]

3. *Center Back Length*—Measure from center back neck joining seams straight down to bottom of garment at center back. If needed, gently lift collar away from back neck to expose joining seam.

4. *Side Length*—Measure from bottom of armhole/side seam straight down to bottom of garment along side of garment. Do not follow natural curve of garment's side seam, unless otherwise indicated. If needed, gently lift sleeve away from armhole/side seam joining seam.

5. *Front Bodice Length (garments with a front opening)*—Measure from high point shoulder at neck straight down, parallel to center front, to top edge of waistband, joining seam, or rib. If garment has a collar, gently lift it away from shoulder-neck measuring point.

6. *Center Front Bodice Length (garments with a plain front; no front opening)*—Measure from center front neck joining seam straight down to top edge of waistband, joining seam, or rib. [Note: A garment without a center opening may still require use of Front Bodice Length if neckline is unusual.]

7. *Center Back Bodice Length*—Measure from center back neck joining seams straight down to top edge of waistband, joining seam, or rib. If needed, gently lift collar away from back neck to expose joining seam.

8. *Side Seam Bodice Length*—Measure from bottom of armhole/side seam straight down to top edge of waistband, joining seam, or rib, along side of garment, following natural curve of garment's side seam, unless otherwise indicated. If needed, gently lift sleeve away from armhole/side seam joining seam. [Note: You can take side seam bodice measurement straight rather than contoured if joining seam/rib can be extended, but indicate change on spec sheet.]

10. *Chest Width Circumference (woven)*—Measure from edge of garment/side seam to edge of garment/side seam straight across garment at a point 1" below armhole. Double this measurement.

11. *Chest Width (raglan sleeve, knit)*—Measure from edge of garment/side seam to edge of garment/side seam straight across garment at a point _____" below high point shoulder. [Note: You will have to determine number of inches down from high point shoulder for each raglan sleeve style based on depth of sleeve. Then indicate this number on spec sheet.]

12. *Chest Width Circumference (raglan sleeve, woven)*—Measure from edge of garment/side seam to edge of garment/side seam straight across garment at a point _____" below high point shoulder. Double this measurement. [Note: You will have to determine number of inches down from high point shoulder for each raglan sleeve style based on depth of sleeve. Then indicate this number on spec sheet.]

13. *Across Shoulder*—Measure straight across front from armhole seam/edge to armhole seam/edge at shoulder seam or across natural shoulder fold line created if there is no seam.

14. *Shoulder Width*—Measure from neckband/collar/ribbing joining seam or neckline edge to top of armhole seam at shoulder, taken along shoulder seam or across natural shoulder fold line created if there is no seam.

15. *Across Chest*—Measure $2\frac{1}{2}$" down from collar/rib joining seam at center front straight across front of

garment from armhole seam/edge to armhole seam/edge. [Note: The $2\frac{1}{2}$" measurement point is for missy-wear only and may need to be adjusted up or down $\frac{1}{4}$" to $\frac{1}{2}$" accordingly for men's, children's, junior's, and large/plus womenswear. Indicate any changes on spec sheet.]

16. *Across Back*—Measure 4" down from collar/rib joining seam at center back straight across back of garment from armhole seam/edge to armhole seam/edge. [Note: The 4" measurement point is for missy-wear only and may need to be adjusted up or down $\frac{1}{4}$" to $\frac{1}{2}$" accordingly for men's, children's, junior's, and large/plus womenswear. Indicate any changes on the spec sheet.]

17. *Across Chest/Center Armhole*—Measure at one-half depth of armhole straight across front of garment from armhole seam/edge to armhole seam/edge.

18. *Across Back/Center Armhole*—Measure at one-half depth of armhole straight across back of garment from armhole seam/edge to armhole seam/edge.

20. *Waist Width Circumference (woven)*—Measure from edge of garment/side seam to edge of garment/side seam straight across garment on seam or at narrowest point of waist taper at a point _____" below high point shoulder. Double this measurement. [Note: You will have to determine number of inches down from high point shoulder for each raglan sleeve style based on depth of sleeve. Then indicate this number on spec sheet.]

32. *Yoke Width Front*—Measure from armhole seam/edge to armhole seam/edge straight across front of garment, ignoring contours or points, at yoke-body joining seams. [Note: If yoke is asymmetrical, indicate changes in measuring as needed on spec sheet.]

33. *Yoke Width Back*—Measure from armhole seam/edge to armhole seam/edge straight across back of garment, ignoring contours or points, at yoke-body joining seams. [Note: If yoke is asymmetrical, indicate changes in measuring as needed on spec sheet.]

34. *Yoke Depth Front*—Measure from high point shoulder at neck straight down to bottom of front yoke-body joining seam. Be sure to gently lift collar away from shoulder-neck joining seam if needed.

35. *Yoke Back Depth*—Measure from center back neck joining seam straight down to bottom of back yoke-body joining seam. Gently lift collar away from back neck joining seam if needed.

36. *Sleeve Length Top Armhole*—Measure along top of sleeve/fold, following contour of sleeve from armhole seam at shoulder to bottom of sleeve opening, including cuff.

37. *Sleeve Length Top Neck*—Measure along top of sleeve/fold, following contour of sleeve from sleeve-neck joining seam/edge to edge of sleeve opening, including cuff. Gently lift collar at sleeve-neck joining seam if needed.

38. *Sleeve Length Center Back*—Measure from center back neck joining seam or from a point above neck at an imaginary line, that of a joining seam, along top of sleeve/fold, following contour of sleeve to edge of sleeve opening, including cuff.

39. *Sleeve Length Underarm*—Measure straight from bottom of armhole along sleeve seam to edge of sleeve opening, including cuff.

41. *Straight Armhole Width Circumference (woven)*—Measure from top of shoulder joining seam/edge straight down to bottom of armhole. Double this measurement.

43. *Curved Armhole Width Circumference (woven)*—Measure from top of shoulder joining seam/edge to bottom of armhole, following contour of armhole. Double this measurement.

44. *Armhole Front*—Measure on front of garment from top of shoulder at neckline joining seam/edge to bottom of armhole, following contour of armhole. Gently lift collar away from neckline joining seam if needed.

45. *Armhole Back*—Measure on back of garment from top of shoulder at neck joining seam/edge to bottom of armhole, following contour of armhole. Gently lift collar away from neck joining seam if needed.

47. *Armhole Width Circumference Straight (woven)*—Measure from top of shoulder seam at a point _____" below neckline joining seam/edge straight down to bottom of armhole. Double this measurement. [Note: Gently move collar away from neck joining seam if needed when measuring down _____" to armhole start point. Indicate the number of inches measured down on spec sheet.]

49. *Muscle Width Circumference (woven)*—Measure from inner sleeve edge/seam to outer sleeve edge/fold at a point 1" below armhole and parallel to sleeve opening. Double this measurement.

51. *Elbow Width Circumference (woven)*—Measure from inner sleeve edge/seam to outer sleeve edge/fold straight across sleeve at a point one-half of underarm sleeve length and parallel to sleeve opening at wrist or cuff. Double this measurement. [Note: If sleeve is three-quarter length, indicate new point of measure on spec sheet.]

53. *Sleeve Opening Width Circumference (woven)*—Measure from inner sleeve edge/seam to outer sleeve edge/fold straight across bottom edge of sleeve opening. Double this measurement.

55. *Sleeve Opening Width Circumference, Stretched (woven)*—Measure from inner sleeve edge/seam to outer sleeve edge/fold straight across bottom edge of sleeve opening in a fully extended position. Double this measurement.

56. *Cuff Length Sleeve*—Measure from outside end of buttonhole to center of button straight along center of cuff. Open cuff out as flat as possible when measuring. [Note: If cuff length is contoured, measure along center-most point.]

57. *Cuff/Ribbing Height Sleeve*—Measure from cuff joining seam or top of ribbing straight down to bottom edge of cuff or rib opening. [Note: If cuff is contoured, indicate changes made as needed to measurement on spec sheet.]

58. *Neck Depth Front (garments with a plain front/asymmetrical front opening)*—Measure from center back neck joining seam/edge straight down to center front neck joining seam/edge.

59. *Neck Depth Center Front (garments with a center front opening)*—Measure from center back neck joining seam/edge straight down to center of first button at center front of garment.

60. *Neck Drop Front*—Measure from an imaginary line connecting neckline edges straight down to center front neck opening edge. Use a ruler if needed to connect top neckline edges.

61. *Neck Drop Back*—Measure from an imaginary line connecting neckline edges straight down to center back neck opening edge. This measurement is taken with front of garment facing up. Use a ruler to connect top neckline edges if needed.

62. *Neck Width, No Collar*—Measure from inside neck edge/seam to inside neck edge/seam straight across back neck at widest point. This measurement is taken with front of garment faceup.

63. *Neck Width, Collar*—Measure straight across back neck from neck-shoulder joining seam to neck-shoulder joining seam or natural shoulder line if no seam. This measurement is taken with back of garment faceup.

65. *Neck Edge Width Circumference (woven)*—Measure from neck edge/seam/fold to neck edge/seam/fold along top opening edge, following natural contour of neck opening. Garment should be positioned with one shoulder on top of the other and with front and back neck edges meeting. Double this measurement.

67. *Neck Edge Width Circumference, Stretched (woven)*—Measure from neck edge/seam/fold to neck edge/seam/fold along top opening edge in a fully extended position. Garment should be positioned with one shoulder on top of the other and with front and back neck edges meeting. Double this measurement.

69. *Neck Base Circumference (woven)*—Measure from neck edge/seam to neck edge/seam along collar/rib joining seam or neckline edge, following natural contour of neck opening. Garment should be buttoned or zippered, if applicable, with one shoulder seam positioned on top of the other and with front and back neck edges meeting. Double this measurement.

70. *Neckband Length*—Measure from outside end of buttonhole to center of buttonhole across neckband, following contour of neckband.

71. *Collar Length*—Measure from one end of collar to other end of collar along neck joining seam.

72. *Collar Height*—Measure from collar/rib joining seam at center back neck straight up to outer edge of collar/rib.

73. *Collar Band Height*—Measure from collar joining seam at center back straight up to neckband joining seam at center back.

74. *Collar Point Length*—Measure from collar joining seam to outer edge of collar along collar point edge. [Note: If collar is rounded, measure at a point parallel to center back and indicate change on spec sheet.]

75. *Collar Point Spread (pointed collars only)*—Measure, with collar band buttoned and collar in place, from collar point straight across collar edge to collar point.

76. *Lapel Width*
A. *Notched*—Measure from lower lapel notch straight across to lapel fold at a point perpendicular to garment center front.
B. *Without Notches*—Measure from lapel edge straight across widest point of lapel to lapel fold at a point _____" down from center back collar joining seam and perpendicular to front of garment.

77. *Center Front Extension*—Measure from an imaginary line at center front of garment horizontally to finished outer edge of front extended piece.

78. *Placket Length*—Measure from top edge of placket straight down to bottom of placket opening along center of placket.

79. *Placket Width*—Measure from placket joining seam straight across placket to placket edge at fold.

80. *Keyhole Length*—Measure from outer edge of neckline straight down to bottom of keyhole opening.

81. *Waistband Depth*—Measure from top of waistband edge straight down to bottom of waistband at waistband joining seam. [Note: If waistband is contoured, indicate measurement change on spec sheet.]

83. *Waistband Circumference (woven)*—Measure from side of bottom band to side of bottom band along center of band, following natural contour of waistband. Double this measurement.

85. *Waistband Width Circumference, Stretched (woven)*—Measure from side of bottom band to side of bottom band straight across center of band in a fully extended position. Double this measurement.

87. *High Hip Width Circumference (woven)*—Measure from edge of garment/side seam to edge of garment/side seam at a point 4" below bottom edge of waistband/seam, following contour of waist. Double this measurement. [Note: The 4" point is for missywear only; adjust as needed $\frac{1}{2}$" to 1" up or down for children's, petite's, junior's, or large/plus womenswear. Indicate change on spec sheet.]

89. *Low Hip Width Circumference from Waist (woven)*—Measure from edge of garment/side seam to edge of garment/side seam at a point 7" below bottom edge of waistband/seam, following contour of waist. Double this measurement. [Note: The 7" point is for missywear only; adjust as needed $\frac{1}{2}$" to 1" up or down for children's, petite's, junior's, or large/plus womenswear. Indicate change on spec sheet.]

91. *Hip Width from High Point Shoulder Circumference (woven)*—Measure from edge of garment/side seam to edge of garment/side seam straight across at a point _____" below high point shoulder. Double this measurement. [Note: You will have to estimate low hip point on garment if there is no waistband and fill in _____" from high point shoulder. This measurement will vary from children's, junior's, missy, and large/plus womenswear.]

93. *Hip Seat Width Circumference (woven pant)*—Measure from edge of garment/side seam to edge of garment/side seam at a point _____" up from crotch seam, following contour of waist. Double this measurement. [Note 1: This measurement is useful when the waistband sits below the natural waistline. Note 2: Adjust the _____" up from crotch as needed for junior's and large/plus womenswear. Note 3: A hip seat width of $2\frac{1}{2}$" up for children's and 3" up for menswear can take place of low hip width.]

103. *Skirt/Pant Yoke Depth Front*—Measure from bottom of waistband/seam (top edge if not banded or stitching if self-elastic/drawstring casing) straight down to bottom of yoke joining seam at center front.

[Note: If yoke is contoured, indicate point of measure on spec sheet.]

104. *Skirt/Pant Yoke Depth Back*—Measure from bottom of waistband/seam (top edge if not banded or stitching if self-elastic/drawstring casing) straight down to bottom of yoke joining seam at center back. [Note: If yoke is contoured, indicate point of measure on spec sheet.]

105. *Inseam*—Measure from crotch joining seam to bottom of leg opening, following inseam/inner fold.

106. *Outseam*—Measure from bottom edge of waistband/seam (top edge if not banded or stitching if self-elastic/drawstring casing) to bottom of garment along side seam/fold of garment.

107. *Front Rise*—Measure from bottom edge of waistband/seam (top edge if not banded or stitching if self-elastic/drawstring casing) to crotch joining seam, following curve of front rise seam. [Note: Measure over zipper if in front rise seam.]

108. *Back Rise*—Measure from bottom edge of waistband/seam (top edge if not banded or stitching if self-elastic/drawstring casing) to crotch joining seam, following curve of back rise seam. [Note: Measure over zipper if in front back seam.]

110. *Thigh Width Circumference (woven)*—Measure from pant leg edge/seam to pant leg edge/seam straight across pant leg at a point 1" below crotch and parallel to leg opening. Double this measurement. [Note: If leg opening is asymmetrical, measure to a point that would be parallel to leg opening.]

112. *Knee Width Circumference (woven)*—Measure from pant leg edge/seam to pant leg edge/seam at a point one-half of the inseam and parallel to leg opening. Double this measurement. [Note 1: If leg opening is asymmetrical, measure to a point that would be parallel to leg opening. Note 2: If pant leg is three-

quarter length, indicate point of measure on spec sheet. Note 3: A general knee measurement from crotch seam of missy 12", junior's 11", large/plus women's 13" can be used. Indicated change on spec sheet. Measure children's at one-half inseam minus $1\frac{1}{2}$", and for men's minus 2".]

114. *Leg Opening Width Circumference (woven)*— Measure from pant leg edge/seam to pant leg edge/seam straight across bottom edge of leg opening. Double this measurement. [Note: If leg opening is contoured, follow contour and indicate measurement change on spec sheet.]

116. *Vented Leg Opening Circumference (woven)*— Measure from pant leg edge/seam to pant leg edge/seam straight across pant leg at top of side vents. Double this measurement.

118. *Leg Opening Width Circumference, Stretched (woven)*—Measure from pant leg edge/seam to pant leg edge/seam straight across bottom edge of leg opening in a fully extended position. Double this measurement.

119. *Cuff Height Pants*—Measure from top of cuff edge straight down to bottom of cuff fold and leg opening.

120. *Bottom Band/Ribbing Height Pants*—Measure from cuff joining seam or top of ribbing straight down to bottom edge of cuff or rib opening. [Note: For fashion-forward pants, you may want to include a cuff width. See point of measure 56, Cuff Length Sleeve, for measuring instructions and indicate cuff width pant as needed on spec sheet.]

121. *Fly/Zipper*
A. *Length*—Measure from top of fly/zipper opening straight down to bottom of fly/zipper opening at zipper stop or bar tack.
B. *Fly/Zipper Width*—Measure top of fly/zipper at joining seam from edge/fold straight across to fly/zipper placket stitching.

122. *Vent/Slit*
A. *Height*—Measure from top of vent/slit straight down to bottom of vent/slit along edge of vent/slit.
B. *Width*—Measure top of vent/slit from edge/fold straight across to vent/slit placket stitching at a point parallel to garment hemline.

123. *Pleat Depth*—Measure from outer edge of pleat at fold/crease to inner fold of pleat. [Note 1: It is a good idea to indicate what type of pleat is being measured, e.g., box, inverted, knife, kick, kilt, or envelope. Note 2: If pleats are not parallel or symmetrical, indicate any special instructions on spec sheet.]

124. *Distance Between Pleats*—Measure from start of pleat to start of pleat, excluding pleat depth at a point directly below pleat joining seam. [Note: If pleats are not parallel or symmetrical, indicate any special instructions on spec sheet.]

125. *Applied Pocket Height*—Measure from top edge of pocket to bottom edge of pocket along center of pocket. [Note: For contoured or irregularly shaped pockets, take a second measurement and indicate point of measure on spec sheet.]

126. *Applied Pocket Width*—Measure from side of pocket to side of pocket along top edge of pocket. [Note: For contoured or irregularly shaped pockets, take a second measurement and indicate point of measure on spec sheet.]

127. *Pocket Opening within a Seam*—Measure from top of pocket to bottom of pocket along edge of pocket opening.

128. *Belt Length*
A. *Total*—Measure from end of belt at buckle along center of belt to opposite end of belt, following contour.
B. *Circumference*—Measure from end of belt at buckle along center of belt to middle hole at opposite end.

129. *Belt Width (or Height)*—Measure from edge of belt straight across to edge of belt. [Note: If belt is contoured, indicate points of measure on spec sheet.]

130. *Belt Loop Length*—Measure from top of belt loop straight down/vertically to bottom of belt loop along center of belt loop. [Note: Fashion-forward or irregularly shaped belt loops may require further spec instructions. Indicate points of measure on spec sheet.]

131. *Belt Loop Width*—Measure belt loop from edge of belt loop straight across/horizontally to edge of belt loop. [Note: Fashion-forward or irregularly shaped belt loops may require further spec instructions. Indicate points of measure on spec sheet.]

132. *Tie Length*—Measure from end of tie/joining seam straight down to tie end along center of tie.

133. *Tie Width*
A. *Straight*—Measure from edge of tie straight across to edge of tie.
B. *Contoured*—Measure from edge of tie straight across to edge of tie at widest point of tie.

134. *Flounce/Ruffle Width*—Measure from flounce/ruffle joining seam straight across to outer edge of flounce/ruffle. [Note: If flounce/ruffle is contoured, measure along narrowest and widest points if possible and indicate changes on spec sheet.]

135. *Strap Length*—Measure from strap joining seam along center of strap to end of strap. [Note: If a strap is contoured or has a contoured edge, measure along center, approximating center end point, or indicate instructions as needed on spec sheet.]

136. *Strap Width*—Measure from edge of strap straight across to edge of strap. [Note: If strap is contoured, measure along narrowest and widest points if possible and indicate changes on spec sheet.]

137. *Front Hood Length*—Measure from top of hood to bottom of hood at center front joining seam along opening edge of hood.

138. *Back Hood Length*—Measure from top of hood at center front to bottom of hood at center back joining seam along outside curve of hood fold/seam.

139. *Hood Width*—Measure from front opening edge of hood straight across to back of hood along widest point of hood.

140. *Flange Depth*—Measure from center back neck joining seam straight down to bottom of flange at center back. [Note: If flange is contoured or asymmetrical, indicate point of measure on spec sheet.]

141. *Shoulder Pad Length*—Measure from edge of pad straight across to edge of pad along center of pad or natural shoulder line of pad.

142. *Shoulder Pad Width*—Measure from side of pad straight across to side of pad along edge of pad if straight or at widest point of pad if curved.

143. *Straight Edge Shoulder Pad Height*—Measure from top of pad straight down to bottom of pad along center of pad.

144. *Curved Edge Shoulder Pad Height*—Stick a one-inch straight pin into the thickest part of shoulder pad. Push pin all way through pad until head of pin rests on top of pad. Be sure not to crush pad. Measure portion of pin sticking out of pad. Subtract this figure from one inch (length of pin) to get shoulder pad height.

145. *Shoulder Pad Placement*—Measure from neck edge or joining seam straight across shoulder seam or natural shoulder line to start of shoulder pad.

146. *Pleats Placement*
A. *Front Pleat Top*—Measure distance from center front of garment straight across to start of first

pleat at a point parallel to garment hem. [Note: You may need to use armhole or side seam as a starting point if there is no center front seam or placket.]

B. *Back Pleat Top*—Measure distance from armhole seam/side seam (depending on pleat placement) to first pleat at a point parallel to garment hem.

C. *Front Pleat Skirt/Pant*—Measure distance from center front of garment waistband joining seam/ edge straight across to start of first pleat.

D. *Back Pleat Skirt*—Measure distance from center back of garment waistband joining seam/edge straight across to start of first pleat.

147. *Button Placement*—Refer to measurement point 59, Neck Depth Center Front, for placement of first button. Then measure distance of first button to second button. Be sure when measuring that button at bust point is lined up to apex of bust. Adjust all buttons accordingly and respace as needed.

148. *Pocket Placement*

A. *Top Pocket Vertical*—Measure from shoulder-neck joining seam straight down to top edge of pocket.

B. *Top Pocket Horizontal*—Measure from center front straight across to side of pocket at top edge.

C. *Front Bottom Pocket Vertical*—Measure from waistband/joining seam/edge straight down to top edge of pocket.

D. *Front Bottom Pocket Horizontal*—Measure from center front straight across to side of pocket at top edge.

E. *Back Bottom Pocket Vertical*—Measure from waistband/joining seam/edge straight down to top edge of pocket.

F. *Back Bottom Pocket Horizontal*—Measure from center back straight across to side of pocket at top edge.

G. *Pocket from Side Seam*—Measure from side seam straight across to top of pocket. [Note: If pocket is contoured at sides, a top and bottom pocket size and placement must be measured and added to spec sheet.]

149. *Belt Loop Placement*

A. *Front*—Measure from center front of garment horizontally across to center of first front belt loop.

B. *Back*—Measure from center back of garment horizontally across to center of first back belt loop.

C. *Side Seam to Front*—Measure from center of side seam belt loop to center of front belt loop.

D. *Side Seam to Back*—Measure from center of side seam belt loop to center of back belt loop.

150. *Dart Placement*

A. *High Point Shoulder Bust Dart*—Measure from shoulder-neck joining seam or at a point _____" from shoulder-neck seam straight down, parallel to center front, to top of dart. [Note: The _____" from shoulder seam measurement is to be used for darts that are too short to be measured from high point shoulder. Be sure to indicate _____" measurement on spec sheet.]

B. *Center Front Bust Dart*—Measure from center front of garment straight across to top of dart.

C. *Side Seam Bust Dart*—Measure from underarm/ side seam joining seam down along contour of side seam to bottom of dart.

D. *High Point Shoulder Princess Dart*—Measure from shoulder-neck joining seam straight down to top of dart.

E. *Center Front Princess Dart*—Measure from center front of garment straight across to top of dart.

F. *Center Front Skirt/Pant*—Measure from the center front of the garment at waistband joining seam/edge straight across to top of dart.

G. *Center Back Skirt/Pant*—Measure from center back of garment at waistband joining seam/edge straight across to top of dart.

151. *Front Torso Length (Jumpsuits and One-Piece Garments)*

A. *Garments with a Front Opening, Relaxed*—Measure from high point shoulder at neck straight down to crotch joining seam with garment in a relaxed position.

B. *Garments with a Front Opening, Extended*—Measure from high point shoulder at neck straight down to crotch joining seam with garment in a fully extended position.

C. *Garments with a Plain Front, No Front Opening, Relaxed*—Measure from center front neck joining seam straight down to crotch joining seam with garment in a relaxed position.

D. *Garments with a Plain Front, No Front Opening, Extended*—Measure from center front neck joining seam straight down to crotch joining seam with garment in a fully extended position.

152. *Back Torso Length (Jumpsuits and One-Piece Garments)*

A. *Relaxed*—Measure from center back neck joining seam straight down to crotch joining seam with garment in a relaxed position.

B. *Extended*—Measure from center back neck joining seam straight down to crotch joining seam with garment in a fully extended position.

153. *High Point Shoulder Length (Jumpsuits and One-Piece Garments)*—Measure from high point shoulder straight down to bottom/hem of garment.

154. *Center Back Garment Length (Jumpsuits and One-Piece Garments)*—Measure from center back neckline seam/edge, straight down to bottom hem of garment. [Note: For pant suits this point will intersect at an imaginary line formed by hemlines of pant legs and the center of garment.]

155. *Crotch Width*—Measure straight across crotch from side to side along seam/bottom edge/fold.

CHAPTER 13 TERMS

When working with woven jumpsuits and one-piece garmets, you may come cross the garment terms listed below. If you are unfamiliar with any of them, please look up the definitions in the glossary at the end of this text.

Bib overalls
Body shirt
Jumpsuit
Overalls
Pant jumper

SPEC SHEET: One-piece woven jumpsuit

STYLE

SEASON:	DESCRIPTION:
LABEL: (SIZE CATEGORY)	
DATE:	

TECHNICAL SKETCH

SKETCH/PHOTO

CODE	POINT OF MEASURE	TOL. +/–	4	S/6	8	M/10	12	L/14	16	XL/18
5.	Front bodice length	3/8								
6.	Center front bodice length	3/8								
7.	Center back bodice length	3/8								
8.	Side seam bodice length	3/8								
10.	Chest width circumference	1/2-3/4								
13.	Across shoulder	1/4								
15.	Across chest	1/4								
16.	Across back	1/4								
32.	Yoke width front	1/4								
33.	Yoke width back	1/4								
34.	Yoke depth front	1/8								
35.	Yoke depth back	1/8								

(Tolerance 1/2-3/4 S, M, L, XL = 3/4" 4-18 = 1/2")

The measured garment spec sheets are for ***illustrative purposes only*** and should not be used as industry standards

CODE	POINT OF MEASURE	TOL. +/−	4	S/6	8	M/10	12	L/14	16	XL/18
36.	Sleeve length top armhole	$3/8$								
39.	Sleeve length underarm	$3/8$								
43.	Curved armhole width circumference	$3/8$								
49.	Muscle width circumference	$1/4$								
51.	Elbow width circumference	$1/4$								
53.	Sleeve opening width circumference	$1/4$								
56.	Cuff length sleeve	$1/4$								
57.	Cuff/ribbing height sleeve	$1/8$								
58.	Neck depth front	$1/8$								
63.	Neck width collar	$1/4$								
70.	Neckband length	$1/4$								
71.	Collar length	$1/4$								
72.	Collar height	$1/8$								
73.	Collar band height	$1/8$								
74.	Collar point length	$1/8$								
75.	Collar point spread	$1/4$								
81.	Waistband depth	$1/8$								
83.	Waistband circumference	$1/2$-$3/4$								
85.	Waistband width circumference stretched	$1/2$-$3/4$								
87.	High hip width circumference	$1/2$-$3/4$								
89.	Low hip width circumference	$1/2$-$3/4$								
105.	Inseam	$3/8$								
106.	Outseam	$3/8$								
107.	Front rise	$3/8$								
108.	Back rise	$3/8$								
110.	Thigh width circumference	$3/8$								
112.	Knee width circumference	$3/8$								
114.	Leg opening width circumference	$1/8$								
121.	Fly/zipper A. Length	$1/4$								
	B. Width	$1/8$								
125.	Applied pocket height	$1/8$								

COMMENTS:

The measured garment spec sheets are for *illustrative purposes only* and should not be used as industry standards

CODE	POINT OF MEASURE	TOL. +/−	4	S/6	8	M/10	12	L/14	16	XL/18
126.	Applied pocket width	$1/8$								
127.	Pocket opening	$1/8$								
151.	Front torso length A. Front opening relaxed	$1/2$								
152.	Back torso length	$1/2$								
153.	Total garment length front	$3/4$								
154.	Total garment length back	$3/4$								

COMMENTS:

One-piece woven jumpsuit   **STYLE**

SEASON:	Spring/summer

DESCRIPTION: One-piece madris plaid bathing suit cover-up with contrast piping and back elastic waist

LABEL: (SIZE CATEGORY)	Missy

DATE:	

TECHNICAL SKETCH

SKETCH/PHOTO

CODE	POINT OF MEASURE	TOL. +/–	4	S/6	8	M/10	12	L/14	16	XL/18
5.	Front bodice length	3/8				16½				
6.	Center front bodice length	3/8				10½				
7.	Center back bodice length	3/8				15				
8.	Side seam bodice length	3/8				8½				
10.	Chest width circumference	1/2-3/4				38				
13.	Across shoulder	1/4				14				
15.	Across chest 5" from HPS	1/4				13½				
16.	Across back	1/4				13				
32.	Yoke width front	1/4								
33.	Yoke width back	1/4								
34.	Yoke depth front	1/8								
35.	Yoke depth back	1/8								

(Tolerance 1/2-3/4 S, M, L, XL = 3/4" 4-18 = 1/2")

The measured garment spec sheets are for *illustrative purposes only* and should not be used as industry standards

CODE	POINT OF MEASURE	TOL. +/−	4	S/6	8	M/10	12	L/14	16	XL/18
36.	Sleeve length top armhole	3/8				8				
39.	Sleeve length underarm	3/8				3				
43.	Curved armhole width circumference	3/8				19				
49.	Muscle width circumference	1/4				15				
51.	Elbow width circumference	1/4								
53.	Sleeve opening width circumference	1/4				14				
56.	Cuff length sleeve	1/4								
57.	Cuff/ribbing height sleeve	1/8								
58.	Neck depth front	1/8								
63.	Neck width collar	1/4								
70.	Neckband length	1/4								
71.	Collar length	1/4								
72.	Collar height	1/8								
73.	Collar band height	1/8								
74.	Collar point length	1/8								
75.	Collar point spread	1/4								
81.	Waistband depth	1/8								
83.	Waistband circumference	1/2-3/4				30				
85.	Waistband width circumference stretched	1/2-3/4				35				
87.	High hip width circumference	1/2-3/4				40				
89.	Low hip width circumference	1/2-3/4				43				
105.	Inseam	3/8				6				
106.	Outseam	3/8				17				
107.	Front rise	3/8				12½				
108.	Back rise	3/8				15				
110.	Thigh width circumference	3/8				27				
112.	Knee width circumference	3/8								
114.	Leg opening width circumference	1/8				25				
121.	Fly/zipper A. Length	1/4								
	B. Width	1/8								
125.	Applied pocket height	1/8								

COMMENTS:

The measured garment spec sheets are for *illustrative purposes only* and should not be used as industry standards

CODE	POINT OF MEASURE	TOL. +/−	4	S/6	8	M/10	12	L/14	16	XL/18
126.	Applied pocket width	1/8								
127.	Pocket opening	1/8				7				
151.	Front torso length A. Front opening relaxed	1/2				30 1/4				
152.	Back torso length Straight, do not follow curve	1/2				31				
153.	Total garment length front	3/4				35				
154.	Total garment length back	3/4				33 1/2				
60.	Neck drop front	1/8				6				
61.	Neck drop back	1/8				1 3/4				
62	Neck width, no collar	1/4				7 1/2				
78.	Placket length	1/4				20				
79.	Placket width	1/8				1 1/2				
150.	Dart length front princess	1/8				4 1/2				
150.	Dart placement E.C.F. to princess	1/8				4				
	Piping width	–				1/8				

COMMENTS:

The measured garment spec sheets are for *illustrative purposes only*
and should not be used as industry standards

CHAPTER 14

Blazers and Unconstructed Jackets

207

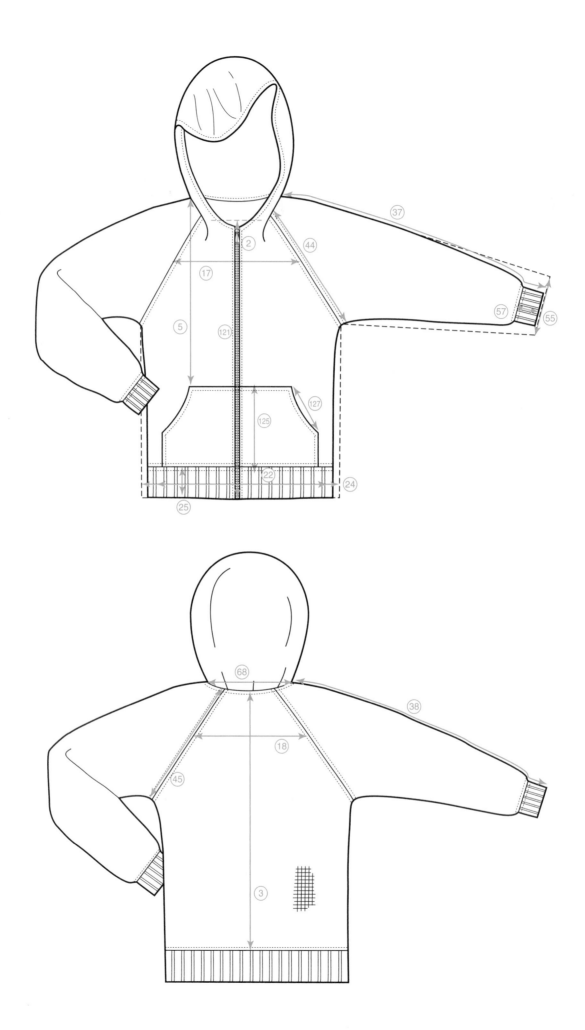

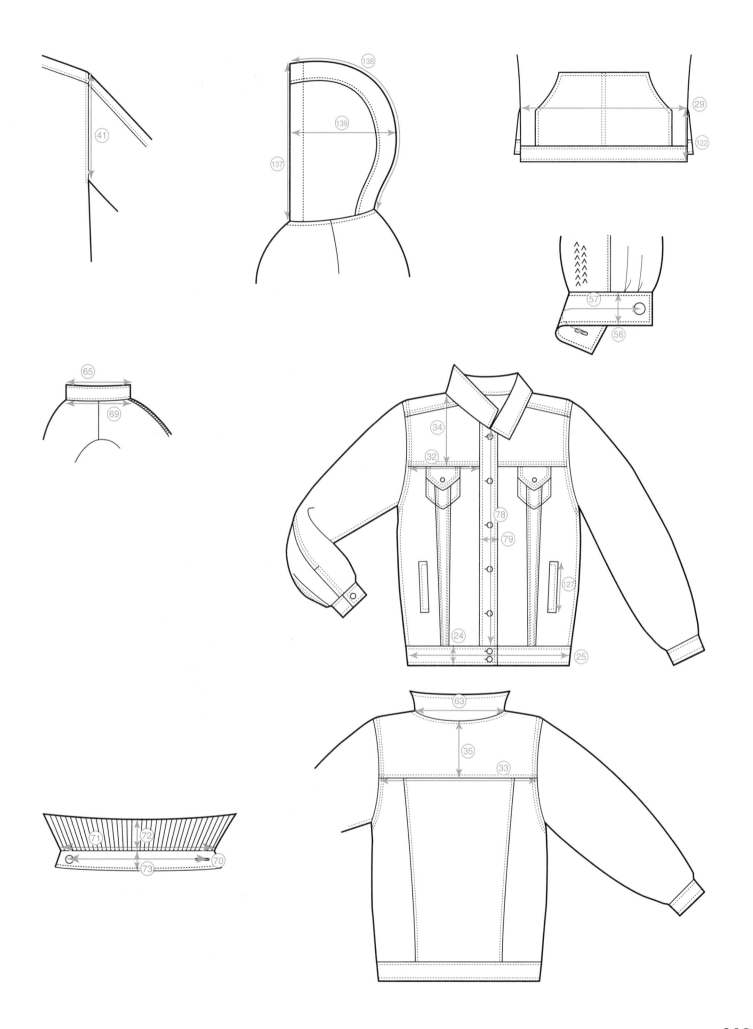

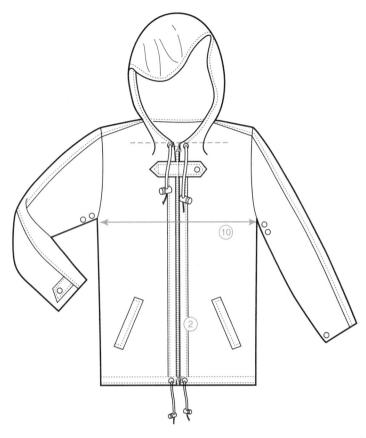

Figure 14.1

Measuring Blazers and Unconstructed Jackets

Blazers and unconstructed jackets, either knitted or woven, are treated as wovens when measuring due to garment construction. Unconstructed knitted jackets are either classified as jackets (Figure 14.1), thus using this category, or as cardigans, therefore using the knit top category.

[Note: Measurement points that previously read "woven top" will read "woven top/jacket" in this section only.]

1. *Front Length (garments with a front opening)*—Measure from high point shoulder at neck straight down, parallel to center front, to the bottom of garment at front. If the garment has a collar, gently lift it away from the shoulder-neck measuring point.

2. *Center Front Length (garments with a plain front; no front opening)*—Measure from center front neck joining seams straight down to bottom of garment at center front. [Note: A garment without a front opening may still require use of Front Length if neckline is unusual.]

3. *Center Back Length*—Measure from center back neck joining seams straight down to bottom of garment at center back. If needed, gently lift collar away from back neck to expose joining seam.

4. *Side Length*—Measure from bottom of armhole/side seam straight down to bottom of garment along side of garment. Do not follow natural curve of garment's side seam, unless otherwise indicated. If needed, gently lift the sleeve away from armhole/side seam joining seam.

5. *Front Bodice Length (garments with a front opening)*—Measure from high point shoulder at neck straight down, parallel to center front, to top edge of waistband, joining seam, or rib. If garment has a collar, gently lift it away from shoulder-neck measuring point.

6. *Center Front Bodice Length (garments with a plain front; no front opening)*—Measure from center front neck joining seam straight down to top edge of waistband, joining seam, or rib. [Note: A garment without a center opening may still require use of Front Bodice Length if neckline is unusual.]

7. *Center Back Bodice Length*—Measure from center back neck joining seams straight down to top edge of waistband, joining seam, or rib. If needed, gently lift collar away from back neck to expose joining seam.

8. *Side Seam Bodice Length*—Measure from bottom of armhole/side seam straight down to top edge of waistband, joining seam, or rib, along side of garment, following natural curve of garment's side seam, unless otherwise indicated. If needed, gently lift sleeve away from armhole/side seam joining seam. [Note: You can take side seam bodice measurement straight rather than contoured if joining seam/rib can be extended, but indicate change on spec sheet.]

10. *Chest Width Circumference (woven)*—Measure from edge of garment/side seam to edge of garment/side seam straight across garment at a point 1" below armhole. Double this measurement.

12. *Chest Width Circumference (raglan sleeve, woven)*—Measure from edge of garment/side seam to edge of garment/side seam straight across garment at a point _____" below high point shoulder. Double this measurement. [Note: You will have to determine number of inches down from high point shoulder for each raglan sleeve style based on depth of sleeve. Then indicate this number on spec sheet.]

13. *Across Shoulder*—Measure straight across front from armhole seam/edge to armhole seam/edge at shoulder seam or across natural shoulder fold line created if there is no seam.

14. *Shoulder Width*—Measure from neckband/collar/ribbing joining seam or neckline edge to top of armhole seam at shoulder, taken along shoulder seam or across natural shoulder fold line created if there is no seam.

15. *Across Chest*—Measure $2\frac{1}{2}$" down from collar/rib joining seam at center front straight across front of garment from armhole seam/edge to armhole seam/edge. [Note: The $2\frac{1}{2}$" measurement point is for missywear only and may need to be adjusted up or down $\frac{1}{4}$" to $\frac{1}{2}$" accordingly for men's, children's, junior's, and large/plus womenswear. Indicate any changes on spec sheet.]

16. *Across Back*—Measure 4" down from collar/rib joining seam at center back straight across back of garment from armhole seam/edge to armhole seam/edge. [Note: The 4" measurement point is for missywear only and may need to be adjusted up or down $\frac{1}{4}$" to $\frac{1}{2}$" accordingly for men's, children's, junior's, and large/plus womenswear. Indicate any changes on spec sheet.]

17. *Across Chest/Center Armhole*—Measure at one-half depth of armhole straight across front of garment from armhole seam/edge to armhole seam/edge.

18. *Across Back/Center Armhole*—Measure at one-half depth of armhole straight across back of garment from armhole seam/edge to armhole seam/edge.

20. *Waist Width Circumference (woven)*—Measure from edge of garment/side seam to edge of garment/side seam straight across garment on seam or at narrowest point of waist taper at a point _____" below high point shoulder. Double this measurement. [Note: You will have to determine the number of inches down from high point shoulder for each raglan sleeve style based on depth of sleeve. Then indicate this number on spec sheet.]

22. *Bottom Band Circumference (woven top/jacket)*—Measure from side of bottom band to side of bot-

tom band along center of band, following natural contour of waistband. Double this measurement.

24. *Bottom Band Width Circumference, Stretched (woven top/jacket)*—Measure from side of bottom band to side of bottom band straight across center of band in a fully extended position. Double this measurement.

25. *Bottom Band/Ribbing Height (knit or woven top/jacket)*—Measure from band/ribbing joining seam straight down to bottom edge of band/rib opening. [Note: If band is shaped or contoured, indicated special measurement instructions on spec sheet.]

27. *Bottom Opening/Sweep Width Circumference (woven top/jacket)*—Measure from edge of garment/side seam to edge of garment/side seam straight across garment at bottom opening. Double this measurement. [Note: If sweep has pleats, measure with pleats closed or relaxed.]

29. *Vented Bottom Opening/Sweep Width Circumference (woven top/jacket)*—Measure from edge of garment/side seam to edge of garment/side seam straight across garment at top of side vents. Do not follow natural curve of garment. Double this measurement. [Note: If vents are too high to measure sweep, indicate opening at appropriate position, e.g., midriff opening.]

31. *Circular Bottom Opening/Sweep Width Circumference (woven top/jacket)*—Measure from edge of garment/side seam to edge of garment/side seam, following natural contour of garment at bottom opening. Double this measurement.

32. *Yoke Width Front*—Measure from armhole seam/edge to armhole seam/edge straight across front of garment, ignoring contours or points, at yoke-body joining seams. [Note: If yoke is asymmetrical, indicate changes in measuring as needed on spec sheet.]

33. *Yoke Width Back*—Measure from armhole seam/edge to armhole seam/edge straight across back of garment, ignoring contours or points, at yoke-body joining seams. [Note: If yoke is asymmetrical, indicate changes in measuring as needed on spec sheet.]

34. *Yoke Depth Front*—Measure from high point shoulder at neck straight down to bottom of front yoke-body joining seam. Be sure to gently lift collar away from shoulder-neck joining seam if needed.

35. *Yoke Back Depth*—Measure from center back neck joining seam straight down to bottom of back yoke-body joining seam. Gently lift collar away from back neck joining seam if needed.

36. *Sleeve Length Top Armhole*—Measure along top of sleeve/fold, following contour of sleeve from armhole seam at shoulder to bottom of sleeve opening, including cuff.

37. *Sleeve Length Top Neck*—Measure along top of sleeve/fold, following contour of sleeve from sleeve-neck joining seam/edge to edge of sleeve opening, including cuff. Gently lift collar away at sleeve-neck joining seam if needed.

38. *Sleeve Length Center Back*—Measure from center back neck joining seam or from a point above neck at an imaginary line, that of a joining seam, along top of sleeve/fold, following contour of sleeve to edge of sleeve opening, including cuff.

39. *Sleeve Length Underarm*—Measure straight from bottom of armhole along sleeve seam to edge of sleeve opening, including cuff.

41. *Straight Armhole Width Circumference (woven)*—Measure from top of shoulder joining seam/edge straight down to bottom of armhole. Double this measurement.

42. *Curved Armhole Width (knit)*—Measure from top of shoulder joining seam/edge to bottom of armhole, following contour of armhole.

44. *Armhole Front*—Measure on front of garment from top of shoulder at neckline joining seam/edge to bottom of armhole, following contour of armhole. Gently lift collar away from neckline joining seam if needed.

45. *Armhole Back*—Measure on back of garment from top of shoulder at neck joining seam/edge to bottom of armhole, following contour of armhole. Gently lift collar away from neck joining seam if needed.

47. *Armhole Width Circumference Straight (woven)*—Measure from top of shoulder seam at a point _____" below neckline joining seam/edge straight down to bottom of armhole. Double this measurement. [Note: Gently move collar away from neck joining seam if needed when measuring down _____" to armhole start point. Indicate number of inches measured down on spec sheet.]

49. *Muscle Width Circumference (woven)*—Measure from inner sleeve edge/seam to outer sleeve edge/fold at a point 1" below armhole and parallel to sleeve opening. Double this measurement.

51. *Elbow Width Circumference (woven)*—Measure from inner sleeve edge/seam to outer sleeve edge/fold straight across sleeve at a point one-half of underarm sleeve length and parallel to sleeve opening at wrist or cuff. Double this measurement. [Note: If sleeve is three-quarter length, indicate new point of measure on spec sheet.]

53. *Sleeve Opening Width Circumference (woven)*—Measure from inner sleeve edge/seam to outer sleeve edge/fold straight across bottom edge of sleeve opening. Double this measurement.

55. *Sleeve Opening Width Circumference, Stretched (woven)*—Measure from inner sleeve edge/seam to outer sleeve edge/fold straight across bottom edge of sleeve opening in a fully extended position. Double this measurement.

56. *Cuff Length Sleeve*—Measure from outside end of buttonhole to center of button straight along center of cuff. Open cuff out as flat as possible when measuring. [Note: If cuff length is contoured, measure along center-most point.]

57. *Cuff/Ribbing Height Sleeve*—Measure from cuff joining seam or top of ribbing straight down to bottom edge of cuff or rib opening. [Note: If cuff is contoured, indicate changes made as needed to measurement on spec sheet.]

58. *Neck Depth Front (garments with a plain front/asymmetrical front opening)*—Measure from center back neck joining seam/edge straight down to center front neck joining seam/edge.

59. *Neck Depth Center Front (garments with a center front opening)*—Measure from center back neck joining seam/edge straight down to center of first button at center front of garment.

60. *Neck Drop Front*—Measure from an imaginary line connecting neckline edges straight down to center front neck opening edge. Use a ruler if needed to connect top neckline edges.

61. *Neck Drop Back*—Measure from an imaginary line connecting neckline edges straight down to center back neck opening edge. This measurement is taken with front of garment facing up. Use a ruler to connect top neckline edges if needed.

62. *Neck Width, No Collar*—Measure from inside neck edge/seam to inside neck edge/seam straight across back neck at widest point. This measurement is taken with front of garment faceup.

63. *Neck Width, Collar*—Measure straight across back neck from neck-shoulder joining seam to neck-shoulder joining seam or natural shoulder line if no seam. This measurement is taken with back of garment faceup.

64. *Neck Edge Width (knit)*—Measure from neck edge/seam/fold to neck edge/seam/fold along top opening edge, following natural contour of neck opening. Garment should be positioned with one shoulder on top of the other and with front and back neck edges meeting. [Note: Occasionally, a knit collar or edge will be put on a woven jacket. You may use this measurement but should measure it in circumference for jacket continuity, noting correction on spec sheet.]

65. *Neck Edge Width Circumference (woven)*—Measure from neck edge/seam/fold to neck edge/seam/fold along top opening edge, following natural contour of neck opening. Garment should be positioned with one shoulder on top of the other and with front and back neck edges meeting. Double this measurement.

66. *Neck Edge Width, Stretched (knit)*—Measure from neck edge/seam/fold to neck edge/seam/fold along top opening edge in a fully extended position. Garment should be positioned with one shoulder on top of the other and with front and back neck edges meeting. [Note: Occasionally, a knit collar or edge will be put on a woven jacket. You may use this measurement but should measure it in circumference for jacket continuity, noting correction on spec sheet.]

67. *Neck Edge Width Circumference, Stretched (woven)*—Measure from neck edge/seam/fold to neck edge/seam/fold along top opening edge in a fully extended position. Garment should be positioned with one shoulder on top of the other and with front and back neck edges meeting. Double this measurement.

68. *Neck Base (knit)*—Measure from neck edge/seam to neck edge/seam along collar/rib joining seam or neckline edge, following natural contour of neck opening. Garment should be buttoned or zippered, if applicable, with one shoulder seam positioned on top of the other and with front and back neck edges meeting. [Note: Occasionally, a knit collar or edge will be put on a woven jacket. You may

use this measurement but should measure it in circumference for jacket continuity, noting correction on spec sheet.]

69. *Neck Base Circumference (woven)*—Measure from neck edge/seam to neck edge/seam along collar/rib joining seam or neckline edge, following natural contour of neck opening. Garment should be buttoned or zippered, if applicable, with one shoulder seam positioned on top of the other and with front and back neck edges meeting. Double this measurement.

70. *Neckband Length*—Measure from outside end of buttonhole to center of buttonhole across neckband, following contour of neckband.

71. *Collar Length*—Measure from one end of collar to other end of collar along neck joining seam.

72. *Collar Height*—Measure from collar/rib joining seam at center back neck straight up to outer edge of collar/rib.

73. *Collar Band Height*—Measure from collar joining seam at center back straight up to neckband joining seam at center back.

74. *Collar Point Length*—Measure from collar joining seam to outer edge of collar along collar point edge. [Note: If collar is rounded, measure at a point parallel to center back and indicate change on spec sheet.]

75. *Collar Point Spread (pointed collars only)*—Measure, with collar band buttoned and collar in place, from collar point straight across collar edge to collar point.

76. *Lapel Width*
A. *Notched*—Measure from lower lapel notch straight across to lapel fold at a point perpendicular to garment center front.

B. *Without Notches*—Measure from lapel edge straight across the widest point of lapel to lapel fold at a point _____" down from center back collar joining seam and perpendicular to front of garment.

77. *Center Front Extension*—Measure from an imaginary line at center front of garment horizontally to the finished outer edge of front extended piece.

78. *Placket Length*—Measure from top edge of placket straight down to bottom of placket opening along center of placket.

79. *Placket Width*—Measure from placket joining seam straight across placket to placket edge at fold.

121. *Fly/Zipper*
A. *Length*—Measure from top of fly/zipper opening straight down to bottom of fly/zipper opening at zipper stop or bar tack.
B. *Fly/Zipper Width*—Measure top of fly/zipper at joining seam from edge/fold straight across to fly/zipper placket stitching.

122. *Vent/Slit*
A. *Height*—Measure from top of vent/slit straight down to bottom of vent/slit along edge of vent/slit.
B. *Width*—Measure top of vent/slit from edge/fold straight across to vent/slit placket stitching at a point parallel to garment hemline.

123. *Pleat Depth*—Measure from outer edge of pleat at fold/crease to inner fold of pleat. [Note 1: It is a good idea to indicate what type of pleat is being measured, e.g., box, inverted, knife, kick, kilt, or envelope. Note 2: If pleats are not parallel or symmetrical, indicate any special instructions on spec sheet.]

124. *Distance Between Pleats*—Measure from start of pleat to start of pleat, excluding pleat depth at a point directly below pleat joining seam. [Note: If pleats are not parallel or symmetrical, indicate any special instructions on spec sheet.]

125. *Applied Pocket Height*—Measure from top edge of pocket to bottom edge of pocket along center of pocket. [Note: For contoured or irregularly shaped pockets, take a second measurement and indicate point of measure on spec sheet.]

126. *Applied Pocket Width*—Measure from side of pocket to side of pocket along top edge of pocket. [Note: For contoured or irregularly shaped pockets, take a second measurement and indicate point of measure on spec sheet.]

127. *Pocket Opening within a Seam*—Measure from top of pocket to bottom of pocket along edge of pocket opening.

128. *Belt Length*
A. *Total*—Measure from end of belt at buckle along center of belt to opposite end of belt, following contour.
B. *Circumference*—Measure from end of belt at buckle along center of belt to middle hole at opposite end.

129. *Belt Width (or Height)*—Measure from edge of belt straight across to edge of belt. [Note: If belt is contoured, indicate points of measure on spec sheet.]

130. *Belt Loop Length*—Measure from top of belt loop straight down/vertically to bottom of belt loop along center of belt loop. [Note: Fashion-forward or irregularly shaped belt loops may require further spec instructions. Indicate points of measure on spec sheet.]

131. *Belt Loop Width*—Measure belt loop from edge of belt loop straight across/horizontally to edge of belt loop. [Note: Fashion-forward or irregularly shaped belt loops may require further spec instructions. Indicate points of measure on spec sheet.]

132. *Tie Length*—Measure from end of tie/joining seam straight down to tie end along center of tie.

133. *Tie Width*

A. *Straight*—Measure from edge of tie straight across to edge of tie.

B. *Contoured*—Measure from edge of tie straight across to edge of tie at widest point of tie.

137. *Front Hood Length*—Measure from top of hood to bottom of hood at center front joining seam along opening edge of hood.

138. *Back Hood Length*—Measure from top of hood at center front to bottom of hood at center back joining seam along outside curve of hood fold/seam.

139. *Hood Width*—Measure from front opening edge of hood straight across to back of hood along widest point of hood.

140. *Flange Depth*—Measure from center back neck joining seam straight down to bottom of flange at center back. [Note: If flange is contoured or asymmetrical, indicate point of measure on spec sheet.]

141. *Shoulder Pad Length*—Measure from edge of pad straight across to edge of pad along center of pad or natural shoulder line of pad.

142. *Shoulder Pad Width*—Measure from side of pad straight across to side of pad along edge of pad if straight or at widest point of pad if curved.

143. *Straight Edge Shoulder Pad Height*—Measure from top of pad straight down to bottom of pad along center of pad.

144. *Curved Edge Shoulder Pad Height*—Stick a one-inch straight pin into thickest part of shoulder pad. Push pin all the way through pad until head of pin rests on top of pad. Be sure not to crush pad. Measure portion of pin sticking out of pad. Subtract figure from one inch (length of pin) to get shoulder pad height.

145. *Shoulder Pad Placement*—Measure from neck edge or joining seam straight across shoulder seam or natural shoulder line to start of shoulder pad.

146. *Pleats Placement*

A. *Front Pleat Top/Jacket*—Measure distance from center front of garment straight across to start of first pleat at a point parallel to garment hem. [Note: You may need to use armhole or side seam as a starting point if there is no center front seam or placket.]

B. *Back Pleat Top/Jacket*—Measure distance from armhole seam/side seam (depending on pleat placement) to first pleat at a point parallel to garment hem.

147. *Button Placement*—Refer to measurement point 59, Neck Depth Center Front, for placement of first button. Then measure distance of first button to second button. Be sure when measuring that button at bust point is lined up to apex of bust. Adjust all buttons accordingly and respace as needed.

148. *Pocket Placement*

A. *Top Pocket Vertical*—Measure from shoulder-neck joining seam straight down to top edge of pocket.

B. *Top Pocket Horizontal*—Measure from center front straight across to side of pocket at top edge.

C. *Front Bottom Pocket Vertical*—Measure from waistband/joining seam/edge straight down to top edge of pocket. [Note: The bottom pocket on a jacket or unconstructed jacket can use this measurement code, but it is measured from bottom of garment up to bottom of pocket. Make this correction on spec sheet.]

D. *Front Bottom Pocket Horizontal*—Measure from center front straight across to side of pocket at top edge.

149. *Belt Loop Placement*

A. *Front*—Measure from center front of garment horizontally across to center of first front belt loop.

B. *Back*—Measure from center back of garment horizontally across to center of first back belt loop.

C. *Side Seam to Front*—Measure from center of side seam belt loop to center of front belt loop.

D. *Side Seam to Back*—Measure from center of side seam belt loop to center of back belt loop.

150. *Dart Placement*

A. *High Point Shoulder Bust Dart*—Measure from shoulder-neck joining seam or at a point _____" from shoulder-neck seam straight down, parallel to center front, to top of dart. [Note: The _____" from shoulder seam measurement is to be used for darts that are too short to be measured from high point shoulder. Be sure to indicate _____" measurement on spec sheet.]

B. *Center Front Bust Dart*—Measure from center front of garment straight across to top of dart.

C. *Side Seam Bust Dart*—Measure from underarm/ side seam joining seam down along contour of side seam to bottom of dart.

D. *High Point Shoulder Princess Dart*—Measure from shoulder-neck joining seam straight down to top of dart.

E. *Center Front Princess Dart*—Measure from center front of garment straight across to top of dart.

CHAPTER 14 TERMS

When working with blazers and unconstructed jackets, you may come across the garment terms listed below. If you are unfamiliar with any of them, please look up the definitions in the glossary at the end of this text.

Basic blazer
Double-breasted blazer
Jacket:
    Baseball
    Bike
    Denim
    Karate
    Safari
    Sweat
Unconstructed
Windbreaker

SPEC SHEET:	Blazer	STYLE

SEASON:	DESCRIPTION:
LABEL: (SIZE CATEGORY)	
DATE:	

TECHNICAL SKETCH Basic blazer | SKETCH/PHOTO

CODE	POINT OF MEASURE	TOL. +/−	4	S/6	8	M/10	12	L/14	16	XL/18
1.	Front length	$1/2$								
3.	Center back length	$1/2$								
4.	Side length	$1/4$								
10.	Chest width circumference	$1/2$-$3/4$								
13.	Across shoulder	$1/4$								
15.	Across chest _____ "	$1/4$								
16.	Across back	$1/4$								
20.	Waist width circumference _____ " from H.P.S.	$1/2$-$3/4$								
27.	Bottom opening/sweep width circumference	$1/2$-$3/4$								
36.	Sleeve length top armhole	$3/8$								
39.	Sleeve length underarm	$3/8$								
43.	Curved armhole width circumference	$3/2$								
49.	Muscle width circumference	$1/4$								
51.	Elbow width circumference	$1/4$								
53.	Sleeve opening width circumference	$1/4$								
59.	Neck depth center front	$1/8$								
71.	Collar length	$1/4$								
72.	Collar height	$1/8$								

(Tolerance $1/2$-$3/4$ S, M, L, XL = $3/4$" 4-18 = $1/2$")

The measured garment spec sheets are for *illustrative purposes only* and should not be used as industry standards

CODE	POINT OF MEASURE	TOL. +/−	4	S/6	8	M/10	12	L/14	16	XL/18
76.	Lapel width A. Notched	$1/8$								
	B. Without notches	$1/8$								
77.	Center front extension	$1/8$								
78.	Placket length	$1/4$								
79.	Placket width	$1/8$								
122.	Vent/slit A. Height	$1/4$								
	B. Width	$1/8$								
125.	Applied pocket height	$1/8$								
126.	Applied pocket width	$1/8$								
141.	Shoulder pad length	$1/8$								
142.	Shoulder pad width	$1/8$								
143.	Straight edge, shoulder pad height	$1/8$								
144.	Curved edge, shoulder pad height	$1/8$								
145.	Shoulder pad placement	$1/8$								
147.	Button placement (Distance between)	$1/8$								
148.	Pocket placement A. Top pocket vertical	$1/8$								
	B. Top pocket horizontal	$1/8$								
	C. Button pocket vertical	$1/8$								
	D. Button pocket horizontal	$1/8$								
150.	Dart length bust dart	$1/8$								
	Princess dart	$1/8$								
150.	Dart placement A. H.P.S. to bust dart	$1/8$								
	B. C.F. to bust dart	$1/8$								
	C. Underarm to bust dart	$1/8$								
	D. H.P.S. to princess dart	$1/8$								
	E. C.F. to princess dart	$1/8$								

COMMENTS:

The measured garment spec sheets are for *illustrative purposes only* and should not be used as industry standards

BLAZERS AND UNCONSTRUCTED JACKETS 219

SPEC SHEET: Blazer	STYLE

SEASON: Early fall	DESCRIPTION: Classic blazer with pocket flaps
LABEL: (SIZE CATEGORY) Missy	
DATE:	

TECHNICAL SKETCH Basic blazer	SKETCH/PHOTO

CODE	POINT OF MEASURE	TOL. +/–	4	S/6	8	M/10	12	L/14	16	XL/18
1.	Front length	1/2				30				
3.	Center back length	1/2				29³/₄				
4.	Side length	1/4				20¹/₈				
10.	Chest width circumference	1/2-3/4				39¹/₄				
13.	Across shoulder	1/4				16¹/₄				
15.	Across chest __5__ " below hips	1/4				4¹/₄				
16.	Across back	1/4				16¹/₂				
20.	Waist width circumference __16__ " from H.P.S.	1/2-3/4				35¹/₂				
27.	Bottom opening/sweep width circumference	1/2-3/4				41¹/₂				
36.	Sleeve length top armhole	3/8				24³/₄				
39.	Sleeve length underarm	3/8				17				
43.	Curved armhole width circumference	3/2				21				
49.	Muscle width circumference	1/4				14¹/₄				
51.	Elbow width circumference	1/4				13¹/₄				
53.	Sleeve opening width circumference	1/4				10¹/₂				
59.	Neck depth center front	1/8				10¹/₂				
71.	Collar length Follow seam	1/4				17				
72.	Collar height	1/8				2⁷/₈				

(Tolerance 1/2-3/4 S, M, L, XL = 3/4" 4-18 = 1/2")

The measured garment spec sheets are for *illustrative purposes only* and should not be used as industry standards

CODE	POINT OF MEASURE	TOL. +/−	4	S/6	8	M/10	12	L/14	16	XL/18
76.	Lapel width A. Notched	1/8				3				
	B. Without notches	1/8								
77.	Center front extension	1/8				7/8				
78.	Placket length	1/4				3 1/2				
79.	Placket width	1/8				1 1/8				
122.	Vent/slit A. Height	1/4				1 7/8				
	B. Width	1/8								
125.	Applied pocket height Pocket flap	1/8								
126.	Applied pocket width Pocket flap	1/8				5 5/8				
141.	Shoulder pad length	1/8				4 1/2				
142.	Shoulder pad width	1/8				7				
143.	Straight edge, shoulder pad height	1/8				3/8				
144.	Curved edge, shoulder pad height	1/8								
145.	Shoulder pad placement	1/8				1/2				
147.	Button placement (Distance between)	1/8				5 7/8				
148.	Pocket placement A. Top pocket vertical	1/8								
	B. Top pocket horizontal	1/8								
	C. Button pocket vertical	1/8				18 1/8				
	D. Button pocket horizontal	1/8				2 3/4				
150.	Dart length bust dart	1/8								
	Princess dart	1/8								
150.	Dart placement A. H.P.S. to bust dart	1/8								
	B. C.F. to bust dart	1/8								
	C. Underarm to bust dart	1/8								
	D. H.P.S. to princess dart	1/8								
	E. C.F. to princess dart	1/8								
	Button hole pocket binding width	1/8				3/16				
	Distance between front princess seams armhole					14				
	Waist	1/4				8 3/4				
	Hem	1/4				9 5/8				
	Distance between back princess seams armhole					16 1/2				
	Waist	1/4				10 5/8				
	Hem	1/4				12 1/2				

COMMENTS:

The measured garment spec sheets are for *illustrative purposes only* and should not be used as industry standards

CHAPTER 15

Outerwear/Coats

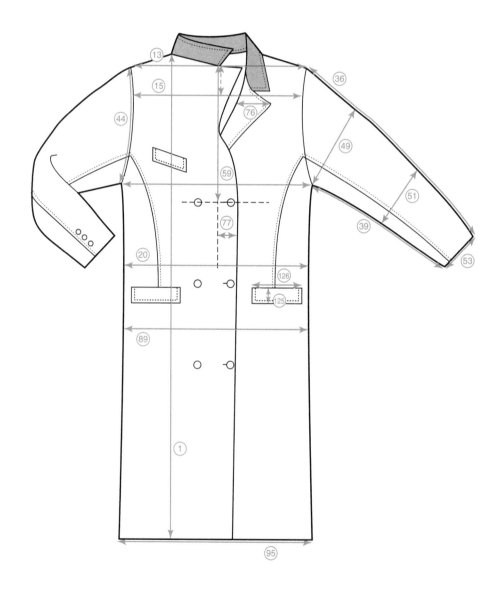

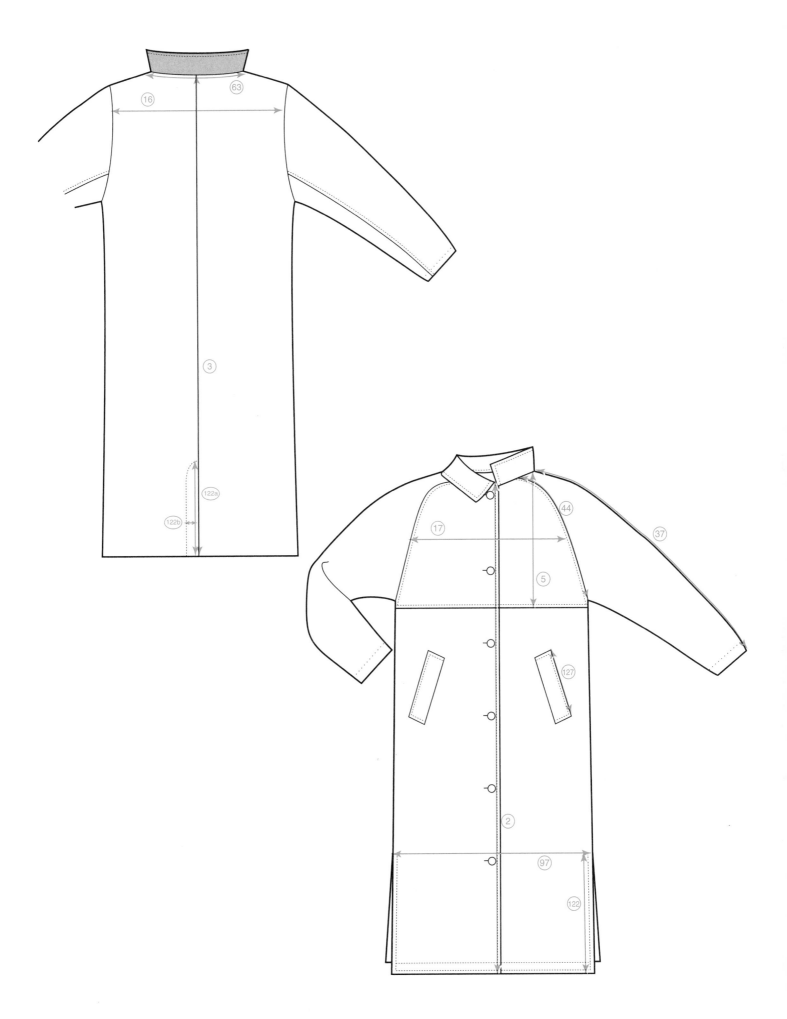

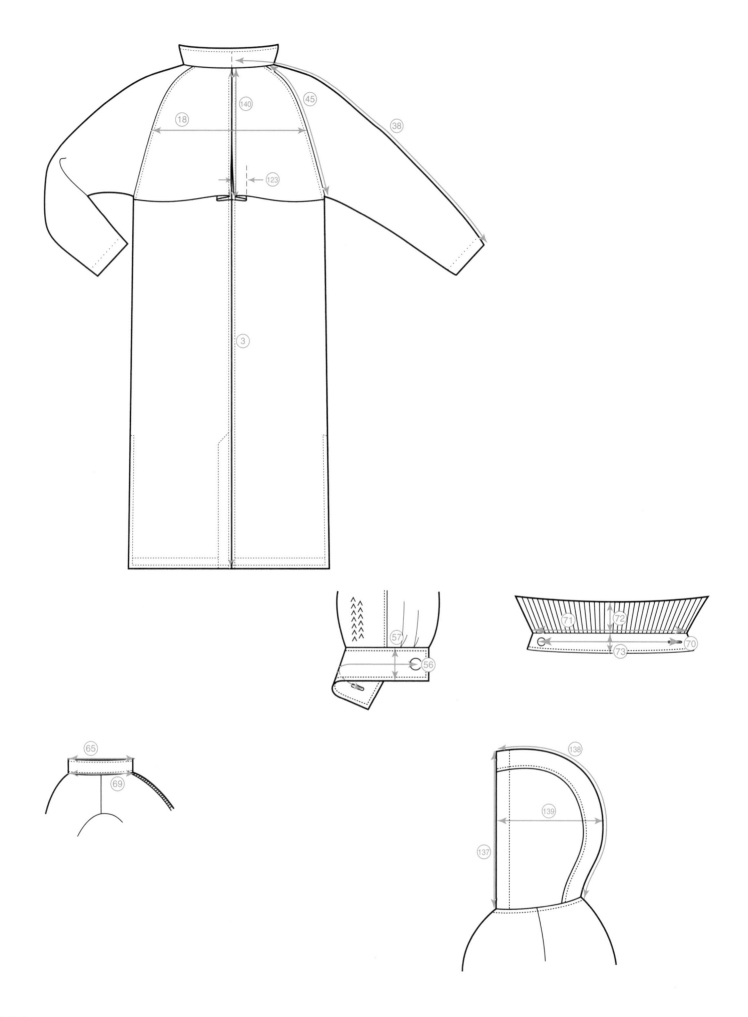

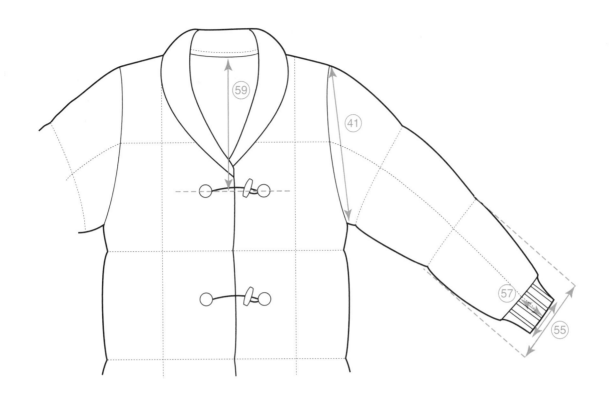

Measuring Outerwear/Coats

Outerwear and coats, either knitted or woven, are treated as wovens when measuring, due to the garment's construction. When measuring a cardigan coat, you should use the knit dress spec sheet if the cardigan coat is not lined, and the outerwear/coat spec sheet if it is lined. Short unlined jackets are usually specced on the blazer and unconstructed jacket spec sheets, while lined jackets are usually specced on the outerwear/coat spec sheets. As you measure these garments, you will have to make that decision based on style features and details. The short pea coat shown below (Figure 15.1) is a good example of a coat that should be specced with the outerwear/coat spec sheet, not the blazer and jacket spec sheet, because it is lined. This section does not contain measurement points for facings, inside pockets, and linings. If you choose to detail these measurements, simply add them to the spec sheet.

[Note: Measurement points that previously read "woven top" will read "woven top/jacket" in this section only.]

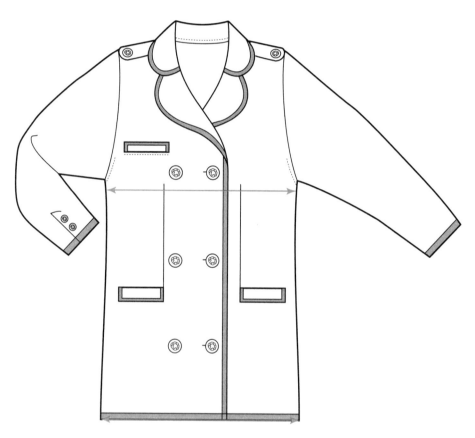

Figure 15.1

1. *Front Length (garments with a front opening)*— Measure from high point shoulder at neck straight down, parallel to center front, to bottom of garment at front. If garment has a collar, gently lift it away from shoulder-neck measuring point.

2. *Center Front Length (garments with a plain front; no front opening)*—Measure from center front neck joining seams straight down to bottom of garment at center front. [Note: A garment without a front opening may still require use of Front Length if neckline is unusual.]

3. *Center Back Length*—Measure from center back neck joining seams straight down to bottom of garment at center back. If needed, gently lift collar away from back neck to expose joining seam.

4. *Side Length*—Measure from bottom of armhole/side seam straight down to bottom of garment along side of garment. Do not follow natural curve of garment's side seam, unless otherwise indicated. If needed, gently lift sleeve away from armhole/side seam joining seam.

5. *Front Bodice Length (garments with a front opening)*—Measure from high point shoulder at neck straight down, parallel to center front, to top edge of waistband, joining seam, or rib. If garment has a collar, gently lift it away from shoulder-neck measuring point.

6. *Center Front Bodice Length (garments with a plain front; no front opening)*—Measure from center front neck joining seam straight down to top edge of waistband, joining seam, or rib. [Note: A garment without a center opening may still require use of Front Bodice Length if neckline is unusual.]

7. *Center Back Bodice Length*—Measure from center back neck joining seams straight down to top edge of waistband, joining seam, or rib. If needed, gently lift collar away from back neck to expose joining seam.

8. *Side Seam Bodice Length*—Measure from bottom of armhole/side seam straight down to top edge of waistband, joining seam, or rib, along side of garment, following natural curve of garment's side seam, unless otherwise indicated. If needed, gently lift sleeve away from armhole/side seam joining seam. [Note: You can take side seam bodice measurement straight rather than contoured if joining seam/rib can be extended, but indicate change on spec sheet.]

10. *Chest Width Circumference (woven)*—Measure from edge of garment/side seam to edge of garment/side seam straight across garment at a point 1" below armhole. Double this measurement.

12. *Chest Width Circumference (raglan sleeve, woven)*—Measure from edge of garment/side seam to edge of garment/side seam straight across garment at a point _____" below high point shoulder. Double this measurement. [Note: You will have to determine number of inches down from high point shoulder for each raglan sleeve style based on depth of sleeve. Then indicate this number on spec sheet.]

13. *Across Shoulder*—Measure straight across front from armhole seam/edge to armhole seam/edge at shoulder seam or across natural shoulder fold line created if there is no seam.

14. *Shoulder Width*—Measure from neckband/collar/ribbing joining seam or neckline edge to top of armhole seam at shoulder, taken along shoulder seam or across natural shoulder fold line created if there is no seam.

15. *Across Chest*—Measure $2\frac{1}{2}$" down from collar/rib joining seam at center front straight across front of garment from armhole seam/edge to armhole seam/edge. [Note: The $2\frac{1}{2}$" measurement point is for missy-wear only and may need to be adjusted up or down $\frac{1}{4}$" to $\frac{1}{2}$" accordingly for men's, children's, junior's, and large/plus womenswear. Indicate any changes on spec sheet.]

16. *Across Back*—Measure 4" down from collar/rib joining seam at center back straight across back of garment from armhole seam/edge to armhole seam/edge. [Note: The 4" measurement point is for missy-wear only and may need to be adjusted up or down $\frac{1}{4}$" to $\frac{1}{2}$" accordingly for men's, children's, junior's, and large/plus womenswear. Indicate any changes on spec sheet.]

17. *Across Chest/Center Armhole*—Measure at one-half depth of armhole straight across front of garment from armhole seam/edge to armhole seam/edge.

18. *Across Back/Center Armhole*—Measure at one-half depth of armhole straight across back of garment from armhole seam/edge to armhole seam/edge.

20. *Waist Width Circumference (woven)*—Measure from edge of garment/side seam to edge of garment/side seam straight across garment on seam or at narrowest point of waist taper at a point _____" below high point shoulder. Double this measurement. [Note: You will have to determine number of inches down from high point shoulder for each raglan sleeve style based on depth of sleeve. Then indicate this number on spec sheet.]

22. *Bottom Band Circumference (woven top/jacket)*—Measure from side of bottom band to side of bottom band along center of band, following natural contour of waistband. Double this measurement.

24. *Bottom Band Width Circumference, Stretched (woven top/jacket)*—Measure from side of bottom band to side of bottom band straight across center of band in a fully extended position. Double this measurement.

25. *Bottom Band/Ribbing Height (knit or woven top/jacket)*—Measure from band/ribbing joining seam straight down to bottom edge of band/rib opening. [Note: If band is shaped or contoured, indicate special measurement instructions on spec sheet.]

27. *Bottom Opening/Sweep Width Circumference (woven top/jacket)*—Measure from edge of garment/side seam to edge of garment/side seam straight across garment at bottom opening. Double this measurement. [Note: If sweep has pleats, measure with pleats closed or relaxed.]

29. *Vented Bottom Opening/Sweep Width Circumference (woven top/jacket)*—Measure from edge of garment/side seam to edge of garment/side seam straight across garment at top of side vents. Do not follow the natural curve of the garment. Double this measurement. [Note: If vents are too high to measure sweep, indicate opening at appropriate position, e.g., midriff opening.]

31. *Circular Bottom Opening/Sweep Width Circumference (woven top/jacket)*—Measure from edge of garment/side seam to edge of garment/side seam, following natural contour of garment at bottom opening. Double this measurement.

32. *Yoke Width Front*—Measure from armhole seam/edge to armhole seam/edge straight across front of garment, ignoring contours or points, at yoke-body joining seams. [Note: If yoke is asymmetrical, indicate changes in measuring as needed on spec sheet.]

33. *Yoke Width Back*—Measure from armhole seam/edge to armhole seam/edge straight across back of garment, ignoring contours or points, at yoke-body joining seams. [Note: If yoke is asymmetrical, indicate changes in measuring as needed on spec sheet.]

34. *Yoke Depth Front*—Measure from high point shoulder at neck straight down to bottom of front yoke-body joining seam. Be sure to gently lift collar away from shoulder-neck joining seam if needed.

35. *Yoke Back Depth*—Measure from center back neck joining seam straight down to bottom of back yoke-body joining seam. Gently lift collar away from back neck joining seam if needed.

36. *Sleeve Length Top Armhole*—Measure along top of sleeve/fold, following contour of sleeve from armhole seam at shoulder to bottom of sleeve opening, including cuff.

37. *Sleeve Length Top Neck*—Measure along top of sleeve/fold, following contour of sleeve from sleeve-neck joining seam/edge to edge of sleeve opening, including cuff. Gently lift collar away at sleeve-neck joining seam if needed.

38. *Sleeve Length Center Back*—Measure from center back neck joining seam or from a point above neck at an imaginary line, that of a joining seam, along top of sleeve/fold, following contour of sleeve to edge of sleeve opening, including cuff.

39. *Sleeve Length Underarm*—Measure straight from bottom of armhole along sleeve seam to edge of sleeve opening, including cuff.

41. *Straight Armhole Width Circumference (woven)*—Measure from top of shoulder joining seam/edge straight down to bottom of armhole. Double this measurement.

42. *Curved Armhole Width (knit)*—Measure from top of shoulder joining seam/edge to bottom of armhole, following contour of armhole.

44. *Armhole Front*—Measure on front of garment from top of shoulder at neckline joining seam/edge to bottom of armhole, following contour of armhole. Gently lift collar away from neckline joining seam if needed.

45. *Armhole Back*—Measure on back of garment from top of shoulder at neck joining seam/edge to bottom of armhole, following contour of armhole. Gently lift collar away from neck joining seam if needed.

47. *Armhole Width Circumference Straight (woven)*—Measure from top of shoulder seam at a point _____"

below neckline joining seam/edge straight down to bottom of armhole. Double this measurement. [Note: Gently move collar away from neck joining seam if needed when measuring down _____" to armhole start point. Indicate number of inches measured down on spec sheet.]

49. *Muscle Width Circumference (woven)*—Measure from inner sleeve edge/seam to outer sleeve edge/fold at a point 1" below armhole and parallel to sleeve opening. Double this measurement.

51. *Elbow Width Circumference (woven)*—Measure from inner sleeve edge/seam to outer sleeve edge/fold straight across sleeve at a point one-half of the underarm sleeve length and parallel to sleeve opening at wrist or cuff. Double this measurement. [Note: If sleeve is three-quarter length, indicate new point of measure on spec sheet.]

53. *Sleeve Opening Width Circumference (woven)*—Measure from inner sleeve edge/seam to outer sleeve edge/fold straight across bottom edge of sleeve opening. Double this measurement.

55. *Sleeve Opening Width Circumference, Stretched (woven)*—Measure from inner sleeve edge/seam to outer sleeve edge/fold straight across bottom edge of sleeve opening in a fully extended position. Double this measurement.

56. *Cuff Length Sleeve*—Measure from outside end of buttonhole to center of button straight along center of cuff. Open cuff out as flat as possible when measuring. [Note: If cuff length is contoured, measure along center-most point.]

57. *Cuff/Ribbing Height Sleeve*—Measure from cuff joining seam or top of ribbing straight down to bottom edge of cuff or rib opening. [Note: If cuff is contoured, indicate changes made as needed to measurement on spec sheet.]

58. *Neck Depth Front (garments with a plain front/asymmetrical front opening)*—Measure from

center back neck joining seam/edge straight down to center front neck joining seam/edge.

59. *Neck Depth Center Front (garments with a center front opening)*—Measure from center back neck joining seam/edge straight down to center of first button at center front of garment.

60. *Neck Drop Front*—Measure from an imaginary line connecting neckline edges straight down to center front neck opening edge. Use a ruler if needed to connect top neckline edges.

61. *Neck Drop Back*—Measure from an imaginary line connecting neckline edges straight down to center back neck opening edge. This measurement is taken with front of garment facing up. Use a ruler to connect top neckline edges if needed.

62. *Neck Width, No Collar*—Measure from inside neck edge/seam to inside neck edge/seam straight across back neck at widest point. This measurement is taken with front of garment faceup.

63. *Neck Width, Collar*—Measure straight across back neck from neck-shoulder joining seam to neck-shoulder joining seam or natural shoulder line if no seam. This measurement is taken with back of garment faceup.

64. *Neck Edge Width (knit)*—Measure from neck edge/seam/fold to neck edge/seam/fold along top opening edge, following natural contour of neck opening. Garment should be positioned with one shoulder on top of the other and with front and back neck edges meeting. [Note: Occasionally, a knit collar or edge will be put on a woven jacket. You may use this measurement, but you should measure it in circumference for jacket continuity, noting correction on spec sheet.]

65. *Neck Edge Width Circumference (woven)*—Measure from neck edge/seam/fold to neck edge/

seam/fold along top opening edge, following natural contour of neck opening. Garment should be positioned with one shoulder on top of the other and with front and back neck edges meeting. Double this measurement.

66. *Neck Edge Width, Stretched (knit)*—Measure from neck edge/seam/fold to neck edge/seam/fold along top opening edge in a fully extended position. Garment should be positioned with one shoulder on top of the other and with front and back neck edges meeting. [Note: Occasionally, a knit collar or edge will be put on a woven jacket. You may use this measurement, but you should measure it in circumference for jacket continuity, noting correction on spec sheet.]

67. *Neck Edge Width Circumference, Stretched (woven)*—Measure from neck edge/seam/fold to neck edge/seam/fold along top opening edge in a fully extended position. Garment should be positioned with one shoulder on top of the other and with front and back neck edges meeting. Double this measurement.

68. *Neck Base (knit)*—Measure from neck edge/seam to neck edge/seam along collar/rib joining seam or neckline edge, following natural contour of neck opening. Garment should be buttoned or zippered, if applicable, with one shoulder seam positioned on top of the other and with front and back neck edges meeting. [Note: Occasionally, a knit collar or edge will be put on a woven jacket. You may use this measurement, but you should measure it in circumference for jacket continuity, noting correction on spec sheet.]

69. *Neck Base Circumference (woven)*—Measure from neck edge/seam to neck edge/seam along collar/rib joining seam or neckline edge, following natural contour of neck opening. Garment should be buttoned or zippered, if applicable, with one shoulder seam positioned on top of the other and with front and back neck edges meeting. Double this measurement.

70. *Neckband Length*—Measure from outside end of buttonhole to center of buttonhole across neckband, following contour of neckband.

71. *Collar Length*—Measure from one end of collar to other end of collar along neck joining seam.

72. *Collar Height*—Measure from collar/rib joining seam at center back neck straight up to outer edge of collar/rib.

73. *Collar Band Height*—Measure from collar joining seam at center back straight up to neckband joining seam at center back.

74. *Collar Point Length*—Measure from collar joining seam to outer edge of collar along collar point edge. [Note: If collar is rounded, measure at a point parallel to center back and indicate change on spec sheet.]

75. *Collar Point Spread (pointed collars only)*—Measure, with collar band buttoned and collar in place, from collar point straight across collar edge to collar point.

76. *Lapel Width*
A. *Notched*—Measure from lower lapel notch straight across to lapel fold at a point perpendicular to garment center front.
B. *Without Notches*—Measure from lapel edge straight across the widest point of lapel to lapel fold at a point _____" down from center back collar joining seam and perpendicular to front of garment.

77. *Center Front Extension*—Measure from an imaginary line at center front of garment horizontally to finished outer edge of front extended piece.

78. *Placket Length*—Measure from top edge of placket straight down to bottom of placket opening along center of placket.

79. *Placket Width*—Measure from placket joining seam straight across placket to placket edge at fold.

87. *High Hip Width Circumference (woven)*—Measure from edge of garment/side seam to edge of garment/side seam at a point 4" below bottom edge of waistband/seam following contour of waist. Double this measurement. [Note: The 4" point is for missywear only; adjust as needed $\frac{1}{2}$" to 1" up or down for children's, petite's, junior's, or large/plus womenswear. Indicate change on spec sheet.]

89. *Low Hip Width Circumference from Waist (woven)*—Measure from edge of garment/side seam to edge of garment/side seam at a point 7" below bottom edge of waistband/seam, following contour of waist. Double this measurement. [Note: The 7" point is for missywear only; adjust as needed $\frac{1}{2}$" to 1" up or down for children's, petite's, junior's, or large/plus womenswear. Indicate change on spec sheet.]

91. *Hip Width from High Point Shoulder Circumference (woven)*—Measure from edge of garment/side seam to edge of garment/side seam straight across at a point _____" below high point shoulder. Double this measurement. [Note: You will have to estimate low hip point on garment if there is no waistband and fill in the _____" from high point shoulder. This measurement will vary from children's, juniors, missy, and large/plus womenswear.]

95. *Bottom Opening/Sweep Width Circumference (woven skirt)*—Measure from edge of garment/side seam to edge of garment/side seam straight across garment at bottom opening. Double this measurement. [Note: If sweep has pleats, measure with pleats closed or relaxed.]

97. *Vented Bottom Opening/Sweep Width Circumference (woven skirt)*—Measure from edge of garment/side seam to edge of garment/side seam straight across garment at top of side vents. Double this measurement. [Note: Indicate on spec sheet if

there is only one vent or if vent hits at a point other than sweep, e.g., thigh opening.]

99. *Circular Bottom Opening/Sweep Width Circumference (woven skirt)*—Measure from edge of garment/side seam to edge of garment/side seam, following natural contour of garment at bottom opening. Double this measurement.

100. *Center Front Skirt Length*—Measure from bottom of waistband/seam (top edge if not banded or stitching if self-elastic/drawstring casing) straight down to bottom of garment at center front. [Note: A fashion-forward skirt may have an asymmetrical waist. Indicate top point of measure on spec sheet.]

101. *Center Back Skirt Length*—Measure from bottom of waistband/seam (top edge if not banded or stitching if self-elastic/drawstring casing) straight down to bottom of garment at center front. [Note: A fashion-forward skirt may have an asymmetrical waist. Indicate top point of measure on spec sheet.]

102. *Side Skirt Length*—Measure from bottom edge of waistband/seam (top edge if not banded or stitching if self-elastic/drawstring casing) to bottom of garment along side seam/fold of garment, following any contour.

121. *Fly/Zipper*
A. *Length*—Measure from top of fly/zipper opening straight down to bottom of fly/zipper opening at zipper stop or bar tack.
B. *Fly/Zipper Width*—Measure top of fly/zipper at joining seam from edge/fold straight across to fly/zipper placket stitching.

122. *Vent/Slit*
A. *Height*—Measure from top of vent/slit straight down to bottom of vent/slit along edge of vent/slit.
B. *Width*—Measure top of vent/slit from edge/fold straight across to vent/slit placket stitching at a point parallel to garment hemline.

123. *Pleat Depth*—Measure from outer edge of pleat at fold/crease to inner fold of pleat. [Note 1: It is a good idea to indicate what type of pleat is being measured, e.g., box, inverted, knife, kick, kilt, or envelope. Note 2: If pleats are not parallel or symmetrical, indicate any special instructions on spec sheet.]

124. *Distance Between Pleats*—Measure from start of pleat to start of pleat, excluding pleat depth at a point directly below pleat joining seam. [Note: If pleats are not parallel or symmetrical, indicate any special instructions on spec sheet.]

125. *Applied Pocket Height*—Measure from top edge of pocket to bottom edge of pocket along center of pocket. [Note: For contoured or irregularly shaped pockets, take a second measurement and indicate point of measure on spec sheet.]

126. *Applied Pocket Width*—Measure from side of pocket to side of pocket along top edge of pocket. [Note: For contoured or irregularly shaped pockets, take a second measurement and indicate point of measure on spec sheet.]

127. *Pocket Opening within a Seam*—Measure from top of pocket to bottom of pocket along edge of pocket opening.

128. *Belt Length*
A. *Total*—Measure from end of belt at buckle along center of belt to opposite end of belt, following contour.
B. *Circumference*—Measure from end of belt at buckle along center of belt to middle hole at opposite end.

129. *Belt Width (or Height)*—Measure from edge of belt straight across to edge of belt. [Note: If belt is contoured, indicate points of measure on spec sheet.]

130. *Belt Loop Length*—Measure from top of belt loop straight down/vertically to bottom of belt loop

along center of belt loop. [Note: Fashion-forward or irregularly shaped belt loops may require further spec instructions. Indicate points of measure on spec sheet.]

131. *Belt Loop Width*—Measure belt loop from edge of belt loop straight across/horizontally to edge of belt loop. [Note: Fashion-forward or irregularly shaped belt loops may require further spec instructions. Indicate points of measure on spec sheet.]

132. *Tie Length*—Measure from end of tie/joining seam straight down to tie end along center of tie.

133. *Tie Width*
A. *Straight*—Measure from edge of tie straight across to edge of tie.
B. *Contoured*—Measure from edge of tie straight across to edge of tie at widest point of tie.

137. *Front Hood Length*—Measure from top of hood to bottom of hood at center front joining seam along opening edge of hood.

138. *Back Hood Length*—Measure from top of hood at center front to bottom of hood at center back joining seam along outside curve of hood fold/seam.

139. *Hood Width*—Measure from front opening edge of hood straight across to back of hood along widest point of hood.

140. *Flange Depth*—Measure from center back neck joining seam straight down to bottom of flange at center back. [Note: If flange is contoured or asymmetrical, indicate point of measure on spec sheet.]

141. *Shoulder Pad Length*—Measure from edge of pad straight across to edge of pad along center of pad or natural shoulder line of pad.

142. *Shoulder Pad Width*—Measure from side of pad straight across to side of pad along edge of pad if straight or at widest point of pad if curved.

143. *Straight Edge Shoulder Pad Height*—Measure from top of pad straight down to bottom of pad along center of pad.

144. *Curved Edge Shoulder Pad Height*—Stick a one-inch straight pin into thickest part of shoulder pad. Push pin all the way through pad until head of pin rests on top of pad. Be sure not to crush pad. Measure portion of pin sticking out of pad. Subtract figure from one inch (length of pin) to get shoulder pad height.

145. *Shoulder Pad Placement*—Measure from neck edge or joining seam straight across shoulder seam or natural shoulder line to start of shoulder pad.

146. *Pleats Placement*
A. *Front Pleat Top/Coat*—Measure distance from center front of garment straight across to start of first pleat at a point parallel to garment hem. [Note: You may need to use armhole or side seam as a starting point if there is no center front seam or placket.]
B. *Back Pleat Top/Coat*—Measure distance from armhole seam/side seam (depending on pleat placement) to first pleat at a point parallel to garment hem.

147. *Button Placement*—Refer to measurement point 59, Neck Depth Center Front, for placement of first button. Then measure distance of first button to second button. Be sure when measuring that button at bust point is lined up to apex of bust. Adjust all buttons accordingly and respace as needed.

148. *Pocket Placement*
A. *Top Pocket Vertical*—Measure from shoulder-neck joining seam straight down to top edge of pocket.
B. *Top Pocket Horizontal*—Measure from center front straight across to side of pocket at top edge.
C. *Front Bottom Pocket Vertical*—Measure from waistband/joining seam/edge straight down to top edge of pocket. [Note: Bottom pocket on a

coat can use this measurement code, but it is measured from bottom of garment up to bottom of pocket. Make correction on spec sheet.]

D. *Front Bottom Pocket Horizontal*—Measure from center front straight across to side of pocket at top edge.

149. *Belt Loop Placement*

A. *Front*—Measure from center front of garment horizontally across to center of first front belt loop.

B. *Back*—Measure from center back of garment horizontally across to center of first back belt loop.

C. *Side Seam to Front*—Measure from center of side seam belt loop to center of front belt loop.

D. *Side Seam to Back*—Measure from center of side seam belt loop to center of back belt loop.

150. *Dart Placement*

A. *High Point Shoulder Bust Dart*—Measure from shoulder-neck joining seam or at a point _____" from shoulder-neck seam straight down, parallel to center front, to top of dart. [Note: The _____" from shoulder seam measurement is to be used for darts that are too short to be measured from high point shoulder. Be sure to indicate _____" measurement on spec sheet.]

B. *Center Front Bust Dart*—Measure from center front of garment straight across to top of dart.

C. *Side Seam Bust Dart*—Measure from underarm/ side seam joining seam down along contour of side seam to bottom of dart.

D. *High Point Shoulder Princess Dart*—Measure from shoulder-neck joining seam straight down to top of dart.

E. *Center Front Princess Dart*—Measure from center front of garment straight across to top of dart.

CHAPTER 15 TERMS

When working with outerwear and coats, you may come across the garment terms listed below. If you are unfamiliar with any of them, please look up the definitions in the glossary at the end of this text.

Coat:
   Balmacaan
   Car
   Chesterfield
   Classic
   Clutch
   Duster
   Military
   Pea
   Peasant
   Princess
   Raglan
   Stadium/Storm
   Tent
   Toggle
   Wrap
Outerwear

SPEC SHEET Outerwear	STYLE
SEASON:	DESCRIPTION:
LABEL: (SIZE CATEGORY)	
DATE:	
TECHNICAL SKETCH Chesterfield coat	SKETCH/PHOTO

CODE	POINT OF MEASURE	TOL. +/−	4	S/6	8	M/10	12	L/14	16	XL/18
1.	Front length	$1/2$								
3.	Center back length	$1/2$								
4.	Side length	$1/4$								
10.	Chest width circumference	$1/2$-$3/4$								
13.	Across shoulder	$1/4$								
15.	Across chest _____" below H.P.S.	$1/4$								
16.	Across back	$1/4$								
20.	Waist width circumference _____" from H.P.S.	$1/2$-$3/4$								
36.	Sleeve length top armhole	$3/8$								
39.	Sleeve length underarm	$3/8$								
43.	Curved armhole width circumference	$3/8$								
49.	Muscle width circumference	$1/4$								

The measured garment spec sheets are for *illustrative purposes only* and should not be used as industry standards

CODE	POINT OF MEASURE	TOL. +/−	4	S/6	8	M/10	12	L/14	16	XL/18
51.	Elbow width circumference	1/4								
53.	Sleeve opening width circumference	1/4								
59.	Neck depth center front	1/8								
71.	Collar length	1/4								
72.	Collar height	1/8								
76.	Lapel width A. With notches	1/8								
	B. Without notches	1/8								
77.	Center front extension	1/8								
78.	Placket length	1/4								
79.	Placket width	1/8								
91.	Hip width from H.P.S. circumference _____ "	1/2 3/4								
95.	Bottom opening/sweep width circumference	1/2 3/4								
122.	Vent/slit A. Height	1/4								
	B. Width	1/8								
125.	Applied pocket height	1/8								
126.	Applied pocket width	1/8								
141.	Shoulder pad length	1/8								
142.	Shoulder pad width	1/8								
143.	Straight edge, shoulder pad height	1/8								
144.	Curved edge, shoulder pad height	1/8								
147.	Button placement (Distance between)	1/8								
148.	Pocket placement A. Top pocket vertical	1/8								
	B. Top pocket horizontal	1/8								
	C. Button pocket vertical	1/8								
	D. Button pocket horizontal	1/8								
150.	Dart length princess	1/8								
150.	Dart placement princess D. H.P.S.	1/8								
	E. C.F.	1/8								

COMMENTS:

The measured garment spec sheets are for *illustrative purposes only* and should not be used as industry standards

SPEC SHEET	Outerwear	STYLE	

SPEC SHEET Outerwear

STYLE

SEASON: Winter

DESCRIPTION: Updated Chesterfield with Turned up cuffs on sleeve and velvet collar

LABEL: (SIZE CATEGORY) Missy

DATE:

TECHNICAL SKETCH   Chesterfield coat

SKETCH/PHOTO

CODE	POINT OF MEASURE	TOL. +/−	4	S/6	8	M/10	12	L/14	16	XL/18
1.	Front length	1/2				49 1/2				
3.	Center back length	1/2				49 1/2				
4.	Side length	1/4				34				
10.	Chest width circumference	1/2-3/4				46				
13.	Across shoulder	1/4				18 1/2				
15.	Across chest __7__" below H.P.S.	1/2-3/4				18				
16.	Across back	1/4				18 1/2				
20.	Waist width circumference __22__" from H.P.S.	1/4				44				
36.	Sleeve length top armhole	3/8				21				
39.	Sleeve length underarm	3/8				17 1/2				
43.	Curved armhole width circumference	3/8				24				
49.	Muscle width circumference	1/4				19				

*The measured garment spec sheets are for **illustrative purposes only** and should not be used as industry standards*

CODE	POINT OF MEASURE	TOL. +/−	4	S/6	8	M/10	12	L/14	16	XL/18
51.	Elbow width circumference	1/4				18				
53.	Sleeve opening width circumference	1/4				16				
59.	Neck depth center front	1/8				19				
71.	Collar length	1/4				22				
72.	Collar height	1/8				3 3/4				
76.	Lapel width A. With notches	1/8				5				
	B. Without notches	1/8								
77.	Center front extension	1/8				2 3/4				
78.	Placket length	1/4								
79.	Placket width	1/8								
91.	Hip width from H.P.S. circumference __25__ "	1/2 3/4				44				
95.	Bottom opening/sweep width circumference	1/2 3/4				44				
122.	Vent/slit A. Height	1/4				21 1/2				
	B. Width	1/8				1 3/4				
125.	Applied pocket height Flap	1/8				2 1/2				
126.	Applied pocket width Flap	1/8				5 1/2				
141.	Shoulder pad length	1/8				7				
142.	Shoulder pad width	1/8				4				
143.	Straight edge, shoulder pad height	1/8								
144.	Curved edge, shoulder pad height	1/8				1/2				
147.	Button placement (Distance between)	1/8				6 1/2				
148.	Pocket placement A. Top pocket vertical	1/8								
	B. Top pocket horizontal	1/8								
	C. Button pocket vertical	1/8				20 3/4				
	D. Button pocket horizontal	1/8				4 1/4				
150.	Dart length princess	1/8				12				
150.	Dart placement princess D. H.P.S.	1/8				-				
	E. C.F.	1/8				4 1/4				
57	Cuff height	1/8				2				

COMMENTS:

PART IV

FITTING AND GRADING

Fitting and grading are for the advanced student or technical designer. However, the novice can use this section to get an overview of the processes involved. A comprehensive understanding of good fit is needed before one tries to evaluate garments and make the necessary adjustments. The same can be said of grading; a comprehensive understanding of patternmaking, pattern adjustments, and alterations and grading patterns is needed. Technology has taken much of the workload out of grading, on a technical design level, as many computer programs have automatized this process.

CHAPTER 16

Achieving the Perfect Fit

Fit Evaluation Sequencing

Fit is a very important aspect of technical design and size specification. Measurements only tell part of the story. It is possible for garment measurements to be accurate but for pattern shapes or slopes to be incorrect. Therefore, every garment that is given numerical specification must also be looked at on a model or dress form. Achieving a perfect fit is sometimes in the eyes of the designer; however, there are some hard-and-fast rules that must be followed for proper movement and comfort.

* A perfect-fitting garment begins with accurate measurements.
* A perfect-fitting garment requires proper garment ease for movement.
* A perfect-fitting garment does not have wrinkles, sagging, gaping, or rippling.
* A perfect-fitting garment enhances the wearer's attractiveness.

Judgment will be your first tool when evaluating a garment for fit. Fashion and styling characteristics, as well as garment function, must be considered when evaluating the appearance and fit elements of a garment. You will use the rules above when sys-

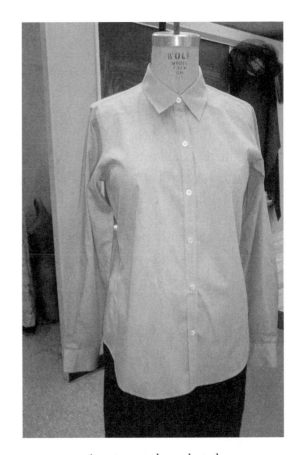

A garment to be evaluated

tematically scrutinizing a garment. Any discrepancies should be conveyed to the manufacturing plant or an overseas agent. The following sequence is suggested when evaluating a garment.

1. Garment Appearance Inadequacies
   a. Inspect the garment when it's lying flat, looking for such things as uneven collars, pockets, or hems. Also look for fabric or sewing defects that affect the quality of the garment.
2. Model or Form Observations
   a. Place the garment on the form correctly. Close any openings/closures. Fit the garment to be evaluated over any garments that might be worn with it; for example, fit a coat over a dress or pants outfit.
   b. A garment that cannot be placed on the body or appear very big once on the body may not be the correct size. Check your spec measurements.
   c. View the garment from the front and the back to get an overall impression of the garment balance. Does it bind, catch, or hang too loose?
   d. Does the garment have enough ease to allow for movement? (See Appendix B for more on body ease.) Note: Live model fitting is the only way to truly check the ease of a garment as it relates to allowances for movement.
   e. Inspect the garment again for such things as uneven collars, pockets, or hems that may not have been seen when the garment was lying flat.
   f. Do all seams lie either parallel or perpendicular to the floor, as designed?
3. Casual Garment Observation
   a. Look at the front view, from top to bottom, for any fit problems.
   b. Look at both side views, from top to bottom, for any fit problems.
   c. Look at the back view, from top to bottom, for any fit problems.
4. Concentrated Garment Observations
   a. Look at the upper front half, including the neck, shoulders, arms, bust, midriff, waist, and trim details for any fit problems.
   b. Look at the upper back half, including the neck, shoulders, arms, across the back, waist, and trim details for any fit problems.
   c. Look at the lower front half, including the hips, rise or sweep, hemline, and any style details for fit problems.
   d. Look at the lower back half, including the hips, rise or sweep, hemline, and any style details for fit problems.

Note: If you are evaluating a dress, long coat, or one-piece garment, you may want to evaluate the front top and bottom before moving to the back.

For practical application, you may use any of the measured garment spec sheets generated so far. Start by putting a measured garment on a body form and use the corresponding spec sheet to evaluate each measurement point one by one. Use the sequencing tips and rules that follow for a good fit. Remember that judgment is your first tool. If a measurement is incorrect, too big or too small, simply cross out the number and place the new number next to it. At first, you may not know how to correct the measurement points. That is why practice and apprenticing under a qualified technician are so important. In the industry, the corrected spec sheet is rewritten and sent back to the manufacturing plant or to the overseas agent with instructions for corrections. When you are ready to begin, look at the fit example (Figure 16.23) at the end of this chapter.

Rules for a Good Fit

Good-fitting garments start with a good understanding of how garments should fit. This section contains more than 30 basic rules for good-fitting garments. Be sure to read and understand all of them before trying to evaluate a garment for fit. Further information relating to specific garment types is listed in the Common Fit Problems and How to Correct Them section that follows.

Necklines—The neckline should always lie nicely around the curve of the base of the neck, unless otherwise designed. The garment should not cut into the neck, wrinkle, pull, or gape. Necklines designed to be wide or lowered should lie flat, but not too snug on the body, unless otherwise designed.

Neckbands—Neckbands and collars must fit the neck comfortably. Check the fit by inserting one finger into the neckband/collar, buttoned. Unless otherwise designed, only one finger should fit easily between the body and the garment.

Lapels—Lapels must lie symmetrical and flat, unless otherwise designed. Lapels should not gape open.

Center Front Seams—Center front seams must be centered on the front of the body and should lie straight from the center front neck down to the bottom of the garment/seam, perpendicular to the floor. They should not pull or shift to either side or buckle at the neck.

Center Back Seams—Center back seams must be centered on the back of the body and should lie straight from the center back neck down to the bottom of the garment/seam, perpendicular to the floor. They should not pull or shift to either side or buckle at the neck.

Center Front and Center Back Closures—Center front and center back closures must hang straight and smooth, without any pulling, puckers, wrinkles, and gaps. A garment top with a full front button/snap/Velcro® opening should always have a closure parallel to the bust apex. A garment bottom with a full front button/snap/Velcro® opening should always have a closure parallel to the fullest part of the abdomen.

Shoulder Seams—Shoulder seams are to lie on top of the shoulder at a point bisecting the shoulder bone and the side neck, unless otherwise designed.

Shoulder Pads—Shoulder pads should be placed on the shoulder seam at a point that appears natural. Generally, the center of the shoulder pads will be placed parallel on the shoulder seam and may ex-

tend lengthwise into the sleeve cap $\frac{1}{4}$" to $\frac{1}{2}$", depending on the design.

Front and Back Armhole Seams—The front armhole seams should cross the body at the end of the shoulder joint (collarbone) but before the end of the shoulder bone, depending on the styling. The back armhole seams should appear to line up with the back arm crease. Jacket seams often extend $\frac{1}{2}$" to 1" beyond this point and coats may extend 1" to $1\frac{1}{2}$" depending on the styling.

Armholes—Armholes must be large enough to allow for easy movement without cutting into the arm/underarm, gaping, or pulling. The lowest point of the armhole should lie approximately 1" to 2" below the armpit, unless otherwise designed.

Sleeve Caps—Sleeve caps should lie smoothly on the end of the shoulders and curve nicely around the armhole without any puckers or wrinkles, unless otherwise designed. Fullness added as a design feature should be evenly distributed and should not extend below a point perpendicular to the cross chest and back chest. The sleeve must be able to lift with the arm without any pulling of the sleeve cap or the garment.

Sleeves—Sleeves must be large enough to hang smoothly around the arm with approximately 2" ease. The elbow must be able to completely bend without binding, wrinkling, or stretching the fabric. If sleeves contain darts or fullness at the elbow, they must be centered over the end of the bone when the arm is bent.

Sleeve Opening—Sleeve openings must be large enough for at least one finger to be easily inserted into hems or cuffs.

Sleeve Length—Sleeve lengths will vary with the design. Short sleeves should be in proportion to the garment and total arm length. Three-quarter-length sleeves should extend below the elbow bone and not rise above the bone when the elbow is bent. Long sleeves should not extend below the bend of the wrist, unless otherwise designed; they should not rise above the wrist bone when the elbow is bent, unless otherwise designed.

Across Chest—Across chest areas and seams should lie smooth, without wrinkles or gaping fabric. There should be no diagonal wrinkling or bulging between the neck and the armhole.

Across Back—Across back areas and seams must lie smooth, without wrinkles or bulges. There should be no wrinkling or bulging below the neckline or between the neck and armholes. The upper back area must have enough ease to allow for movement of the armhole seams when arms are forward, without pulling or straining the seams/fabric.

Darts—Darts should point toward the fullest part of the body. Bust darts should end approximately 1" to 2" from the apex of the bust, depending on the styling. Back darts should end approximately 1" to $1\frac{1}{2}$" from the fullest part of the back, again depending on the styling. Skirt darts should end approximately 1" to $1\frac{1}{2}$" from the fullest part of the abdomen or back, depending on the styling. Darts should always be pressed in an outward or downward position, without wrinkles or bubbles at the dart tip.

Center Front Seams—Center front seams must be centered on the front of the body and should lie straight from the center front neck joining seam to the hem (for tops and dresses) or the waist joining seam down to the bottom of the garment/seam (for skirts), perpendicular to the floor. They should not pull or shift to either side or buckle at the waist.

Center Back Seams—Center back seams, when used, must be centered on the back of the body and should lie straight from the center back neck joining seam (for tops and dresses) or the waist joining seam down to the bottom of the garment/seam (for skirts), perpendicular to the floor. They should not pull or shift to either side or buckle at the waist.

Side Seams—Side seams should always lie straight on the body from the center of the underarm down to the bottom of the garment/seam, perpendicular to the floor. Side seams should never pull to the front or the back of the body.

Grain Lines/Knitted Courses—Grain lines/knitted courses must hang straight on the desired grain, as designed. Lengthwise grain lines/knitted courses should hang straight down the center front and back of the garment, perpendicular to the floor and down the center of the sleeve. Horizontal grain lines/knitted courses should lay at a point parallel to the floor at the shoulders, chest, across back, and hemline. Diagonal/bias grain lines/knitted courses are rare with knits, as extra stretch is generally not needed; however, for styling they may be used and should lie at a 45-degree angle to the shoulders, chest, across back, and hem.

Pockets—Pockets must be sewn on straight in a horizontal, vertical, or biased position and should lie flat to the garment without gaping open, unless otherwise designed.

Slits and Vents—Slits and vents should hang straight on the body and should lie smooth without pulling or gaping open when standing. The slit/vent should be large/long enough to allow for ease of movement when walking, sitting, and climbing stairs.

Pleats—Pleats and tucks should hang flat and straight on the body, without any pulling or gaping, except during movement.

Gathers—Gathers should be small and evenly spaced without any puckering or bulges.

Bottom Bands—Bottom bands on tops should fit comfortably around the body without pulling, gaping, and wrinkling during movement. Two fingers should be able to be easily inserted into the bottom band.

Waistbands—Waistbands should fit comfortably around the waist while standing and sitting without pulling, cutting, or gaping. Two fingers should fit easily between the body and the waistband.

Hems—Hems should always be straight and even, lying parallel to the shoulders, chest, and across back (for tops), or waist and hips (for skirts, dresses, coats, and pants), unless otherwise designed. Classic skirt hemlines are: ultra-mini 14", mini 16", short skirt 18" to 20", knee-length 22", traditional 26" to 28" or 2" to $2\frac{1}{2}$" below the knee, maxi 36" and floor-length 42" below the waistline. Lengths longer or shorter should be styled in proportion to body figures and fabric types. Hems crossing at the widest part of the calf will make the leg look heavier and the woman appear shorter.

Skirts—Skirts should fit comfortably on the body and lie in a smooth, relaxed position. There should be a minimum of 2" ease at the abdomen, hips, and thighs. The skirt fabric should not fall into horizontal folds, wrinkles, or creases at the waist, hips, and thighs, nor should it cup under the stomach, thighs, or buttocks.

Across Front Hip—Across front hip areas and seams should lie smooth, without pulling or fabric gaping. There should be no diagonal pulls or bulging between the waist and the thighs, especially when sitting.

Across Back Hip—Across back hip areas and seams must lie smooth, without wrinkles or bulges. There should be no pulling or bulging between the waist and the thighs, especially when sitting.

Side seams should always lie straight on the body from the side of the waist joining seam down to the bottom of the garment/seam, perpendicular to the floor. Side seams should never pull to the front or the back of the body.

Rise—The rise of a pant must be long enough to be comfortable when standing, sitting, and moving without cutting into the crotch area. A well-sloped rise will not wrinkle or fold around the waist, or wrinkle or pull at the crotch or into the thigh area.

Linings—Linings must fit smoothly under any garments and must follow the same ease rules that apply to that garment for comfort.

Generalized Garment Fitting Tips

As previously stated, fitting garments can be a very difficult process. Most technicians apprentice for several years before conducting a fitting without supervision. One of the reasons behind ill-fitting ready-to-wear in the past few years is a general lack of understanding of pattern construction. When a fit problem is not corrected on a sample garment, it will be repeated as the pattern is graded into a full size range. Unfortunately, ill-fitting patterns are often sent into production to save costs as well. More pattern pieces will fit on a sloper if the rises are long and shallow than if they have a generous curve. Cost aside, a good technician will always strive to achieve a perfect fit.

Designers, buyers, and consumers may have different ideas of what that perfect fit is, how tight or loose a blouse or top should be. However, a top should never be as snug as to pull the weave or knitted loops/yarns beyond their natural relaxed position. For example, a top pulling across the apex of the bust may indicate that there is not enough ease in that area. A knit top generally lacks the darts or seams of a woven top; therefore, bust ease is often gained by increasing the chest width. As a result, the sweep of a knit garment is often increased as well.

Full skirts with ample shirring at the waist generally only need to be adjusted at the waist because the fullness is very forgiving for many body types. However, formfitting skirts can be very difficult to fit. Some women have fuller hips, stomachs, buttocks, and thighs. A woven skirt pulling across the stomach may indicate that there is not enough ease in that area. It can also signal improper dart placement. Most designers will have their customer's ideal figure type and fit to it. For example, a designer fitting a junior's skirt generally fits to a straighter waist and hip, while designers fitting a womenswear skirt generally have to accommodate a protruding stomach or hips.

Knit skirts are usually the easiest garments to fit. The stretch property of the knit allows for ease of movement. However, a woman with fuller hips, stomach, buttocks, and thighs may find that the knit fabric unwittingly clings to her body. A knit skirt pulling across the stomach may indicate that there is not enough ease in that area or that the fabric has been knitted with a different degree of stretch than the designer anticipated.

Knit pants are generally easier to fit than woven pants because they are often less constructed; however, most of the fit rules are the same. Women with fuller hips, stomachs, buttocks, and thighs may find knit and woven pants too tight in these areas if an ample amount of ease has not been added. Designers, buyers, and consumers have a different idea of how tight or loose a pant should be, and many popular designers fit to a taller, slimmer figure. It is important that the pant is comfortable and easy to move in no matter what body prototype is used. A pant should never be so snug as to pull the fabric or side seams. Pleats, rarely used in knits, should lie flat to the body in a natural relaxed position. Pleats are added for garment contouring, not body ease. A pant pulling across the stomach area may indicate that there is not enough ease in that area. Increasing the stomach or hip area does not necessarily mean increasing the thigh as well.

When fitting knit and woven dresses, the fit rules and solutions to fitting tops and skirts should be combined. In many instances, a dress will not have a waistband, but the skirt portions of the dress will follow the skirt rules.

When fitting a jumpsuit or a one-piece garment, the fit rules and problem solutions for a top and pant should be combined. Below is an additional list of rules that should be taken into consideration during the fitting process.

1. There should be enough ease in the bodice length to allow for ease of sitting, without pulling up the bottom portion of the garment.
2. There should be enough ease and/or rise length to allow for movement of the bottom portion of the garment without pulling down on the bodice or top of the garment.

The same techniques for fitting tops and fixing common fitting problems apply to jackets and unconstructed blazers. Keep in mind that the ease allowances must now compensate for the blazer or jacket to fit over a blouse or sweater. Note these differences.

1. The shoulder pad should extend $\frac{1}{2}$" to $\frac{3}{4}$" into the sleeve cap.
2. The lowest point of the armhole should lie approximately 2" to 3" below the armpit, unless otherwise designed.

When fitting outerwear/coats, the fitting rules and solutions to problems for tops and dresses should be applied. Keep in mind that the ease allowances must now compensate for the coat to fit over a blouse or sweater and blazer. Note these differences.

1. The shoulder pad should extend $\frac{3}{4}$" to 1" into the sleeve cap.
2. The lowest point of the armhole should lie approximately 3" to 4" below the armpit, unless otherwise designed.
3. A minimum of 4" ease is required at the abdomen, hips, and thighs.

Common Fit Problems and How to Correct Them

Technical designers often face common fit issues when evaluating garments. Often, solutions for these

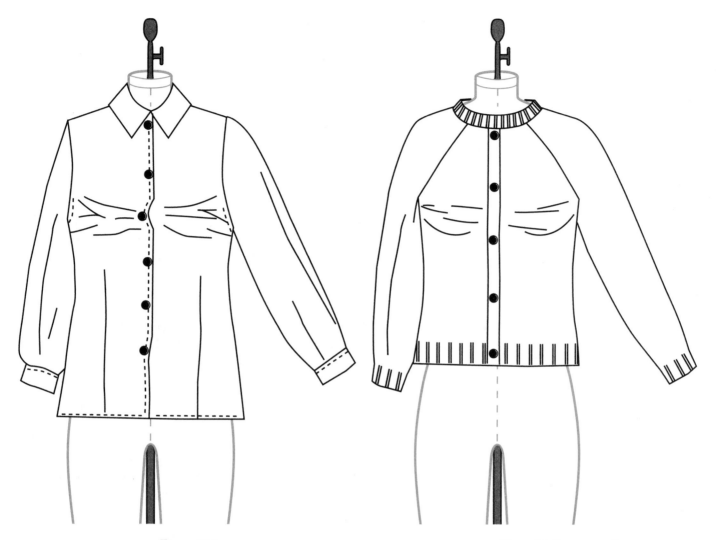

Figure 16.1a

Figure 16.1b

corrections must be sent along with the spec sheet to the man-ufacturing plant or overseas agent. This section addresses some of those common issues with suggestions for correction. On occasion, it is necessary to take the garment apart to check the pattern slope. Do not assume you know what the problem is or that you have the correct solution. It is always a good idea to check with your patternmaker when advising a pattern cor-rection.

Tops and Blouses

Problem Area 1—Chest width—the top pulls across the chest (Figures 16.1a and b).

Solution A—Check the chest width measurement. Is there enough ease allowed in this garment? If not, add the required amount of ease, depending on the results you desire (Figure 16.1c).

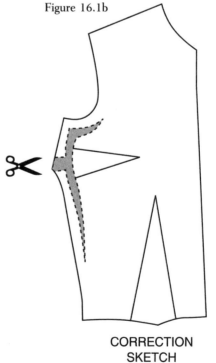

CORRECTION
SKETCH

Figure 16.1c

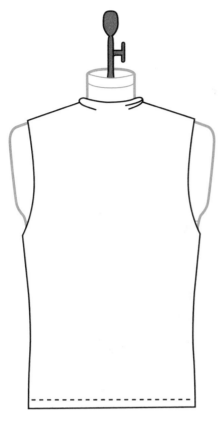

Figure 16.2a

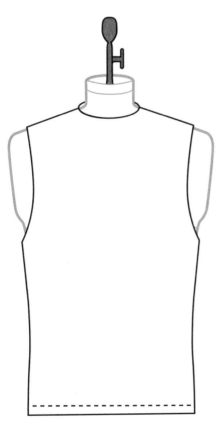

Figure 16.2b

Solution B—Check the dart placement. Does the dart fall at the proper point on or below the apex? If the dart is too high or too low or too long, adjust it accordingly.

Solution C—Check the apex button placement. (This is a common problem with woven blouses. With knits, it is often a combination of too little ease and improper button placement.) The blouse may have enough ease, and the darts placement may be correct, but the button at the bust does not fall parallel to the bust apex. When the bust button is too high or too low, gaping may result, giving the appearance of a garment that is too tight. Align the buttons so that the bust button is aligned with the apex of the bust, then adjust all the other buttons accordingly.

[Note: If the chest width is too large/small, other width measurements may be affected as well. Be sure to make all corrections as needed.]

Problem Area 2—Neck opening circumference is too tight/too loose (Figures 16.2a and b).

Solution A—Often, adding or subtracting to the spec circumference is all that is needed to fix this problem. However, if the neck depth or neck width is not correct, then further investigation is needed. With knits, it is important to check the stretch as well. Knits do not often have buttoned vent openings or zippers; therefore, it is important that the neck opening circumference is large enough to get over the head, yet still looks good on the neck.

Solution B—Check the front and back neck depth measurements. Does the neck opening or joining seam fall at a point that is comfortable for the wearer? If it is too high or too low, adjust it accordingly. Again, check the stretch as stated above.

Solution C—Check the neck width. If the neck width is too narrow, it will draw the shoulders and sleeve cap up. It probably will not fit over the head well. If the neck width is too wide, the neck opening or joining seam will gape along the sides of the neck and look stretched out. Adjust the measurement accordingly (Figures 16.2c and d).

Problem Area 3—Shoulder seams do not lie smoothly on the shoulder (Figures 16.3a, b, and c).

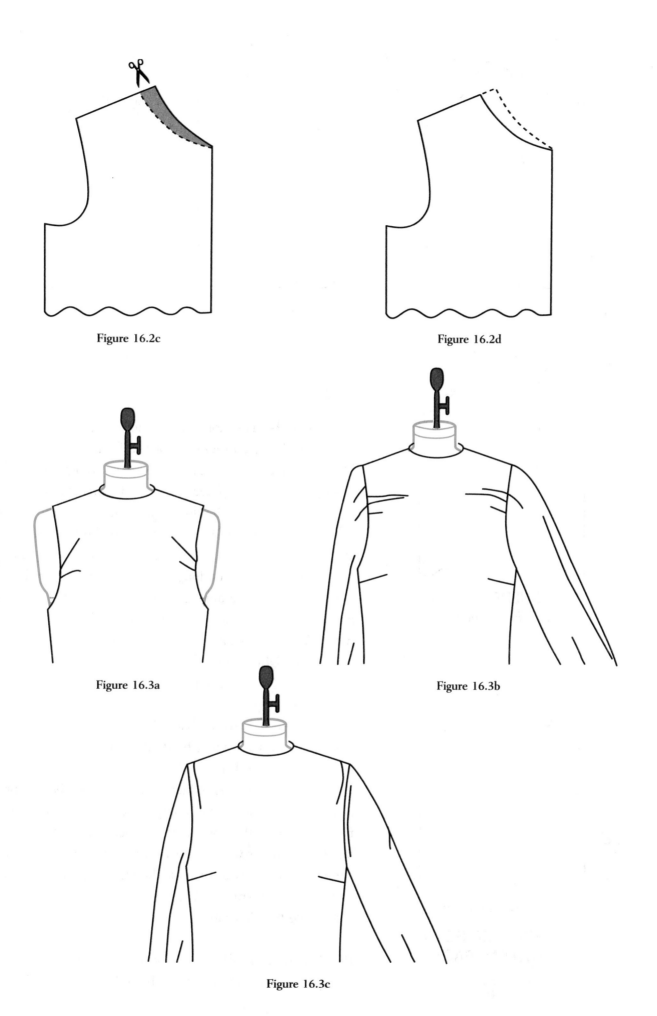

Figure 16.2c

Figure 16.2d

Figure 16.3a

Figure 16.3b

Figure 16.3c

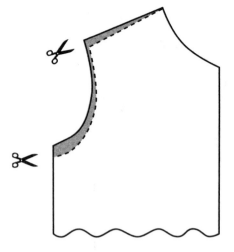

Figure 16.3d

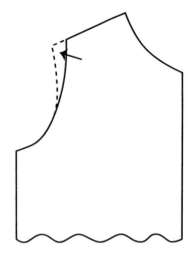

Figure 16.3e

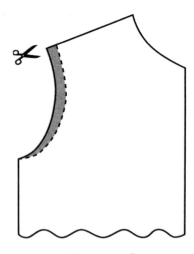

Figure 16.3f

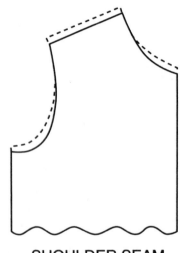

**SHOULDER SEAM
TOO FAR FRONT**

Figure 16.3g

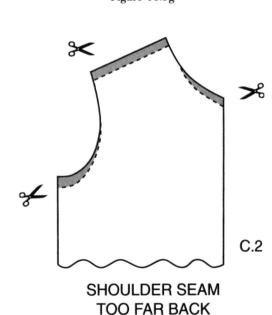

C.2

**SHOULDER SEAM
TOO FAR BACK**

Figure 16.3h

Solution A—The slope of the shoulder seam may be too severe. Check the garment off of the form while it's lying flat. Does the shoulder seam appear to be too straight or too sloped? If so, correct the slope accordingly (Figure 16.3d).

Solution B—The shoulder seam width may be too long or too short. If the shoulder seam is too short, it may pull the sleeve cap up, giving the garment the appearance of being too tight. If the seam is too long, the shoulder cap can droop, giving the garment the appearance of being too big. Sometimes, a shoulder seam is long on purpose for styling reasons. Be sure not to shorten a shoulder seam if, for example, the armhole seam is straight rather than curved (Figures 16.3e and f).

Solution C—The shoulder seam placement is incorrect. The shoulder seam may actually lie too far to the front of the shoulder or too far toward the back. If either of these is the case, a new shoulder seam must be drafted in the corrected position (Figures 16.3g and h).

Solution D—The shoulder seams may not be the problem at all, because the problem may be across chest or across back measurements. If either of these measurement points is too big, the shoulder will appear to droop. If either of these measurement points is too small, the shoulder may be drawn in and appear too small. (A tighter-fitting knit top is especially vulnerable to this problem.)

Problem Area 4—Waist or bottom opening/sweep is pulling or gaping open (Figures 16.4a, b, and c).

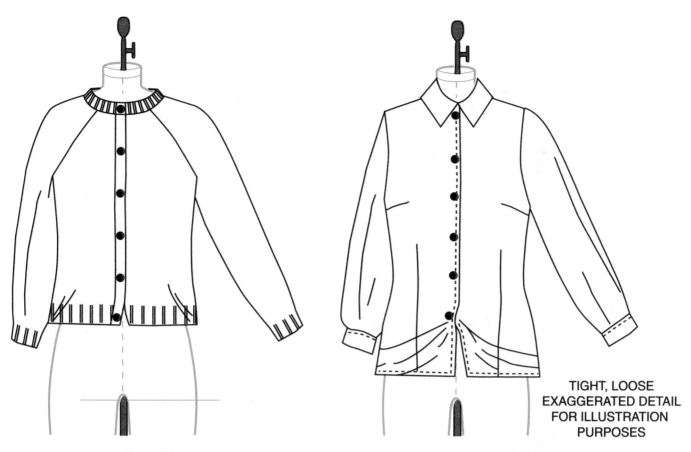

Figure 16.4a

Figure 16.4b

TIGHT, LOOSE
EXAGGERATED DETAIL
FOR ILLUSTRATION
PURPOSES

Figure 16.4c

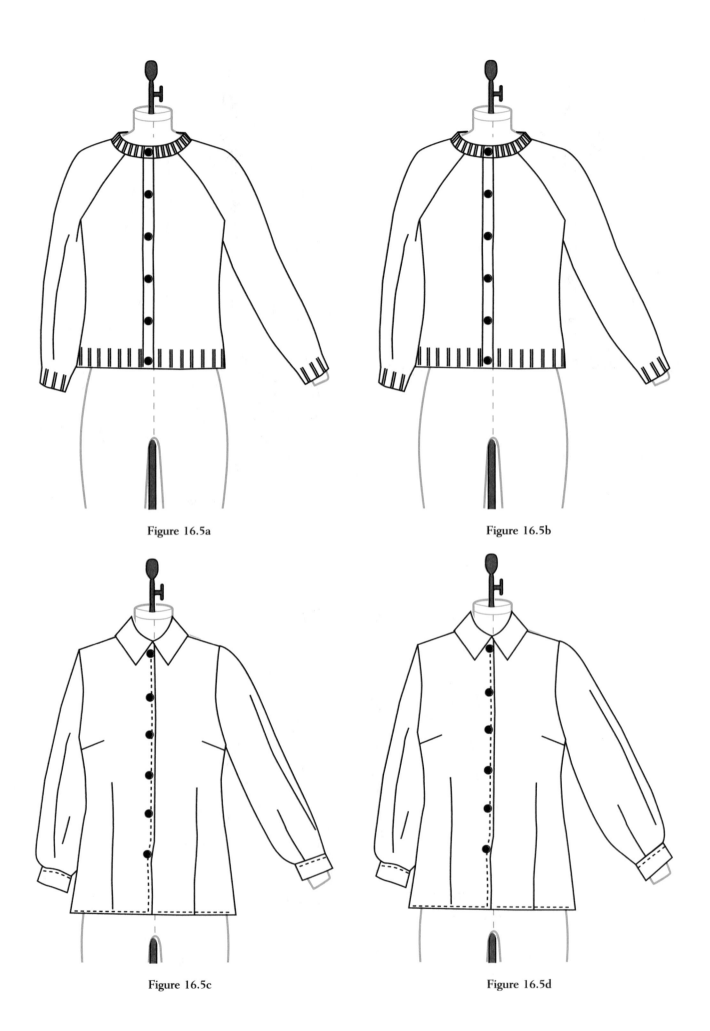

Figure 16.5a

Figure 16.5b

Figure 16.5c

Figure 16.5d

Solution A—Check the waist and bottom opening/ sweep width measurements. Is there enough ease allowed in this garment or is there too much? If not, add or reduce the required amount of ease depending on the results you desire.

[Note: Occasionally, the front opening will be pulling, but the sides or back are loose. This indicates a problem in the bust area. Perhaps not enough ease was allowed or the dart placement is incorrect. Sometimes, diagnosing one problem area leads to a different area or solution.]

Problem Area 5—Sleeve length is too long/short (Figures 16.5a–d).

Solution A—The problem may be simply that the sleeve length needs to be lengthened or shortened.

Solution B—The sleeve length is longer on either the outer or inner seams or the sleeve opening does not lie parallel on the hand/wrist. Either of these problems is due to an improperly sloped sleeve cap. If the sleeve cap is too long, the sleeve length will pull up on the underarm seam (Figure 16.5e). If the sleeve cap is too short, the sleeve will droop along the outer edge (Figure 16.5f). I recommend removing the sleeve from the garment and looking at the sleeve cap slope, then adjusting accordingly.

Solution C—The shoulder seam may be too short, pulling the sleeve up, or it may be too long, making the sleeve appear too long. Check the sleeve width. Does it lie properly? If not, adjust accordingly.

Problem Area 6—Sleeve is too tight on the upper arm (Figures 16.6a and b).

Solution A— Rule out the possibility that there is not enough ease in the sleeve. If this is the case, adjust the entire sleeve width (Figure 16.6c).

Solution B—The more common problem is the sleeve cap slope. If the sleeve cap is too long, the sleeve width at the armhole will be too small, causing the sleeve to be too tight. A good way to check this problem without removing the sleeve from the garment is to lift the arm. If the sleeve pulls across the upper arm and pulls the chest, the sleeve cap is definitely cut with too long a cap. Some manufacturers will often cut sleeve caps this way to save fabric on the width of the sleeve without affecting any of the other measurements (Figure 16.6d).

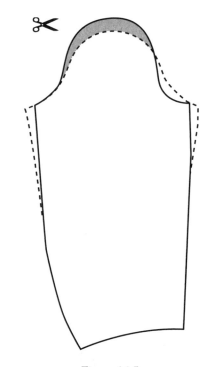

Figure 16.5e

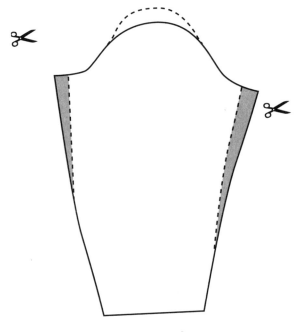

Figure 16.5f

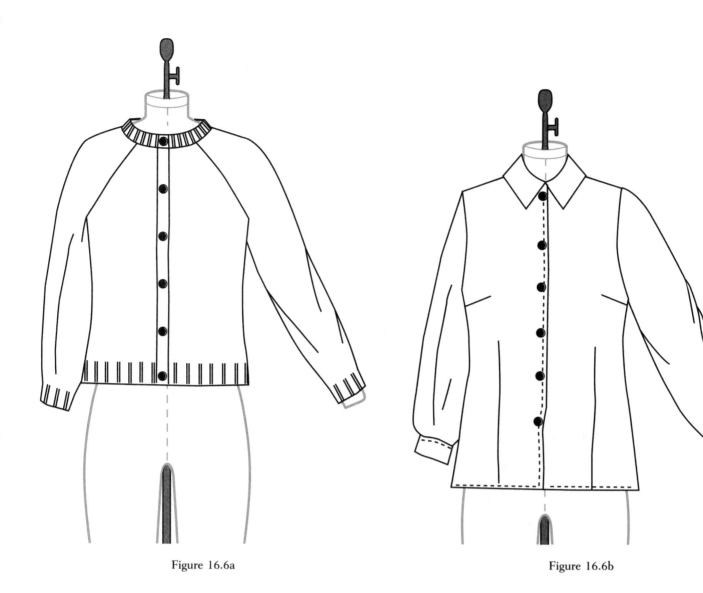

Figure 16.6a

Figure 16.6b

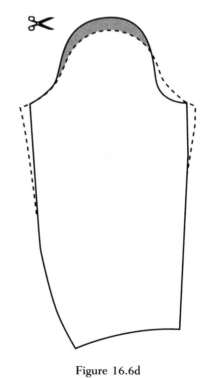

Figure 16.6c

Figure 16.6d

Problem Area 7—Armhole is too tight/too loose (Figures 16.7a and b).

Solution A—Simply check the spec measurement. Is the armhole too small or too big? Make the necessary adjustments (Figures 16.7c and d).

Solution B—The armhole has not been cut with the proper curve. If the front or back armhole curve is too severe, the underarm seam may ride too high under the arm and appear too small. If the front or back armhole has not been cut with enough curve, then the armhole will droop under the arm and appear too small. Adjust accordingly.

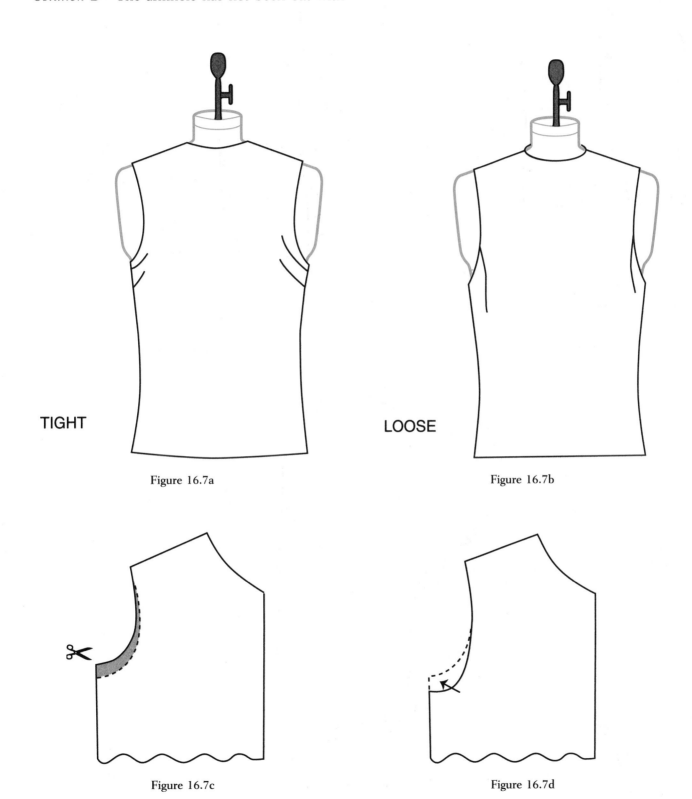

TIGHT

Figure 16.7a

LOOSE

Figure 16.7b

Figure 16.7c

Figure 16.7d

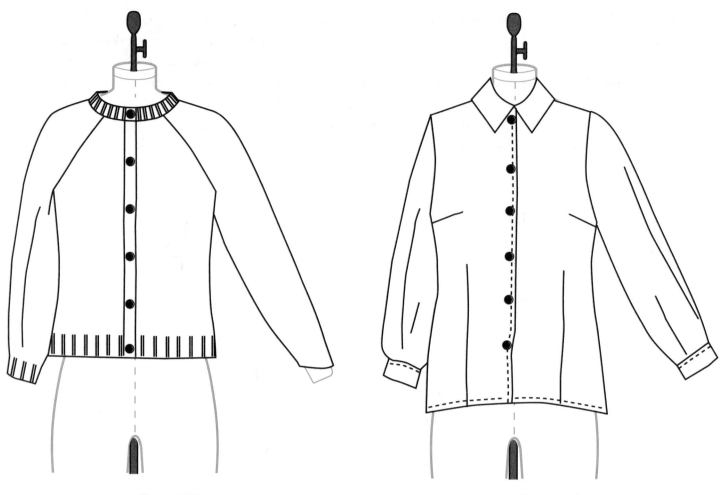

Figure 16.8a

Figure 16.8b

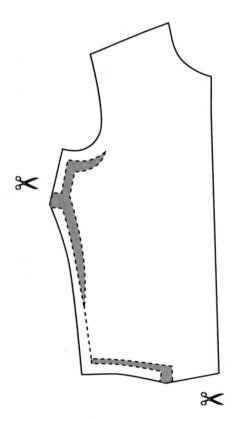

Figure 16.8c

Problem Area 8—The front bodice is shorter than the back bodice (Figures 16.8a and b).

Solution A—This is a common mistake and sometimes difficult to correct for knits because not enough ease has been allowed to accommodate the bust and darts cannot be added. The pattern either needs to be slashed and spread more in this area or more allowance can be added at the front shoulder area and at the dart area (Figure 16.8c). This will mean that the front armhole will be slightly longer than the back armhole. Lying flat, the shoulder seam will appear to fall toward the back; however, this will give a little extra fabric to the front of the garment to accommodate the chest. Always have the patternmaker recheck the pattern.

Problem Area 9—The garment does not fit over the head.

Solution A—A majority of knit tops are designed without buttoned or zippered neck openings. As a result, it is imperative that there is enough stretch in the neck opening to allow the garment to be slipped over the head. This is especially crucial for turtleneck styles. Double-check the neck width and neck drop measurements to make sure they are correct.

Solution B—If the spec measurements are correct and the neck opening is still too tight, the manufacturer may have to be notified. They may have to adjust their knitting machines to allow for more stretch.

Solution C—On rare occasions, the specs are correct and the knitting cannot be adjusted without adversely affecting the garment in other fit areas. In this case, the neck shape of the garment will have to be redesigned.

Skirts

Problem Area 1—Skirt pulls across the abdomen (Figures 16.9a and b).

Solution A—This is a common problem for fitted skirts when there is not enough ease added across the abdomen. If the skirt has darts, simply add more depth to the dart curve. If it has princess seams, add more ease at the princess joining seam. If it has pleats or gathers, add more depth to the pleat width or to the shirring area. If the side seam is too straight, adjust the curve accordingly (Figure 16.9c). Since few knitted skirts have darts, pleats, or shirring, the skirt construction must be looked at very closely. Is the skirt full fashioned, meaning

Figure 16.9a

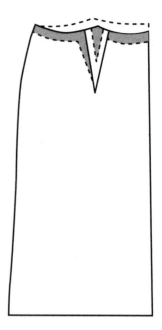

Figure 16.9c

Figure 16.9b

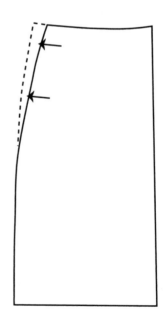

Figure 16.9d

adding or reducing knit stitches has created the shape? If it is, then the actual knitting must be looked at and stitches must be added as needed. This process is common in flat-knit weft knitting.

Solution B—Does the hemline also pull up? If so, slash and spread the pattern horizontally at the center front waist, over but not through the waist at the side seam. Add the required ease (Figure 16.9d).

Solution C—There may not be enough length in the abdomen. Does the hemline also pull up? If so, slash and spread the pattern horizontally at the center front waist, over but not through the waist at the side seam. Add the required ease (Figures 16.9e and f).

Solution D—If the dart, princess, pleat, or shirred areas seem to have enough depth, then check the side seam hip curve. If the side seam is too straight, adjust the curve accordingly. If the skirt has darts, simply add more depth to the dart curve. If it has princess seams, add more ease at the princess joining seam. If it has pleats or gathers, add more depth to the pleat width or to the shirring area. If the side seam is too straight, adjust the curve accordingly.

Problem Area 2—The skirt is too big, sags across the abdomen (Figures 16.10a and b).

Solution A—This is a common problem for fitted skirts when there is too much ease added across the abdomen. Again, since few knitted skirts have darts, pleats, or shirring, the skirt construction must be looked at very closely. If the skirt is full fashioned, then the actual knitting process must be looked at and stitches must be reduced as needed. Again, since few knitted skirts have darts, pleats, or shirring, the skirt construction must be looked at very closely. If it has princess seams, reduce the ease at the princess joining seam. If it has pleats or gathers, reduce the depth to the pleat width or to the shirring area (Figure 16.10c).

Solution B—If the dart, princess, pleat, or shirred area depths are correct, then check the side seam hip curve. If the side seam is too full, straighten the curve accordingly (Figure 16.10d).

Solution C—There may be too much length in the abdomen. Does the hemline also sag at the center front? If so, slash and pinch or fold the pattern horizontally at the center front waist, over but not through the waist at the side seam. Reduce the ease (Figure 16.10e and f).

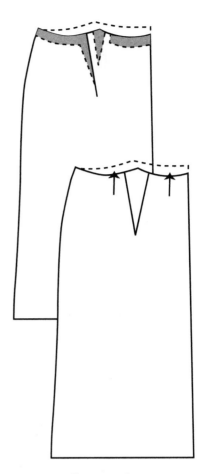

Figure 16.9e

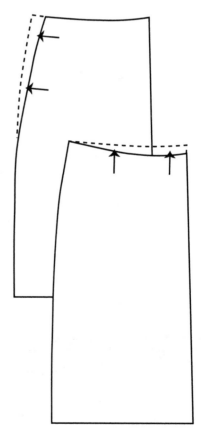

Figure 16.9f

Figure 16.10a

Figure 16.10b

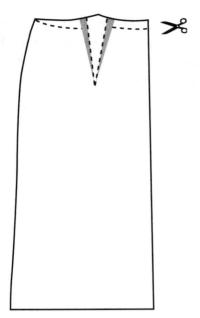

Figure 16.10c

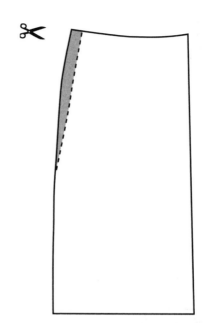

Figure 16.10d

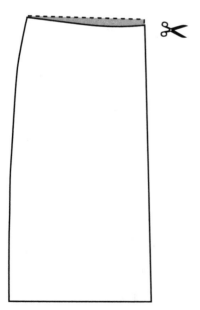

Figure 16.10e

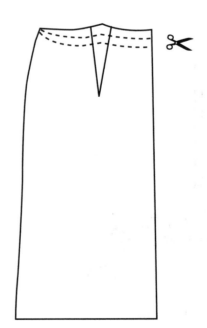

Figure 16.10f

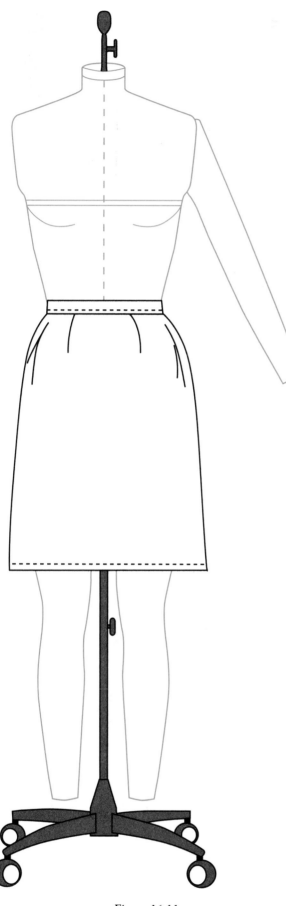

Figure 16.11

Solution D—This is a common problem for fitted skirts when there is too much ease added across the abdomen. If the skirt has darts, simply reduce the depth of the dart curve. If it has princess seams, reduce the ease at the princess joining seam. If it has pleats or gathers, reduce the depth to the pleat width or to the shirring area.

Problem Area 3—Fabric at the side seam, abdomen, and hip areas bulges (Figure 16.11).

Solution A—The ease has been placed at the side seam and not distributed evenly throughout the body. See solutions A through D in Problem Area 1 and adjust accordingly.

Problem Area 4—There is horizontal folding below the back waist and above the buttocks (Figures 16.12a and b).

Solution A—The skirt needs less fabric in the length between the waist and hip area. Tuck the pattern horizontally at the center back, without distorting the side seam length (Figures 16.12c and d).

Solution B—The back darts are too long. Shorten accordingly (Figure 16.12e).

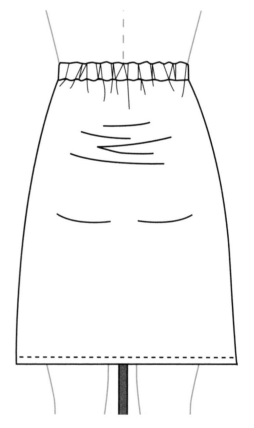

Figure 16.12a

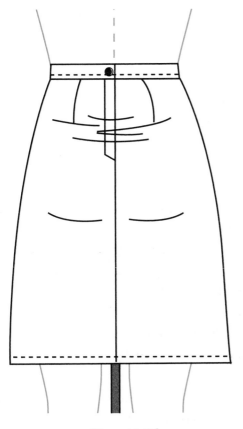

Figure 16.12b

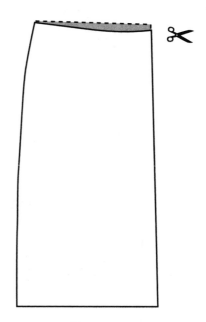

Figure 16.12c

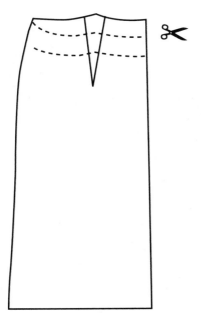

Figure 16.12d

Figure 16.12e

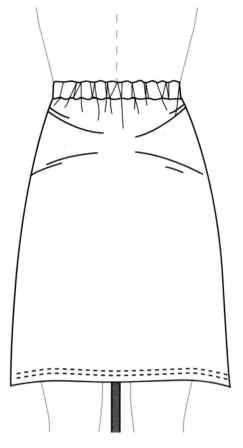

Figure 16.13a

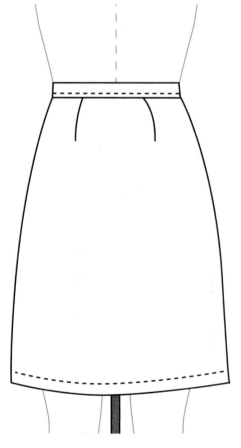

Figure 16.13b

Problem Area 5—Hemline does not hang straight (Figures 16.13a and b).

Solution A—The hem is pulling up at the center front; more ease needs to be added across the abdomen. Check the pattern and adjust accordingly.

Solution B—The hem is pulling up at the center back; more ease needs to be added across the buttocks. Check the pattern and adjust accordingly.

Solution C—The hem is pulling up on the side seams; the side seam at the hip may be too short. Check the pattern length between the waist and the thigh and adjust accordingly.

Solution D—The hem sags at the center front; too much ease has been added to the abdomen. Check the pattern and adjust accordingly.

Solution E—The hem sags at the center back; too much ease has been added to the buttocks. Check the pattern and adjust accordingly.

Solution F—The hem is sagging at the side seams; the side seam at the hip may be too long. Check the pattern length between the waist and the thigh and adjust accordingly.

Solution G—The hem is simply not straight. Check the pattern. If the hemline is straight on the pattern, and none of the problems exist in solutions A through F, then the garment may have been cut or sewn unevenly.

Pants

Problem Area 1—Pant pulls across the abdomen (Figure 16.14a and b).

Solution A—This is a common problem for knit pants when there is not enough ease for the abdomen. Since few knitted pants have darts, pleating, or shirring, the pant construction must be looked at very closely. Is the pant full fashioned, meaning that the shape is achieved by adding or removing stitches? If it is, then the actual knitting process must be looked at and stitches must be added as needed. This process is common in flat-knit weft knitting (Figure 16.14c).

Solution B—The front rise may not be long enough. The garment may need more length and/or width at the abdomen. Lengthen or raise the garment at the front waist and widen or move out the garment at the center front. Be sure to taper both corrections back to the original side seam and front rise (Figure 16.14d).

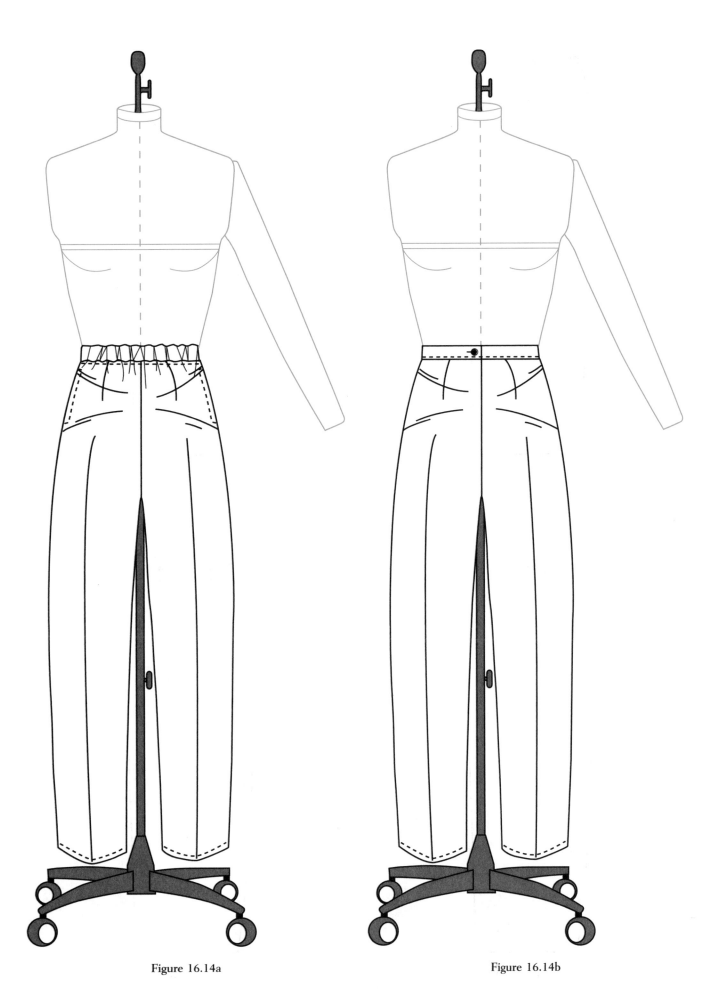

Figure 16.14a

Figure 16.14b

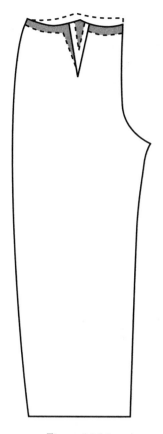

Figure 16.14c

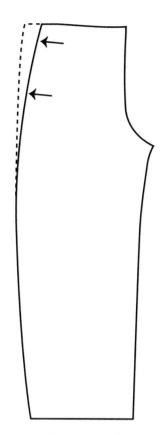

Figure 16.14d

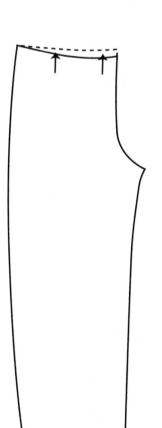

Figure 16.14e

Figure 16.14f

Solution C—If the pant has darts, simply add more depth to the dart curve. If it has pleats or gathers, add more depth to the pleat width or to the shirring area (Figures 16.14e and f).

Solution D—If the dart, pleat, or shirred areas seem to have enough depth, then check the side seam hip curve. If the side seam is too straight, adjust the curve accordingly.

Problem Area 2—The pant is too big, sagging across the abdomen (Figures 16.15a and b).

Solution A—This is a common problem for knit pants when there is too much ease for the abdomen. Again, since few knitted pants have darts, pleating, or shirring, the pant construction must be looked at very closely. If the pant is full fashioned, then the actual knitting process must be looked at and stitches must be reduced as needed. This process is common in flat-knit weft knitting (Figure 16.15c).

Solution B—The front rise may be too long. The garment may need less length and/or width at the abdomen. Shorten or lower the garment at the front waist and narrow or move the seam in at the center front. Be sure to taper both corrections back to the original side seam and front rise (Figure 16.15d).

Solution C—If the pant has darts, simply reduce the depth of the dart curve. If it has pleats or gathers, reduce the depth to the pleat width or to the shirring area (Figures 16.15e and f).

Solution D—If the dart, pleat, or shirred area depths are correct, then check the side seam hip curve. If the side seam is too full, straighten the curve accordingly.

Refer to Figures 16.15a–f on the next page.

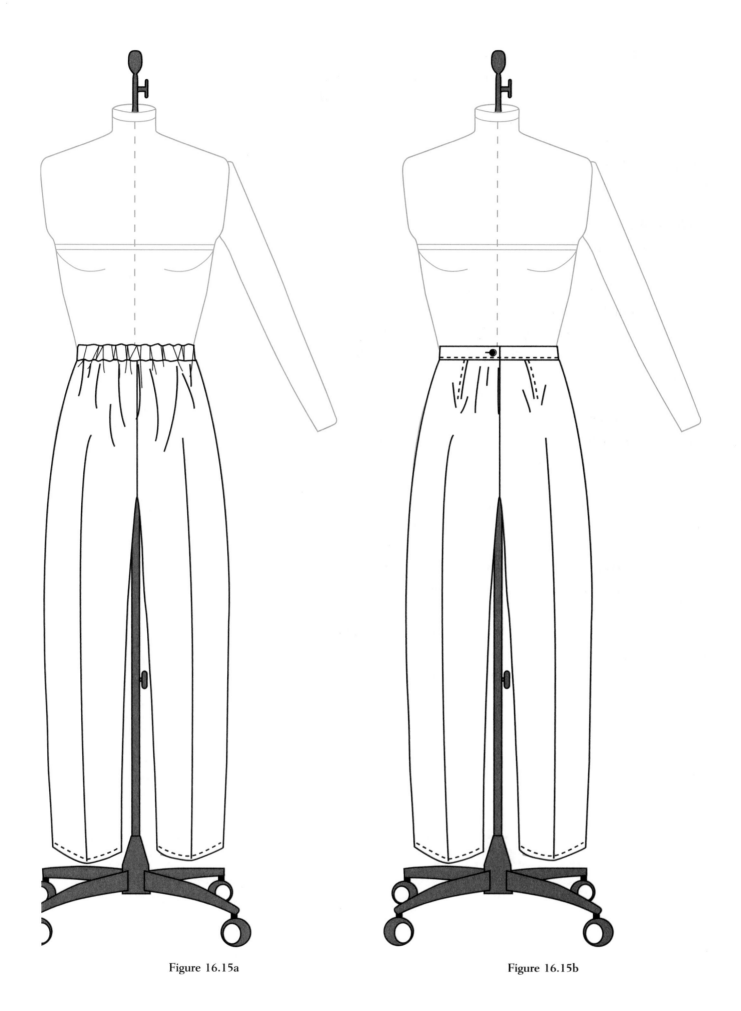

Figure 16.15a

Figure 16.15b

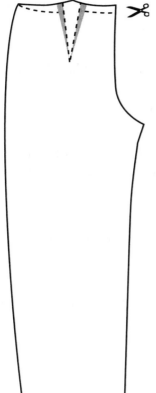

Figure 16.15c

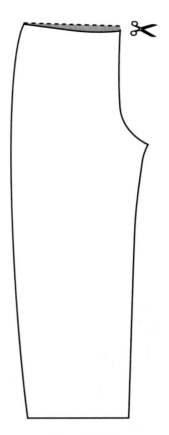

Figure 16.15e

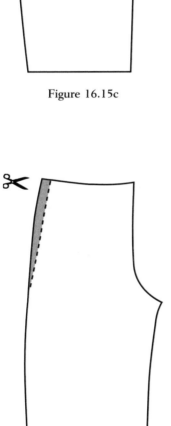

Figure 16.15d

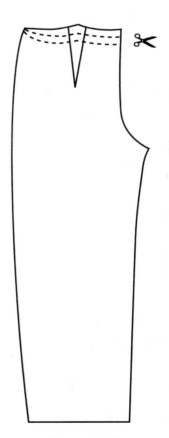

Figure 16.15f

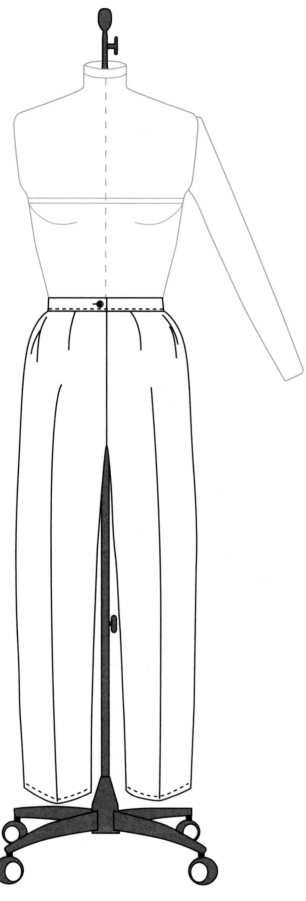

Figure 16.16

Problem Area 3—Fabric at the side seam, abdomen, and hip areas bulge (Figure 16.16).

Solution A—The ease has been placed at the side seam and not distributed evenly throughout the body. See solutions A through D in Problem Area 1 and adjust accordingly.

Problem Area 4—There is horizontal folding below the back waist and above the buttocks (Figure 16.17a).

Solution A—The pant needs less fabric in the length between the waist and hip area. Tuck the pattern horizontally at the center back, without distorting the side seam length (Figures 16.7b and c).
Solution B—The back darts are too long. Shorten accordingly (Figure 16.17d).

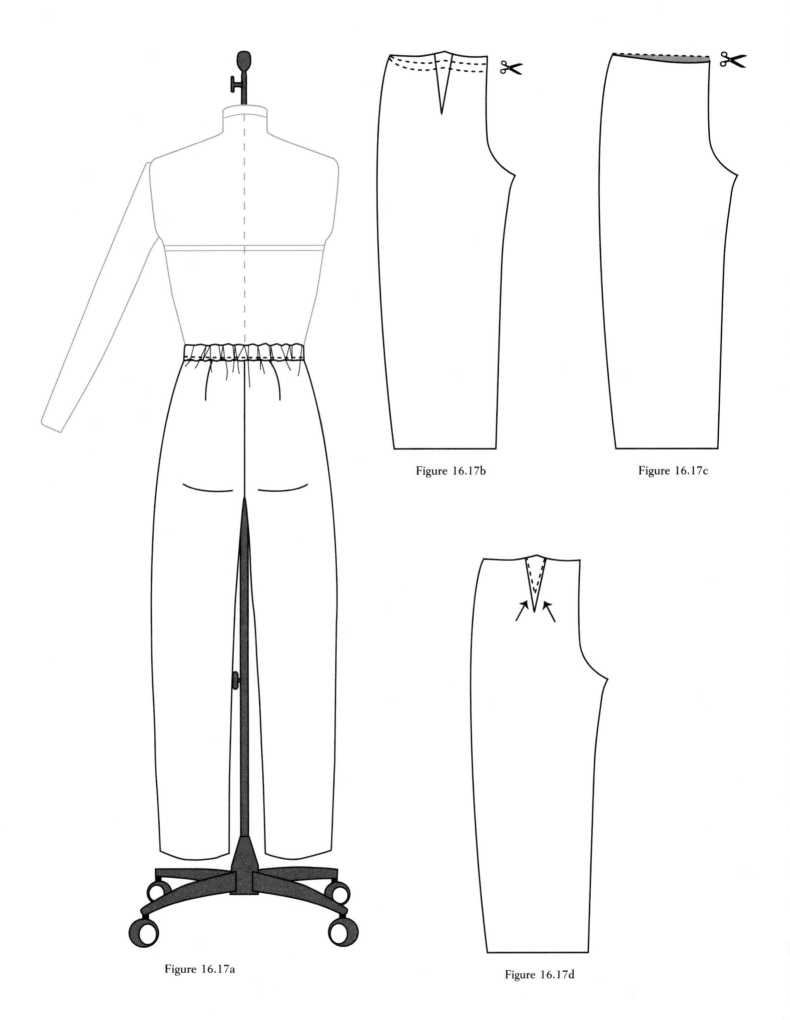

Figure 16.17b

Figure 16.17c

Figure 16.17a

Figure 16.17d

Problem Area **5**—The front rise does not fit well. It sags (Figure 16.18a).

[Note: Rises are the most difficult area to fit. Always check the rise curve first. You will know if the rise is ill fitting if the pant hangs flat at the crotch. The measurement of the rise may be to spec, but the pant is still ill fitting. An easy way to check for a poor rise is to sit. Does the pant leg pull up on the body to allow movement for sitting? Is the thigh measurement narrow? Is the inseam shorter than the outseam? These are all indicators for a poorly shaped rise.]

Solution A—Check the rise measurement first. If the measurement is too big, then too much fabric has been added to the pattern at the abdomen and waist. Does the garment sag in this area? Shorten the rise above the curve (Figure 16.18b).

Solution B—If the measurement is correct, yet the pant sags at the crotch, check the rise curve. Lay the pant front side up on the table and manipulate the curve so that it lays flat. If you have a sloper, check the garment's curve against the pattern. If not, use your judgment. Does the curve turn at a good angle or is it too straight? A good indicator that the curve is too shallow is that the front thigh width is shorter than the back thigh width. To correct the rise, fabric must be taken from the front and added into the curve (Figure 16.18c).

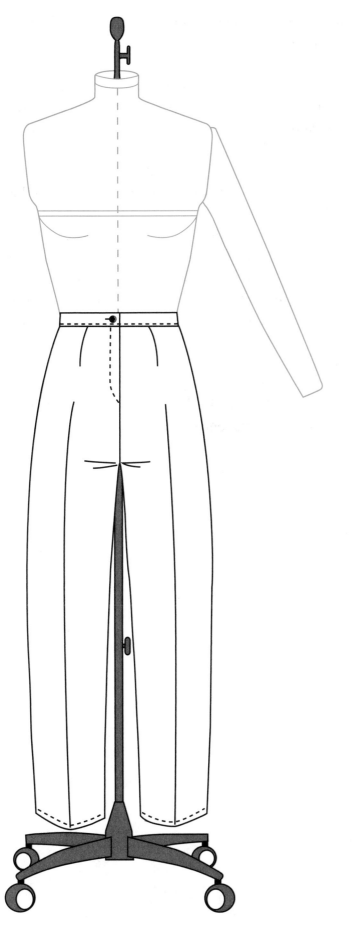

Figure 16.18a

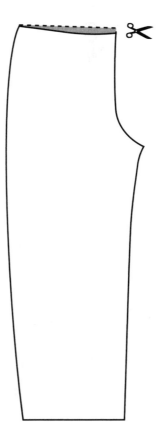

Figure 16.18b

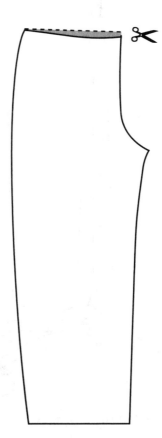

Figure 16.18c

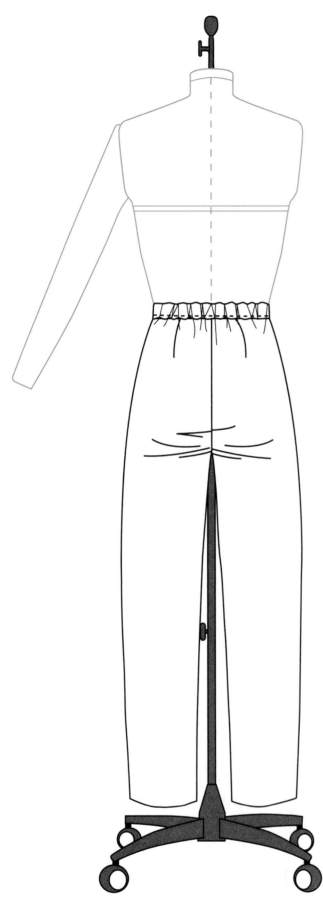

Figure 16.19a

Problem Area 6—The pant is too tight across the buttocks (Figure 16.19a).

Solution A—This is a common problem for knit pants when there is not enough ease for the buttocks. Since few knitted pants have darts, the pant construction must be looked at very closely. Is the pant full fashioned? If it is, then the actual knitting process must be looked at and stitches must be added as needed. This process is common in flat-knit weft knitting (Figure 16.19b).

Solution B—The back rise may not be long enough. The garment may need more length and/or width at the buttocks. Lengthen or raise the garment at the back waist and widen or move out the garment at the center back. Be sure to taper both corrections back to the original side seam and back rise (Figure 16.19c).

Solution C—If the pant has darts, simply add more depth to the dart curve (Figure 16.19d).

Solution D—If the dart depth is OK, see if the side seam is too straight. Adjust the curve accordingly.

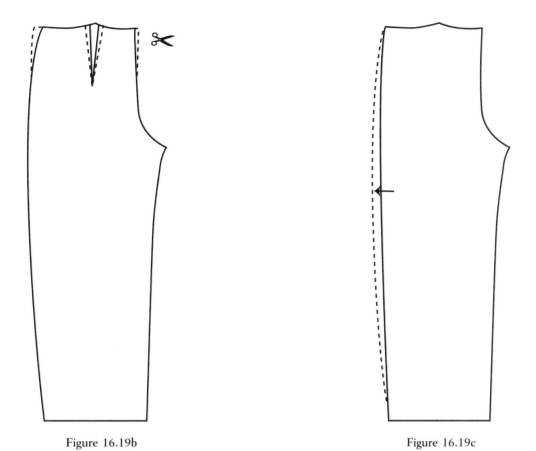

Figure 16.19b

Figure 16.19c

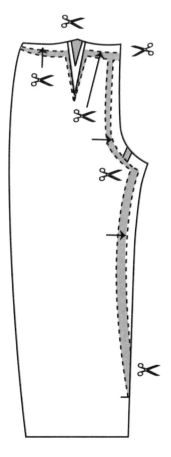

Figure 16.19d

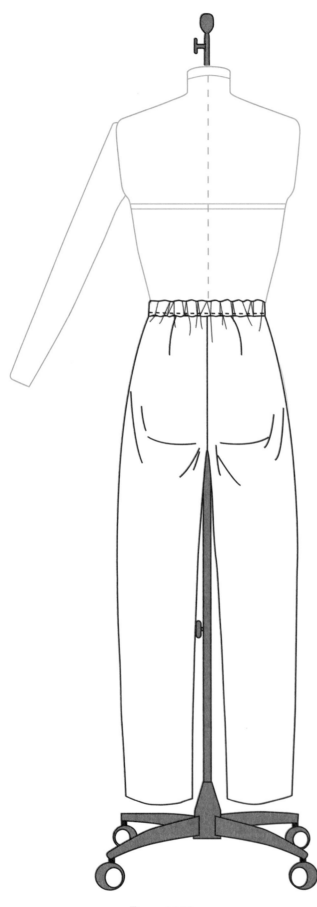

Figure 16.20a

Problem Area 7—The pant is too loose across the buttocks (Figure 16.20a).

Solution A—This is a common problem for knit pants when there is too much ease for the buttocks. Again, few knitted pants have darts; therefore, the pant construction must be looked at very closely. Is the pant full fashioned? If it is, then the actual knitting process must be looked at and stitches must be reduced as needed. This process is common in flat-knit weft knitting (Figure 16.20b).

Solution B—The back rise may be too long. The garment may need less length and/or width at the buttocks. Shorten or lower the garment at the back waist and narrow or move in the garment at the center back. Be sure to taper both corrections back to the original side seam and back rise (Figure 16.20c).

Solution C—If the pant has darts, simply add more depth to the dart curve (Figure 16.20d).

Solution D—If the dart depth is OK, see if the side seam is too straight. Adjust the curve accordingly.

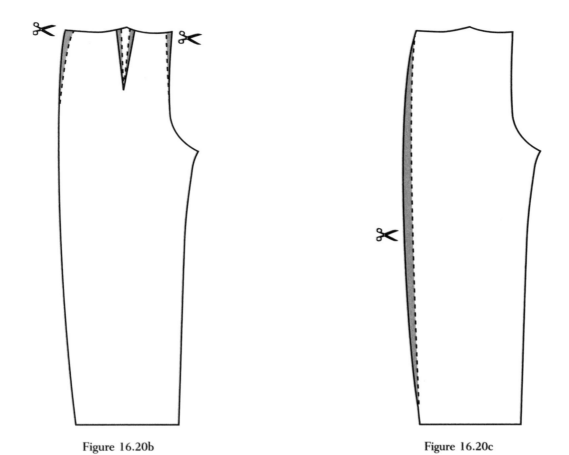

Figure 16.20b

Figure 16.20c

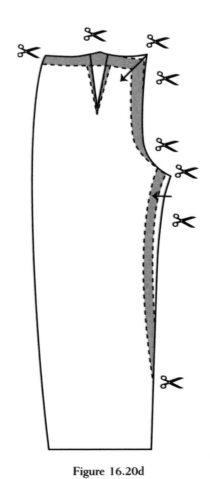

Figure 16.20d

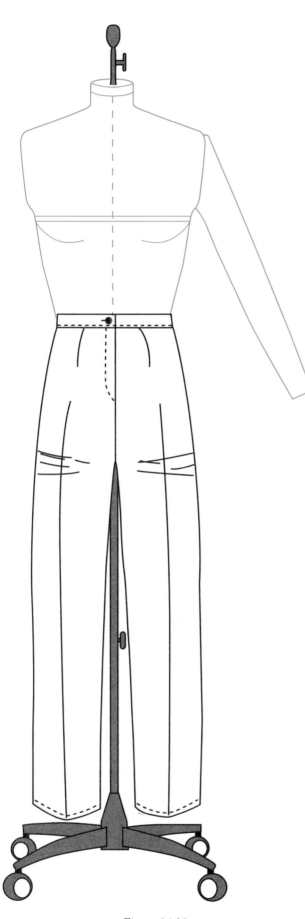

Figure 16.21a

Problem Area 8—Thigh area is too tight (Figure 16.21a).

Solution A—Check the rise and correct as instructed in Problem Area 5, Solution B. This will give more ease to the thigh area.

Solution B—If the rise is correct, add width to the side seams at the thigh area and taper into the hip and leg (Figure 16.21b).

Problem Area 9—Thigh area is too big (Figure 16.22a).

Solution A—Check the rise. It is rare for too much curve to be added to the rise, but it is possible. Shorten the rise curve at the crotch, which will reduce the width of the thigh (Figure 16.22b).

Solution B—If the rise is correct, reduce the width of the side seams at the thigh area and taper into the hip and leg (Figure 16.22c).

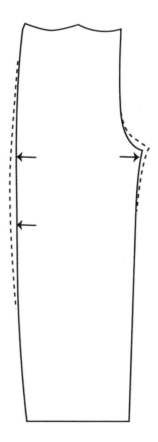

Figure 16.21b

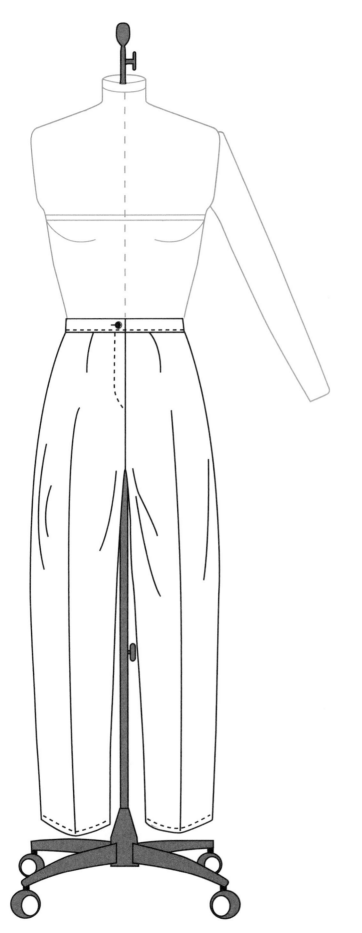

Figure 16.22a

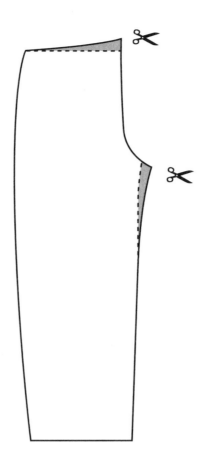

Figure 16.22b

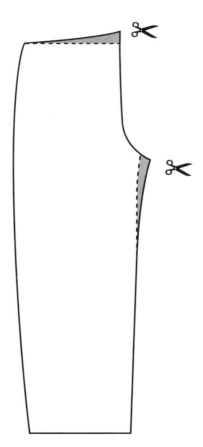

Figure 16.22c

Over the course of your career, you may encounter these and many other fit issues. Figure 16.23 has been added as a visual example of the fitting process on a spec sheet.

CHAPTER 16 TERMS

When working with fitting and grading, you may come across the garment terms listed below. If you are unfamiliar with any of them, please look up the definitions in the glossary at the end of this text.

Ease
Fit
Slope

SPEC SHEET:	Knit top	STYLE	
SEASON: Early fall		DESCRIPTION: Sleeveless Turtleneck	
LABEL: (SIZE CATEGORY) Missy			
DATE:			

TECHNICAL SKETCH   Turtleneck

SKETCH/PHOTO

CODE	POINT OF MEASURE	TOL. +/−	4	S/6	8	M/10	12	L/14	16	XL/18
1.	Front length	1/2				23				
3.	Center back length	1/2				21 1/2				
4.	Side length	1/4				14				
9.	Chest width	1/4-3/8				18 1/2				
13.	Across shoulder	1/4				14 3/4	15			
15.	Across chest	1/4				13 3/4	14			
16.	Across back	1/4				13 3/4	14			
25.	Bottom band/ribbing height	1/8				3/8				
26.	Bottom opening/sweep	1/4-3/8				18 1/2				
36.	Sleeve length top armhole	3/8								
39.	Sleeve length underarm	3/8								
42.	Curved armhole width (opening)	1/4				9				
48.	Muscle width	1/8								
50.	Elbow width	1/8								
52.	Sleeve opening width	1/8								
54.	Sleeve opening width stretched	1/8								
57.	Cuff/ribbing height sleeve (armhole)	1/8				3/8				
58.	Neck depth front	1/8				1				

(Tolerance 1/4-3/8 S, M, L, XL = 3/8" 4-18 = 1/4")

The measured garment spec sheets are for *illustrative purposes only* and should not be used as industry standards

CODE	POINT OF MEASURE	TOL. +/−	4	S/6	8	M/10	12	L/14	16	XL/18
63.	Neck width collar	1/4				6½				
64.	Neck edge width	1/4				6½				
66.	Neck edge width stretched	1/4				13				
68.	Neck base	1/4				7½				
72.	Collar height	1/8				6				
73.	Collar band height	1/8				3/8				
122.	Side vent A. Height	1/4				2½				
	B. Width rib	1/8				3/8				
	POINT OF MEASURE	TOL. +/−	4	S/6	8	M/10	12	L/14	16	XL/18

COMMENTS:

The measured garment spec sheets are for *illustrative purposes only* and should not be used as industry standards

CHAPTER 17

Grading

How to Grade a Spec Sheet

A sample garment, once approved for production, must be graded or converted into all of the other sizes that will be produced. In other words, each piece of the sample pattern must be made either smaller or larger (graded) to achieve the rest of the patterns in that size range. For example, if the top evaluated and approved is a size medium, it must then be converted to sizes small, large, and extra large.

Many private labels and most merchandising companies send their patterns out to jobbers to be produced. In order to get the exact size conversions desired, it is imperative for the spec sheet to contain grading information. This information sheet is called a Fully Graded Specification. A jobber may convert the patterns by hand or may have computer systems such as Lectra E-manufacturing products; GERBERsuite, a patternmaking, grading, and marker making system; or Gerber Pattern Design 2000, by Gerber Technologies (a division of Gerber Scientific), which allows the operators to do size customizations. Regardless of the system used, the operator/grader needs to know the desired proportions to use, which he or she will get from your graded spec sheet.

Garment grading is another one of those difficult processes. Most graders apprentice as patternmakers for several years before grading their own patterns. Many companies have set up or purchased mathematical formulas for grading and most of it is done by computers; however, there are occasions when the numbers will not convert correctly. It takes years of trial and error, plus working closely with a grading expert, for the technician to be able to troubleshoot these instances. For now, simply use the charts provided for practice.

Grading Guidelines for Misses/Missy Sizes

The following charts offer grading guidelines for the most common measurement points used in this text. Simply add or subtract measurements from your sample size, as shown on the chart. Please note that these guidelines are an average of popular industry grades; because they averaged measurements, they will not work for everyone. Most technical designers round grades to the closest eighth or quarter of an inch; however, many graders will grade as precisely as one-sixteenth of an inch. Therefore, I would like to caution the reader not to presume that the mea-

Many companies use computer systems to grade patterns.

surements given are industry standards; they are simply a re-flection of popular standards used within the industry. These charts also include tolerance levels. Tolerances are the differ-ential allowed between a given measurement and the actual measurement, an acceptable allowance for human sewing error.

CHAPTER 17 TERMS

When grading a garment, you may come across the terms listed below. If you are unfamiliar with any of them, please look up the definitions listed in the glossary at the end of this text.

Fully graded specification
Grading
Tolerance

CODE AND TERM	4	6	8	10	12	14	16	18	TOL. +/−
1. Front Length	−1/4	−1/4	−1/4	X	+1/4	+1/4	+1/4	+1/4	1/2
2. Center Front Length	−1/4	−1/4	−1/4	X	+1/4	+1/4	+1/4	+1/4	1/2
3. Center Back Length	−1/4	−1/4	−1/4	X	+1/4	+1/4	+1/4	+1/4	1/2
4. Side Length	−1/4	−1/4	−1/4	X	+1/4	+1/4	+1/4	+1/4	1/4
5. Front Bodice Length	−1/4	−1/4	−1/4	X	+1/4	+1/4	+1/4	+1/4	1/4
6. Center Front Bodice length	−1/4	−1/4	−1/4	X	+1/4	+1/4	+1/4	+1/4	1/4
7. Center Back Bodice length	−1/4	−1/4	−1/4	X	+1/4	+1/4	+1/4	+1/4	1/4
8. Side Seam Bodice Length	−1/4	−1/4	−1/4	X	+1/4	+1/4	+1/4	+1/4	1/4
9. Chest Width (knit)	−1/2	−1/2	−1/2	X	+3/4	+3/4	+3/4	+3/4	1/4
10. Chest Width Circumference (woven)	−1	−1	−1	X	+1 1/2	+1 1/2	+1 1/2	+1 1/2	1/2
11. Chest Width (raglan sleeve, knit)	−1/2	−1/2	−1/2	X	+3/4	+3/4	+3/4	+3/4	1/4
12. Chest Width Circumference (raglan sleeve, woven)	−1	−1	−1	X	+1 1/2	+1 1/2	+1 1/2	+1 1/2	1/2
13. Across Shoulder	−1/4	−1/4	−1/4	X	+3/8	+3/8	+3/8	+3/8	1/4
14. Shoulder Width	−0	−1/8	−0	X	+1/8	+1/8	+1/8	+1/8	1/4
15. Across Chest	−1/4	−1/4	−1/4	X	+3/8	+3/8	+3/8	+3/8	1/4
16. Across Back	−1/4	−1/4	−1/4	X	+3/8	+3/8	+3/8	+3/8	1/4
17. Across Chest Center Armhole	−1/4	−1/4	−1/4	X	+3/8	+3/8	+3/8	+3/8	1/4
18. Across Back Center Armhole	−1/4	−1/4	−1/4	X	+3/8	+3/8	+3/8	+3/8	1/4
19. Waist Width (knit)	−1/2	−1/2	−1/2	X	+3/4	+3/4	+3/4	+3/4	1/4
20. Waist Width Circumference (woven)	−1	−1	−1	X	1 1/2	1 1/2	1 1/2	1 1/2	1/2
21. Bottom Band Width (knit top)	−1/2	−1/2	−1/2	X	+3/4	+3/4	+3/4	+3/4	1/4
22. Bottom Band Circumference (woven top)	−1	−1	−1	X	+1 1/2	+1 1/2	+1 1/2	+1 1/2	1/2
23. Bottom Band Width Stretched (knit top)	−1/2	−1/2	−1/2	X	+3/4	+3/4	+3/4	+3/4	1/4
24. Bottom Band Width Circumference Stretched (woven top)	−1	−1	−1	X	+1 1/2	+1 1/2	+1 1/2	+1 1/2	1/2
25. Bottom Band/Ribbing Height (knit or woven top)	−0	−0	−0	X	+0	+0	+0	+0	1/8
26. Bottom Opening/Sweep (knit top)	−1/2	−1/2	−1/2	X	+3/4	+3/4	+3/4	+3/4	1/4
27. Bottom Opening/Sweep Width Circumference (woven top)	−1	−1	−1	X	+1 1/2	+1 1/2	+1 1/2	+1 1/2	1/2

(continued)

Grading Chart for Missy and Misses Sizes Continued

CODE AND TERM	S	M	L	XL	TOL. +/-
1. Front Length	$-1/2$	X	$+1/2$	$+1/2$	$1/2$
2. Center Front Length	$-1/2$	X	$+1/2$	$+1/2$	$1/2$
3. Center Back Length	$-1/2$	X	$+1/2$	$+1/2$	$1/2$
4. Side Length	$-1/2$	X	$+1/2$	$+1/2$	$1/4$
5. Front Bodice Length	$-1/2$	X	$+1/2$	$+1/2$	$1/4$
6. Center Front Bodice length	$-1/2$	X	$+1/2$	$+1/2$	$1/4$
7. Center Back Bodice length	$-1/2$	X	$+1/2$	$+1/2$	$1/4$
8. Side Seam Bodice Length	$-1/2$	X	$+1/2$	$+1/2$	$1/4$
9. Chest Width (knit)	-1	X	$+1 1/2$	$+1 1/2$	$3/8$
10. Chest Width Circumference (woven)	-2	X	$+3$	$+3$	$3/4$
11. Chest Width (raglan sleeve, knit)	-1	X	$+1 1/2$	$+1 1/2$	$3/8$
12. Chest Width Circumference (raglan sleeve, woven)	-2	X	$+3$	$+3$	$3/4$
13. Across Shoulder	$-1/2$	X	$+3/4$	$+3/4$	$1/4$
14. Shoulder Width	$-1/8$	X	$+1/4$	$+1/4$	$1/4$
15. Across Chest	$-1/2$	X	$+3/4$	$+3/4$	$1/4$
16. Across Back	$-1/2$	X	$+3/4$	$+3/4$	$1/4$
17. Across Chest Center Armhole	$-1/2$	X	$+3/4$	$+3/4$	$1/4$
18. Across Back Center Armhole	$-1/2$	X	$+3/4$	$+3/4$	$1/4$
19. Waist Width (knit)	-1	X	$+1 1/2$	$+1 1/2$	$3/8$
20. Waist Width Circumference (woven)	-2	X	$+3$	$+3$	$3/4$
21. Bottom Band Width (knit top)	-1	X	$+1 1/2$	$+1 1/2$	$3/8$
22. Bottom Band Circumference (woven top)	-2	X	$+3$	$+3$	$3/4$
23. Bottom Band Width Stretched (knit top)	-1	X	$+1 1/2$	$+1 1/2$	$3/8$
24. Bottom Band Width Circumference Stretched (woven top)	-2	X	$+3$	$+3$	$3/4$
25. Bottom Band/Ribbing Height (knit or woven top)	-0	X	$+0$	$+0$	$1/8$
26. Bottom Opening/Sweep (knit top)	-1	X	$+1 1/2$	$+1 1/2$	$3/8$
27. Bottom Opening/Sweep Width Circumference (woven top)	-2	X	$+3$	$+3$	$3/4$

(continued)

Grading Chart for Missy and Misses Sizes Continued

CODE AND TERM	4	6	8	10	12	14	16	18	TOL. +/-
28. Vented Bottom Opening/Sweep Width (knit top)	-1/2	-1/2	-1/2	X	+3/4	+3/4	+3/4	+3/4	1/4
29. Vented Bottom Opening/Sweep Width Circumference (woven top)	-1	-1	-1	X	+1 1/2	+1 1/2	+1 1/2	+1 1/2	1/2
30. Circular Bottom Opening/Sweep Width (knit top)	-1/2	-1/2	-1/2	X	+3/4	+3/4	+3/4	+3/4	1/4
31. Circular Bottom Opening/Sweep Width Circumference (woven top)	-1	-1	-1	X	+1 1/2	+1 1/2	+1 1/2	+1 1/2	1/2
32. Yoke Width Front	-1/4	-1/4	-1/4	X	+3/8	+3/8	+3/8	+3/8	1/4
33. Yoke Width Back	-1/4	-1/4	-1/4	X	+3/8	+3/8	+3/8	+3/8	1/4
34. Yoke Depth Front	-0	-0	-0	X	+0	+0	+0	+0	1/8
35. Yoke Back Depth	-0	-0	-0	X	+0	+0	+0	+0	1/8
36. Sleeve Length Top Armhole (Short Sleeve to Long Sleeve)	-1/8-1/4	-1/8-1/4	-1/8-1/4	X	-1/8-1/4	-1/8-1/4	-1/8-1/4	-1/8-1/4	3/8
37. Sleeve Length Top Neck (Short Sleeve to Long Sleeve)	-1/4-1/2	-1/4-1/2	-1/4-1/2	X	-1/4-1/2	-1/4-1/2	-1/4-1/2	-1/4-1/2	3/8
38. Sleeve Length Center Back (Short Sleeve to Long Sleeve)	-1/4-1/2	-1/4-1/2	-1/4-1/2	X	-1/4-1/2	-1/4-1/2	-1/4-1/2	-1/4-1/2	3/8
39. Sleeve Length Underarm (Short Sleeve to Long Sleeve)	-1/8-1/4	-1/8-1/4	-1/8-1/4	X	-1/8-1/4	-1/8-1/4	-1/8-1/4	-1/8-1/4	3/8
40. Straight Armhole Width (knit)	-1/4	-1/4	-1/4	X	+3/8	+3/8	+3/8	+3/8	1/4
41. Straight Armhole Width Circumference (woven)	-1/2	-1/2	-1/2	X	+5/8	+5/8	+5/8	+5/8	3/8
42. Curved Armhole Width (knit)	-1/4	-1/4	-1/4	X	+3/8	+3/8	+3/8	+3/8	1/4
43. Curved Armhole Width Circumference (woven)	-1/2	-1/2	-1/2	X	+5/8	+5/8	+5/8	+5/8	3/8
44. Armhole Front (Or Use: Grade Accordingly)	-1/4	-1/4	-1/4	X	+1/4	+1/4	+1/4	+1/4	1/4
45. Armhole Back (Or Use: Grade Accordingly)	-1/4	-1/4	-1/4	X	+1/4	+1/4	+1/4	+1/4	1/4
46. Armhole Width Straight (knit)	-1/4	-1/4	-1/4	X	+3/8	+3/8	+3/8	+3/8	1/4
47. Armhole Width Circumference Straight (woven)	-1/2	-1/2	-1/2	X	+5/8	+5/8	+5/8	+5/8	3/8
48. Muscle Width (knit) (Regular Sleeve vs Dolman Sleeve)	-1/8-1/4	-1/8-1/4	-1/8-1/4	X	+1/4-3/8	+1/4-3/8	+1/4-3/8	+1/4-3/8	1/8
49. Muscle Width Circumference (woven) (Regular Sleeve vs Dolman Sleeve)	-1/8-1/4	-1/8-1/4	-1/8-1/4	X	+1/4-3/8	+1/4-3/8	+1/4-3/8	+1/4-3/8	1/4
50. Elbow Width (knit)	-1/8	-1/8	-1/8	X	+1/8	+1/8	+1/8	+1/8	1/8
51. Elbow Width Circumference (woven)	-1/4	-1/4	-1/4	X	+3/8	+3/8	+3/8	+3/8	1/4
52. Sleeve Opening Width (knit) (Long Sleeve to Short & Capped)	-1/8-1/4	-1/8-1/4	-1/8-1/4	X	+1/8-1/4	+1/8-1/4	+1/8-1/4	+1/8-1/4	1/8
53. Sleeve Opening Width Circumference (woven) (Long Sleeve to Short & Capped)	-1/4-1/2	-1/4-1/2	-1/4-1/2	X	+1/4-1/2	+1/4-1/2	+1/4-1/2	+1/4-1/2	1/4
54. Sleeve Opening Width Stretched (knit) (Long Sleeve to Short & Capped)	-1/8-1/4	-1/8-1/4	-1/8-1/4	X	+1/8-1/4	+1/8-1/4	+1/8-1/4	+1/8-1/4	1/8

(continued)

Grading Chart for Missy and Misses Sizes Continued

CODE AND TERM	S	M	L	XL	TOL. +/-
28. Vented Bottom Opening/Sweep Width (knit top)	−1	X	+1½	+1½	⅜
29. Vented Bottom Opening/Sweep Width Circumference (woven top)	−2	X	+3	+3	¾
30. Circular Bottom Opening/Sweep Width (knit top)	−1	X	+1½	+1½	⅜
31. Circular Bottom Opening/Sweep Width Circumference (woven top)	−2	X	+3	+3	¾
32. Yoke width Front	−½	X	+¾	+¾	¼
33. Yoke Width Back	−½	X	+¾	+¾	¼
34. Yoke Depth Front	−0	X	+0	+0	⅛
35. Yoke Back Depth	−0	X	+0	+0	⅛
36. Sleeve Length Top Armhole (Short Sleeve to Long Sleeve)	−1/4-1/2	X	+1/4-1/2	+1/4-1/2	⅜
37. Sleeve Length Top Neck (Short Sleeve to Long Sleeve)	−3/8-5/8	X	+3/8-5/8	+3/8-5/8	⅜
38. Sleeve Length Center Back (Short Sleeve to Long Sleeve)	−3/8-5/8	X	+3/8-5/8	+3/8-5/8	⅜
39. Sleeve Length Underarm	−1/4-1/2	X	+1/4-1/2	+1/4-1/2	⅜
40. Straight Armhole Width (knit)	−½	X	+¾	+¾	¼
41. Straight Armhole Width Circumference (woven)	−1	X	+1¼	+1¼	⅜
42. Curved Armhole Width (knit)	−½	X	+¾	+¾	¼
43. Curved Armhole Width Circumference (woven)	−1	X	+1¼	+1¼	⅜
44. Armhole Front (Or Use: Grade Accordingly)	−½	X	+½	+½	¼
45. Armhole Back (Or Use: Grade Accordingly)	−½	X	+½	+½	¼
46. Armhole Width Straight (knit)	−½	X	+¾	+¾	¼
47. Armhole Width Circumference Straight (woven)	−1	X	+1¼	+1¼	⅜
48. Muscle Width (knit) (Regular Sleeve vs Dolman Sleeve)	−1/4-1/2	X	+3/8-5/8	+3/8-5/8	⅛
49. Muscle Width Circumference (woven) (Regular Sleeve vs Dolman Sleeve)	−1/4-1/2	X	+3/8-5/8	+3/8-5/8	¼
50. Elbow Width (knit)	−¼	X	+½	+½	⅛
51. Elbow Width Circumference (woven)	−½	X	+¾	+¾	¼
52. Sleeve Opening Width (knit) (Long Sleeve to Short & Capped)	−1/4-1/2	X	+1/4-1/2	+1/4-1/2	⅛
53. Sleeve Opening Width Circumference (woven) (Long Sleeve to Short & Capped)	−1/2-1	X	+1/2-1	+1/2-1	¼
54. Sleeve Opening Width Stretched (knit) (Long Sleeve to Short & Capped)	−1/4-1/2	X	+1/4-1/2	+1/4-1/2	⅛

(continued)

Grading Chart for Missy and Misses Sizes Continued

CODE AND TERM	4	6	8	10	12	14	16	18	TOL. +/-
55. Sleeve Opening Width Circumference Stretched (woven) (Long Sleeve to Short & Capped)	−1/4-1/2	−1/4-1/2	−1/4-1/2	X	−1/4-1/2	−1/4-1/2	−1/4-1/2	−1/4-1/2	1/4
56. Cuff Length Sleeve	−1/4	−1/4	−1/4	X	+1/4	+1/4	+1/4	+1/4	1/4
57. Cuff/Ribbing Height Sleeve	−0	−0	−0	X	+0	+0	+0	+0	1/8
58. Neck Depth Front (garments with a plain front/asymmetrical front opening)	−0-1/4	−0-1/4	−0-1/4	X	−0-1/4	−0-1/4	−0-1/4	−0-1/4	1/8
59. Neck Depth Center Front (garments with a center front opening)	−0-1/4	−0-1/4	−0-1/4	X	−0-1/4	−0-1/4	−0-1/4	−0-1/4	1/8
60. Neck Drop Front	−0-1/4	−0-1/4	−0-1/4	X	−0-1/4	−0-1/4	−0-1/4	−0-1/4	1/8
61. Neck Drop Back *Depending on Style*	−0-1/4	−0-1/4	−0-1/4	X	−0-1/4	−0-1/4	−0-1/4	−0-1/4	1/8
62. Neck Width, No Collar	−1/8	−1/8	−1/8	X	+1/4	+1/4	+1/4	+1/4	1/8
63. Neck Width, Collar	−1/8	−1/8	−1/8	X	+1/4	+1/4	+1/4	+1/4	1/8
64. Neck Edge Width (knit)	−1/8	−1/8	−1/8	X	+1/4	+1/4	+1/4	+1/4	1/8
65. Neck Edge Width Circumference (woven)	−1/4	−1/4	−1/4	X	+3/8	+3/8	+3/8	+3/8	1/4
66. Neck Edge Width, Stretched (knit)	−1/8	−1/8	−1/8	X	+1/4	+1/4	+1/4	+1/4	1/8
67. Neck Edge Width Circumference, Stretched (woven)	−1/4	−1/4	−1/4	X	+3/8	+3/8	+3/8	+3/8	1/4
68. Neck Base (knit)	−1/8	−1/8	−1/8	X	+1/4	+1/4	+1/4	+1/4	1/8
69. Neck Base Circumference (woven)	−1/4	−1/4	−1/4	X	+3/8	+3/8	+3/8	+3/8	1/4
70. Neckband Length	−1/4	−1/4	−1/4	X	+3/8	+3/8	+3/8	+3/8	1/4
71. Collar Length	−1/4	−1/4	−1/4	X	+3/8	+3/8	+3/8	+3/8	1/4
72. Collar Height	−0	−0	−0	X	+0	+0	+0	+0	1/8
73. Collar Band Height	−0	−0	−0	X	+0	+0	+0	+0	1/16
74. Collar Point Length	−0	−0	−0	X	+0	+0	+0	+0	1/8
75. Collar Point Spread (pointed collars only) *(Or Use: Grade Accordingly)*	−1/16	−1/16	−1/16	X	+1/16	+1/16	+1/16	+1/16	1/4
76. Lapel Width	—	—	—	X	—	—	—	—	—
A. Notched	−0	−0	−0	X	+0	+0	+0	+0	1/8
B. Without Notches	−0	−0	−0	X	+0	+0	+0	+0	1/8
77. Center Front Extension *(Or Use: Grade Accordingly)*	−0	−0	−0	X	+0	+0	+0	+0	1/8
78. Placket Length *(Or Use: Grade Accordingly)*	−0	−0	−0	X	+0	+0	+0	+0	1/4
79. Placket Width	−0	−0	−0	X	+0	+0	+0	+0	1/8

(continued)

Grading Chart for Missy and Misses Sizes Continued

CODE AND TERM	S	M	L	XL	TOL. +/-
55. Sleeve Opening Width Circumference Stretched (woven) (Long Sleeve to Short & Capped)	$-^1/_2$-1	X	$+^1/_2$-1	$+^1/_2$-1	$^1/_4$
56. Cuff Length Sleeve	$-^1/_2$	X	$+^1/_2$	$+^1/_2$	$^1/_4$
57. Cuff/Ribbing Height Sleeve	-0	X	$+0$	$+0$	$^1/_8$
58. Neck Depth Front (garments with a plain front/asymmetrical front opening)	-0-$^1/_4$	X	$+0$-$^1/_4$	$+0$-$^1/_4$	$^1/_8$
59. Neck Depth Center Front (garments with a center front opening)	-0-$^1/_4$	X	$+0$-$^1/_4$	$+0$-$^1/_4$	$^1/_8$
60. Neck Drop Front	-0-$^1/_4$	X	$+0$-$^1/_4$	$+0$-$^1/_4$	$^1/_8$
61. Neck Drop Back	-0-$^1/_4$	X	$+0$-$^1/_4$	$+0$-$^1/_4$	$^1/_8$
62. Neck Width, No Collar	$-^3/_8$	X	$+^3/_8$	$+^1/_2$	$^1/_8$
63. Neck Width, Collar	$-^3/_8$	X	$+^3/_8$	$+^1/_2$	$^1/_8$
64. Neck Edge Width (knit)	$-^3/_8$	X	$+^3/_8$	$+^1/_2$	$^1/_8$
65. Neck Edge Width Circumference (woven)	$-^3/_4$	X	$+^3/_4$	$+1$	$^1/_8$
66. Neck Edge Width, Stretched (knit)	$-^3/_8$	X	$+^3/_8$	$+1$	$^1/_8$
67. Neck Edge Width Circumference, Stretched (woven)	$-^3/_4$	X	$+^3/_4$	$+1$	$^1/_4$
68. Neck Base (knit)	$-^3/_8$	X	$+^3/_8$	$+^1/_2$	$^1/_8$
69. Neck Base Circumference (woven)	$-^3/_4$	X	$+^3/_4$	$+1$	$^1/_4$
70. Neckband Length	$-^3/_4$	X	$+^3/_4$	$+1$	$^1/_4$
71. Collar Length	$-^3/_4$	X	$+^3/_4$	$+1$	$^1/_4$
72. Collar Height	-0	X	$+0$	$+0$	$^1/_8$
73. Collar Band Height	-0	X	$+0$	$+0$	$^1/_{16}$
74. Collar Point Length	-0	X	$+0$	$+0$	$^1/_8$
75. Collar Point Spread (pointed collars only)	$-^1/_8$	X	$+^1/_8$	$+^1/_8$	$^1/_4$
76. Lapel Width	—	—	—	—	—
A. Notched	-0	X	$+0$	$+0$	$^1/_8$
B. Without Notches	-0	X	$+0$	$+0$	$^1/_8$
77. Center Front Extension	-0	X	$+0$	$+0$	$^1/_8$
78. Placket Length	-0	X	$+0$	$+0$	$^1/_4$
79. Placket Width	-0	X	$+0$	$+0$	$^1/_8$

(Or Use: Grade Accordingly) — 75. Collar Point Spread (pointed collars only)

(Or Use: Grade Accordingly) — A. Notched / B. Without Notches

Depending on Style — 58–61

(continued)

Grading Chart for Missy and Misses Sizes Continued

CODE AND TERM	4	6	8	10	12	14	16	18	TOL. +/-
(Or Use: Grade Accordingly)									
80. Keyhole Length	−0	−0	−0	X	+0	+0	+0	+0	1/8
81. Waistband Depth	−0	−0	−0	X	+0	+0	+0	+0	1/8
82. Waistband Width (knit)	−1/2	−1/2	−1/2	X	+3/4	+3/4	+3/4	+3/4	1/4
83. Waistband Circumference (woven)	−1	−1	−1	X	+1 1/2	+1 1/2	+1 1/2	+1 1/2	1/2
84. Waistband Width Stretched (knit)	−1/2	−1/2	−1/2	X	+3/4	+3/4	+3/4	+3/4	1/4
85. Waistband Width Circumference Stretched (woven)	−1	−1	−1	X	+1 1/2	+1 1/2	+1 1/2	+1 1/2	1/2
86. High Hip Width (knit)	−1/2	−1/2	−1/2	X	+3/4	+3/4	+3/4	+3/4	1/4
87. High Hip Width Circumference (woven)	−1	−1	−1	X	+1 1/2	+1 1/2	+1 1/2	+1 1/2	1/2
88. Low Hip Width From Waist (knit)	−1/2	−1/2	−1/2	X	+3/4	+3/4	+3/4	+3/4	1/4
89. Low Hip Width Circumference From Waist (woven)	−1	−1	−1	X	+1 1/2	+1 1/2	+1 1/2	+1 1/2	1/2
90. Hip Width From HPS (knit)	−1/2	−1/2	−1/2	X	+3/4	+3/4	+3/4	+3/4	1/4
91. Hip Width From HPS Circumference (woven)	−1	−1	−1	X	+1 1/2	+1 1/2	+1 1/2	+1 1/2	1/2
92. Hip Seat Width (knit pant)	−1/2	−1/2	−1/2	X	+3/4	+3/4	+3/4	+3/4	1/4
93. Hip Seat Width Circumference (woven pant)	−1	−1	−1	X	+1 1/2	+1 1/2	+1 1/2	+1 1/2	1/2
94. Bottom Opening/Sweep Width (knit skirt)	−1/2	−1/2	−1/2	X	+3/4	+3/4	+3/4	+3/4	1/4
95. Bottom Opening/Sweep Width Circumference (woven skirt)	−1	−1	−1	X	+1 1/2	+1 1/2	+1 1/2	+1 1/2	1/2
96. Vented Bottom Opening/Sweep Width (knit skirt)	−1/2	−1/2	−1/2	X	+3/4	+3/4	+3/4	+3/4	1/4
97. Vented Bottom Opening/Sweep Width Circumference (woven skirt)	−1	−1	−1	X	+1 1/2	+1 1/2	+1 1/2	+1 1/2	1/2
98. Circular Bottom Opening/Sweep Width (knit skirt)	−1/2	−1/2	−1/2	X	+3/4	+3/4	+3/4	+3/4	1/4
99. Circular Bottom Opening/Sweep Width Circumference (woven skirt)	−1	−1	−1	X	+1 1/2	+1 1/2	+1 1/2	+1 1/2	1/2
100. Center Front Skirt Length	−0	−0	−0	X	+0	+0	+0	+0	3/8
101. Center Back Skirt Length	−0	−0	−0	X	+0	+0	+0	+0	3/8
102. Side Skirt Length	−0	−0	−0	X	+0	+0	+0	+0	3/8
103. Skirt/Pant Yoke Depth Front	−0	−0	−0	X	+0	+0	+0	+0	1/4
104. Skirt/Pant Yoke Depth Back	−0	−0	−0	X	+0	+0	+0	+0	1/4
105. Inseam	−0	−0	−0	X	+0	+0	+0	+0	3/8
106. Outseam	−1/8	−1/4	−1/4	X	+1/4	+1/4	+1/4	+1/4	3/8

Or grade accordingly if an inseam length grade is desired (add above length to this measurement)

(continued)

CODE AND TERM	S	M	L	XL	TOL. +/-
(Or Use: Grade Accordingly)					
80. Keyhole Length	-0	X	+0	+0	1/8
81. Waistband Depth	-0	X	+0	+0	1/8
82. Waistband Width (knit)	-1	X	+1 1/2	+1 1/2	3/8
83. Waistband Circumference (woven)	-2	X	+3	+3	3/4
84. Waistband Width Stretched (knit)	-1	X	+1 1/2	+1 1/2	3/8
85. Waistband Width Circumference Stretched (woven)	-2	X	+3	+3	3/4
86. High Hip Width (knit)	-1	X	+1 1/2	+1 1/2	3/8
87. High Hip Width Circumference (woven)	-2	X	+3	+3	3/4
88. Low Hip Width From Waist (knit)	-1	X	+1 1/2	+1 1/2	3/8
89. Low Hip Width Circumference From Waist (woven)	-2	X	+3	+3	3/4
90. Hip Width From HPS (knit)	-1	X	+1 1/2	+1 1/2	3/8
91. Hip Width From HPS Circumference (woven)	-2	X	+3	+3	3/4
92. Hip Seat Width (knit pant)	-1	X	+1 1/2	+1 1/2	3/8
93. Hip Seat Width Circumference (woven pant)	-2	X	+3	+3	3/4
94. Bottom Opening/Sweep Width (knit skirt)	-1	X	+1 1/2	+1 1/2	3/8
95. Bottom Opening/Sweep Width Circumference (woven skirt)	-2	X	+3	+3	3/4
96. Vented Bottom Opening/Sweep Width Circumference (knit skirt)	-1	X	+1 1/2	+1 1/2	3/8
97. Vented Bottom Opening/Sweep Width Circumference (woven skirt)	-2	X	+3	+3	3/4
98. Circular Bottom Opening/Sweep Width (knit skirt)	-1	X	+1 1/2	+1 1/2	3/8
99. Circular Bottom Opening/Sweep Width Circumference (woven skirt)	-2	X	+3	+3	3/4
100. Center Front Skirt Length	-0	X	+0	+0	3/8
101. Center Back Skirt Length	-0		+0	+0	3/8
102. Side Skirt Length	-0	X	+0	+0	3/8
103. Skirt/Pant Yoke Depth Front	-0	X	+0	+0	1/4
104. Skirt/Pant Yoke Depth Back	-0	X	+0	+0	1/4
105. Inseam	-0	X	+0	+0	3/8
106. Outseam	-1/2	X	+1 1/2	+1 1/2	3/8

Or grade accordingly if an inseam length grade is desired (add above length to this measurement)

(continued)

CODE AND TERM	4	6	8	10	12	14	16	18	TOL. +/-
107. Front Rise	−1/4	−3/8	−3/8	X	+3/8	+3/8	+3/8	+3/8	3/8
108. Back Rise	−1/4	−3/8	−3/8	X	+3/8	+3/8	+3/8	+3/8	3/8
109. Thigh Width (knit)	−1/4	−3/8	−3/8	X	+1/2	+1/2	+1/2	+1/2	1/4
110. Thigh Width Circumference (woven)	−1/2	−3/4	−3/4	X	+1	+1	+1	+1	3/8
111. Knee Width (knit) *(Or use: Grade accordingly)*	−1/4	−1/4	−1/4	X	+3/8	+3/8	+3/8	+3/8	1/4
112. Knee Width Circumference (woven) *(Or use: Grade accordingly)*	−3/8	−1/2	−1/2	X	+3/4	+3/4	+3/4	+3/4	3/8
113. Leg Opening Width (knit)	−1/8	−1/8	−1/8	X	+1/4	+1/4	+1/4	+1/4	1/8
114. Leg Opening Width Circumference (woven)	−1/4	−1/4	−1/4	X	+3/8	+3/8	+3/8	+3/8	1/4
115. Vented Leg Opening Width (knit)	−1/8	−1/8	−1/8	X	+1/4	+1/4	+1/4	+1/4	1/8
116. Vented Leg Opening Circumference (woven)	−1/4	−1/4	−1/4	X	+3/8	+3/8	+3/8	+3/8	1/4
117. Leg Opening Width Stretched (knit)	−1/8	−1/8	−1/8	X	+1/4	+1/4	+1/4	+1/4	1/8
118. Leg Opening Width Stretched Circumference (woven)	−1/4	−1/4	−1/4	X	+3/8	+3/8	+3/8	+3/8	1/4
119. Cuff Height Pants	−0	−0	−0	X	+0	+0	+0	+0	1/8
120. Bottom Band/Ribbing Height pants	−0	−0	−0	X	+0	+0	+0	+0	1/8
121. Fly/Zipper	—	—	—	X	—	—	—	—	—
A. Length *(Or use: Grade accordingly)*	−0	−0	−0	X	+0	+0	+0	+0	1/4
B. Fly/Zipper width	−0	−0	−0	X	+0	+0	+0	+0	1/8
122. Vent/Slit	—	—	—	X	—	—	—	—	—
A. Height *(Or use: Grade accordingly)*	−0	−0	−0	X	+0	+0	+0	+0	1/4
B. Width	−0	−0	−0	X	+0	+0	+0	+0	1/8
123. Pleat Depth	−0	−0	−0	X	+0	+0	+0	+0	1/8
124. Distance Between Pleats	*	*	*	X	*	*	*	*	1/16
125. Applied Pocket Height	−0	−0	−0	X	+0	+0	+0	+0	1/8
126. Applied Pocket Width	−0	−0	−0	X	+0	+0	+0	+0	1/8
127. Pocket Opening	−0	−0	−0	X	+0	+0	+0	+0	1/4
128. Belt Length	—	—	—	X	—	—	—	—	—
A. Total	−1	−1	−1	X	+1 1/2	+1 1/2	+1 1/2	+1 1/2	1/2

* *Grade Accordingly*

(continued)

Grading Chart for Missy and Misses Sizes Continued

CODE AND TERM	S	M	L	XL	TOL. +/-
107. Front Rise	-3/4	X	+3/4	+3/4	3/8
108. Back Rise	-3/4	X	+3/4	+3/4	3/8
109. Thigh Width (knit)	-3/4	X	+1	+1	1/4
110. Thigh Width Circumference (woven)	-1 1/2	X	+2	+2	3/8
111. Knee Width (knit) *(Or use: Grade accordingly)*	-3/8	X	+3/4	+3/4	1/4
112. Knee Width Circumference (woven) *(Or use: Grade accordingly)*	-1	X	+1 1/2	+1 1/2	3/8
113. Leg Opening Width (knit)	-1/4	X	+3/8	+3/8	1/8
114. Leg Opening Width Circumference (woven)	-1/2	X	+3/4	+3/4	1/4
115. Vented Leg Opening Width (knit)	-1/4	X	+3/8	+3/8	1/8
116. Vented Leg Opening Circumference (woven)	-1/2	X	+3/4	+3/4	1/4
117. Leg Opening Width Stretched (knit)	-1/4	X	+3/8	+3/8	1/8
118. Leg Opening Width Stretched Circumference (woven)	-1/2	X	+3/4	+3/4	1/4
119. Cuff Height Pants	-0	X	+0	+0	1/8
120. Bottom Band/Ribbing Height pants	-0	X	+0	+0	1/8
121. Fly/Zipper	—	—	—	—	—
A. Length *(Or use: Grade accordingly)*	-0	X	+0	+0	1/4
B. Fly/Zipper width	-0	X	+0	+0	1/8
122. Vent/Slit	—	—	—	—	—
A. Height *(Or use: Grade accordingly)*	-0	X	+0	+0	1/4
B. Width	-0	X	+0	+0	1/8
123. Pleat Depth	-0	X	+0	+0	1/8
124. Distance Between Pleats	*	*	*	*	1/16
125. Applied Pocket Height	-0	X	+0	+0	1/8
126. Applied Pocket Width	-0	X	+0	+0	1/8
127. Pocket Opening	-0	X	+0	+0	1/4
128. Belt Length	—	—	—	—	—
A. Total	-2	X	+3	+3	3/4

* Grade Accordingly

(continued)

Grading Chart for Missy and Misses Sizes Continued

CODE AND TERM	4	6	8	10	12	14	16	18	TOL. +/–
B. Circumference	−1	−1	−1	X	+1½	+1½	+1½	+1½	½
129. Belt Width (or height)	−0	−0	−0	X	+0	+0	+0	+0	⅛
130. Belt Loop Length	−0	−0	−0	X	+0	+0	+0	+0	⅛
131. Belt Loop Width	−0	−0	−0	X	+0	+0	+0	+0	⅛
132. Tie Length	*	*	*	X	*	*	*	*	¼
133. Tie Width	—	—	—	—	—	—	—	—	—
A. Straight	−0	−0	−0	X	+0	+0	+0	+0	⅛
B. Contoured	−0	−0	−0	X	+0	+0	+0	+0	⅛
134. Flounce/Ruffle Width	−0	−0	−0	X	+0	+0	+0	+0	⅛
135. Strap Length	*	*	*	X	*	*	*	*	¼
136. Strap Width	−0	−0	−0	X	+0	+0	+0	+0	⅛
137. Front Hood Length	−0	−0	−0	X	+0	+0	+0	+0	¼
138. Back Hood Length	−0	−0	−0	X	+0	+0	+0	+0	¼
139. Hood Width	*	*	*	X	*	*	*	*	¼
140. Flange Depth	*	*	*	X	*	*	*	*	⅛
141. Shoulder Pad Length	−0	−0	−0	X	+0	+0	+0	+0	⅛
142. Shoulder Pad Width	−0	−0	−0	X	+0	+0	+0	+0	⅛
143. Straight Edge Shoulder Pad Height	−0	−0	−0	X	+0	+0	+0	+0	1/16
144. Curved Edge Shoulder Pad Height	−0	−0	−0	X	+0	+0	+0	+0	1/16
145. Shoulder Pad Placement	*	*	*	X	*	*	*	*	⅛
146. Pleats Placement	—	—	—	—	—	—	—	—	—
A. Front Pleat Top	*	*	*	X	*	*	*	*	¼
B. Back Pleat Top	*	*	*	X	*	*	*	*	¼
C. Front Pleat Skirt/Pant	*	*	*	X	*	*	*	*	¼
147. Button Placement	*	*	*	X	*	*	*	*	⅛
148. Pocket Placement	—	—	—	—	—	—	—	—	—
A. Top Pocket Vertical	*	*	*	X	*	*	*	*	⅛

(Rows 141–144) (May use: Grade accordingly or give a spec grade if a certain size is desired)

* Grade accordingly

(continued)

Grading Chart for Missy and Misses Sizes Continued

CODE AND TERM	S	M	L	XL	TOL. +/–
B. Circumference	-2	X	+3	+3	3/4
129. Belt Width (or height)	-0	X	+0	+0	1/8
130. Belt Loop Length	-0	X	+0	+0	1/8
131. Belt Loop Width	-0	X	+0	+0	1/8
132. Tie Length	*	X	*	*	1/4
133. Tie Width	—	—	—	—	—
A. Straight	-0	X	+0	+0	1/8
B. Contoured	-0	X	+0	+0	1/8
134. Flounce/Ruffle Width	-0	X	+0	+0	1/8
135. Strap Length	*	X	*	*	1/4
136. Strap Width	-0	X	+0	+0	1/8
137. Front Hood Length	-0	X	+0	+0	1/4
138. Back Hood Length	-0	X	+0	+0	1/4
139. Hood Width	*	X	*	*	1/4
140. Flange Depth	*	X	*	*	1/8
141. Shoulder Pad Length	-0	X	+0	+0	1/8
142. Shoulder Pad Width	-0	X	+0	+0	1/8
143. Straight Edge Shoulder Pad Height	-0		+0	+0	1/16
144. Curved Edge Shoulder Pad Height	-0	X	+0	+0	1/16
145. Shoulder Pad Placement	*	X	*	*	1/8
146. Pleats Placement	—	—	—	—	—
A. Front Pleat Top	*	X	*	*	1/4
B. Back Pleat Top	*	X	*	*	1/4
C. Front Pleat Skirt/Pant	*	X	*	*	1/4
147. Button Placement	*	X	*	*	1/8
148. Pocket Placement	—	—	—	—	—
A. Top Pocket Vertical	*	X	*	*	1/8

(May use: Grade accordingly or give a spec grade if a certain size is desired)

* Grade accordingly
(continued)

Grading Chart for Missy and Misses Sizes Continued

CODE AND TERM	4	6	8	10	12	14	16	18	TOL. +/-
B. Top Pocket Horizontal	*	*	*	X	*	*	*	*	1/8
C. Front Bottom Pocket Vertical	*	*	*	X	*	*	*	*	1/8
D. Front Bottom Pocket Horizontal	*	*	*	X	*	*	*	*	1/8
E. Back Bottom Pocket Vertical	*	*	*	X	*	*	*	*	1/8
F. Back Bottom Pocket Horizontal	*	*	*	X	*	*	*	*	1/8
G. Pocket From Side Seam	*	*	*	X	*	*	*	*	1/8
149. Belt Loop	—	—	—	—	—	—	—	—	—
A. Length	-0	-0	-0	X	+0	+0	+0	+0	1/8
B. Width	-0	-0	-0	X	+0	+0	+0	+0	1/8
C. Placement C.F.	*	*	*	X	*	*	*	*	1/8
D. Placement C.B.	*	*	*	X	*	*	*	*	1/8
150. Dart Length Front	*	*	*	X	*	*	*	*	1/8
Dart Placement: Center Front & Center Back	*	*	*	X	*	*	*	*	1/8
A. High Point Shoulder Bust Dart	*	*	*	X	*	*	*	*	1/8
B. Center Front Bust Dart	*	*	*	X	*	*	*	*	1/8
C. Side Seam Bust Dart	*	*	*	X	*	*	*	*	1/8
D. High Point Shoulder Princess Dart	*	*	*	X	*	*	*	*	1/8
E. Center Front Princess Dart	*	*	*	X	*	*	*	*	1/8
F. Center Front Skirt/Pant	*	*	*	X	*	*	*	*	1/8
G. Center Back Skirt/Pant	*	*	*	X	*	*	*	*	1/8
151. Front Torso Length (Jumpsuits and One-Piece Garments)	—	—	—	—	—	—	—	—	—
A. Garments With a Front Opening Relaxed	-1/2	-1/2	-1/2	X	+1	+1	+1	+1	5/8
B. Garments With a Front Opening Extended	-1/2	-1/2	-1/2	X	+1	+1	+1	+1	5/8
C. Garments With a Plain Front, No front Opening, Relaxed	-1/2	-1/2	-1/2	X	+1	+1	+1	+1	5/8
D. Garments With a Plain Front, No Front Opening, Extended	-1/2	-1/2	-1/2	X	+1	+1	+1	+1	5/8
152. Back Torso Length (Jumpsuits and One-Piece Garments)	—	—	—	—	—	—	—	—	—
A. Relaxed (Or use "adjust accordingly" if other length measurements have already been given.)	-1/2	-1/2	-1/2	X	+1	+1	+1	+1	5/8

(For 151 A–D: Or use "adjust accordingly" if other length measurements have already been given.)

* Grade accordingly

(continued)

Grading Chart for Missy and Misses Sizes Continued

CODE AND TERM	S	M	L	XL	TOL. +/-
B. Top Pocket Horizontal	*	X	*	*	1/8
C. Front Bottom Pocket Vertical	*	X	*	*	1/8
D. Front Bottom Pocket Horizontal	*	X	*	*	1/8
E. Back Bottom Pocket Vertical	*	X	*	*	1/8
F. Back Bottom Pocket Horizontal	*	X	*	*	1/8
G. Pocket From Side Seam	*	X	*	*	1/8
149. Belt Loop	—	—	—	—	—
A. Length	-0	X	+0	+0	1/8
B. Width	-0	X	+0	+0	1/8
C. Placement C.F.	*	X	*	*	1/8
D. Placement C.B.	*	X	*	*	1/8
150. Dart Length Front	*	X	*	*	1/8
Dart Placement: Center Front & Center Back	*	X	*	*	1/8
A. High Point Shoulder Bust Dart	*	X	*	*	1/8
B. Center Front Bust Dart	*	X	*	*	1/8
C. Side Seam Bust Dart	*	X	*	*	1/8
D. High Point Shoulder Princess Dart	*	X	*	*	1/8
E. Center Front Princess Dart	*	X	*	*	1/8
F. Center Front Skirt/Pant	*	X	*	*	1/8
G. Center Back Skirt/Pant	*	X	*	*	1/8
151. Front Torso Length (Jumpsuits and One-Piece Garments)	—	—	—	—	—
A. Garments With a Front Opening Relaxed	-1		+2	+2	5/8
B. Garments With a Front Opening Extended	-1	X	+2	+2	5/8
C. Garments With a Plain Front, No front Opening, Relaxed	-1	X	+2	+2	5/8
D. Garments With a Plain Front, No Front Opening, Extended	-1	X	+2	+2	5/8
152. Back Torso Length (Jumpsuits and One-Piece Garments)	—	—	—	—	—
A. Relaxed	-1	X	+2	+2	5/8

(Or use "adjust accordingly" if other length measurements have already been given.)

(Or use "adjust accordingly" if other length measurements have already been given.)

* Grade accordingly

(continued)

Grading Chart for Missy and Misses Sizes Continued

CODE AND TERM	4	6	8	10	12	14	16	18	TOL. +/−
B. Extended (Or use adjust accordingly if other length measurements have already been given.)	−1/2	−1/2	−1/2	X	+1	+1	+1	+1	5/8
153. Total Garment Length Front	−1/2	−1/2	−1/2	X	+1	+1	+1	+1	7/8
154. Total Garment Length Back	−1/2	−1/2	−1/2	X	+1	+1	+1	+1	7/8
155. Crotch Width	−1/8	−1/8	−1/8	X	+1/8	+1/8	+1/8	+1/8	1/8

(continued)

Grading Chart for Missy and Misses Sizes Continued

CODE AND TERM	S	M	L	XL	TOL. +/−
B. Extended (Or use *adjust accordingly if other length measurements have already been given.*)	−1	X	+2	+2	$5/8$
153. Total Garment Length Front	−1	X	+2	+2	$7/8$
154. Total Garment Length Back	−1	X	+2	+2	$7/8$
155. Crotch Width	$-1/4$	X	$+1/4$	$+1/4$	$1/8$

APPENDIX A

Basic Garment Croquis

How to Use a Garment Croquis

When many people think of a fashion illustration, they think of the creative sketches often seen in magazines. Technical sketches are not those. Technical sketches must be drawn in a format called flat, in other words, without dimension. Every detail from a collar, placket, pocket, button, and topstitch must be illustrated in order to ensure garment accuracy. When creating sketches for size specification and technical design, detail is very important. First garment samples may be drafted from size specifications where the only references are the sketch and the measurements. This section contains 126 flat sketches of the most commonly designed garments. They are all uniform in missy proportion, size 8/10

or medium, so the user can trace or copy the garment body to be used as needed. Practical application of the croquis can be expedited as follows:

❖ They may be used as a guide for illustrating garments under evaluation. Simply trace the croquis that is closest to your garment into the sketch/photo section of your spec sheet, changing style features as needed.

❖ They may be used to set up a new spec sheet. Trace the croquis into the technical sketch section of your spec sheet. Add the appropriate measurement arrows, fill in the points of measure, and you have a custom-made spec sheet. A blank spec sheet has been added to this section for your use (Figure A.1 on the next page).

GENERIC SPEC SHEET   **STYLE**

SEASON:	DESCRIPTION:
LABEL: (SIZE CATEGORY)	
DATE:	

TECHNICAL SKETCH   SKETCH/PHOTO

CODE	POINT OF MEASURE	TOL. +/−	4	S/6	8	M/10	12	L/14	16	XL/18

Figure A.1

(continued)

GENERIC SPEC SHEET   **STYLE**

CODE	POINT OF MEASURE	TOL. +/–	4	S/6	8	M/10	12	L/14	16	XL/18

COMMENTS:

CODE	POINT OF MEASURE	TOL. +/–	4	S/6	8	M/10	12	L/14	16	XL/18

Figure A.1 *Continued*

Woven Tops

Basic or front buttoning
Body shirt or fitted
Bow
Cossack
Cowboy (Western)
Drawstring
Dress
Epaulet
Guayabera
Hawaiian
Jabot
Nautical or Middy
Peasant
Stock-tie
Tunic
Oversized
Wrap

Basic or front-buttoning

Body shirt or fitted

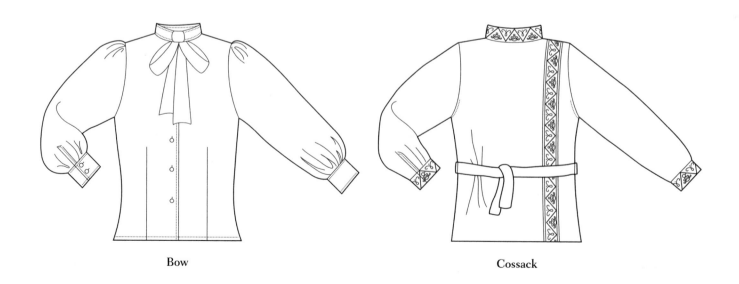

Bow   Cossack

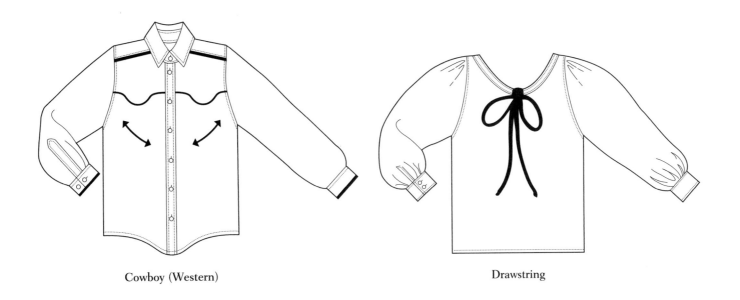

Cowboy (Western)

Drawstring

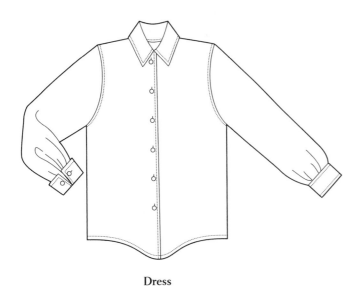

Dress

Epaulet

Guayabera

Hawaiian

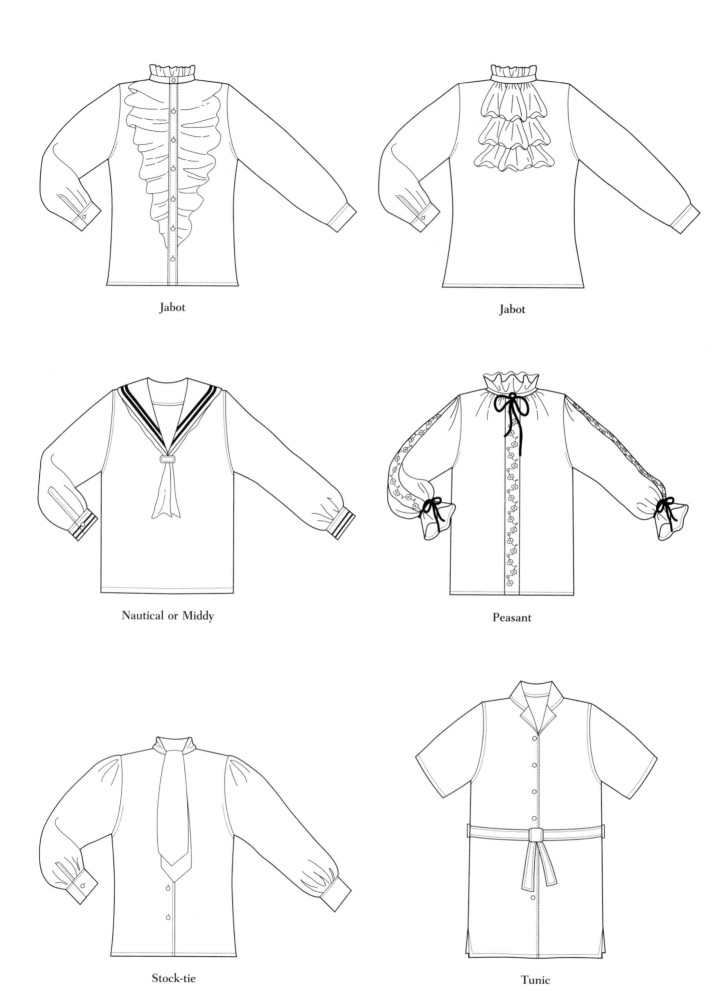

Jabot

Jabot

Nautical or Middy

Peasant

Stock-tie

Tunic

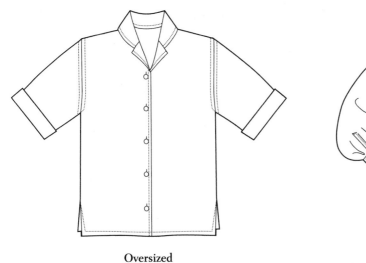

Oversized

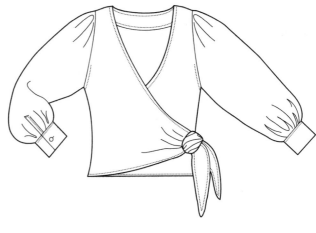

Wrap

Knit Tops

Belted cardigan
Boat neck sweater
Boat neck T-shirt
Capped sleeve
Classic cardigan
Crew neck sweater
Crew neck T-shirt
Cropped
Cowl neck
Dolman Sleeve
Flashdance
Golf shirt
Henley
Mock turtleneck
Oversized T-shirt
Sweatshirt
Tank top
Turtleneck
V neck sweater
V neck T-shirt
V neck cardigan
Vest

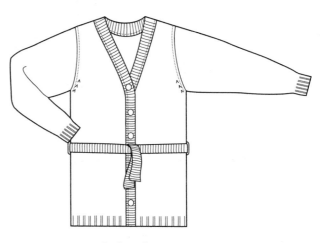

Belted cardigan

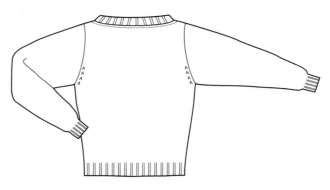

Boat neck sweater

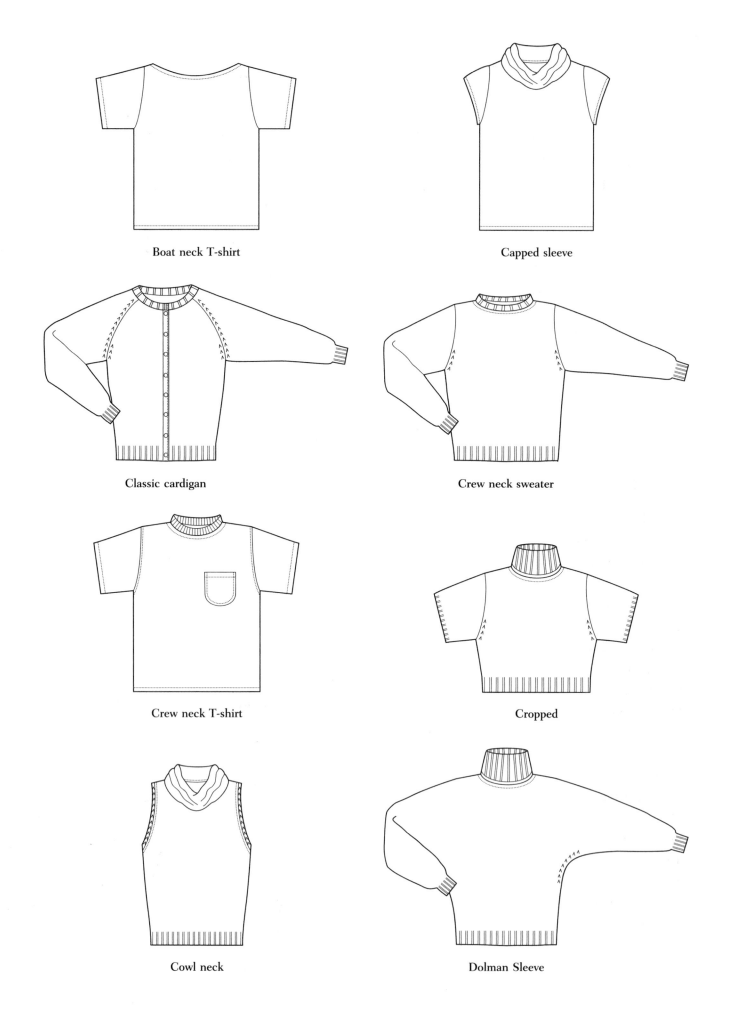

Boat neck T-shirt

Capped sleeve

Classic cardigan

Crew neck sweater

Crew neck T-shirt

Cropped

Cowl neck

Dolman Sleeve

Flashdance

Golf shirt

Henley

Mock turtleneck

Oversized T-shirt

Sweatshirt

Tank top

Turtleneck

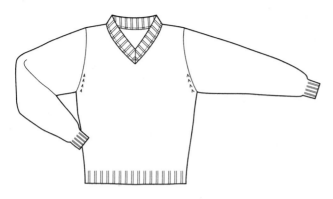

V neck sweater

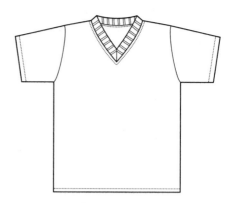

V neck T-shirt

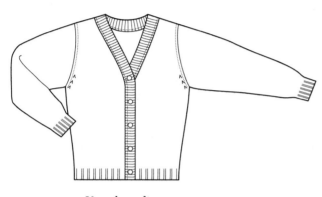

V neck cardigan

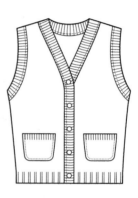

Vest

Skirts

A-line
Asymmetric
Denim
Drawstring
Granny
Gored
Kick pleated
Layered/Tiered
Pleated
Pull-on
Skirt lengths
Slit
Straight
Yoke
Wrap

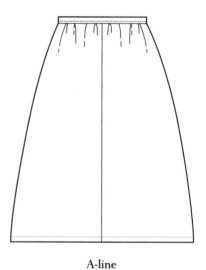

A-line

Asymmetric

Denim

Drawstring

Granny

Gored

Kick pleated

Layered/Tiered

Pleated

Pull-on

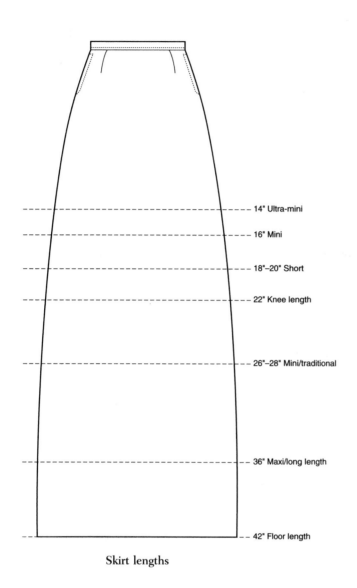

14" Ultra-mini

16" Mini

18"–20" Short

22" Knee length

26"–28" Mini/traditional

36" Maxi/long length

42" Floor length

Skirt lengths

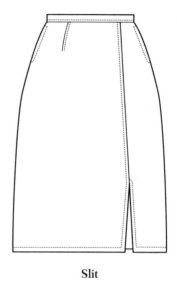

Slit

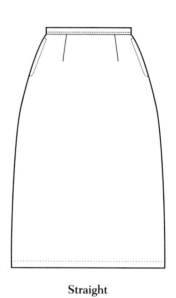

Straight

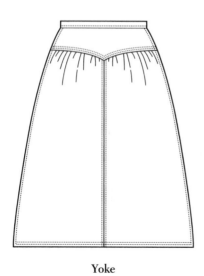

Yoke

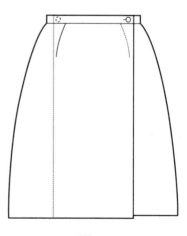

Wrap

Pants

Baggy
Bell-bottom/Flares
Blue jean/Denim
Cargo
Continental
Cropped
Cuffed
Drawstring
Hip-hugger
Jodhpur
Knickers
Oxford
Palazzo
Parachute/Zippered
Pull-on, Elastic/Warm-up
Sailor
Stirrup
Stovepipe
Surfer/Biker
Western

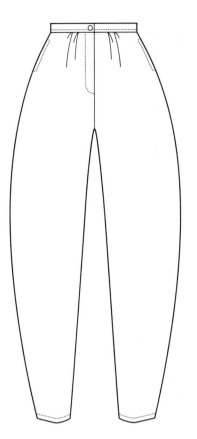

Baggy

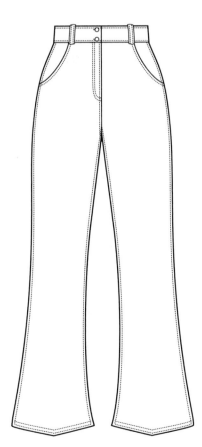

Bell-bottom/Flares

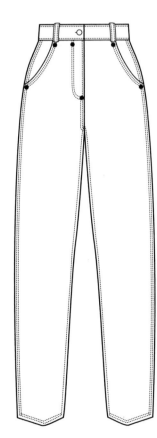

Blue jean/Denim

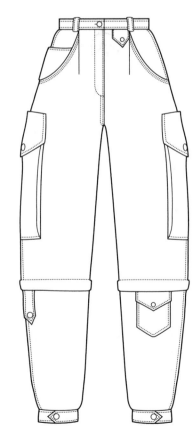

Cargo

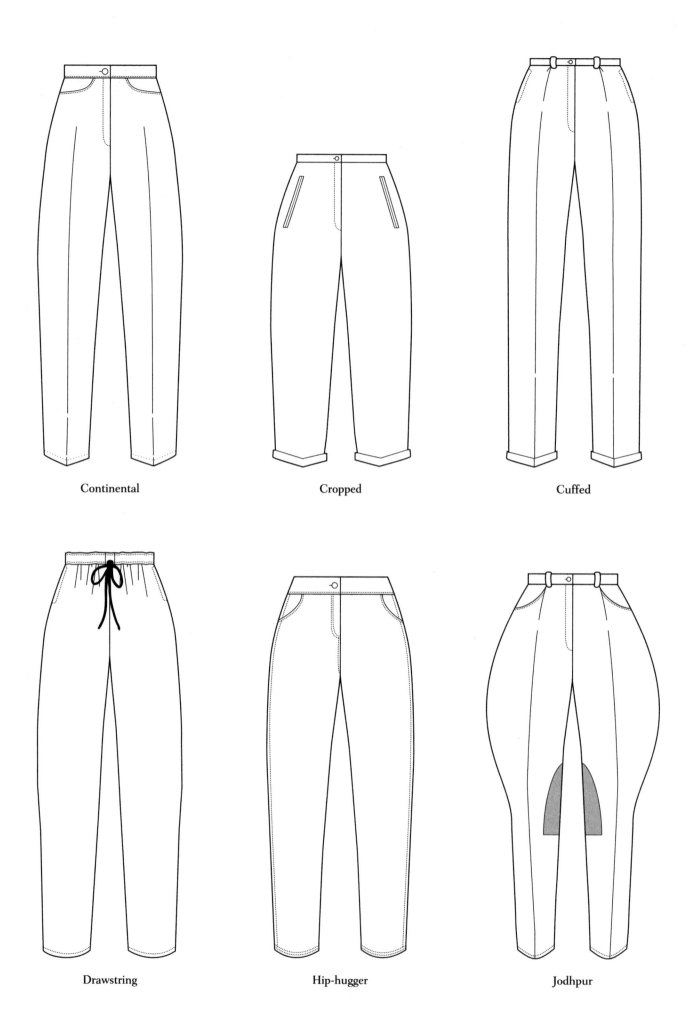

Continental

Cropped

Cuffed

Drawstring

Hip-hugger

Jodhpur

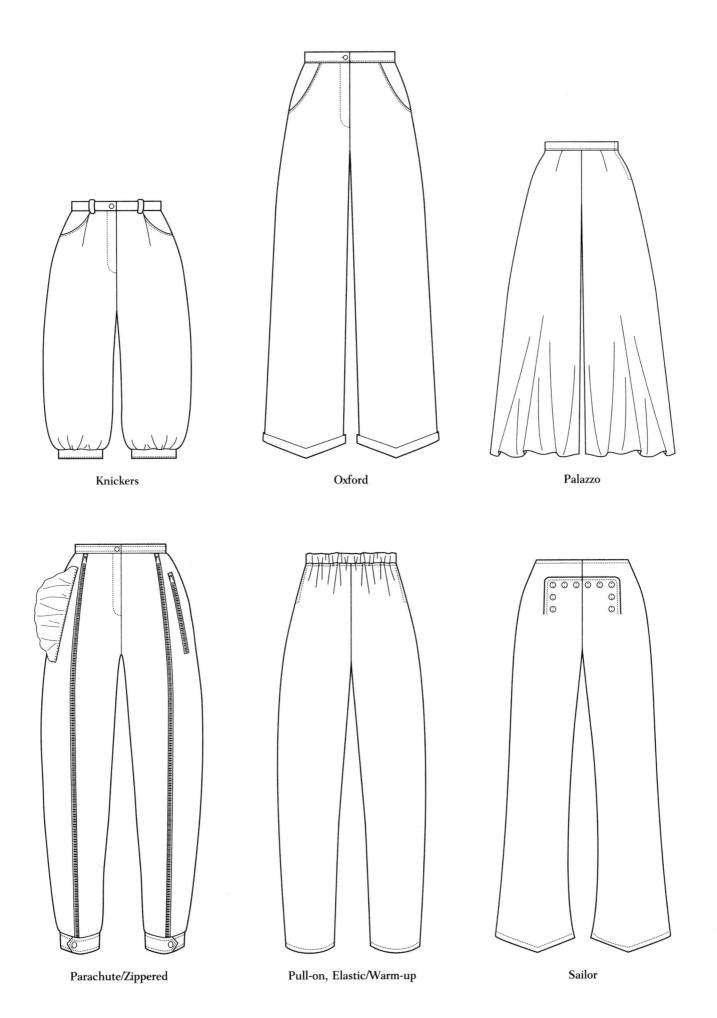

Knickers

Oxford

Palazzo

Parachute/Zippered

Pull-on, Elastic/Warm-up

Sailor

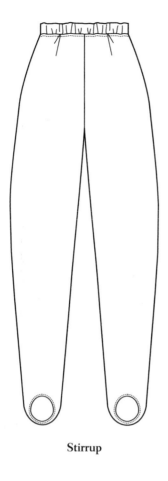

Stirrup

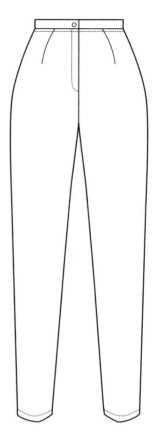

Stovepipe

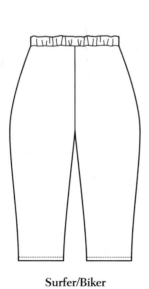

Surfer/Biker

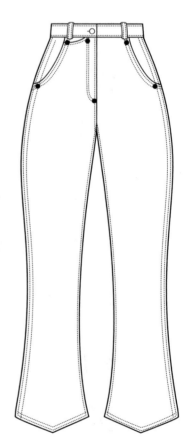

Western

Dresses

A-line jumper
Basic/Shift
Caftan
Cardigan
Coat
Empire
Granny
One-shoulder
Princess
Safari
Shirt
Slip
Sheath
Sweater
T-shirt
Tank
Trumpet
Torso
Wrap
Wedge

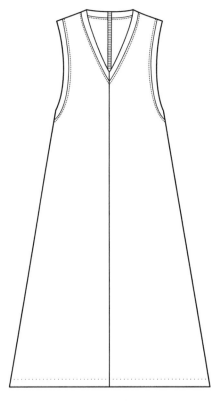

A-line jumper

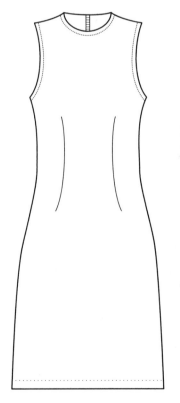

Basic/Shift

Caftan

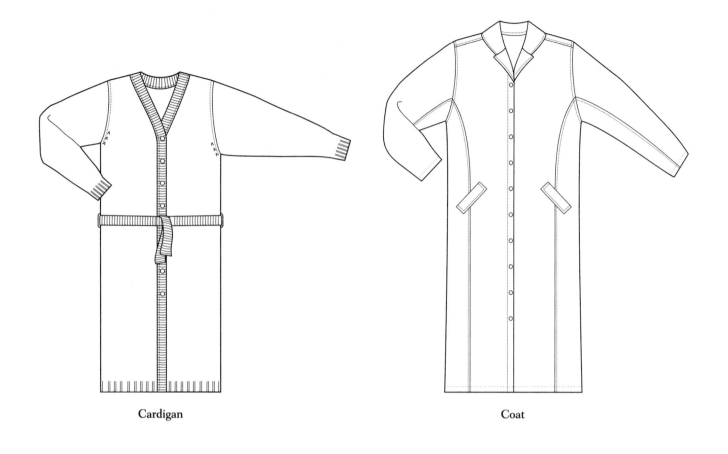

Cardigan

Coat

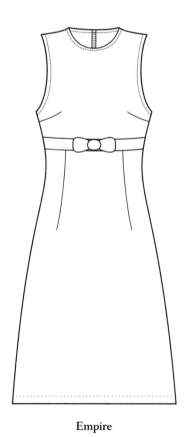

Empire

Granny

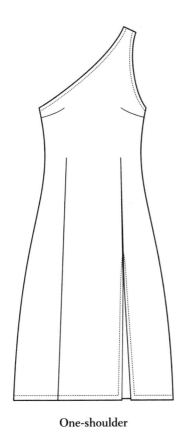

One-shoulder

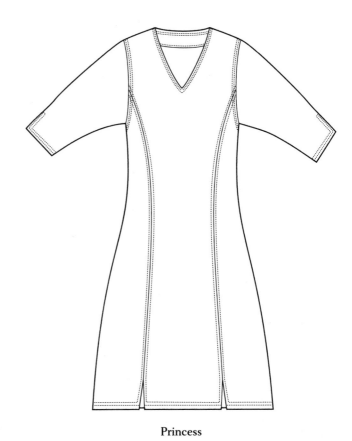

Princess

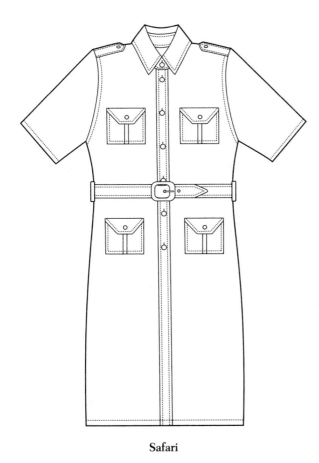

Safari

Shirt

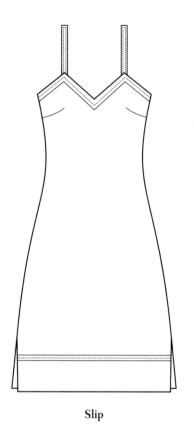

Slip

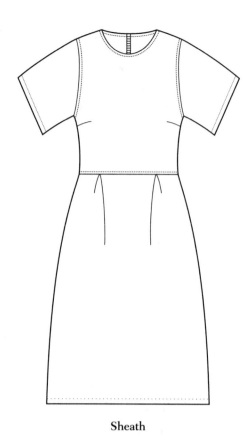

Sheath

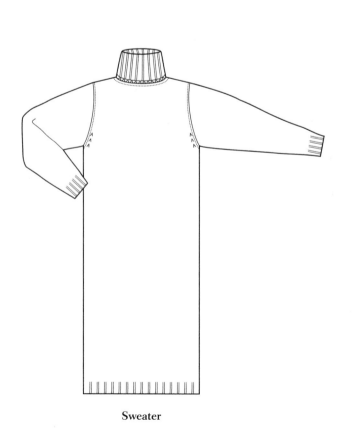

Sweater

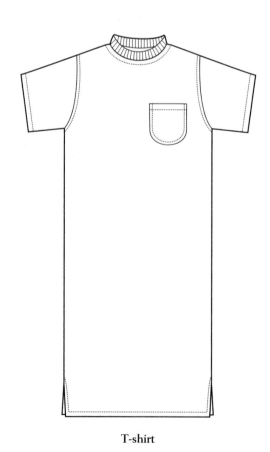

T-shirt

Tank

Trumpet

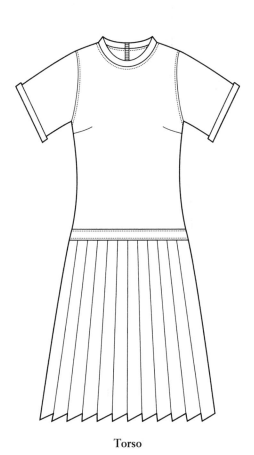

Torso

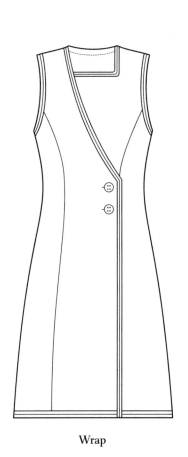

Wrap

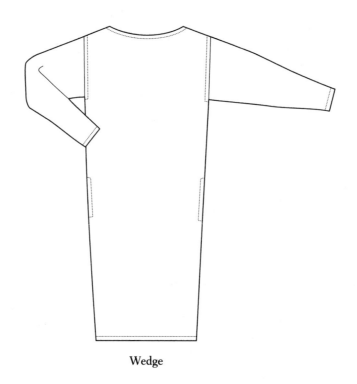

Wedge

One-Piece Outfits/Jumpsuits

Bib-overall
Bodyshirt
Body stocking
Bodysuit
Bunny suits
Jumpsuit
One-piece swimsuit
Pant jumper

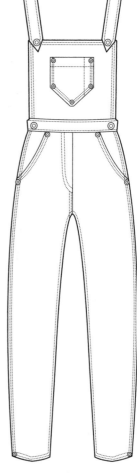

Bib-overall

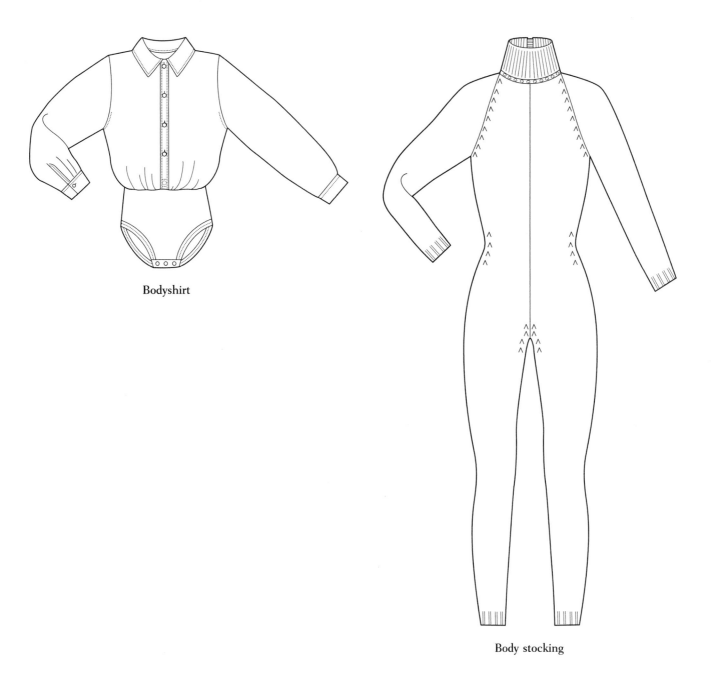

Bodyshirt

Body stocking

Bodysuit

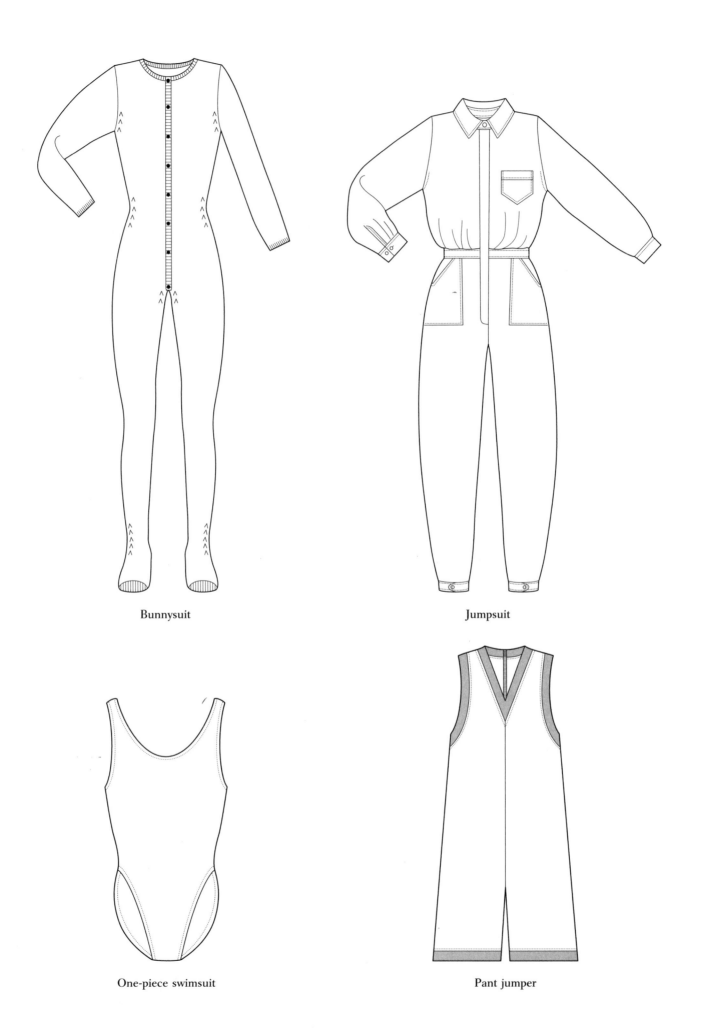

Bunnysuit

Jumpsuit

One-piece swimsuit

Pant jumper

Blazers and Unconstructed Jackets

Baseball
Basic Blazer
Bike
Denim
Double-breasted
Golf
Karate
Safari
Sweat jacket
Windbreaker

Baseball

Basic Blazer

Bike

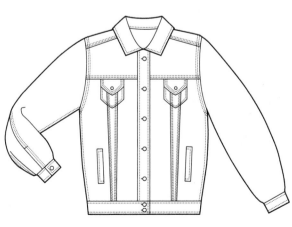

Denim

Double-breasted

Golf

Karate

Safari

Sweat jacket

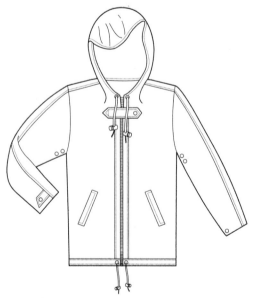

Windbreaker

Coats

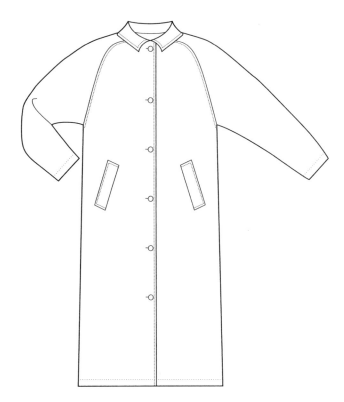

Balmacaan

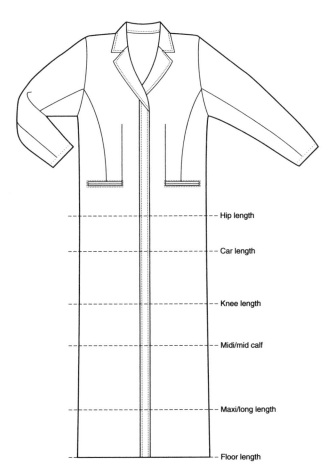

Basic coat lengths

- Hip length
- Car length
- Knee length
- Midi/mid calf
- Maxi/long length
- Floor length

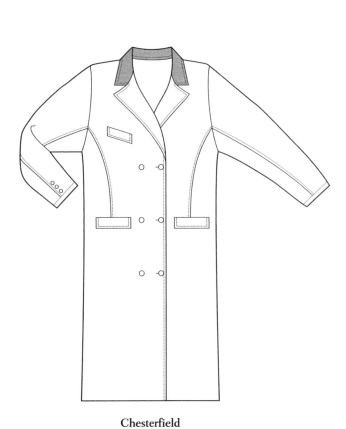

Chesterfield

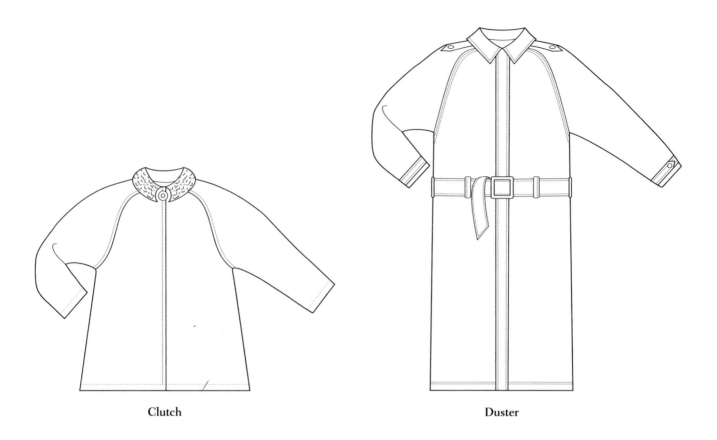

Clutch

Duster

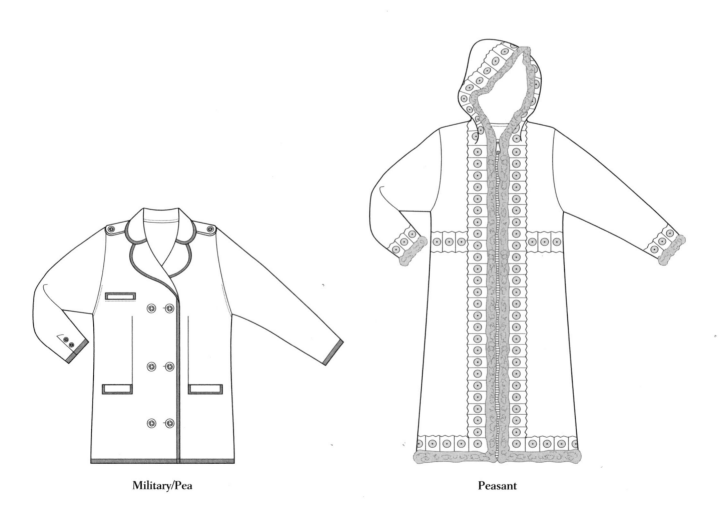

Military/Pea

Peasant

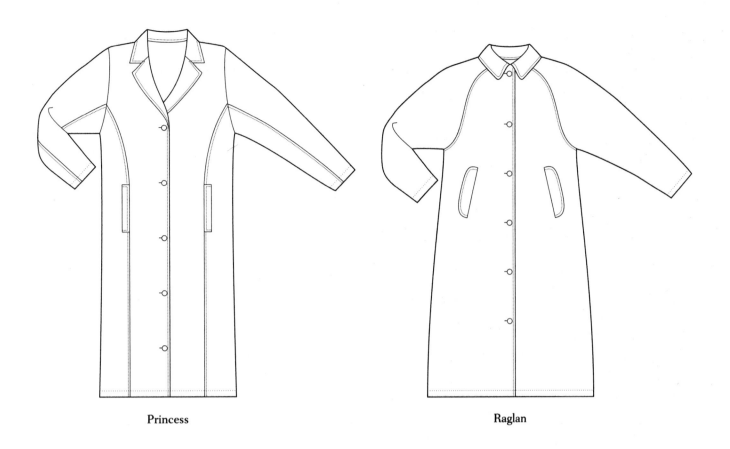

Princess

Raglan

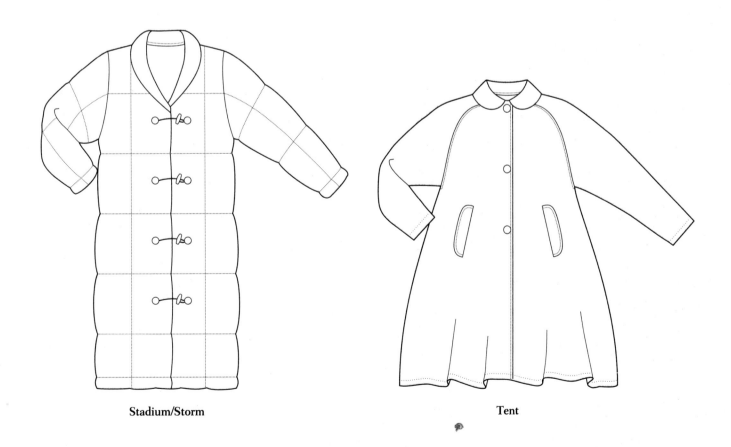

Stadium/Storm

Tent

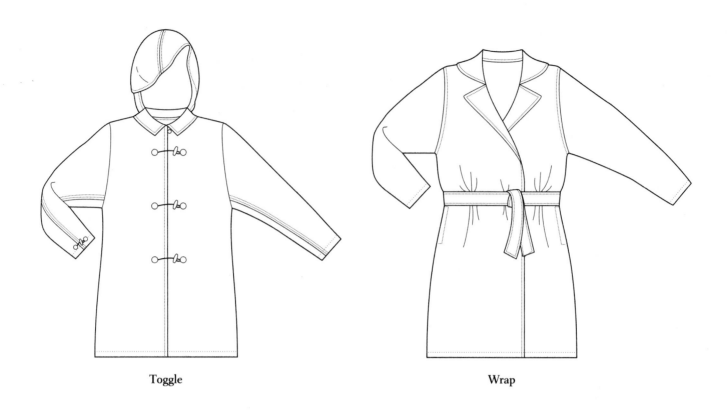

Toggle

Wrap

APPENDIX B

Body Ease

What Is Ease?

Ease is the measurable difference between the measurement of the body and the measurement of the garment. Every garment must have a certain amount of ease, in other words, a larger measurement, to allow for movement and comfort. The amount of ease required depends on the design of the garment, the fabric, the body type, the end use of the garment, and of course, personal preference. The amount of ease allowed for movement is called the wearing ease. The amount of ease chosen for style is called the design ease.

Wearing ease follows the basic rule that the wearer must be able to move, bend, breathe, sit, raise arms, and walk without the garment pulling, pinching, binding, stretching, or straining beyond a natural relaxed position. Fashion trends will affect the accepted amounts of wearing ease, but regardless of design it is imperative that all garments fit and hang well on the body. In order for every garment to have the ease allowance needed for movement, it is important to know those allowances.

The chart on the next page lists wearing ease in what has become accepted as design ease for five different types of fit: close fitting, fitted, semifitted, loose fitting, and oversized. Close-fitting measurements are used for the extreme of fashion-forward styles. Fitted and semifitted measurements are used for basic styles; loose-fitting measurements are used for garments or styles with gathers or excess ease. Oversized measurements are used for garments that appear to be larger than usually sized. You may need to refer to these measurements when evaluating fit.

	Close-fitting	Fitted	Semifitted	Loose fitting	Oversized
Bust	$\frac{1}{2}$"–2"	2"–4"	4"–5"	5"–8"	over 8"
Waist/Hip	$\frac{1}{2}$"–2"	2"–3"	3"–4"	4"–6"	over 6"
Waistband	$\frac{1}{4}$"–$\frac{1}{2}$"	$\frac{1}{2}$"–$\frac{3}{4}$"	$\frac{3}{4}$"–1"	1"–2"	over 2"
Crotch Depth	$\frac{3}{4}$"–1"	1"–1$\frac{1}{2}$"	1$\frac{1}{2}$"–2"	2"–2$\frac{1}{2}$"	over 2$\frac{1}{2}$"
Armhole	1"–2"	2"–3"	3"–4"	4"–5"	over 5"
Upper Arm/Sleeve	1"–2"	2"–3"	3"–4"	4"–5"	over 5"
Elbow	$\frac{1}{2}$"–1"	1"–2"	2"–3"	3"–4"	over 4"
Wrist	1/2"	$\frac{1}{2}$"–1"	1"–2"	2"–3"	over 3"
Thigh/Knee/Leg Opening	1"–2"	2"–3"	3"–4"	4"–5"	over 5"
Shoulder Seams	0"–$\frac{1}{4}$"	$\frac{1}{4}$"–$\frac{1}{2}$"	$\frac{1}{2}$"–1"	1"–1$\frac{1}{2}$"	over 1$\frac{1}{2}$"
Across Back	$\frac{1}{2}$"–$\frac{3}{4}$"	$\frac{3}{4}$"–1$\frac{1}{4}$"	1$\frac{1}{4}$"– 2$\frac{1}{2}$"	2$\frac{1}{2}$"–3$\frac{1}{2}$"	over 3$\frac{1}{2}$"

[Note: Blazer/jacket ease minimums should use the semifitted measurements, and coat/outerwear ease minimums should use the loose-fitting measurements.]

APPENDIX C

Care Labeling

The following is adapted from the American Textile and Manufacturers Institute's Website. http://www.atmi.org/Standards/labeling.asp#Care

❖ The <u>U.S. Federal Trade Commission</u> enforces the *Care Labeling of Textile Wearing Apparel and Certain Piece Goods*. The U.S. Congress created the Act in 1971 to protect a consumer's right to know how to care for a garment.

❖ The Act requires a permanent label attached to the garment with care instructions. Other products such as home furnishings are not required to provide a care label, but most manufacturers provide this information on a voluntary basis.

❖ From 1971 to June 30, 1997, the care instructions were required to be conveyed to the consumer in English words. The use of care symbols was allowed during this time period but words had to accompany the symbols.

❖ On July 1, 1997, the FTC modified the rule to allow the option of using care symbols only on the label. However, from July 1, 1997, through December 31, 1998, manufacturers that use care symbols only are required to provide consumers with educational materials (i.e., in the form of a hangtag, sticker, or handout) to decipher the meaning of the symbols.

❖ The use of care symbols is not mandatory, but optional, so consumers may continue to see products with written care instructions.

❖ ATMI supported the change to allow the use of care symbols for these reasons:

1. Consumers have indicated their dissatisfaction with the increasing size of product labels as some individuals have sensitive skin and have irritation problems because of the large labels.

2. As companies increase their export business and distribute their products throughout the world, the market demands numerous language labeling requirements (i.e., English, French, Spanish). This has lead to increased manufacturing costs to produce separate labels for each country, and for inventory management control. Products are inventoried by color, style, and labels. If a manufacturer can eliminate inventory categories, their manufacturing costs go down. Consumers will gain from this, as products' prices should remain the same and in some cases be lower.

3. If words can be eliminated from the label, the manufacturer can use a larger point size for the printed information, therefore making it easier for the consumer to read the label.

ATMI participates in the activities and development of care symbols in the <u>American Society for Testing and Materials (ASTM) D-13.62</u>

333

ASTM GUIDE TO CARE SYMBOLS

Wash

Machine wash cycles

normal | permanent press | delicate / gentle | hand wash

Water temperatures (maximum)

	(200F)	(160F)	(140F)	(120F)	(105F)	(65F-85F)
symbol(s)	95C	70C	60C	50C	40C	30C

Bleach

any bleach when needed | only non-chlorine bleach when needed

Dry

Tumble dry cycles

normal | permanent press | delicate / gentle

Tumble dry heat setting

any heat | high | medium | low | no heat / air

line dry / hang to dry

drip dry

dry flat

Iron

Iron--dry or steam

maximum temperature	200 C (390 F) high	150 C (300F) medium	110 C (230 F) low

Dryclean

Dryclean - normal cycle

A — any solvent | P — any solvent except trichloroethylene | F — petroleum solvent only | do not dryclean

Dryclean - additional instructions

short cycle | reduce moisture | low heat | no steam finishing

This figure has been reproduced by Fairchild Books under license from ASTM International. This figure is reprinted from ASTM Standard D5489-01a, Standard Guide for Care Symbols for Care Instructions on Textile Products, © ASTM International, 100 Barr Harbor Drive, West Conshohocken, PA 19428, USA (Phone: 610-832-9585, fax: 610-832-9555, e-mail: service@astm.org, Web site: www.astm.org). Copies of the official Standard should be obtained directly from ASTM.

APPENDIX D

Ordering a Body Form

The following is a checklist that can be used when ordering a quality body form. Form measurements/dimensions can be developed from the ASTM statistical body dimensions (Chapter 2), exclusive company body dimensions, a popular fit model, or average size dimensions sold by a particular body form manufacturer.

_____ Full Body Form
 Full-length (ankle-length) form—bifurcated
 Collapsible shoulders
 Stationary padded arm piece/pair.
 Sole, ankle, waist, and optional hips/bust marked with tape for location
_____ Stand
 Slotted
 Automatic raise-and-lower mechanism with floor pedal
 Wheeled
_____ Identification Markings
 Date (e.g., 2003)
 Size marking (e.g., Misses Size–8)
_____ Form measurement/dimensions
 Bust =
 Waist =
 Upper Hip =
 Lower hip =
 Midneck =

Armseye =
Upper arm =
Elbow =
Wrist =
Thigh maximum =
Thigh mid =
Knee =
Calf =
Ankle =
Vertical trunk =
Cross back width =
Cross chest width =
Bust point to bust point =
Armseye to waist =
Waist to hip =
Shoulder length =
Arm length, shoulder to wrist =
Arm length, shoulder to elbow =
Underarm length =
Waist length, front =
Waist length, back =
Stature =
Shoulder height =
Bust height =
Waist height =
High hip height =
Lower hip height =
Crotch height =
Knee height =
Ankle height =

335

GLOSSARY

Important Terms and Definitions

Apex The highest or culminating point of the bust.

Apparel A general or blanket term that applies to all men's, women's, and children's clothing.

Apparel manufacturer A broad spectrum of fashion industry companies that may develop, produce, and sell garments.

Applied pocket Any pocket stitched or applied onto the garment, e.g., a patch pocket.

Assistant designer A person who works for the designer and may do illustrating, patternmaking, or sewing.

Assistant merchandiser A person working for a merchandiser who is primarily responsible for clerical duties.

Assistant size specification analyst A person who performs clerical duties for a specification analyst. This person knows how to measure and is apprenticing in fit analysis.

Assistant technical designer A person who performs clerical duties for the technician. This person knows how to measure and is apprenticing in fit analysis and design.

Basic blazer A slightly fitted, single-breasted sport jacket.

Basket weave A variation of the plain weave construction accomplished by passing filling yarns over and under warp yarns, two or more warp yarns up and two or more warp yarns down, in alternating rows.

Belted cardigan A slightly fitted hip-length jacket or sweater that may or may not button, worn with a matching belt. See *Cardigan*.

Bib overalls A pant with a piece of cloth attached to the waistline/band, often held in place by shoulder straps. See *Overalls*.

Bifurcated body form A form that is divided by branches or parts. The best forms are solid and bifurcated with twill tape.

Blazer A single-breasted sport jacket.

Blouse

> *Basic or front buttoning* A traditional front-buttoning garment or top often styled after a man's dress shirt, and may or may not have a separate placket, chest pocket, and/or shoulder yoke.
>
> *Body shirt or fitted* See *Body shirt* or *Fitted* under their alphabetical listing.
>
> *Bow* A blouse generally having a band around the neck with two long ends attached that tie in a bow formation at the front of the neck.

Cossack A long blouse or overblouse often made with an embroidered high-standing collar, cuffs, and asymmetrical front placket, secured with a belt.

Cowboy (Western) A version of the basic blouse often styled with curved or V-shaped yokes, fancy buttonhole pockets, and piping trim; a look that is synonymous with Western United States cowboys.

Drawstring A blouse with a drawstring closure at the neckline. See *Drawstring* under its alphabetical listing.

Dress shirt Traditional front buttoning shirt with conservative menswear details.

Epaulet A blouse with shoulder epaulets and patch pockets.

Guayabera A shirt with pin tucks running down the front from the shoulder to the yoked hem, patch pockets, and button-trimmed shoulder yokes that is often associated with Cuba.

Hawaiian A floral-patterned shirt associated with Hawaii. It usually has two patch chest pockets.

Jabot A front or back-buttoning blouse with jabot-styled ruffles at the neck or front placket.

Nautical/Middy An over-the-head or slip-on blouse of traditional U.S. Navy/sailor styling. It has a large collar, neckerchief, and two or three rows of trim on the collar and cuffs.

Oversized A blouse that generally fits loosely on the body and may give the appearance of being sized too big.

Peasant A blouse styled after European folkloric tops with long or three-quarter puffed sleeves and embroidered and ruffled trims.

Stock-tie Generally a plain blouse with an ascot or flip-tie neckline.

Tunic A blouse styled after the loose-fitting garments of ancient Rome and Greece. It may be front-buttoning or pullover styled and may or may not have a belt.

Wrap A blouse that is generally cut on the bias, crosses over in the front or back, and ties at the waist. It may not have sleeves or they may be of varying lengths.

Boat neck (Bateau) A neckline slit over the shoulders in a boat shape that rests high on the front and back neck. A boat-neck top or dress would have this neck shape.

Bodice A close-fitting, upper-chest portion of a woman's dress or blouse.

Body dimension The actual measurement, the number in inches/centimeters, of a body at a body point of measurement.

Body form A dressmaking form made in the shape of a human body with legs on which a technical designer fits garments and a fashion designer or home sewer drapes fabric. These are also called dummy or model forms. Dress forms or dressmaker's dummies are generally body forms made without legs.

Body point of measure (body measurement) A measurement of a person's body at a specific point, e.g., the chest, waist, or hip.

Body prototype The model or body on which a dress form is patterned. A full-scale copy of a model's body.

Body shirt Refers to two different shirt styles: 1. a shirt that is fitted (also known as a fitted shirt) to conform to the body by slightly shaping the side seams or adding fitting darts/princess lines; 2. a blouse and leotard/bodysuit combination often seamed at or below the waist.

Body stocking A one-piece knitted garment with legs worn as an undergarment, sleep garment, or fashion garment. It may or may not have feet or sleeves and varying necklines.

Bodysuit A one-piece formfitting garment made without legs, often having a snap crotch opening.

Brand/Branded merchandise A wholesale label or trade name used for distinguishing products to that of a particular company.

Bunny suit A one-piece garment often worn for sleeping or lounging, fashioned after the trademarked childrenswear sleeper by Dr. Denton's.

Cardigan A slightly fitted hip-length jacket or sweater that buttons, sometimes having a small rolled collar. See *Classic cardigan*.

Center back (CB) The center of the garment, in back.

Center front (CF) The center of the garment, in front.

Circular knit/knitting The construction of a knitted fabric or garment on a knitting machine in circular or tubular form.

Circular web A fabric knitted in a tubular form, then cut and sewn to construct a garment.

Circumference The perimeter of the garment, including the front and back measurements, in other words, the total measurement. [Note: To get the circumference measurement, the garment is measured once, across the front, then that number is doubled.]

Classic cardigan Named after the seventh Earl of Cardigan, this is a slightly fitted hip-length jacket or sweater generally made out of wool, buttons, and sometimes having a small rolled collar.

Close fitting A broad term used for a garment that fits very close or tight to the body, generally of fashion-forward design.

Coat An outerwear garment (with sleeves) designed to be worn over other clothing.

Balmacaan A loose-fitting coat with raglan sleeves and a turn-down collar, buttoning up to the neck. It may be made in wool or rain-resistant fabrics.

Car A hip- to three-quarter-length coat styled for comfort while riding in a car.

Chesterfield A classic overcoat made of wool with a velvet collar, and can be single or double breasted.

Classic A term that fits any basic coat style or a coat that has been in fashion for a long period of time.

Clutch A coat without front fasteners. It is generally held together by hand and may have a flared hemline.

Duster Generally water-repellent or raincoat made with a smock/flange on the back, raglan sleeves, shoulder epaulets, and a belt. Originally named for a vintage car coat to keep the dust off one's clothing.

Military Generally any coat that borrows details from coats worn by persons in the military, usually styles with gold buttons, epaulets, and a double-breasted front opening.

Pea A short military-styled coat/jacket often of navy officer design.

Peasant A midlength coat trimmed with real or fake fur and embroidered ribbon on the borders and cuffs.

Princess A long coat with princess-seamed detail.

Raglan A coat with raglan-styled sleeves.

Stadium/Storm A coat often of quilted design made for warmth. It is often three-quarters in length and can have toggle front closures or a zip front.

Tent A knee-length coat with a widely flared hem and raglan sleeves.

Toggle Any coat with toggle closures or a short car coat with toggle closures and a hood.

Wrap A coat of any length with a wrap closure and belt.

Codes The numbering (or lettering) system given to each of the measurement points.

Constructed (constructed garment) A term used for a garment that employs one or more of the following advanced sewing construction techniques: facings, linings, collars, sleeves, pockets, and/or waistbands.

Constructed waistband A waistband that is sewn with two or more parts.

Costing The process of achieving a total cost of goods by evaluating the materials, labor, shipping, and markup.

Cost sheet A name given to the page of calculations for the total cost of goods.

Cowl neck A draped neckline falling in soft folds and may be of a bias cut. A cowl-neck shirt or dress would have this neckline.

Crew neck A round neckline often finished with a self-bias or knit ribbing, originally derived from the neckline on crew racing shirts.

Cropped top A top with a shortened or cutoff hemline, generally falling above the waistline.

Department merchandise manager (DMM) A person who manages a division or department of merchandise. This person manages several merchandisers and reports to a general merchandise manager.

Design ease Ease that is added to a garment for design or style, not fit.

Designer A person engaged in creating new and original clothing or accessories.

Designer merchandise A term used for merchandise that is designed by a well-known or branded designer.

Dolman sleeve A sleeve that is fitted at the wrist and cut with a deep armhole, sometimes starting at the waist. The dolman sleeve is often cut as one piece with the bodice. A dolman-sleeve dress or blouse would have this sleeve.

Double-breasted blazer A slightly fitted blazer with a lapped-over front opening, fastened with two rows/sets of buttons.

Drafted/Drafting An industry term for the process of making a new pattern from a basic pattern or sloper.

Draping An industry term for the process of creating a garment by arranging and pinning fabric over a dress form to conform to the design of that garment.

Drawstring A closure for hems, necklines, waistlines, and cuffs made by inserting a cord or ribbon into a band of fabric, which is then pulled and tied. A drawstring skirt would have this closure on the waistband.

Dress Predominately a woman's or children's item of clothing, made in one piece, or pieced at the waist, to resemble a top and a skirt.

> **Basic A-line (shift)** A dress with a slightly flared skirt, having the illusion of the letter A in silhouette.
>
> **Caftan** Traditionally a Moroccan-styled long and loose fitting dress with an embroidered, slit neckline.
>
> **Cardigan** A dress that resembles the cardigan sweater in styling.
>
> **Coat** A classic dress resembling a coat in styling. It may be single or double breasted and belted or unbelted.
>
> **Empire** A dress having an empire or high waistline ending just under the bosom.
>
> **Granny** An ankle-length dress often styled with a high collar, long sleeves, full skirt, and ruffled hem. It may have embroidered or ribbon trim.
>
> **One-shoulder** A dress with an asymmetrical neckline with one shoulder bare.
>
> **Princess** A dress styled with princess seams for shaping.
>
> **Polo shirt** A dress that resembles a polo shirt in styling.
>
> **Poor-boy shift** A dress resembling that of the early 1900s newsboy/poor-boy sweater.
>
> **Safari** Generally a tailored dress resembling a bush shirt or jacket, as worn on safari hunts.

> **Sheath** A straight and narrow-fitting dress that is shaped to the body with vertical darts, princess seams, or a set-in waistline.
>
> **Shirt (shirtdress)** A dress that resembles a blouse or man's shirt. It can be worn with or without a belt.
>
> **Slip** A simple dress that is usually cut on the bias, fitted at the bust, is constructed with shoulder straps, and may resemble a slip or undergarment.
>
> **Sweater** A generic term for any knitted dress that resembles a sweater in styling.
>
> **T-shirt** A dress that resembles a T-shirt in styling.
>
> **Tank** A dress resembling a tank top in styling.
>
> **Torso/Dropped waist** A loose-fitting dress that has an attached skirt below the waist.
>
> **Trumpet:** A slightly fitted dress with a flared flounce starting at the knees.
>
> **Waisted** A generic term for any dress that has a constructed waistline.
>
> **Wedge** A dress that is cut very full or wide at the shoulders, tapering down to a narrow or slim hemline, in a wedge/pie shape.
>
> **Wrap** A generic term for any dress wrapping to either the front or the back, where an extension forms the closure.

Dress form A dressmaking form in the shape of a human body, used as a substitution for the body when draping or fitting clothing. It's also known as a dressmaker's dummy, dressmaker's form, dummy, and model form.

Ease The allowance added to patterns to accommodate for comfortable fit and ease of movement. See *Wearing ease*.

Elastic waist (elasticized waistband): A waistline/band used for pull-on garments, made by either inserting elastic into a casing, stitching elastic directly on to the fabric at the waistline, or shirring fabric to the elastic with two or more rows of stitching.

Exclusive Limiting a style, fabric, or name to a single company or group.

Extended measurement A measurement taken when the garment is stretched beyond the relaxed position, but not further than the natural extended position.

Factory Building or facilities for manufacturing.

Fashion director (coordinator) A person who works closely with the merchandisers, supplying important forecast information on color, trends, new fabrications, and market insights.

Fashion-forward A broad term for a garment (or person) more fashionable than most.

Fiberglass tape measure A narrow strip or tape (made more commonly of plastic than fiberglass) marked off in units of inches or centimeters for measuring.

Figure types Common combinations of typical body shapes or figure variations.

First patternmaker A person who works with the designer or may be an assistant to the designer, who can construct actual pattern pieces for a new style by adjusting a sloper (basic pattern) for sample making.

Fit (n) The manner in which clothing is designed to look when worn; (v) adjust or adapt to an end design.

Fitted A general term referring to a garment that fits closely to or hugs the body.

Fitted skirt A skirt that fits closely to or hugs the body. See *Body shirt*.

Flashdance Generally referring to the neckline of a top or dress popularized by the 1983 film *Flashdance*. These garments are often cut at the neck so that the garment falls off the shoulder on one side.

Flat knit The construction of a knitted fabric on a knitting machine in a flat form.

Fractional math Mathematical equations involving fractions.

Full fashioned A process of flat knitting in which fabric is shaped by adding or reducing stitches.

Fully graded specification A specification sheet listing the measurement points for pattern construction, including all applicable sizes.

Gathered skirt A skirt made from straight or full panels, shirred or gathered at the waist for shaping.

General merchandise manager A person who manages several divisions or departments of merchandise.

Gerber system A generic name used in the industry for all Gerber Technology, a division of Gerber Industry, hardware and software.

Grading Increasing or decreasing pattern pieces and slope to achieve different sizes.

Gross margin The retail industry's measure of profitability, using a percent of total sales (before expenses) as profit.

Global sourcing Locating manufacturing facilities/factories to produce apparel merchandise worldwide.

High point shoulder The highest point on the shoulder seam slope, not including neck bindings or collars.

Illustrator A person who illustrates for the designer, product development team, or technical team. Many illustrators work freelance. In the past, illustrators were known for creating illustrations for ads, catalogs, or presentations, while sketchers did sketches for design, product development, and technical teams. The terms *illustrator* and *sketcher* have sometimes blurred in their definition as some illustrators sketch and some sketchers illustrate. See *Sketcher*.

Inert elastic Elastic in a relaxed position, before it has been stretched.

Jacket

    Baseball A jacket resembling those worn by major league baseball players. It has a snap or zippered front opening, ribbed cuffs and waist, and often carries a team insignia.

    Bike A traditionally styled jacket resembling those worn by a motorcyclist. It may be of leather or cloth and have shoulder epaulets, a buttoned sleeve cuff, and a ribbed waistband.

    Denim Any western-style jacket or any jacket made out of denim.

    Golf A jacket resembling those worn by golf players. It has a snap or zippered front opening and elastic cuffs and waist.

    Karate A jacket originally styled like a short kimono worn for the sport of karate, also worn as a fashion styled jacket.

    Safari A jacket styled after the bush jacket for safari hunts, introduced as a fashion item in the late 1960s.

    Sweat (Sweat jacket) Similar to a sweatshirt in design, with a front opening and a hood.

Jumper A sleeveless dress meant to be worn over a blouse or sweater. It may or may not be belted.

Jumpsuit A one-piece garment that is a combination of a shirt and trouser, also known as a *Coverall*.

Junior's A division of apparel aimed at female teenage customers who are too old for childrenswear and too youthful for missy. Sizes generally range from 1 to 13.

Jobber A manufacturer who generally does production work for several labels and customers. It may or may not own its own label.

Knit (n) A fabric that has been constructed by interlocking a series of loops (of one or more yarns); (v) to construct fabric by interlocking a series of loops (of one or more yarns).

Knitted course (also spelled coarse) A row of interlooping loops.

Knitting in the round A term for circular or tubular knitting.

Knockoff A copy of another's idea or design.

Large/Plus women's A size or segment of the industry for women with an ample girth or fit. Sizes generally range from 14W to 26W.

Line A designer's, manufacturer's, or retailer's collection of clothing offered for a specific season, linked by a common theme, such as color, fabric, or style. See *Product line*.

Loose fitting A general term referring to a garment that fits loosely on the body.

Manufacturer A company that produces clothing or clothing components, also called a contractor or jobber.

Manufacturing The process of making clothing or clothing components from raw materials, also a segment of the industry known for making clothing or clothing components from raw materials.

Manufacturing plant A place, factory, or workshop used for the manufacture of goods. See *Production plant*.

Marker A paper pattern, containing a fully graded size run, that provides the cutting lines for cutting stacked fabric in clothing production.

Marker yardage The amount of fabric needed to cut a fully graded size run.

Market 1. A segment of the fashion industry; 2. A place where buyers and sellers meet to potentially trade ownership of goods; 3. A demographic group of potential customers.

Measurement method The instructions or procedure for which a specific measurement is taken.

Measurement point A furnished point or position of which a measurement is taken. See *Point of measure*.

Measurer The title given to a person in the fashion industry whose sole responsibility is to measure garments and record those measurements on a spec sheet.

Merchandiser A person who makes decisions concerning the direction of the company's line. The merchandiser will study market trends, conduct market research, work with the sales staff, and oversee product development. This person is responsible for merchandise numbers in terms of the product and the stockkeeping units (SKUs).

Middleman A dealer or an agent who intermediates between a producer of goods, a manufacturer, and a retailer or consumer.

Missy (misses) A size or segment of the industry for women with an average girth or fit. Sizes generally range from 6 to 16.

Mock turtleneck A neckline/collar that stands on and fits close to the neck, but does not roll over like a turtleneck. A mock turtleneck sweater would have this neckline.

Natural relaxed position A garment set at ease or resting in a state that the inherent properties of the fabric or style allow.

One-piece swimsuit (bathing suit) Any bathing/swim garment for women or children made in one piece. Classic one-piece suits include the tank and the maillot.

Outerwear Another name for a coat generally styled hip-length to full-length and designed to be worn over other clothing, also called an outercoat.

Overalls Pants with a bib top and shoulder straps, traditionally worn by farmers in denim blue or by painters (painter pants) in natural or white, and common styles in many fabrics for children.

Oversized A general term referring to a garment that fits very loosely on the body and may give the appearance of being sized too big.

Pants

> **Baggy (baggies)** A pant that is cut full through the hips and tapers to a narrow opening at the ankle.

> **Bell-bottom (bell-bottoms)** A pant that is cut with fullness at the hem on both the inner and outer seam, causing a perceived bell shape.

> **Blue jean/denim** Pants originally styled for work, with topstitching, hip pockets, back pockets, a back yoke, and rivets, and now refers to any pant made of denim.

> **Cargo** Pants designed with several hip pockets and large below-thigh pockets, often banded at the bottom. Pant legs may or may not zip off into shorts.

Continental A pant with a man's trouser styling, fitted at the waistband without a belt. The pockets are often curved from the waist to the side seams.

Cropped A pant cut at a length ranging anywhere between the knee and the ankle.

Cuffed Generally refers to any classic pant with cuffs.

Hip-hugger (low rise) A pant that sits at any point below the waistline, usually resting on the hip bones.

Jodhpur Riding pant that flair at the side of the hips, are narrow through the calves and ankles, and have reinforced patches on the inseams at the knee.

Knickers A full pant of varying width fastened at the knee with a cuff.

Oxford A pant that follows a 1920s men's styling, with wide cuffed legs.

Palazzo A voluminous long wide-leg pant often worn for evening or loungewear.

Parachute/Zippered A pant made of parachute cloth, nylon, or "swishy" cloth, adorned with zippers and cuffs.

Sailor A pant styled after a navy sailor's pant, with flared/bell-bottom legs, a ten-button center front flap, and center back lacing.

Stirrup Pants generally made slim in design, with attached or detachable strap extensions under the instep, and made to be worn with boots.

Stovepipe A narrow-fitting pant with leg openings the same from the knee down.

Surfer/Bike Close-fitting pants extending to the knee, traditionally worn by surfers, bikers, and for exercise.

Western A slightly low-rising pant made traditionally of denim or gabardine, with topstitching accents and riveted detailing, named after the look of the pant worn by the Western United States cowboy.

Pant jumper A garment similar to a sleeveless pantdress, worn with or without a blouse.

Pattern A paper model designed and made into pieces to be used for making clothing.

Patternmaker A person who is in charge of making a sample pattern or final pattern for grading and production.

Plain weave The construction of a woven fabric by passing filling yarns over and under warp yarns, one warp up and one warp down, in alternating rows.

Pleat Folds of fabric stitched into a garment.

> **Box** Two pleats, one folded to the left, one folded to the right; the fabric in between forms the appearance of a box.

> **Envelope** A large inverted pleat, often placed on the side of a garment, which generally reveals a pocket underneath.

> **Inverted** Two pleats, one folded to the right and one folded to the left, that touch in the center.

> **Kick** A flat pleat on the front or center back of a narrow skirt, which generally reveals a slit to make walking easier.

Kilt A series of flat pleats, covering one-half of the next pleat, all folded in the same direction.

Knife A series of pleats traditionally spaced one-half to one inch apart, all facing the same direction.

Point of measure A specific point or name of a point at which a garment is measured. See *Measurement point*.

Private label merchandise A category/line of merchandise that carries the name of or is owned exclusively by a retail store and meets its standards.

Product developer A person who develops exclusive product lines, brands, or private label merchandise.

Product development The processes of developing a particular product line, brand, or private label merchandise.

Product development manager A person who oversees the development of an exclusive line and monitors its production to assure those garments meet the company's expectations.

Product line (collection) A designer's, manufacturer's, or retailer's collection of clothing offered for a specific season, linked by a common theme, such as color, fabric, or style. See *Line*.

Product manager An executive who heads the product development team and is responsible for helping to plan, develop, and oversee the consistency of a style message for an exclusive product, product line, brand, or private label.

Production plant A place, factory, or workshop used for the manufacture of goods. See *Manufacturing plant*.

Prototype An original model in which something is patterned or copied.

Pull-on (pullover, skirt/pant) A garment, without traditional openings and closures, that can be pulled on or pulled over a part of the body, e.g., a pull-on pant or pullover sweater.

Retail buying office (resident buying office) An association or group of retail stores working together under one organization for the purpose of sharing and providing services to member stores.

Retail standard Size and quality standards unique to a retailer's customer.

Rise The front and back seams on a pair of pants from the crotch to the waistband.

Romper A one-piece garment resembling a pajama-styled jumpsuit, with short legs or elastic-gathered leg openings.

Satin weave The construction of a woven fabric by passing filling yarns over and under warp yarns. This weave is generally constructed with five warps up and one warp down, repeating to create a smooth surface.

Season The apparel calendar for which a new line is presented, e.g., fall, winter, resort, holiday, spring, and summer.

Seat 1. The buttock portion of a pair of pants; 2. A hip measurement taken at a predetermined number of inches up from the crotch.

Semifitted A general term referring to a garment that is somewhat fitted in style, yet hangs a little loose on the body.

Selvage The finished edge on a cloth that prevents raveling or fraying.

Senior technical design manager A person who manages several technical design managers, makes executive department decisions, works with the divisional merchandise managers, and writes specification sheets as needed.

Shirring Multiple rows of gathering fabric.

Shrink A waist-length sweater or knit top, which may or may not have a ribbed hem and may or may not have sleeves, that looks as though it had been shrunk in the wash.

Side Seam Any garment seam running along the side of the body from under the arm to the ankle bone.

Silhouette The outline or contour of a figure or garment.

Size range The range of sizes to be cut within a size scale, e.g., small, medium, large.

Size scale The number of each size cut within a marker, e.g., three small, six medium, three large.

Size specification Accurate garment measurements.

Size specification analyst A person who analyzes garments, checking and adjusting fit as required and writing specification sheets. This person knows how to measure garments.

Sketch In fashion, a garment or silhouette drawing.

Sketcher A person who sketches for the designer, product development team, or technical team. Many sketchers work freelance. See *Illustrator*.

Skirt

A-line A slightly flared skirt having the illusion of the letter A in silhouette.

Asymmetric A skirt with a hemline that differs in length from the right to the left, often in a diagonal line. It may or may not have ruffles or flounces attached to the hemline.

Fitted (straight) A skirt that is close fitting, or is shaped to fit the body closely, any slim skirt.

Gored A skirt that is generally fitted through the waist, flaring out at the hem. It may be made by sewing together four to 24 gored skirt sections.

Granny A full-length gathered skirt, often styled with a ruffled hem.

Jean/Denim A skirt with blue jean styling or any skirt made of denim.

Kick pleated A skirt with a flat pleat on the front or center back of a narrow skirt, which generally reveals a slit to make walking easier.

Layered/Tiered A skirt with varying layers or tiers sewn together and placed on top of each other.

Pleated A skirt with pleats. It may have box pleats, envelope pleats, inverted pleats, knife pleats, or kick pleats. See *Pleats*.

Slit A straight skirt made with a slash or slit for walking.

Straight (Fitted) A skirt that is close fitting, or is shaped to fit the body closely, any slim skirt. See *Fitted (straight)*.

Yoke A skirt made with a yoke just under the waistband. The lower portion of the skirt is often gathered.

Wrap A skirt that wraps around the body and fastens with buttons or ties. It is open from the waist to the hem and usually overlaps across the front or the back.

Skirt length The length of the skirt measured from under the waistband seam or stitching.
14" = Ultra-Mini
16" = Mini
18–20" = Short
22" = Knee length
26–28" = Midi/Traditional
36" = Maxi/Long
42" = Floor length

Slashed and spread A method of pattern alteration, cutting the pattern apart in the area that needs to be adjusted, spreading the pieces to obtain the desired results, then trueing the new line.

Sleeve cap 1. The extension of a shoulder seam into the sleeve; 2. The top curved portion of a sleeve pattern.

Sleeve cap slope The sleeve cap's degree of slant or curve.

Slide fastener (zipper) A fastener consisting of two rows of (metal or plastic) teeth or spirals, which draw closed or open by moving a sliding piece.

Slope The slant or incline of a garment or pattern.

Sloper A basic or foundation pattern created after standard body measurements have been designated. This pattern becomes the template for stylized patterns.

Softly tailored A term originally used for a garment of predominately curved lines and rounded shapes. It's now also used for a garment that possesses lightly tailored techniques, such as specialized cutting, fitting, sewing, and finishing. See *Tailored*.

Sourcing 1. Locating manufacturing facilities/factories to produce or assemble apparel merchandise; 2. Determining how and where merchandise or their components will be obtained.

Sourcing agent A person who locates manufacturing facilities/factories to produce or assemble apparel merchandise, or a person who determines how and where merchandise or their components will be obtained.

Specification (spec) sheet A standardized list of garment measurements. It consists of style information, technical renderings, points of measure, size ranges, and garment measurements.

Stockkeeping unit (SKU) Merchandise within a classification of merchandise to which an identifying number is assigned for the purpose of keeping sales and stock records.

Straight skirt Any slim, close-fitting, fitted, or semifitted skirt without fullness.

Style (n) The distinctive characteristics or appearance of a garment; (v) to give fashion features to a garment or line.

Style clerk A person working in a spec office who checks and records the style numbers of the garment for analysis.

Style Name A name assigned to and used for identifying a particular style or garment.

Style number A number assigned to and used for identifying a particular style or garment.

Stylist A person who shops the market for style ideas that will fit the company's image, may translate those style ideas to fit the company's needs, giving direction to the design department or product development staff, and possesses a thorough knowledge of textiles and color.

Sweep The circumference of a hem, following the edge, straight or curved.

T-shirt (tee) A long- or short-sleeve knitted sport/casual shirt or dress with a ribbed, round, or V neck neckline.

Tailored A term originally used for a garment of predominately straight lines and angled shapes and now also used for a garment that possesses tailoring techniques such as specialized cutting, fitting, sewing, and finishing. See *Softly tailored*.

Technical design The process of analyzing garments, checking and adjusting fit and writing specification sheets.

Technical designer A person who analyzes garments, checking and adjusting fit as required and writing specification sheets. This person also has a design background and can offer style changes as needed to solve production problems.

Technical design manager A person who manages several technical designers, makes final fit decisions, writes specification sheets, and evaluates potential production risks. This person works closely with the general merchandise manager, may offer style or design changes as needed for production, and sets the fit schedule.

Technical sketch A flat, proportioned drawing of a garment including all style details.

Thread count (count of cloth) The number, or count, of warp and weft yarns per inch.

Tolerance The amount of acceptable measurement deviation, plus or minus, allowed during sewing.

Total measurement The perimeter of the garment, including the front and back measurements, in other words, the circumference. [Note: To get the total measurement, the garment is measured once, across the front, then that number is doubled.]

Tube top A strapless top made of tight-fitting stretch or elastic-shirred fabric.

Turtleneck A neckline/collar that stands on and fits close to the neck and rolls over once or twice. A turtleneck sweater would have this neckline.

Twill weave The construction of a woven fabric by passing filing yarns over and under warp yarns, two warps up and one warp down, creating a diagonal effect.

Unconstructed jacket A jacket that is not constructed with advanced sewing techniques for facings, linings, collars, sleeves and/or pockets.

Union suit A one-piece, front-buttoned, knitted garment of 1880s design worn for warmth. It may or may not have a drop seat.

V neck A neckline that is cut down in the front or back of a garment to a sharp point in the shape of a V. A V-neck T-shirt or dress would have this neckline.

V neck cardigan A slightly fitted hip-length jacket or sweater that is cut down in the front to a point in the shape of a V. See *Cardigan*.

Vest A jacket- or sweater-style garment made without sleeves, meant to be worn over a blouse or knit top.

Wales The series of lengthwise loops or vertical stitches in knitted fabric.

Warm-up pant A casual pant generally made with a pull-on waist construction, often worn for exercise.

Warp knitting Knit produced with yarns running lengthwise, as warp-on beams are prepared with one or more yarns per needle.

Warp yarns (filling yarns) The set of yarns in a woven fabric that run from selvage edge to selvage edge.

Wearing ease The allowance added to patterns to accommodate for comfortable fit and ease of movement. See *Ease*.

Weft knitting Knitting produced on both flat and circular knitting machines using one continuous thread (yarn) making all of the loops in a course.

Weft yarns The set of yarns in a woven fabric that run lengthwise or parallel to the selvage.

Windbreaker A trademarked nylon jacket made for warmth and wind protection. It generally has a zip front opening, a hood, and a fitted waistband and cuffs. It has now become synonymous with any wind-protecting jacket.

Womenswear A size or segment of the industry for women with an ample girth or fit. Sizes generally range from 14W to 26W.

Work sketch or work photo A sketch or photo of a garment using the principles and elements of a style, without being a necessarily finalized design.

Yoke A separate seamed portion of the garment across the front and back shoulders.

Index